THE WOMAN QUESTION

IN EUROPE

THE WOMAN QUESTION

IN EUROPE

A SERIES OF ORIGINAL ESSAYS

EDITED BY
THEODORE STANTON, M.A.

SOURCE BOOK PRESS

All rights reserved. No part of this book may be reproduced
in any form without permission from the publisher.
Library of Congress Catalogue Card No. 74-134195
ISBN 0-87681-075-X
SOURCE BOOK PRESS, a Division of Collectors Editions Ltd.,
185 Madison Avenue, New York, N.Y. 10016
Unabridged republication of the 1884 New York edition: First printing 197◖
Manufactured in the United States of America

THE WOMAN QUESTION

IN EUROPE

A SERIES OF ORIGINAL ESSAYS

EDITED BY

THEODORE STANTON, M.A.

WITH AN INTRODUCTION BY

FRANCES POWER COBBE

"If you would know the political and moral status of a people, demand what place its women occupy."—L. AIMÉ MARTIN, "On the Education of Mothers," Book I., Chapter VI.

"There is nothing, I think, which marks more decidedly the character of men or of nations, than the manner in which they treat women."—HERDER, "Philosophy of History " (French Edition), Vol. II., Book VIII., Chapter IV.

G. P. PUTNAM'S SONS

NEW YORK : 27 AND 29 WEST 23D STREET
LONDON : 25 HENRIETTA STREET, COVENT GARDEN
PARIS : G. FISCHBACHER, 33 RUE DE SEINE

1884

I DEDICATE THIS WORK

TO MY MANY COLLABORATORS, AND, ABOVE ALL, TO MARGUERITE
BERRY, MY WIFE, WHOSE PARTICIPATION HAS NOT BEEN LIMITED TO
A SINGLE CHAPTER, BUT EXTENDS THROUGHOUT EVERY PAGE OF THE
VOLUME.   T. S.

EDITOR'S PREFACE.

I BEGAN collecting the materials for this volume in the winter of 1880–'81. It was my wish to secure, in each country of Europe, the collaboration of one or more women, who, in connection with a literary training, had participated, either actively or in spirit, in some phase of the women's movement,—that remarkable social revolution now going on in old Europe as well as in young America. With the exception of the chapter on Portugal and a portion of the chapter on France, all the contributions are from the pens of women.

One of the most distinguished Portuguese authoresses, Mrs. Maria Amalia Vaz de Carvalho, had promised to speak for her country, when a sudden illness interrupted her work. Mr. Rodrigues de Freitas, the well-known Portuguese publicist and republican, kindly came forward to fill the gap.

The chapter on France differs materially from the others, both as regards its form and its amplitude. France, while accomplishing less than almost any other country in the practical amelioration of woman's condition, has, in the field of ideas, always led the world. What her thinkers and reformers have written and spoken, other nations have put into practice. France has already solved theoretically the woman question, as she has all the other great problems of the nineteenth cent-

ury.   Hence it is that so much space has been devoted
to this one country.   It is hoped that the brief historical retrospect with which the chapter begins will explain
and complete the other chapters.   It has been my endeavor, as far as possible, to have each separate topic
treated by a writer possessing special information on such
topic.   It is therefore believed that the statements and
conclusions will be found trustworthy and important.

It will be noticed that England has the first place and
the lion's share of the volume.   But, as it is in Great
Britain of all Europe that, on the whole, the most marked
progress has been made, especially in the direction of political rights, the *summum bonum* of the age, the largest
space and the post of honor justly belong to the Mother
Country.

In the arrangement of the chapters, I have striven to
observe an ethnological order.   First comes Anglo-Saxon
England, followed by the Teutonic countries—Germany,
Holland and Austria; then Scandinavia, embracing Nor-
way, Sweden and Denmark; next the Latin nations—
France, Italy, Spain and Portugal; then Latin-Teutonic
Belgium and Switzerland; afterward the Slavonic States
—Russia, Poland and Bohemia; and, finally, the Orient.

Hungary should have had its separate place in the Slavonic group; but, after repeated efforts, I was unable to
find a collaborator in that country, and the reader, unfortunately, must be contented with the few words devoted
to Hungarian women in the chapter on Austria.   However, as Hungary is an integral part of the empire of the
Hapsburgs, much of what is said in the chapters given
to Austria and Bohemia applies equally well to Hungary.

I have endeavored to make this volume on the European movement for women a storehouse of facts rather than a philosophical study. The latter itself presents, however, a theme of the deepest interest, and one which, if I may be permitted to say so, might well be based on the material found in the following pages. Exactness, therefore, has been one of the chief cares of the editor. In order to secure this end, the translated portions of this work were, before being sent to the printer, submitted to the authors in the English form. The first proofs, and, in some cases, the second proofs also, were passed under their eyes, and, in many instances, were carefully examined by third parties, natives of the countries treated therein. It is hoped that, by this means, accuracy has been secured, not only as regards the facts, but also in the orthography of proper names, so often disfigured in passing through a foreign press.

I beg, however, the indulgence of the reader for any errors which may be discovered in these pages; for, with the editor on one side of the Atlantic, and the publisher on the other, the difficulties of proof-reading have been greatly increased. The double translation which some of the essays have undergone may have occasioned a few misconstructions. Without counting the English, the contributions to this volume came to the editor in six different languages, viz., German, Italian, Spanish, Norwegian, Polish and modern Greek. But, as has already been said, the English text has been examined more than once by the authors, who—a fact worthy of note, by the way— are, with but two exceptions, conversant with the English tongue.

My work has not been simply that of a translator, but the more difficult one of an editor. The principal object of this volume was, as has just been stated, to furnish facts. The style in which these facts were to be presented was to be free from extravagance of every kind. I did not wish to take as my guide Diderot, who says: "When woman is the theme, the pen must be dipped in the rainbow and the pages must be dried with the dust of the butterfly's wing."   Nor was the "vile-wretchman" spirit to prevail.   But rather Horace's golden mean was to be observed. In order to stick to facts and the *juste milieu*, the editor greatly increased his labors. With the exception of the biographical notices, and of the English essays, to which I have added a few notes, no chapter appears in its original form.   Each has been subjected to severe pruning, some having been abridged one-half. In several chapters the order of the matter has been changed, paragraphs have been remodeled, and new sentences introduced. But in every case the English arrangement has received the final approval of the author. And I hasten to add that in every instance this approval was cheerfully given, my collaborators readily perceiving that in this way only could we hope to produce a work which would be homogeneous and, at the same time, acceptable to a public three thousand miles away, of whose character all foreign writers are more or less ignorant.

Besides other matter, the editor is responsible for most of the foot-notes. With the exception of those in the chapter on France, all the foot-notes are signed with the initials of their respective authors.   In this chapter, those not signed belong to the editor.   It will be thought, perhaps, that many foot-notes would more properly appear in the body of the text than at the bottom of the page.   But as the text was the composition of a particular author, additional matter could be added only in the form of notes. Although continuity is thus often sacrificed, no better plan suggested itself.

I have been considerably puzzled as to what titles of address to use before names of persons. It would not do to adopt a different method in each chapter as a new country was taken up. The following rule has, therefore, been observed: Except in the chapter on France, the ordinary English forms have been employed in all cases. It would have been more uniform to have done the same throughout the whole volume, but such an expression as "*Mrs.* de Staël," for example, shocked the ear too much to admit of such a practice.

I cannot close this preface without returning thanks to a few at least of the many persons who have aided me in the preparation of this volume. Mention is not made of the various collaborators whose names appear at the head of the chapters or in the notes thereto. Suffice it to say, that without their generous aid this preface would have no *raison d'être,*—this volume would not exist.

The list is as follows: England—The Rev. W. H. Channing, Mrs. Peter A. Taylor, wife of the member for Leicester; Mrs. Katharine L. Thomasson, wife of the member for Bolton; Miss Emily Faithfull, Mrs. Laura McLaren, wife of the member for Stafford; Mrs. Fanny Hertz, Miss Caroline A. Biggs, Editor of the *Englishwoman's Review;* Miss Agnes Blatch, and Mrs. Stanton-Blatch, B.A., who has read the larger part of the proofs. France—Mme. Jules Favre, M. Gréard, Vice-Rector of the Academy of Paris; M. Molinier, Professor at the Toulouse Law School; Dr. Nicholas Joly, corresponding member of the Institute; Mme. Caroline de Barrau; M. Joseph Fabre, deputy; Mlle. Verneuil, M.D.; M. Alphonse Rodière, Mme. Olympe Audouard, Mlle.

Hubertine Auclert, M. Desmoulins, of the Paris Municipal Council; Mme. Griess-Traut and M. Paul Dubuisson. Germany—Mrs. Louis Otto-Peters. Italy—Mrs. Christine Lazzati-Rossi, Mrs. Ernesta Napollon, and Mr. Charles François Gabba, Professor at the University of Pisa. Spain—Mr. Fernando G. Arenal and Miss Thérès Roaldès. Portugal—Mr. Antonio da Costa. Belgium— Mr. Jules Pagny. Switzerland—Mr., Mrs., and Miss Z. Milkowski. Denmark—The Baroness Astrid Stampe-Feddersen and Mr. Fredrick Bajer, member of the Danish Parliament. Norway—Mr. H. E. Berner, member of the Norwegian Parliament, and Miss Charlotte Jacobsen. Holland—Mr. R. C. Nieuwenhuys, of Deventer. Poland— Mrs. M. Abdank-Abakanowiez. Russia—the late Ivan Tourguéneff and Mr. Pierre Lavroff. Bohemia—Mrs. Charlotte Garrigue Masaryk. Greece—Mr. A. R. Rangabé, Greek Minister at Berlin and Dr. X. Zographos. United States—Mr. Theodore Tilton, Mrs. Laura Curtis Bullard and Mrs. Elizabeth Cady Stanton.

THEODORE STANTON.

59, RUE DE CHAILLOT, PARIS,
  December, 1883.

CONTENTS.

CHAPTER VIII.

INTRODUCTION.

BY FRANCES POWER COBBE.

[Miss Frances Power Cobbe, daughter of Charles Cobbe, D.L., of New-bridge House, Co. Dublin, was born in 1822, and is the author of the following works : " An Essay on Intuitive Morals," " Religious Duty," " Broken Lights," " Darwinism in Morals," "The Hopes of the Human Race," " The Duties of Women," " The Peak in Darien," etc. Of late Miss Cobbe has devoted herself almost exclusively to the work of the Victoria Street Society for the Protection of Animals from Vivisection, of which she is the foundress and Honorary Secretary.]

THERE have been many movements in the world—some of them recorded in history as portentous events, others forgotten within a few years of their occurrence—which may each be compared to a wave on the surface of the Mediterranean. From the insignificant ripple to the wave-high billow flecked with foam and breaking in cataracts, they have arisen only to subside to their original level, leaving the boundaries of land and sea where they have stood for a thousand years. There are other movements, on the contrary, which resemble the tides of the Ocean, wherein each wave obeys one uniform impetus, and carries the waters onward and upward along the shore.

Of all the movements, political, social and religious, of past ages there is, I think, not one so unmistakably tide-like in its extension and the uniformity of its impulse, as that which has taken place within living memory among the women of almost every race on the globe. Other agitations, reforms and revolutions have pervaded and lifted up classes, tribes, nations, churches. But this movement has stirred an entire sex, even half the human race. Like the incoming tide, also, it has rolled in separate waves, and each one has obeyed the same law, and has done its part in carrying forward all the rest. The waves of the Higher Education of Women all over the world; the waves which lifted women over the sand-bars of the medical and (in America) of the legal and clerical professions; the waves which seated them on the School Boards and Boards of Guardians of the Poor; the wave which gave them the English Municipal Vote; the wave which restored to Married Women a right to their own property; every one of these waves, great and small, has been rolled forward by the same advancing tide.

But the crown and completion of the progress must be the attainment of the Political Franchise in every country wherein representative government prevails, and till that point be reached, there can be no final satisfaction in any thing which has been achieved. It has been repeated till it has become a commonplace, that "the Suffrage is the key of woman's position." Obtaining it, every privilege she can reasonably desire must follow. Failing to obtain it, nothing,—not even such installments of her rights as she has hitherto enjoyed,—is secure. An easily-raised storm of prejudice and selfishness, whether of trade or party or sect, passing over the masculine population, might sweep away her few privileges, while she remained helpless and unable to protect them by a single vote. On a small scale such confiscations of the rights of women in trades and other matters have occurred again and again. The sufferers had no appeal from injustice, and, because they were unrepresented, their wrongs were overlooked.

The most difficult problem in that great branch of
Ethics which we call Politics regards the place which
ought to be assigned under each constitutional government to alien races of men. The system of Representation itself, with Trial by Jury and the whole scheme of
civil and political liberty, as we, in our day, understand
it, has grown up through a thousand years of

> " Freedom slowly broadening down
> From precedent to precedent,"

among our law-abiding Anglo-Saxon race ; and either the
hasty adoption of it by other nations with different
tendencies and untrained to self-government, or else the
sudden admission of aliens in large numbers to a share
in the working of our own machinery, are experiments
fraught with difficulty and danger. In the Greek, Italian,
French and Spanish Chambers we see examples of the
first ; and, in the Irish Parliamentary " Obstruction " and
misuse of the jury system to defeat justice, of the second.
Noble and righteous as was the act by which the government of the United States extended the suffrage to the
emancipated negroes, the perils of such a step could
scarcely have been encountered by any sane statesman
had the lately freed slaves borne a much larger proportion to the whole white population of the Republic ; and
not even American democracy will contemplate for many
a year to come following up this heroic act by enfranchis-
ing Chinese immigrants ; nor English radicalism ask for
the admission of Hindoos to a share in the Legislative,—
scarcely even in the Executive,—government of India.

Statesmen, even of the broadest views, may not only be
pardoned, but praised, for hesitating and taking time for
deep consideration, when it is proposed to introduce a

new element into the constitution of their country. In my humble judgment, as a Conservative, there has been culpable recklessness on the part of those who, to serve party interests, have, in England, thrown open the gates of our sacred "*polis*" to a rabble of "illiterates," and in America have admitted hordes of immigrants to the ballot-box, before it was possible for them to acquaint themselves with American politics, or to imbibe American principles.

These considerations should induce women, and their generous advocates, to regard without impatience all opposition to their claims to the suffrage which they believe to be honestly intended and grounded on patriotic anxiety lest the introduction of a new force should disturb the working of the machine of State. They should teach them also to frame their arguments with the paramount object of allaying the fears and encouraging the confidence of such worthy opponents, who, when once convinced that the enfranchisement of women will tend to the stability and prosperity of the State, and to the maintenance of social order and religion, will become the most earnest advocates of the measure. The difference—nay, rather the contrast—should likewise be insisted on between proposals to admit the dregs of a population to the franchise, and those to admit the mothers, daughters and sisters of the men who already exercise it ; and again, between proposals to admit aliens of another race, and those to admit women who have the same hereditary tendencies, attachments, creeds and interests ; and who are the inevitable partakers of the nation's prosperity, and the deepest sufferers by its disasters, or misrule. In short, it ought to be the care of the advocates of women to point out that not a single one of the reasons for caution

in the case of the admission of aliens affect their claims;
while there exist a multitude of valid reasons, why, being
by nature part of the nation, they should also be, by law,
citizens of the State; bringing with them, not an element
of weakness and disintegration, but a completer union,
and a contribution to the nation's counsels of something more than " mother-wit," even of mother-wisdom.

The man is not to be envied who can view the struggle of women for political rights with contempt or indifference. That those struggles may not always have
been guided by infallible taste and wisdom, and that they
have often been met—for lack of sensible argument—with
silly derision, need not blind us to the fact that they constitute one of the bravest battles, one of the most pathetic movements, the world has ever seen. Other strifes
have been carried on between rival races, rival classes, rival
sects; but here we have only the patient, persistent appeal of daughters to fathers; of sisters to brothers; of
wives to husbands; of the women, who make the charm
of society, to the men who call them friends. There are
no " garments rolled in blood " in the battle of these war-
riors. The combatants command neither cannon nor bay-
onets. They cannot even break down iron palings, like
the populace of London, when the rights they demanded
were withheld; or threaten dynamite and petroleum like
Nihilists and Fenians. They have not the minutest political influence at their disposal wherewith to coerce their
opponents. Never was there a case of such pure and simple Moral Pressure,—of an appeal to justice, to reason, to
men's sense of what is due, and right, and expedient for
all. When the time comes to look back on the slow, universal awakening of women all over the globe, on their
gradual entrance into one privileged profession after

another, on the attainment by them of rights of person and property, and, at last, on their admission to the full privileges of citizenship, it will be acknowledged that of all the " Decisive Battles of History," this has been, to the moralist and philosopher, the most interesting ; even as it will be (I cannot doubt) the one followed by the happiest Peace which the world has ever seen.

I feel myself honored in being called on to introduce a worthy and adequate record of this great contest to the public of England and America.

CHAPTER I.

ENGLAND.

I. THE WOMEN'S SUFFRAGE MOVEMENT.

BY MILLICENT GARRETT FAWCETT.

[Mrs. Fawcett is a daughter of Mr. Newson Garrett, of Aldeburg, Suffolk, where she was born in 1847. In 1867 she married Mr. Henry Fawcett, then Member for Brighton, and now Member for Hackney and Postmaster General in the present Administration (1883). Mr. Fawcett is also Professor of Political Economy in the University of Cambridge; and Mrs. Fawcett was led, through reading to her husband, who is blind, to study the same subject. She published in 1870 her "Political Economy for Beginners," and a year or two later "Tales in Political Economy." Mrs. Fawcett has also written a novel, "Janet Doncaster," and is joint author with her husband of a volume of essays and lectures on political and social subjects. She was one of the earliest among lady speakers and lecturers in England on behalf of the political enfranchisement of women, and she has also frequently lectured on other political, literary and economic subjects in many of the principal towns of Great Britain and Ireland. Many members of Mrs. Fawcett's family have taken an active part in promoting the removal of the disabilities of women. Her eldest sister, the late Mrs. J. W. Smith, was the secretary of the first society formed in London to promote women's suffrage; another of her sisters is Mrs. Garrett-Anderson, the well-known physician; a third, Mrs. Cowell, was for several years a member of the London School Board; and her cousin, the late Miss Rhoda Garrett, an excellent speaker and lecturer on behalf of women's suffrage, was also well known in artistic circles as a designer and decorator.]

It is very difficult in tracing the history of any great social movement to point to one particular date and say, on this day or in this year the movement began. The claim of women for education, for political enfranchisement, for social and industrial freedom, is one that is generally regarded as essentially modern. But it owes its origin in England to a date at least as far back as 1792, when Mary Wollstonecraft published her " Vindication of the Rights of Woman." Another weighty blow was struck for women in 1810, when Sydney Smith published his well-known and witty essay urging the claim of women to a sound literary education. Shelley's name must also be recorded as among those of the earliest of our friends. As late as the first thirty years of this century, the movement must be regarded as one of the results of the upheaval of the human mind of which the French Revolution was the most portentous manifestation. The awakening of the democratic spirit, the rebellion against authority, the proclamation of the rights of man, were almost necessarily accompanied by the growth of a new ideal concerning the position of women, by the recognition, more or less defined and conscious, of the rights of women. The growth of this movement and its adaptation to the practical spirit of the nineteenth century are to a very large extent due to the life-long advocacy and guidance of the late John Stuart Mill.* Not only in his book on the Subjection of Women,

---

* An English lady, whom I shall have occasion to quote several times in the foot-notes to this essay, writes me as follows : The train of events which led to John Stuart Mill's conversion to the cause of Women's Suffrage is worthy of note. The vague enthusiasm for the Rights of Man which convulsed society in Europe, at the end of the eighteenth century, soon assumed in England a more practical shape. Bentham, the father of modern Radicalism, published his philosophical essays upon Government, and founded a school of followers called Philosophic Radicals, who exercised a marked influence on thought at the beginning of this century. Amongst the most distinguished of the disciples of Bentham was James Mill, father of John Stuart Mill. As

but in the Principles of Political Economy, in his Essays
and Dissertations, in the books on Liberty, Utilitarianism
and Representative Government he attacked the fortress
of world-old custom and prejudice, and claimed for women
the fullest liberty in the practical affairs of life, and showed
the mischief, folly and misery of withholding from half the
human race the opportunity of development which nothing but freedom can give.   Mr. Mill was always careful

---

a keen, hard-headed thinker, James Mill stands pre-eminent amongst the little band of reformers, and his trenchant pen did much to impress the genius
and logic of Bentham upon the enthusiasts of his time.   About 1824 James
Mill published an article on Government in the " Encyclopædia Britannica "
which excited much attention by its novel and lucid argument.   After commenting upon the love of power common to our race he argues that the safeguard of the elective franchise is necessary to protect our liberties from en-
croachment.   " But," he continues, " all those individuals whose interests are
included in those of other individuals may be struck off " the electoral roll.   " In
this light *women* may be regarded, the interest of *almost all* of whom is involved in that of their fathers, or in that of their husbands."   Upon the publication of this article, William Thompson, another disciple of Bentham, wrote
to John Mill, pointing out that " almost all " women did not include " all
women," and that therefore, by his own argument, *some women* at least should
be enfranchised.   Thompson demanded that this logical inaccuracy should
be amended.   James Mill refused to alter the article, whereupon Thompson
and Mrs. Wheeler published in 1825, as a joint production, a substantial
volume called " The Appeal of Women," in which James Mill is attacked in
scathing terms, and the whole position of women is treated with a thoroughness which no writer of the present day has surpassed.   There is no
doubt that John Stuart Mill, young as he was at the time, must have seen
the controversy in which his father was so fiercely attacked, and it is probably from a consideration of these arguments that his attention was directed
to the question of Women's Suffrage.   His book on the Subjection of
Women, published thirty years later, follows very much the lines laid down
in " The Appeal of Women ; " but, instead of the vehemence and indignation of the earlier work, we find a cool, dispassionate statement of facts
which disarms opposition, and has proved far more alluring to our practical
politicians.—T. S.

to disclaim having been the originator of the women's rights question; in a speech at Greenwich in 1870 he corrected a previous speaker who had alluded to him as having been the first to advocate the enfranchisement of women. "Several of the most eminent philosophers," he said, "and many of the noblest of women for ages have done this." But there can be no dispute that Mr. Mill's influence marks an epoch in the history of the women's movement. He was a master and formed a school of thought. Just as in art, a master forms a school and influences his successors for generations, so the present leaders and champions of the women's movement have been influenced, and to a great extent formed, by Mr. Mill. Even those who are opposed to the enfranchisement of women are unconsciously influenced by the movement of which Mr. Mill was the leader. Sir James Stephen admits that in the making of laws which directly affect the relations between men and women, men have made rules for their own supposed advantage which are in fact greatly to the injury of both parties. Even Mr. Goldwin Smith admits that "if there is any wrong to half humanity, which cannot be righted in any other way, we must at once accept Female Suffrage, whatever perils it may entail;" and leading members of Parliament aver, in opposing the bill to remove the electoral disabilities of women, that women are as fit as men to exercise the political franchise with intelligence and care. In this, as much as in the advocacy of our friends, we see the fruit of the seed sown by Mill between the years 1848 and 1869.

One great service of Mill to the women's movement in England has been, I conceive, in impressing upon it from the first, the character of practical good sense and moderation which has been its distinguishing feature. The suffrage has not been claimed for women in England as an abstract and inalienable right, but it has been claimed upon the ground of expediency; that is to say, on the ground that the good resulting from it would far outweigh any evils that might possibly attend it. This note was struck by Mr. Mill in his speech in the House of Commons in May, 1867, and the whole movement from the first has kept in harmony with the tenor of this speech. He then said : " I do not mean that the elective franchise, or any other public function, is an abstract right, and that to withhold it from any one, on sufficient grounds of expediency, is a personal wrong; it is a complete misunderstanding of the principle I maintain, to confound this with it ; my argument is entirely one of expediency. But there are different orders of expediency; all expediencies are not exactly on the same level; there is an important branch of expediency called justice, and justice, though it does not necessarily require that we should confer political functions on every one, does require that we should not capriciously and without cause withhold from one what we give to another." He proceeded to state that the only grounds on which the political suffrage could be justly withheld were personal unfitness or public danger, and these, he contended, did not exist in the case of the women it was proposed to enfranchise.

This basis of expediency on which the women's suffrage movement in England has rested, has led every women's suffrage society, without exception, to seek for the suffrage on behalf of those women, and those women only, who fulfill all the qualifications which the law demands of the male elector ; that is for householders in boroughs, the owners of freeholds, and the renters of land and houses, above a certain value, in counties. The societies have held steadfastly by this principle, and have refused to be drawn either by friends or foes into complicating their position by claiming the suffrage for those women who, by marriage, or any other circumstance, are prevented from fulfilling the conditions imposed by the legislature on the possessors of the suffrage. Whether these conditions are themselves expedient, that is, conducive on the whole to the public good, is another matter which it concerns the community very seriously to consider; it is, however, the principle on which the women's suffrage societies have always acted, not to enter in any way into the general question of the conditions imposed on electors; but to say to Parliament and to the English people, "You have fixed these conditions as you believe to be for the best; you have spent years in considering what they shall be; we accept your decision, and only ask that all who fulfill these conditions shall be admitted to the privileges they confer." This character of practical moderation and rather humdrum common sense, which has stamped the movement in England, has prevented a good deal of what strikes one as rather comic about the movement in other countries. We talk about "women" and "women's suffrage;" we do not talk about Woman with a capital W. That we leave to our enemies. A recent diatribe by Mr. Goldwin Smith in the *Nineteenth Century*, upon "Woman," shows how completely he has lost his touch upon English politics and the English tone of approaching this question. If, in his article, the word "Woman" were struck out wherever it occurred, and the word "Man" were inserted, a great part of it would read like a caricature of the fulminations against the "vile wretch man" which appear to have been the laughing-stock of the American public some twenty years ago. It must not be supposed, however, that Mr. Smith is able to vent all his wrath in general terms; he goes on to speak of women in particular in a way that recalls Vivien's talk to Merlin, when she

> "let her tongue
> Rage like a fire among the noblest names,
> .   .   .   .   .
> till she left
> Not even Lancelot brave nor Galahad clean."

The studious moderation of the societies, the absence of tall talk, is one great secret of the progress the women's movement has made in England. The words Man, Woman, Humanity, etc., send a cold shudder through the average Briton, but talk to him of John and Elizabeth and he is ready to be interested and, up to his lights, just.

The agitation on the subject of parliamentary reform which preceded the passing of the reform bill of 1867, naturally led to the consideration of the claims of women to representation. The death of Lord Palmerston in 1865 made reform a practical political question of the first importance; the general election of the same year, when Mr. Mill was returned as member for Westminster, gave the women's suffrage movement a parliamentary leader of the first intellectual rank. These events led to the formation in London in 1866 of a society for promoting the extension of the suffrage to women. The members were Mrs. Peter Taylor, Mr. Hastings, now member for Worcestershire, the late Dean of Canterbury (Dean Alford), the late Professor Cairnes, the well-known political economist; Mrs. Knox, better known by her maiden name of Isa Craig, Miss Emily Davies, the originator of Girton College; Miss J. Boucherett,* Rev. W. L. Clay, Lady Gold-

---

* Miss Boucherett is the author of the essay on "The Industrial Movement," at the end of this chapter.—T. S.

smid, Mr. James Heywood, Miss Manning, and Mrs. Hens-
leigh Wedgewood. The honorary secretary was Mrs. J.
W. Smith. It is an interesting and touching list for us
who are left, for many of the names are now dear and
honored memories, " precious friends hid in death's date-
less night." The society was instrumental in getting
signatures to a petition in favor of the extension of the
suffrage to women who were possessed of the legal qualifications, and this petition, signed by 1,499 women, was
presented during the session of 1866. A member of the
society, Madame Bodichon (*née* Miss Barbara Leigh
Smith), read a paper at the meeting of the Social Science
Congress at Manchester in October, 1866, entitled, " Reasons for the Enfranchisement of Women."

The first London Committee was dissolved in 1867 and
reformed by Mrs. Peter Taylor under the name of the
London National Society for Women's Suffrage. Societies in correspondence with the London society, but entirely independent of it and of one another, were almost
simultaneously formed at Manchester, Edinburgh, Bristol,
Birmingham, Belfast and Dublin, and subsequently smaller societies were formed in more than forty towns in Great
Britain and Ireland. Mr. Mill was the president of the
London National Society, Mrs. Peter Taylor was its honorary secretary and treasurer, and, I may add, its presiding
genius. The meetings were held at her house, and she
devoted herself with all the enthusiasm of her gentle and
courageous spirit to the objects of the society. Mrs. Peter
Taylor was greatly assisted in her labors by Miss Caroline
A. Biggs, who has ever since been an indefatigable worker
for the cause of women's suffrage.* The Manchester soci-

---

* " A few years later," writes the lady to whom I have already referred, " a
large share of the active work of the movement was undertaken by another

ety was so fortunate as to secure from the outset the services of Miss Becker as its able and zealous secretary.* Mrs. Duncan McLaren, sister of Mr. Bright, was the president of the Edinburgh society. Lady Amberley presided over the Bath and Bristol society, where she was aided by the untiring energy and self devotion of the Miss Ashworths, members of another branch of the Bright family.

Immediately previous to the formation of these societies, a great impetus had been given to the movement by the first discussion upon it in Parliament, which was raised by Mr. Mill on May 20, 1867, in the form of an amendment to the fourth clause of Mr. Disraeli's reform bill. The amendment took the form of moving to leave out the word "man" in order to insert the word "person." Eighty-one members, counting the tellers, either voted or paired in favor of Mr. Mill's amendment, and from this date the parliamentary history of the movement begins. Among Mr. Mill's supporters were eleven Conservatives, one of whom, Mr. Russell Gurney, the late Recorder of London, was a teller; Mr. Gurney was throughout his life a tried and valued friend of every movement for the benefit of women. Mr. John Bright, who has since gone over to the enemy, was one of Mr. Mill's band of eighty-one. Others, alas! have gone over to the majority in a different sense. Death has deprived us of Lord Amberley, Sir

---

committee, composed mainly of delegates from provincial centres. The first meetings of this committee were held at the house of Mrs. Frederick Pennington, wife of the present member for Stockport. Under the name of the Central Committee it afterwards became united with the London National Society."—T. S.

* " Miss Becker has since then devoted her whole time and energy to the work, and has, by her untiring efforts, continued for sixteen years, become the most active leader of the organization."—T. S.

Francis Goldsmid, Mr. Mill himself, and others whose names are less widely known.

The year 1868 was marked by what has since become quite common, the presence of ladies as speakers at public meetings on behalf of the enfranchisement of women. In April, 1868, a meeting was held in the Assembly rooms, Manchester, at which Mrs. Pochin,* the wife of the Mayor of Salford ; Miss Robertson, of Dublin, and Miss Becker, spoke.†

The Mayor, Mr. Pochin, was in the chair. This meeting was followed by one in May, 1868, at Birmingham ; but it was not until more than a year later, namely, July, 1869, that a meeting with lady speakers was ventured upon in London. The meeting was held at some rooms in Conduit street. Mrs. Peter Taylor was in the chair, and the speakers were, besides herself, Mr. Hare, Mr. Boyd Kinnear, Mr. Mill, the Rev. Charles Kingsley, Mr. Henry Fawcett, Mrs. Henry Fawcett, Lord Houghton, Mr. John Morley, Sir Charles W. Dilke, Mr. P. A. Taylor, Professor Masson, and Mr. Stansfeld. The presence of lady speakers is now so common at similar meetings as to call forth no remark either of commendation or the reverse, but fourteen years ago lady speakers had to endure an ordeal of ridicule from foes and remonstrance from friends such

---

* "Of all the advocates now living of the claims of women to the suffrage, Mrs. Pochin occupies the earliest place, having, in the year 1855, published a pamphlet entitled ' The Right of Women to Exercise the Electoral Franchise,' one of the most brilliant defences of their cause."—T. S.

† It may be mentioned as illustrative of the change which has taken place in public opinion with regard to the propriety of women speaking on the platform, that, at this first meeting in Manchester, it was believed that the utmost public opinion would endure was that the ladies should *read papers ;* they therefore each read a short address, instead of making a speech in the ordinary way."—M. G. F.

as can hardly now be conceived. Shortly after these meetings a member of Parliament referred in his place to the ladies who had taken part in them as having disgraced themselves and their sex.

After the passing of the English reform bill, in 1867, followed in 1868 by the passing of similar bills for Scotland and Ireland, it was believed by many friends of the movement for women's suffrage, especially by members of the Manchester society, that the new reform acts as they stood included the enfranchisement of women. They took their stand upon the existing law, desisted from holding meetings and getting signatures to petitions, and resolved that the legal status of a female householder as regards the parliamentary suffrage should be tested at the next election. At a by-election at Manchester, in 1867, a woman's name, that of Lily Maxwell, had been accidentally allowed to remain on the register, and she, under the escort of Miss Becker, went to the poll and voted in favor of Mr. Jacob Bright. Previous to the general election of 1868, after the passing of Mr. Disraeli's reform bill, a large number of women householders claimed, before the revising barristers, to be put upon the roll of the parliamentary electors. In Manchester alone 5,346 women householders signed the claim to be put upon the register. The revising barristers were not unanimous in the interpretation of the law ; in a few places the claim of women to be put on the register was allowed ; in the great majority it was disallowed. At Scarisbrick, Lady Scarisbrick and twenty-seven women farmers, her tenants, were allowed by the revising barristers for South West Lancashire to remain on the register, and they came to the poll in a body, and voted for Mr. Gladstone. These, it must be remembered, were the days of open voting. In Man-

chester, the claim of the women was disallowed. **The**
Salford overseers placed the names of 1,400 women on
the register, but these were struck out by the revising
barristers. In November, 1868, the claim that women
were enfranchised by the acts of 1867-8, was heard in the
Court of Common Pleas, and judgment was given against
allowing the claim of women householders to the parliamentary franchise, on the ground that, whatever the
wording of the statute and of Lord Brougham's act,
whereby in all acts of Parliament words importing the
masculine gender shall be deemed and taken to include
the feminine unless the contrary is expressly provided, it
was clearly the intention of Parliament, as demonstrated
by the division on Mr. Mill's motion of May, 1867, not to
admit women to the parliamentary suffrage. From the
date of this adverse decision the more active and strenu-
ous labors of the various societies for women's suffrage
may be said to begin. All the usual means of influencing
public opinion were adopted by the societies; public meetings were held and lectures were delivered in almost every
town in Great Britain; petitions to Parliament were circulated, to which the number of signatures appended were
unprecedentedly numerous;* articles were written for
the magazines and newspapers; every opportunity was
eagerly seized for showing that women did want the suffrage and why they wanted it. In 1870, the Manchester
society started the publication of the *Women's Suffrage
Journal,* under the editorial charge of Miss Becker. The
Journal has appeared monthly since its first publication

---

* In 1874, 1,427 petitions in favor of women's suffrage, with 445,564
signatures, were presented. In 1873, 248 meetings were held ; and up to th'
present time the number of meetings held each year remains at a ver}
high figure.—M. G. F.

and forms a very valuable record of all that concerns the development of the women's suffrage movement.

In 1871 special memorials signed by over 9,000 women in favor of the extension of the suffrage were addressed to Mr. Gladstone and to the Earl of Beaconsfield, then Mr. Disraeli. Another means of ventilating the subject was adopted by raising debates on the removal of the electoral disabilities of women in Town Councils. This was done by some member friendly to the movement proposing a resolution that the Council to which he belonged should petition Parliament in its favor. In 1871 the town councils of Manchester, Salford, and Burnley adopted these resolutions by substantial majorities, and a large number of similar petitions were presented in succeeding years.

More recently, with a view of reaching a class that is very seldom to be found at public meetings, a very large number of drawing-room meetings have been held; both lady and gentlemen speakers attend and discussion is usually invited. The object of the drawing-room meetings is not to make a demonstration of the numbers of those who approve of the movement, but to attract those who are either hostile or indifferent to it; and in this object I believe they have been remarkably successful. From the very nature of these meetings, however, addressing as they do a limited class and very limited numbers, it is impossible to rely on them alone for the spread of the movement. Ward and District meetings among the working classes, to which working women were specially invited, leading up to a monster meeting of women in the principal hall in the town, have been held in Manchester, London (St. James's Hall), Bristol, Birmingham, Bradford, Glasgow, and Nottingham. These great demonstrations of the keen desire which exists among women to possess the

parliamentary franchise far surpass as expressions of public
opinion anything of the same kind which has taken place
since the reform agitation prior to 1867. The agricultural
laborers and the other unrepresented classes among the
male population have never been able to show anything
like such evidence of the demand among themselves for
electoral power. At Manchester the Free Trade Hall, in
February, 1880, was not only filled, but an overflow meeting had to be held at the Memorial Hall, Albert Square.
The local newspapers spoke of the demonstration as an
occurrence entirely unprecedented in the history of public
meetings, and averred that the Free Trade Hall was
crowded as it is only crowded when public feeling is deeply
stirred. A similar success attended a similar gathering of
women in St. James's Hall, London. Here also an overflow meeting had to be quickly arranged, and in fact at
all the places previously mentioned where these monster
meetings of women have been held, the result has been
the same :—an overwhelming crowd, great enthusiasm,
accompanied by perfect order and good temper.*   The
remark, so common at one time, that women themselves
do not want the suffrage, is silenced by these huge demonstrations ; but how long it will be before the legislature
listens to the demands of those who urge their claims
without blowing up prisons or knocking down park rails

* " Among the women who took a prominent part in these demonstrations
were Viscountess Harberton, Mrs. Scatcherd, Mrs. Shearer, Miss Becker, Miss
Lord, of Belfast ; Miss Biggs, Mrs. Alfred Osler, Mrs. McLaren, and her sister, Mrs. Lucas ; Mrs. Helen Clark, eldest daughter of Mr. John Bright ;
Mrs. Fawcett, Miss Jessie Craigen, Miss Jane Cobden, Miss Rhoda Garrett
and many others. Perhaps the best known of the women speakers, after
Miss Becker, have been Mrs. Scatcherd and Mrs. Shearer, who have by
their eloquence and enthusiasm done much to influence public opinion in
favor of the claims of women."—T. S.

is a question which only the future can solve. Nothing is more marked in the present phase of the women's suffrage movement than the fact that it is supported by the rank and file of women themselves. At first and from the first it was supported, almost without exception, by every woman who had earned a name for herself by intellectual distinction or by the achievement of excellence in any department of art, literature or philanthropy. It is difficult to choose names when the list is so long, but it is right to mention among the distinguished women who have been with this movement from the outset, the names of Mrs. Somerville, Harriet Martineau, Florence Nightingale, Mrs. Browning, Miss Anna Swanwick, Miss Cobbe, Mrs. Grote, Mrs. Ritchie (Miss Thackeray,) Miss Mary Carpenter and Mrs. Jameson.* These women have been, some of them unconsciously, the leaders of their sex in this question, and, having led the way, hundreds and thousands of women are following them in their aspirations for freer development of all the various faculties with which nature may have endowed them.

I have here anticipated in part the social history of the movement by speaking of its later developments. It is

---

* The Rev. W. H. Channing, of London, writes me: "But there are a large company of nobly gifted, and highly cultivated women scattered throughout Great Britain, quite apart from the well-known leaders of the so-called Women's Suffrage Party. My reference is to such grand women as Mrs. Josephine Butler, of Liverpool; Miss S. Winkworth, of Clifton, Bristol; Miss Anna Swanwick, the distinguished translator of 'Faust' and 'Æschylus'; Mrs. Augusta Webster, the translator of 'Euripides,' etc." And he closes by referring to "the splendid work which women are engaged in here, in education, literature, art, industry, philanthropy, social reform, etc." Mr. Channing's tribute to English women is fully deserved. I know of no centre in the world containing so many remarkable and progressive women as London.—T. S.

now however necessary, if we are to trace its parliamentary history, to go back to the year when Mr. Mill first introduced it into the House of Commons in 1867.

Mr. Mill's parliamentary career was very short: he was elected for Westminster in 1865, and he lost his seat in 1868. He never entered Parliament again, and death closed his labors in 1873. The general election in November, 1868, resulted in a very large Liberal majority, and although the question of women's suffrage was not brought forward during the session of 1869, that year deserves to be remembered as one in which a most important step was made in the direction of women's complete political enfranchisement. A municipal reform act was passed which conferred upon women householders the right to take part in municipal elections.* This was followed by another step in the same direction in 1870, when Mr. W. E. Forster introduced and carried his Education bill, and then conferred upon women householders the power to vote at school-board elections, and also qualified women to sit as members of school-boards, a qualification of which the electors have availed themselves in an ever-increasing number at each succeeding school-board election.

In 1870, the principle of Mr. Mill's resolution of 1867 was embodied in a bill which was introduced by Mr. Jacob Bright, Sir Charles Dilke and Mr. Eastwick. The second reading took place on May 4th, and was carried by 124 against 91. The government remained neutral in

---

* " The bill as originally introduced did not confer this franchise upon women, but an amendment in that sense was, at the suggestion of Mr. Jacob Bright, member for Manchester, accepted by the Government, and passed without a division in both Houses of Parliament. In 1881 and 1882 Dr. Cameron, member for Glasgow, carried a similar measure through Parliament, to confer the privilege of the same municipal franchise on the women of Scotland."—T. S.

this division, and its members were to be found some on one side and some on the other of the division list. When, however, the second reading of the bill was found to have been carried, the alarm seems to have gone forth that if women had votes, the days of the Liberal administration would be numbered. The Liberal government of that day thought they had more to fear from their countrywomen than from their own blunders. The mistake was committed of timidly hesitating to intrust the franchise to a hitherto untried body in the constituencies. Politicians are generally more mistaken in their fears than in anything else.* However, the word went forth. All members of the Liberal government were compelled to desist from giving their support to Mr. Jacob Bright's bill on the motion for going into committee, and all Liberals who were amenable to government influence were urged to vote against the bill. The result was what might have been anticipated: the motion for going into committee was lost by 220 votes to 74.

The women's disabilities removal bill was reintroduced in 1871 by Mr. Jacob Bright, the gentlemen sharing with him the charge of the bill being Mr. Eastwick (Conservative) and Mr. Lyon Playfair (Liberal), afterward Post-master General, and now (1882) Chairman of Committees. The de-

---

* The Duke of Wellington, in 1832, said in a letter to Lord Melville, "I don't in general take a gloomy view of things, but I confess that, knowing all that I do, I cannot see what is to save the Church, or property, or colonies, or union with Ireland, or eventually monarchy, if the reform bill passes." Despatches of Field Marshal the Duke of Wellington, Vol. ii. p. 451. In the Greville Memoirs we find that the astute and well-informed man of the world who wrote them thought that the passing of the reform bill would be the beginning of a revolution, and he even forecast that the future had in store for poor old William IV. the fate of Charles I !—Greville Memoirs, Vol. ii., pp. 136-7.—M. G. F.

2

bate on the bill in the year 1871 was rendered remarkable by a speech from Mr. Gladstone, in which, although declaring that he did not feel able to vote for the bill, he adduced such cogent arguments in its favor, that the speakers who followed him predicted his speedy enrolment among the list of its supporters. Mr. Gladstone, referring to the various laws which regulate the relations between men and women, confessed that in many most important matters women obtain far less than justice. Alluding to the divorce act, he called the attention of the house to the fact that this act introduced a " new and gross inequality against women, and in favor of men," and that in other matters connected with the subject of matrimonial infidelity, " the English law does women much less than justice, and great mischief, misery, and scandal result from that state of things in many of the occurrences and events of life." He concluded by calling upon those who wished well to their country to devise some means by which women could exercise political influence through " a safe and well-adjusted alteration of the law as to political power." This speech excited much comment at the time, both from the friends and from the opponents of the women's suffrage movement. Sir Henry James, who was not then a member of the government, attacked it in a vigorous speech. He is the most distinguished and the ablest among the prominent opponents of the bill, who have not usually been found in the ranks of leading politicians. It is to be observed that whereas the bill has at different times been introduced by Sir Charles Dilke, Mr. Playfair and Mr. Leonard Courtney, who are now (1882) all members of the present government, its leading opposers have rarely attained a first-rate political position. The Hon. E. P. Bouverie has never succeeded in getting any constituency to elect him as their representative after his defeat at Kilmarnock in 1874 ; his nephew, Lord Folkestone, although securely seated in the House of Commons, is quite unknown to parliamentary fame, and the same thing may be said of Earl Percy, Mr. Hanbury, and other aristocratic gentlemen who have taken a leading part in opposing this bill. Mr. Newdegate, Mr. Beresford Hope, Mr. Smollett, and Mr. Scourfield, who have also been active in resisting this bill, have, it is true, a kind of notoriety, but it is on the whole of the sort that one can with great cheerfulness see enlisted in the ranks of one's opponents.

In the division which followed the debate of 1871 the supporters of the bill * numbered 159, the opponents 228. The minority included the names of Mr. Disraeli (afterward the Earl of Beaconsfield), Mr. Ward Hunt, Mr. Selwin Ibbetson, Lord John Manners, and Mr. Russell Gurney, all leading members of the Conservative party, while the then Liberal government and the present government were represented by Sir Charles Dilke, Mr. Fawcett, Mr. Osborne Morgan, Mr. Playfair, Mr. Stansfeld, Mr. Trevelyan, and Mr. Villiers.

In the session of 1872 the women's disabilities bill was again in charge of the same gentlemen who introduced it in 1871, and its rejection was again moved by Mr. Bouverie. The debate does not appear to have had any very remarkable features, save perhaps that Mr. Osborne Morgan, who had voted for the bill in 1871, announced his intention to vote against it in 1872, on account of the prominent part taken by some ladies in the agitation which was then commencing for the repeal of the contagious

---

* In citing the numbers in parliamentary divisions, I have throughout this article included tellers and pairs on each side.—M. G. F.

diseases acts. He did not, however, propose to disfranchise or otherwise punish the gentlemen who were devoting themselves to the same agitation. On a division the numbers were: for the bill, 163, against, 242.

In 1873 the debate was chiefly memorable for a speech of about two minutes' length from the Right Hon. J. W. Henley, the Conservative member for Oxfordshire, one of the oldest and most respected members of the House. He said that, having watched the effect of women's suffrage in municipal and school-board elections, he believed it to be beneficial, and as he could not see why it should not also be beneficial in parliamentary elections, he intended for the first time to support the bill. This characteristically English and common-sense declaration was not without its effect upon the division, in which the minority in favor of the bill included for the first time Sir Stafford Northcote, the present leader of the Conservative party in the House of Commons. The numbers were 172 to 239.

The general election in the spring of 1874 resulted in a large majority for the Conservative party. The changes which the election caused in the *personnel* on both sides of the House were very marked in their effect upon the women's suffrage question. The leading advocate (Mr. Jacob Bright) and the leading opponent (Mr. E. P. Bouverie) lost their seats. The former was re-elected for Manchester in 1876; the latter, as previously remarked, has never been re-elected at all. These changes necessitated a search on the part of the women's suffrage movement for a new parliamentary leader, and Mr. Forsyth, Conservative member for Marylebone, a gentleman of high legal and academic distinction, took charge of the bill. Associated with him as sponsors for it were Sir Robert

Anstruther (Liberal,) Mr. Russell Gurney (Conservative,) and Mr. Stansfeld (Liberal).

The session of 1874 passed without a debate, Mr. Forsyth failing to secure a day for the second reading; but in 1875 he reintroduced the bill, which came on for second reading in April; and the first division in the newly elected House of Commons showed a decided improvement in the parliamentary position of the bill. The numbers were: for the bill, 170, and against, 205. The rejection of the bill was moved by Mr. Chaplin, followed by Mr. Leatham, and later in the debate by Mr. Smollett, in a speech characterized, even by the opponents of the bill, as one of "incredible coarseness." *Punch*, alluding to this speech, said: "We understand Mr. Smollett is descended from the novelist. We hope he will not descend any lower." The disgust caused by this painful exhibition did a good deal, especially among women, to make them believe in the necessity of intrusting to women the power of influencing the laws by which they are governed. "If this is how men speak of us," I heard more than one lady say, "it is not fit that they should have uncontrolled power of making laws for women." A lady, living in the town Mr. Smollett represented, who had not previously signed the petition, signed it with the remark: "A few insults I have received lately have convinced me that women do need representation." It is only fair to say that the more respectable opponents of the women's suffrage bill in the House of Commons were heartily ashamed of Mr. Smollett's contribution in their aid, and the friends of the bill, although they knew that Mr. Smollett had really promoted their cause, felt that a heavy price had been paid for the benefit they had gained.

On March 1, 1876, Mr. Jacob Bright was, as has already

been said, re-elected as member for Manchester. He was therefore present to assist Mr. Forsyth in the House of Commons when the bill came on for second reading on April 26th in that year. Mr. John Bright for the first and only time took part in the debate. To the great regret of the promoters of the bill and the great joy of its opponents, he spoke against the enfranchisement of women. His main argument was that women did not need representation because they were not a separate class. The reply to this argument seems to be that women are not a separate class as long as they are treated with strict and equal justice, but that they are created artificially into a separate class as long as special legal penalties and disabilities are attached to their sex. A life devoted to setting free the oppressed, to extending the boundaries of constitutional liberty, to bringing home to all minds the priceless blessing of freedom and self-government, more than outweighs a single speech. Mr. Bright's influence is with us, though his speech, and recently his votes, have been against us. No one can read his speeches on the extension of the suffrage to men without feeling that almost every argument he uses so forcibly applies with equal weight to women. It was, however, a great blow to the movement when the old leader of reform lifted his voice against it. It gave an excuse to all weak-kneed and half-hearted Liberals to turn against us; it enabled Tories to say that the bill was too revolutionary even for Mr. John Bright. The division which followed Mr. Bright's speech was 161 for the bill, 248 against it.*

---

* The following letter, which, I need scarcely say, the writer gives me permission to make public, will be read with interest in connection with the remarks in the text :

"ONE ASH, ROCHDALE, Oct. 21, '82.

"Dear Sir :—I have never *changed* my opinion on the question of women's

In 1877 Mr. Jacob Bright resumed charge of the bill, his coadjutors being Sir R. Anstruther, Mr. Russell Gurney and Mr. Stansfeld. There was no division, as the debate was not over when the hour (5.50) for the adjournment of the House was reached. In this debate Mr. Leonard Courtney, who had been elected for Liskeard in the previous December, took part. He had during his election contest spoken more than once with all the force of his powerful intellect on behalf of the enfranchisement of women, and the hopes that were entertained of him as a powerful friend and future leader were not disappointed.

Mr. Jacob Bright, so long the trusted and courageous champion of the bill in the House of Commons, was compelled towards the close of 1877 to go abroad for several months for the benefit of his health. Early in 1878 it became necessary to obtain another parliamentary leader, and the friends of the movement were so fortunate as to obtain the services of Mr. Courtney. The English people

---

suffrage. I voted with great doubt and reluctance with Mr. Mill, and more out of sympathy with him than from agreement with him on the subject before us. I have always regretted the vote, and explained the whole matter in a speech against women's suffrage in a subsequent session of Parliament. I cannot give you the date of this speech, but it is fully reported in Hansard's Debates. I cannot give you all the reasons for the view I take, but I act from a belief that to introduce women into the strife of political life would be a great evil to them, and that to our own sex no possible good could arrive. If women are not safe under the charge and care of fathers, husbands, brothers and sons, it is the fault of our non-civilization and not of our laws. As civilization, founded on Christian principle, advances, women will gain all that is right for them, although they are not seen contending in the strife of political parties. In my experience I have observed evil results to many women who have entered hotly into political conflict and discussion. I would save them from it. If all the men in a nation do not and cannot adequately express its will and defend its interests, to add all the women will not better the result, and the representative system is a mistake. But I cannot discuss the question in a note. I give you an

are said never to pay attention to more than one political question at a time, and at this moment they were devoting all their attention to the consideration of the fate of Eastern Europe. Notwithstanding the absorbed state of the public mind upon foreign politics, Mr. Courtney succeeded in raising a very good debate on the second reading of the bill on June 19, 1878. His speech in introducing the bill was a model of well-reasoned eloquence, but the result of the division showed, as usual, that the appeal to nonsense had been more powerful that the appeal to sense, and the numbers were 155 to 234.

The year 1879 is unfortunately the last in which it is possible to record the result of a debate and division in the House of Commons. The subject this year was raised by Mr. Courtney in the form of an amendment on going into committee. In his speech he referred with great effect to the result of women's suffage in the Territory of Wyoming.

---

idea merely of the view I take of it. There is more in my speech, but even that very lightly touches upon the whole subject.

"I am, respectfully yours,
"JOHN BRIGHT.

"Theodore Stanton, Esq.
"à Jacournassy,
"par Sorèze,
"Tarn."

When in London in the autumn of 1882 I had the pleasure of meeting Mr. Bright, and, the conversation turning on the subject of women's suffrage, he developed more at length the same lines of argument contained in the above note written a few weeks before. It is a curious fact, however, that John Bright stands almost alone in his views on this question among the members of his very large family. For instance, his sisters, Mrs. McLaren, wife of the member for Edinburgh, and Mrs. Lucas ; his brother, Mr. Jacob Bright, M.P. ; his daughters, Mrs. Helen Bright Clark, Mrs. R. F. Curry and Mrs. Bernard Roth ; his neices, Mrs. Ashworth Hallett, Mrs. Joseph Cross and Mrs. John P. Thomasson, wife of the member for Bolton ; and his nephews, Mr. Charles B. McLaren, M.P., and Mr. Walter B. McLaren, not to speak of almost as many more relatives by marriage, are advocates of women's suffrage, and several of them active workers in the movement.—T. S.

He quoted from a letter written by the Speaker of the House of Representatives of Wyoming in which, after confessing that at first he had been strongly opposed to women's suffrage, he adds: " I can now say that the more I have seen of the results of women's suffrage, the less have my objections been realized and the more has the thing commended itself to my judgment and good opinion ; and I now frankly acknowledge, after all my distrust, that it has worked well and been productive of much good to the Territory, and no evil that I have been able to discern. Women are more interested in good government and its moral influence upon our future sons and daughters than men. They look above and beyond mere party questions or influences in deciding their vote." The debate was unusually long, and, mainly I believe from accidental causes, the division was unusually bad : only 134 voted and paired for Mr. Courtney's resolution, 248 being on the other side.

The general election of 1880 did a great deal directly and indirectly for women. Large numbers of the supporters of women's suffrage were among the successful candidates, while a host of the old opponents of the measure lost their seats. Indirectly the movement for women's suffrage was advanced by the fact that the share which women took in the electoral campaign was quite unprecedented. There were few constituencies in which there were not lady canvassers, and there were a great many in which there were lady speakers. Mr. Gladstone did not appeal in vain when he called upon his country-women to play their own part in this political crisis. Addressing his country-women he besought them to use their influence in the electoral contest, assuring them that to do so was the "performance of a duty, the neglect of which would be in future times a source of pain and mortification, and the accomplishment of which would serve to gild your own future years with sweet remembrances, and to warrant you in hoping that each in your own place and sphere has raised your voice for justice, and has striven to mitigate the sorrows and misfortunes of mankind." The questions that were decided at the late election were of a character that was certain to call forth the enthusiasm of women. It is needless to say that women were not on these, nor on any questions, all on one side. The opinion of the Baroness Burdett Coutts was placarded all over London and Middlesex, in support of the Tory government. Still the organized strength of the women was exerted for the Liberal party, and in the north and in many of the metropolitan constituencies many worked hard and with great effect on behalf of the Liberal candidates. The session of 1881 was so disturbed by the general election and by the subsequent formation of the present government, that no opportunity arose for the introduction of the women's suffrage bill, and before the beginning of another session the acceptance by Mr. Courtney of the post of Under Secretary for the Home Department, deprived the movement of its parliamentary chief. Mr. Courtney's successor has been found in the person of Mr. Hugh Mason, member for Ashton-under-Lyne. He has not up to the present time (February, 1883) succeeded in getting a day for the discussion of the bill. It is believed that the women's suffrage party gained a large accession of strength at the last election, but up to the present this impression has not been brought to the test of a division.

Reference has just been made to the experience of the Territory of Wyoming in the matter of women's suffrage. England has within the last two years had the benefit of seeing the experiment of giving votes to women tested in a sort of English Wyoming, *i. e.*, the Isle of Man.

After a spirited contest between the two branches of the Manx legislature in the year 1880, the representative chamber, the House of Keys, prevailed upon the upper chamber to consent to the enfranchisement of women owners of real estate of the annual value of £4 and upwards. Women occupiers and lodgers are still excluded ; but the feeling in the House of Keys was so strong in favor of giving women some share of representation that they at last consented as a compromise to accept the limited measure of enfranchisement which was offered by the other House. The bill received the royal assent early in 1881, and the first election in which women took part was held immediately afterward (March 21, 1881). The women showed the most marked appreciation of their new privilege by polling in large numbers, and the universal opinion in the island seems to have been expressed by one of the gentlemen who was returned, viz., "that the new political element had acted in the most admirable manner."

As I have suggested that the Isle of Man may be regarded as occupying in relation to England a somewhat similar position to that of Wyoming in relation to the United States, I ought, perhaps, for American readers, to point out some of the reasons which make the extension of the parliamentary suffrage to women in the Isle of Man even more important as a political experiment than the enfranchisement of women in Wyoming.

The Manx constitution is of very great antiquity; the island has never been incorporated with Great Britain ; the governor is nominated by the queen, and certain dues, such as customs, royalties on mines, etc., are paid to Great

Britain. But the island has complete legislative independence. It sends no representative to the House of Commons. It has a miniature Parliament of its own, which is
of even greater antiquity than the Parliament of Great
Britain. The population of the island is 54,042, its area,
180,000 acres. In area, Wyoming greatly surpasses the
Isle of Man, for the Territory covers 62,645,120 acres.
The population, however, of Wyoming is only 9,118 ; *
therefore, whereas the island has one person to (approximately) every three and one-third acres, there are about
6,870 acres to every person in the Territory. An example
set by an old established and comparatively thickly peopled
community like the Isle of Man has, I think, more significance than a similar example set by the youngest and
smallest of the members which make up the corporate
body of the American nation. It is a thing to be expected that the newly settled regions of the United States
should become the field for making all kinds of social and
political experiments. The freedom which the American
Constitution admits in this direction is one of its greatest
merits. But I think it may be claimed that when a similar experiment is tried with success in a place that is
rigidly conservative of its ancient institutions, the history
of which can be traced back to the sixth century, the example is one that is entitled to even greater respect than
that set by the good people of Wyoming.

The universal feeling among those engaged in working
the women's suffrage question in England is, that with
the general public great progress is being made ; but that

---

* This was the population of 1870, but the new census, according to the
Tribune Almanac, gives 20,789 souls. This does not in the least affect,
however, Mrs. Fawcett's argument, for women's suffrage was in operation
in Wyoming in 1870.—T. S.

in Parliament the progress is much less rapid and assured. The great object of all concerned in this movement in England must be to keep it well to the front, so that when the reform question is opened again, as it must be before many years have passed, politicians may be made to feel that women have earned some share of representation. As I write these lines a letter on this subject appears in the London papers, addressed to Mrs. Ashworth Hallett by Sir Stafford Northcote, in which he says: " If we should be called upon to pass a measure for that purpose " (lowering the qualifications for the suffrage) " the case of the women rate-payers ought certainly to be dealt with." With powerful friends on both sides of the House, it may, I hope, be predicted with some confidence that women will not be left out of the next English reform bill.*

---

* Although the Married Women's Property Act, which was passed by Parliament in the summer of 1882, does not properly belong to the subject of this essay, still, as several of the advocates of women's suffrage, were prominent in securing the enactment of this important measure, and as it has wrought such a revolution in the condition of married women in England, it deserves at least a few words of notice. " When the bill becomes law " (as it did on January 1, 1883), says the London *Times* of August 18, 1882 (weekly edition), " a married woman will be capable of acquiring, holding and disposing, by will or otherwise, of real or personal property as her separate estate, just as if she were single. . . . It probably portends indirect social efforts much greater than the disposition of property, and it may in the end pulverize some ideas which have been at the basis of English life. Measures which affect the family economy are apt to be 'epoch-making'; and probably when the most talked of bills of the session are clean forgotten this obscure measure may be bearing fruit." I was in London in November, 1882, when the meeting was held at Willis's Rooms, to hear the report of the committee—Mrs. Jacob Bright and Mrs. E. W. Elmy—who had had the measure in charge, and to formally thank them for their untiring labors. Mr. Shaw Lefevre, M.P., presided, and speeches were made by Mr. Jacob Bright, M.P.; Mrs. Jacob Bright, Mr. Hinde Palmer, M.P.; Mr. Osborne Morgan, M.P., and others. I was forcibly

II. THE WOMEN'S EDUCATIONAL MOVEMENT.

BY MARIA G. GREY.

[Emily Anne Eliza Shirreff, born November 3, 1814, and Maria Georgina Grey, born March 7, 1816, are the elder daughters of the late Admiral William Henry Shirreff and Elizabeth Anne Murray, his wife. Admiral Shirreff, son of General William Henry Shirreff, claimed collateral descent through his mother, Margaret Bayard, of New York, with the Chevalier Bayard *sans peur et sans reproche*, the Protestant branch of whose family left France after the revocation of the edict of Nantes. His wife also claimed French Huguenot blood through the marriage of her grandfather, the Rev. Dr. Gideon Murray, brother of the sixth and father of the seventh Lord Elibank, Premier Baron of Scotland, with Elizabeth, daughter of General David Montolieu, Baron de St. Hypolite. Maria Georgina Shirreff married in January, 1841, her first cousin, William Thomas Grey, eldest son of the Hon. William, Lieutenant-Colonel Grey, and nephew of the second Earl Grey, who carried the reform bill of 1832. She and her sister composed together first a novel, " Passion and Principle," published in 1841, and later on " Thoughts on Self Culture," published in 1850. In 1858 Miss Shirreff brought out her work on "The Intellectual Education of Women." In 1868 Mrs. Grey published a novel, " Love's Sacrifice." In 1870 she was a candidate as a member for her own borough, Chelsea, in the first election for the School Board of London, but was defeated by a few votes. In 1871 she formed the National Union for the Education of Women of all Classes, of which Princess Louise, Marchioness of Lorne, became the president, and Mrs. Grey held the post of Hon. Organizing Secretary till her health broke down in the winter of 1878–9. In that capacity she was instrumental in forming the Girl's Public Day School Co. (limited), incorporated in July, 1872, and the Teachers' Training and Registration Society, incorporated in 1877. Her sister, Miss Shirreff, who worked hand in hand with her in all these undertakings, was also an Hon. Secretary of the Union and joint editor, with Mr. George C. T. Bartley, of the *Journal of the Women's*

---

struck at this gathering, as I have often been since, by the large number of prominent persons who take an active part in the English women's movement.—T. S.

Education Union, till it ceased to appear at the end of 1881. In 1876, Miss Shirreff, having previously given much attention to the Kindergarten system, was elected president of the Froebel Society, in succession to the late lamented Miss Doreck, its founder and first president. In the same year Miss Shirreff published her "Principles of the Kndergarten System;" and in 1877 her "Sketch of Friedrich Froebel's Life," was first read as a lecture before the meeting of the Froebel Society. She is now (1882) issuing a series of papers entitled "The Kindergarten at Home," in the monthly periodical, *The Governess*, published by Joseph Hughes. The other literary work of the two sisters, besides that mentioned above, consists of numerous papers on educational subjects read first at Social Science Congresses, meetings of the British Association, and various educational societies, and afterward published as pamphlets or in educational journals; and of articles on social and other subjects in *Fraser's Magazine*, the *Contemporary Review*, the *Nineteenth Century*, and the *Fortnightly Review*.]

THE first and most striking fact to note, in giving an account of the movement on behalf of the education of women in England, is its extremely recent origin, and the shortness of the period which has seen its birth and its culminating success. Perhaps no movement of equal importance and involving such far-reaching results ever developed so rapidly, or attained its object so completely, within a fraction of the life-time of one generation. Forty years ago the question of women's education did not exist, and only within the last twenty years has it taken its place among the public and active interests of the day. When the question of popular education came to the front, no difference was made between the girls and the boys; elementary instruction, especially the religious instruction, which was its basis at that time, being admitted as equally necessary to both sexes. But of education, as the development of human faculty and the pursuit of knowledge for its own sake, there was no question for women, or indeed for men either. Boys of all classes were sent to school because it was the necessary preparation for active life. When the progress of civilization after the Renaissance had made a certain amount of culture the necessary accomplishment of a gentleman, it became the fashion for the sons of gentlemen to go from school to the university; and the universities changed their character from being the fountains of higher knowledge to the students, rich and poor, who came to them for knowledge only, into high schools for the sons of the wealthy landed gentry and aristocracy, while also providing poorer men with the necessary preparation, the *brodstudien*, for the so-called learned professions, the church, the bar, and medicine. As women did not go into these professions, and the finishing process with them required accomplishments, not culture, of course any higher instruction than that of the school-room was held to be quite unnecessary in their case, and every attempt to approximate their education to that of men was stigmatized as a departure from the proprieties of their sex.

The first public action taken to place within the reach of girls of the middle and upper classes better school-teaching, both as regarded quality and quantity, was initiated in 1846–7, by one who was in the vanguard of so many other fruitful movements for the propagation of "sweetness and light" in regions where they had never before penetrated, the Rev. F. D. Maurice, at that time a professor of King's College, London. "He took compassion on the sisters of his boy pupils," says the Dowager Lady Stanley of Alderley,* who was his able and zealous colleague then, as she has been since, of all who have taken up the work of women's education, "and with the Rev. R. C. Trench, the present Archbishop of Dublin, and

---

* Personal Recollections of Women's Education.—*Nineteenth Century,* August, 1879.—M. G. G.

some other fellow workers, elaborated the plan of Queen's College. . . . . . The first idea of the founders was that governesses only were to be educated in this college;" (another proof how entirely education was governed by bread-winning necessities); "but this limited plan soon gave place to one including all who could and would come to the classes. . . . . For such a purpose no endowment could be got, and Queen's College was a venture, depending for its success on the unselfish devotion and energy of its founders. Good workers were not wanting. The college was modestly opened in a house in Harley Street, on the 1st of May, 1848; and in 1853 a royal charter was obtained, at that time the only means of forming a corporation, except by an Act of Parliament. This charter was the first formal public sanction given in modern times to the principle that the education of Englishwomen was not less important or less worthy of honor than that of men." . . . .*

In addition to the systematic classes of the college, free evening classes were opened to governesses only, in arithmetic, mathematics, geography, Latin, history, theology, and mental and moral philosophy. Of these classes, the first of their kind, Miss Buss, the head-mistress of the North London Collegiate School, herself one of the students, says: "To young beginners they opened, as it were, a new life." And Miss Beale, principal of the Ladies' College, Cheltenham, expresses in equally strong terms her debt of gratitude to them. That these two women, who have since led the van in the practical work of improving the education of women, should have both owed their training to Queen's College, is alone sufficient

---

* Ibid., page 305.

to stamp its value and justify the position assigned to it as a real and powerful, though silent, agent in the great reform that followed. A year after the foundation of Queen's College, 1849, the example was followed in the foundation of Bedford College, on the same lines and with the same purposes, with this difference only, that whereas Queen's, like King's College, London, to which its founders belonged, was placed distinctly under Church of England patronage, Bedford College stood as distinctly aloof from connection with any religious denomination.

After this the whole question seems to have dropped out of sight and out of mind, and it was not till seventeen years later that the next great step was taken. This was the admission of girls to the Local Examinations of the University of Cambridge.* The object for which these examinations had been instituted was to raise the standard of middle-class instruction, known to be lamentably low, by setting up both a standard and a test of attainment. The want of such means not only of testing the instruction given, but of impressing a steady direction toward a well-defined aim on the character of the teaching, was even more needed in girls' than in boys' schools ; since even the lowest of the latter gains something from the influence of the great public schools and universities. Accordingly a movement was set on foot, of which Miss Emily Davies was the life and soul, to obtain the admission of girls to the local examinations. In 1862 a committee was formed for this purpose, of which Miss Davies was

---

* For the benefit of foreign readers it may be well to explain that these are Examinations of young people of school age, under fourteen for the Junior and under sixteen for the Senior, which were instituted first by the University of Oxford and soon after by that of Cambridge, and which are conducted by Examiners appointed by the University wherever a local centre can be formed.—M. G. G.

elected Honorary Secretary; and in December, 1863, an experimental examination was held in London, with the co-operation of the Syndicate, for conducting the local examinations; the regulations for boys being strictly observed. Forty senior and forty-three junior girls were examined; and as only six weeks' notice could be given, it is not surprising that only six senior and twenty-seven junior girls were successful.* The experiment had, however, shown that no practical difficulty stood in the way of the scheme. Miss Davies redoubled her efforts, and in the following year a memorial, signed by about one thousand ladies and gentlemen officially engaged, or connected with educational work, and supported by other influential persons, was presented to the Vice-Chancellor and the Senate of the University of Cambridge. The answer was favorable, and in 1865 the Cambridge Local Examinations were finally thrown open to girls, and six local centres were formed. In 1881 that number had increased to eighty-seven, and the number of candidates to 1,554 Juniors and 1,139 Seniors,—total 2,693. Of these, 75 per cent. of the Juniors and 57.5 of the Seniors passed successfully.

Oxford was not long in following the example of Cambridge, and so far bettered it that, instead of classing the girls separately, as in the Cambridge plan, all the candidates take their places on the list giving the results of the examination irrespective of sex; and thus affording a perfectly fair standard of comparison between the girls and the boys, both in the several subjects and in the general average of success and failure.

It is worth noting that as the percentage of girls sent up has increased, and the improvement in girls' schools

* Ibid. Page 312.—M. G. G.

and their methods of teaching have had time to make themselves felt, there is a marked tendency toward equality of results between the sexes; * indicating, like the similar tendency observable in the results of the other examinations in which both sexes compete on equal terms, that the intellectual differences between them are probably rather accidental than inherent, and that under similar conditions of training and exercise there is no congenital impediment to the success of women in any field of intellectual labor.†

About the same time that the University of Cambridge thus recognized the claims of girls to share in the advantages offered to boys, these claims received their first recognition as a matter of national interest by the inclusion of girls' schools within the scope of the Royal Commis-

---

* The percentage of failures given in the report above quoted is 32 for Junior boys, 25 for Junior girls; 45 for Senior boys, 42.5 for Senior girls. —M. G. G.

† Mr. Alfred P. Hensman, of The Temple, writing to the editor of the London *Standard* on November 15, 1882, says: "Will you allow me to draw the attention of your readers to a remarkable result of the recent Examination for the Degree of Bachelor of Arts in the University of London? There were two hundred and thirty-seven candidates altogether, of whom two hundred and fifteen were men. Of these two hundred and fifteen men, ninety, or about forty-two per cent., obtained the degree. Of the twenty-two women who presented themselves no fewer than sixteen, or about seventy-three per cent., were successful. But, further, only fifty-eight of the two hundred and fifteen men, or twenty-seven per cent., were placed in the first division, whereas fifteen of the twenty-two women, or sixty-eight per cent., succeeded in obtaining places in that division. To put it in another way, more than one in every three of the men who obtained their degrees was in the second division; only one of the sixteen women who became graduates failed to be placed in the first division. Upon inquiry I find that the average age of the women was not higher, probably it was slightly lower, than that of the men. As one who took an active part in the movement which ended in the admission of women to the Degrees of the University, I am desirous that these striking facts should be generally known."—T. S.

sion, opened in 1864, for inquiring into the education
given in schools not included in the former commissions,
and also for " considering and reporting what measures,
if any, were required for the improvement of such education, having special regard to all endowments applicable,
or which can rightly be made applicable, thereto." The
reports of this Commission, consisting of a General Report
and the several reports of the Assistant Commissioners, to
each of whom had been assigned one of the eight districts
into which England and Wales had been divided, together with the evidence given before the Commissioners
by men and women engaged or interested in educational
work, were published in 1868–9. The portion of the
reports and of the evidence referring to the education of
girls was reprinted separately, with the sanction of the
Commissioners, by Miss Dorothea Beale, Principal of the
Ladies' College, Cheltenham, who added a very valuable
preface, giving the results of her own large experience,
and adding all the weight of her testimony to the truth
of the sad picture presented by the reports. To this
volume the present writer has often referred as the Dooms-
day book of women's education,—recording, however, not
its possessions, but its deficiencies ; and a few extracts
from it will best illustrate the condition of things which
the initiators of the reform movement had to deal with ;
and, at the same time, afford the best measure of the
ground gained in the interval between that and the
present day.

The Commissioners in their general report sum up the
result of the Assistant Commissioners' inquiries in the
following words:—" Want of thoroughness and foundation ;
want of system ; slovenliness and showy superficiality ;
inattention to rudiments ; undue time given to accom-

plishments, and those not taught intelligently, or in any scientific manner; want of organization."

Mr. Norris's evidence, quoted in the above report as the most concise and accurate view of the state of girls' schools, is to this effect :—" We find, as a rule, a very small amount of professional skill, an inferior set of school-books, a vast deal of dry, uninteresting task-work, rules put into the memory with no explanation of their principles, no system of examination worthy of the name, a very false estimate of the relative value of the several kinds of acquirement, a reference to effect rather than to solid worth, a tendency to fill and adorn rather than to strengthen the mind."

"It is no exaggeration to say," states the Assistant Commissioner, Mr. Fitch, "that in the mass of girls' schools the intellectual aims are very low, and the attainments lower than the aims."

The districts allotted to Mr. Fearon and Mr. Giffard, embracing London and its neighborhood, Surrey and Sussex, contained the highest grade girls' schools in the country. This is Mr. Fearon's conclusion in regard to them :—(1) " The provision in London is most inadequate." (2) " The cost of education is very high." (3) " The buildings and premises of almost all these schools, whether day or boarding, are most unsatisfactory." "Except Queen's and Bedford Colleges, where gentlemen are employed in teaching, and at a very few private schools whose principals have determined to make a stand against the frivolous character of girls' education, the quality of the visiting teachers of language and science is very inferior in girls' schools of the first grade." Mr. Giffard sums up the impressions he derived from his visits to girls' schools thus :—" That the mental training of the best girls' schools is unmistakably inferior to that of the best boys' schools; and the great and obvious feature of all girls' schools, except those of the very humblest, is the enormous preponderance given to accomplishments."

The damaging conclusions of the Assistant Commissioners were more than borne out by the evidence given before the Commissioners. Mr. Sargant states that the education of girls in Birmingham, of what he terms the middle class, is "disgracefully bad; that they are very much worse educated than their brothers—very much worse than those who go to any school under H. M.'s. Inspectors"—that is, elementary schools. Miss Emily Davies, mentioned above as one of the earliest and most active movers in the cause of woman's education, says:— "I have come across the best school-mistresses. They always speak a great deal of the bad preparation of the girls who come to them. They say they are perfectly ignorant. Their ignorance is unfathomable."

Miss Beale, the editor of these reports, states of female education in the class of life to which her pupils belong, *i. e.*, independent gentlemen and professional men, that "it is defective in an extraordinary degree. . . . Evidence is afforded that there are expensive schools where pupils who have naturally fair abilities may remain for years without obtaining the rudiments of education."

Miss Buss, one of the highest authorities on the subject, and of whose work we shall speak further on, says in answer to the question put to her by the Commissioners, whether she thought that the girls who came to her from the preparatory schools were in a better or worse state of instruction than boys similarly circumstanced :—"I do not know about the boys ; I know the girls could not be worse prepared than they are."

The evidence quoted above applies mainly to the middle class in its three strata, lower, middle and upper; but there was good reason to believe that in the highest classes, who are mostly educated at home, although the instruction given might be better and the standard of information somewhat higher, there was really as little systematic training of the intellectual powers, as little appreciation of knowledge, of the higher forms of literature, or of real excellence in the pursuit of any art.*   And it must further be noted that the education of which these reports gave the results, was exceedingly expensive;—"nearly twice as expensive," says Mr. Bryce, "as that far more solid and practically useful education which a boy receives."

While the education of girls was so much more costly than that of boys, it received none of that help from endowments which has done so much to save the education of boys from falling into an equal abyss of triviality and vulgarity. Miss Buss says in her evidence before the Commission:—"I feel most strongly from the people I have had to do with—professional men with comparatively small incomes—that they can obtain help in the education of their boys, but that no assistance whatever is given in the case of their girls; and that even when willing and able to pay for a good education, they cannot get it." From the tables of endowed schools given in the general report of the Commission, it appears that while the endowments applied to boys' schools amounted to £177,000 a year, exclusive of the great public schools, those allotted to girls were under £3,000 a year; and in every case the endowed girls' schools gave only elementary instruction, and were intended for the servant class only; while among

* Paper read by Mrs. M. G. Grey at the meeting of the Society of Arts. May 31, 1871.—M. G. G.

the endowed schools for boys rank the highest in the land.

The disclosures respecting the education of women in these reports coming so soon after the general impetus given to it by the admission of girls to the University Local Examinations, and at a time when the subject of education generally was occupying more and more of public attention, led to various associations being formed with a view to supplement the deficiencies so startlingly revealed, and to bring the means both of better and larger instruction within the reach of women of the middle and upper classes. Among these the North of England Council for the higher education of women and the Ladies' Council of the Yorkshire Council of Education, which was practically an off-shoot of the former, were among the earliest and most important, as taking the lead in the movement and representing considerable areas of the country. The movement rapidly spread, and in almost every large town in England and in University centres both in Scotland and Ireland, similar associations were formed.

The principal aim of all these associations was to obtain for women, through the means of lectures and classes, the more advanced instruction which men receive at a University. They prepared the public mind in the only way then possible, to accept the idea of education for women beyond that of school, to be carried on through the years which had hitherto been considered as those of emancipation from all serious study and occupation. Their modest beginnings, with lectures on two or three popular subjects, such as history and English literature, gradually expanded into classes for systematic teaching, and finally, in many cases, into complete courses of college education;

sometimes merging the original association for women only into one of the older or newer institutions for men also,—as in the case of the Clifton classes merged in the New University College, Bristol; the London Ladies' Association in University College, London; or as the Cambridge Association in the Newnham Resident College for women; and they are largely superseded now by the ample means of instruction opened to men and women alike, by the Cambridge and London Societies for the extension of University teaching, and the new Victoria University. Their original work received its natural seal and sanction through the University Examinations for women over eighteen, first instituted in 1873, by the University of Cambridge; an example followed within a few years with scarcely an exception by the other universities of the United Kingdom. There was considerable variety in the standard adopted and the lines of examination; but all agreed in the fundamental point that the candidates should have passed the school age, and the standard be that of higher than school instruction.

Meanwhile, Miss Emily Davies, already so often mentioned in these pages, being dissatisfied with these imperfect substitutes for the higher education given to men by a university college course, had conceived the bold idea of giving to women a precisely similar education, under similar conditions of college life; to be tested at its close by the same examination as that by which the university tests its under-graduates. The idea was, of course, scouted at first, and many even of the best friends of women's education opposed it, on the ground that, considering the great and recognized imperfection of the existing university system, it was unwise to adopt it in founding a wholly new institution for the other sex. Miss Davies, whose singular clearness of judgment, tenacity of purpose, and untiring energy, specially fitted her for the task she had undertaken, maintained the ground she had taken up, *i. e.*, that the question of woman's fitness for the higher education, represented by the university course, could be fairly solved only by submitting the women students to precisely the same course, under precisely the same tests, as the men. The university tests were known and recognized; they were current coin. A fancy test invented for women only, even if really higher, would never possess more than a fancy value. She enlisted in her cause many Cambridge men,—without whose generous help, indeed, success would have been impossible,—and many others, both men and women, amongst the most active workers for women's education; and in October, 1869, the college for women, organized in all respects as one of the Cambridge colleges and getting its tuition from Cambridge tutors, was opened in a small hired house at Hitchin, with five students. In 1873, it was removed to Girton, close to Cambridge, where proper buildings had been erected for it from funds raised by subscriptions and donations, which constitute its only endowment; and those buildings, twice enlarged since,* now contain fifty-eight students. To quote again Lady Stanley of Alderley, who in the case of Girton as of Queen's College was among its earliest and most generous supporters : " Girton is in all respects a college on the old model. The students have their own rooms for private reading, their class-rooms for lectures, their public dining-hall; and if no grand old library is theirs, much earnest enthusiasm for study has proved them

---

* It is about to be enlarged again now (January, 1883) the applications being far in advance of the accommodation and continually increasing.—M. G. G.

worthy of richer opportunities than they yet possess. The university did not recognize, nor has it yet* recognized in any official sense the existence of the women's college, but the help and favor of individual members has never failed. The teaching has been Cambridge teaching ; and the Girton students have been yearly examined from the same papers, and under the same conditions as the under-graduates, both for the previous examination, and for examinations for degrees, with or without honors."

Side by side with Girton, another institution has grown up in Cambridge, which has met the educational wants of numbers of women to whom Girton, with its strict collegiate organization, high standard of matriculation and also higher terms, would have been inaccessible. In 1870, a system of lectures for women was established under the management of a mixed committee of men and women residing in Cambridge, the men being all members of the university, and Professor Maurice once more taking a prominent part in the movement. The educational opportunities thus offered soon attracted students from various parts of the country, and in October, 1871, Miss A. J. Clough opened a house for the reception of these students, whose numbers rapidly increased from five at the time of the opening to twenty-six in the Easter term of 1874. In 1873, the Association for Promoting the Higher Education of Women in Cambridge was formed, and Newnham Hall was built for the reception of the rapidly increasing number of students, the funds being obtained in the form of shares in a limited liability company. The success of Newnham Hall has equaled that of Girton ; and though the first object of both Association and Hall was

---

* This ceased to be true in February, 1881, as we shall see further on.— M. G. G.

to afford students thorough preparation for the Cambridge Higher Local Examinations, many of them have desired and obtained more advanced instruction, and have shared the privilege granted to the Girton students of informal examination in the Tripos subjects. In 1880, a further step was taken. The Association and Newnham Hall were amalgamated as Newnham College ; a second building was added to accommodate the largely increased number of students, remaining under the superintendence of Miss Clough, to whose initiative in the first instance, and unwearied care throughout, the College mainly owes its present prosperity. It was recognized, together with Girton, by the Senate of the University, as a place of residence for students intending to present themselves for the Tripos Examinations.

Two other institutions founded about the same time in the sister island, must be mentioned here ; Alexandra College, Dublin, presided over and owing largely its success to the late lamented Mrs. Jellicoe, and the Queen's Institute, Dublin, similarly indebted to its principal, Miss Corlett. The latter was at first intended as a technical school only, but the want of instruction and culture in the students making itself more and more felt, classes to supply it were added to the technical classes, and the Institute became the rival of the College as a place for the higher education of women.

It will be seen that all these various movements for the education of women sprang up sporadically as it were, supported, indeed, in large measure by the same active and devoted group of friends to the cause, but having no connection and no bond of common action. The North of England Council for improving the education of women, and the Ladies' Council of the Yorkshire Council of Education did, indeed, represent comparatively large local areas, but neither of them was, nor pretended to be, in any sense national. The need of some wider organization which should offer the means of communication and co-operation to all throughout the three kingdoms interested or actively concerned in the movement, pressed with great force on the mind of the present writer, and in June, 1871, she brought before a meeting of the Society of Arts, in a paper on the Education of Women, a scheme for a national society affording the desired means of co-operation between all workers in the cause, and obtained the promise, afterward amply redeemed, of the support of the Society. During the meeting of the Social Science Congress at Leeds, in October of the same year,*—the intervening months having been spent in obtaining the names as members of every well-known friend of the cause, whether man or woman,—the new organization took definite shape under the name of the National Society for Improving the Education of Women of All Classes; shortened afterward into Women's Education Union. In November of that year it was inaugurated in London at a public meeting, presided over by the late Lord Lyttelton, whose support was a tower of strength. Through his good offices, Princess Louise, Marchioness of Lorne, consented to be President of the society, and it numbered among its Vice Presidents besides Lord Lyttelton himself and the Dowager Lady Stanley of Alderley, already so often mentioned in these

---

* I gladly take this opportunity of acknowledging the great debt o gratitude the women's education movement owes to this Association, and to the President of its Council, Mr. Hastings. The opportunities of public advocacy and discussion afforded by its annual Congresses, and the cordial help and sympathy of its Education Section Committee were invaluable to the women, excluded at that time from all other means of public action.—M. G. G.

pages, representative names in both Scotland and Ireland; such as Sir Alexander Grant, of the University of Edinburgh, the Archbishop of Dublin, the late lamented Provost of Trinity College, Dublin, Dr. Lloyd, etc., thereby stamping its national character. The objects of the society were as follows: (1) To bring into communication and co-operation all individuals and associations engaged in promoting the education of women, and to collect and register, for the use of members, all information bearing on that education. (2) To promote the establishment of good schools, at a moderate cost, for girls of all classes above those provided for by the Elementary Education Act. (3) To aid all measures for extending to women the means of higher education after the school period, such as colleges and lectures for women above eighteen, and evening classes for women already earning their own maintenance. (4) To provide means for training female teachers, and for testing their efficiency by examinations of recognized authority, followed by registration according to fixed standard. (5) To improve the tone of public opinion on the subject of education itself, and on the national importance of the education of women.

After a lapse of eleven years we venture to affirm that those objects have in the main been attained. The English jealousy of centralization and love of local independence did, indeed, baffle in a great degree the efforts toward organized co-operation of all the various movements on foot toward their common end; but the Union did undoubtedly, though in an informal way, largely promote intercommunication and concentration of effort; and it can boast that every name of note in the roll of friends of women's education has been included in its list of members, and every step in advance has been either led or powerfully backed by its wide-spread influence. Its Journal, under the joint editorship of Miss Shirreff and Mr. G. T. C. Bartley,—both well-known writers on education, Mr. Bartley on that of the people, Miss Shirreff on that of women,*—by recording every movement affecting women's education, not only in England but abroad ; by keeping the work done or doing throughout the country before the public, and by its series of papers on educational subjects both by Miss Shirreff and other writers of weight, which may almost raise it to the rank of an educational manual, has been a real force in aid of liberal education generally and that of women in particular. The Union, by giving scholarships to successful candidates in the various examinations open to girls in the three kingdoms, to be held at some place of higher education, gave an impulse to the latter, and set an example which was largely followed afterward by other bodies. By public and drawing-room meetings wherever opportunity offered, by the publication of papers, by memorials and deputations bringing concentrated influence to bear wherever questions affecting the interests of women's education were being decided, the Union carried on with unwearied energy and no little success its work of propagandism ; and if now it is gradually withdrawing from the field, it is because the work is done and the arms by which the battle has been won may be safely laid down.†

Of its two principal achievements, the formation of the Girls' Public Day School Company and of the Teachers'

---

* "Schools for the People." By G. T. C. Bartley. "Intellectual Education." By Miss Shirreff. " Thoughts on Self-Culture." By Emily Shirreff and Maria G. Grey.—M. G. G.

† Since the above was written the Union has been finally dissolved, and the publication of the Journal, of course, ceased at the same time.—M. G. G.

Training and Registration Society, I must speak with somewhat more detail, as both were initiatory movements of great and far-reaching importance, which entitles them to distinct mention in the history of the general movement for women's education.

The reader will have perceived that up to this time the efforts of the supporters of the movement had been mainly directed to obtaining higher education for women, as the continuation and supplement of school education. But a greater and more pressing want, as shown by the Reports of the Schools Enquiry Commission, was that of good schools to prepare girls not only for this higher education, which must always be the privilege of the few, but for the work and duties of life incumbent on all. It was to supply this want that the Central Committee of the Women's Education Union first turned their attention. Private boarding-schools, with some brilliant exceptions, were not only bad, but so expensive as to put them beyond the reach of all but the wealthier classes; and the young ladies' academies, which took their place as private day-schools in towns, and professed to teach everything for £1 a quarter, were, as a rule, below contempt. A few proprietary schools existed, mostly of a semi-charitable character, with one splendid exception, the Ladies' College at Cheltenham, which had already been raised by the ability and educational genius of its Principal, Miss Dorothea Beale, to the rank of a model institution; and which may now, with its noble central building, its group of boarding-houses, its thorough organization, and its six hundred pupils, fairly be looked upon as the Eton or Harrow for girls. Another woman of genius, Miss Buss, conceived at this time the generous scheme of giving permanence to the work of twenty years of life, the North

4

London Collegiate School, by making over all her interest
in it, though retaining her position as head mistress, to a
body of trustees, who were also to be the future governing
body; and creating at the same time a lower school for
the poorer middle class, unable to pay even the moderate
fee of the Collegiate School.   After several years' arduous
struggle to obtain the necessary financial support for this
scheme, under difficulties to which any lesser energy and
ability than Miss Buss's must have succumbed, her efforts
were crowned with success by the splendid endowment of
the Brewers' Company; and the Camden Schools, with their
noble buildings, their nine hundred pupils,—five hundred in
the Upper, four hundred in the Lower,—and their admirable organization both as to instruction and discipline, stand
in their respective grades at the head of all schools of a similar type throughout the country, and will remain a lasting
monument of the genius and self-devotion of their founder.

It was Miss Buss's original creation, the North London
Collegiate School, that the Women's Education Union
took as their model; but warned by the difficulties she
had encountered in obtaining funds, and feeling, moreover,
that the secondary education of girls in England could
not, and what is more, ought not, to be provided out of
charitable endowments, the Central Committee determined
to raise the money by means of shares in a limited liability company.   In July, 1872, this company was formed
under the title of the Girls' Public Day School Company
(limited), and its first school was opened at Durham House,
Chelsea, in November of the same year.   The experiment
of a public,* undenominational school for girls of the mid-

---

* It may be necessary for American readers to explain that a public school
in England means one open without distinction of classes, to any one who
can pay the fees; not, as in America, a school supported by public funds.—
M. G. G.

dle and upper classes, was an entirely novel, and by many held to be a perilously bold one. On these two points the School Company departed from its model, Miss Buss's school, which before it became an endowed school, admitted pupils only on the recommendation of the Head Mistress and the members of the proprietary body, and was distinctly Church of England in its religious teaching, though with the widest conscience clause. The result has justified the action of the company, and shown how completely it met the great and growing wants of the time ; for at this date, only ten years and a half from its commencement, it has twenty-three schools* at work in London and the provinces, giving a thoroughly good education to an aggregate of over four thousand scholars, at a maximum fee of £15 a year; and before the end of 1882, two more will be opened. For the last four years it has paid a dividend of £5 per cent. to its shareholders ; and while the mixture of classes and denominations has been as complete as possible, not a single difficulty has arisen from it, even in provincial towns, where social and religious distinctions have a much more tenacious life than in London. The Girls' Public Day School Company has thus satisfactorily solved the problem of providing good and cheap education for girls of the classes above those attending the public elementary schools, on terms insuring a fair interest on the capital invested in them. Nor should the beneficent action of the company be measured by its own schools only. Its example has been largely followed throughout the country; schools of the same type have been established by independent local bodies in various places, and it may be safely predicted that, in the course

* Now, January, 1883, increased to twenty-six, with a corresponding increase in the number of scholars, making it close on 5,000.—M. G. G.

of a few years, no town with a sufficient population to maintain a school will remain unprovided with one, either by the Girls' Public Day School Company, or by some local agency of a similar nature. The only real difficulty now embarrassing the executive of the former, is how to meet the increasing demand for schools without outrunning its resources both of capital and teaching power.

The Women's Education Union having thus provided schools, next turned its attention to the training of teachers. In the case of teachers of elementary schools, the necessity for training had been admitted long before ; and thanks to the unwearied energy and self-devotion of the late Sir James Kay-Shuttleworth and Mr. Carleton Tuffnell, training colleges for elementary school-teachers of both sexes had been established, and a certificate of training required from all candidates for appointments in elementary schools receiving the Government grant. But the equal necessity of such training for higher-grade teachers was by no means admitted, and the very fact that it was required for elementary school-masters caused it to be looked upon as the stamp of an inferior grade of teachers. That University graduates, accustomed, if they had taken a brilliant degree, to have the best appointments in the great public schools offered to their acceptance, should be supposed to require training to teach what they knew, seemed almost an insult ; and the general ignorance of the principles of education, both as a science and an art, even among the educational public, favored this assumption that the possession of knowledge was sufficient to secure the power of imparting it.

By slow degrees, however, the question forced itself to the front, through the efforts of such societies as the College of Preceptors and the Scholastic Registration Society, but mainly by those of a few prominent individuals, among whom, besides Sir James Kay-Shuttleworth, should be specially mentioned the late Mr. Joseph Payne, who made the question his own, and who finally received from the College of Preceptors the first appointment to a professorship of the Science and Art of Education ever made in England. With this exception nothing practical had been done till the Women's Education Union took up the question in 1876, and after careful inquiries into the systems adopted in continental countries, formed a Society for the Training and Registration of Teachers, which began its independent existence in December of that year. Teachers of both sexes were contemplated by the Society, but the Council felt that the first claim upon them was that of women, always at a disadvantage in regard to means; and in May, 1878, their first Training College for Teachers in Middle and Higher Schools for Girls was opened in premises kindly lent to them by the Rev. William Rogers, adjoining to the Bishopsgate Middle Class School for Girls; to which the students were admitted as a practicing school. The College opened with only four students, but the numbers rapidly increased, and in 1832 amounted to thirty-six;* and the efficiency of its training has been most satisfactorily tested by the success of the students at the Cambridge University Examinations in the Theory, History and Practice of Education.

This examination, held for the first time in June, 1880, was the result of the efforts made by the various educational bodies and individual educationalists of note, by whom the question of training for higher-grade teachers had been taken up and pressed on the Universities, not only of Cambridge, but also of Oxford and London;

* Now (January, 1883) over forty.—M. G. G.

though only Cambridge has as yet given effect to their demands.*

It must be noted, as marking the great advance already made in public opinion by the women's claim to educational equality, that in this examination no difference is made between the male and female candidates, the conditions of admission, standard, and certificate being precisely the same for both. † This brings me to the last and culminating success of the movement—the admission of women to University degrees. The history of the struggle of women to obtain medical education, and the medical degree which alone could give them professional status, belongs to another part of this volume, but it was a most important and efficient factor in the general movement on behalf of women's education, and undoubtedly accelerated its final triumph by many years. The public, which had little sympathy with women's desire for educational privileges for their own sake, could feel the injustice of excluding them from the same privileges where they constituted the only access to professional position and emolument. The University examinations hitherto open to women were all arranged for women only, excepting the informal Tripos Examination of Girton and Newnham Hall students at Cambridge, which had no value for medical students. The first step taken on behalf of the latter was the passing of the Rt. Hon. Russell Gurney's *enabling* bill, to allow all the nineteen British medical examining bodies to confer their degrees or diplomas upon women. Of these bodies, the Queen's University of Ireland and the King and Queen's College of Physicians, Ireland, were

---

* London has now established a similar examination.—M. G. G.

† This holds good also for all the new teaching and examining bodies created within the last few years.—M. G. G.

the first, to their honor be it spoken, to use the powers
thus conferred, by admitting women who had successfully
passed their examinations as duly qualified physicians to
the Medical Register. In 1876 the Senate of the University of London passed a resolution in favor of admitting women to the examination for medical degrees, under
the powers conferred by the Russell Gurney Act; but the
Convocation of the University protested against the Senate
proceeding under a permissive Act, and against the admission of women to medical degrees, before the question of their admission to all the degrees of the University
had been considered. The Senate then prepared a Sup-
plementary Charter, providing that all the degrees of the
University should be open to women. This charter
was presented to Convocation and passed by a majority
of 241 to 132, nearly 2 to 1, on the 15th of January,
1878, a date to be ever remembered in the history
of women. The final step was taken in January, 1882,
by the admission of women graduates of the University
to vote in Convocation, a right which had before been
reserved. An injudicious attempt was made to include
in this the right to vote for the Members of Parliament
representing the University; which was in effect an attempt by a side-wind to confer the parliamentary suffrage
on women. But this portion of the motion having been
properly set aside, that part of it which gave votes in
Convocation to women was carried by a very large majority, and women were finally placed on a complete equality
with men in every respect within the competence of the
University.

It was natural that the University of London, from its
modern origin and constitution, and consequent freedom
from ancient tradition and social prejudice, should take

the lead in this bold innovation ; but it is another proof
of the rapid advance of public opinion on the subject, that
within two years the ancient University of Cambridge
should have followed the example, and pressed by memorials very largely and influentially signed, one coming
from its own resident members, should have admitted
women formally to the Tripos Examinations, to which
hitherto the students of Girton and Newnham had only
been admitted informally, and as it were *sub rosa.* This
was done on the 24th of February, 1881 ; and it is still
more remarkable that the measure should have been
carried by the extraordinary majority of 258 to 26, including a large number of the non-resident members of
the University, who are generally supposed to constitute
its conservative and retrograde element.

Great as this step is, it still falls far short of the position
of the University of London as regards equality between
men and women. Cambridge has conferred that equality
only in respect of the Tripos Examination, but it has not
acknowledged women as members of the University; and
it is a curious proof of the tenacity of the prejudice against
women following a higher course of education for its own
sake only as a means of general culture, that they are
still excluded from examination for the ordinary degree,
and were admitted to the honors' examination avowedly
on the ground that it alone would confer upon them any
advantage in the race for professional advancement. We
may, however, be satisfied with this partial result, knowing
well that the wedge, already inserted so deeply, will not
fail to be driven home before long. Perhaps Oxford,
which, though always moving more slowly than Cambridge
in the cause of women's education, has made each concession more thorough when granted at last, and which,

like Cambridge, has two resident colleges for women students, Somerville Hall and the Lady Margaret's Hall, may again better the example of the sister University by granting in full what Cambridge is doling out piecemeal: the admission of women to all the privileges of the University on equal terms with the other sex.

A few months after the decision of Cambridge, the University of Durham opened to women its public examinations and first degree in Arts,—the only Faculty besides Theology in which degrees are conferred at Durham, —on the same conditions of residence, etc., as male undergraduates. But till some place of residence and means of instruction have been provided there for women, the privilege will remain practically *nil.* The University of St. Andrews had preceded even London in admitting women to an examination in Arts, of which the standard was the same for men and women in the same subjects, and conferring a degree on the successful candidates; who, however, when women, were entitled Licentiates instead of Bachelors of Arts, from some foolish fear of the ridicule attaching to the latter term applied to women. Last year the foolishness was increased by making the title, L. L. A., Lady Licentiate. It is to be hoped that the proof afforded by the proceedings of the University of London that women can receive and wear the title of B. A., B. Sc., or B. D. with perfect propriety and dignity, will soon dispel these absurd imaginations, and induce the sister Universities to admit the principle that academic distinctions are of no sex, and mark only degrees of learning, whether the wearer be man or woman.

A word must now be said on the application of endowments to the education of girls. Of all the claims made for women, this was the one which met with the bitterest and most persistent opposition, especially in the localities and by the classes interested in the endowments. The idea that girls want secondary education no less than boys has been very slow to penetrate the average British brain, and to apply any part of an educational endowment to their benefit was strenuously resisted as so much robbery of the boys. The Endowed Schools' Commission, presided over by Lord Lyttelton, the never-failing friend of the women's cause, first gave the girls a *locus standi* under their schemes of reconstruction, and by placing women on the governing bodies of endowed schools acknowledged the right of the mother to be represented as well as the father in the direction of the children's education. The dissolution of the Commission and the transference of its work to a department of the Charity Commission, animated by a very different spirit from that of Lord Lyttelton and his colleagues, seriously threatened for a time the interests of girls; but the gradually increasing change of public opinion in their favor, and the efforts of the good friends still left to them in the Department, prevented any permanent reaction, and up to the year 1882 fifty-three schemes for applying a part or the whole of as many local endowments to secondary schools for girls have been sanctioned. Of these, ten are first grade, fourteen second grade, and twenty-nine third grade.*

Nor does this by any means represent all that has been done for girls by the Department. There are many schemes under which scholarships and exhibitions for girls are provided where there were not means or oppor-

---

* It may be necessary to explain that this classification makes only differences in the curriculum of the school and the average age of leaving, which involve difference in the school fees, and has nothing to do with the social position of the scholars.—M. G. G.

tunity for setting up a school, and others where girls get an interest in the endowment contingent upon an expected increase in the value of it. On the whole, we may agree with the Secretary to the Department, Mr. Douglas Richmond, to whom we owe the above statistics and who is himself a staunch friend to the girls, that this is a result by no means calling for self-abasement; and if we contrast it with the state of things when the Endowed Schools Commission began its labors only twelve years ago, when, as we have seen, not a single endowment was applied to the secondary education of girls, and the infinitesimal share they received in the immense educational endowments of the country, went entirely to the support of industrial schools, we shall better measure the ground gained by their cause.

Before leaving this subject, one other endowment for the benefit of women's education must receive special mention for its unique magnificence. It is the college for women planned and now building near Egham, Surrey, by Mr. Holloway, in memory of his mother, at a cost of £237,000 for the building alone, with a further endowment for maintenance, besides the purchase money for the park-like grounds in which it stands. The college, —the idea of which, it will be interesting to American readers to know, was suggested by Vassar College,—is intended to give the highest university education to four hundred students, and will be as unique for the grandeur and beauty of its architecture and the scale of its internal arrangements, as for the lavish generosity of its founder. It is to be completed in 1883, and made over by the founder to the trustees who are to be the future governing body under the provisions of the trust. Some of those provisions, especially that which excludes from the

College women intending to make teaching a profession, we would gladly see altered, and also a larger number of women admitted to the governing body. But it would be ungracious to look so splendid a gift-horse too closely in the mouth, and we can but cordially hope that the spirit which is to dwell in so beautiful a temple, may prove worthy of it in every respect.

The latest step toward supplying university education to women which I have to record, was taken in 1881 by the same body, King's College, London, to which belonged the movers of the first. The Council, presided over by the principal, Canon Barry, always the cordial and able friend of women's education, resolved to commemorate the jubilee of its foundation by founding a Women's Department of the College. Three years previously, following the example given long before by its elder sister, University College,* London, King's College had established classes for women in all the subjects taught at the college, which had proved most successful. University College had, in that same year, admitted women to all its classes on the same terms as men, the junior classes being still separate, the senior mostly common to both sexes. At King's College the complete separation of the sexes was still to be maintained, and it was proposed to raise £20,000 for the necessary buildings—a proposal which, if made on behalf of a scheme for women a few years ago, would have been scouted as preposterous—and £3,000 were actually subscribed toward it

---

* The difference between these colleges, both instituted to give the instruction which the University of London only tests by its examinations, is, that King's College is connected with the Church of England, and gives theological instruction to its students, while University is purely secular.— M. G. G.

before the meeting. Perhaps we cannot better close this history of the women's education movement than by contrasting the tone of some of the speeches made on this occasion with our recollection of that which prevailed at its beginning. Then all the efforts of the advocates of women's education had to be directed to show cause why they should be educated; to meet what Miss Shirreff on one occasion wittily called the "shirt-button and slipper argument," and prove that the comforts of men would not be less carefully attended to if women's thoughts and interests were enlarged beyond the sphere of the kitchen and the workroom. One gentleman who was appealed to for support bluntly expressed what many more implied, that women were getting too much out of hand and wanted, instead of help, "to be taken down a peg." On another occasion, at a meeting to establish classes for the higher education of ladies in one of the metropolitan suburbs, it was urged that the first classes opened should be for cooking and needle-work, as the subjects of paramount importance in the training of future wives. The conception of women as human beings, with moral and intellectual claims and responsibilities in the cultivation of their faculties and the direction of their lives, was looked upon as one of those "advanced" ideas, or rather crotchets, which had no real standing-ground in practical affairs. Listen now to Lord Salisbury, assuredly no partisan of liberal reform in general, speaking at this King's College meeting, presided over by the Archbishop of Canterbury, and having for its express purpose to provide the highest college education for women. Lord Salisbury said: "He had accepted the invitation rather to show his sympathy with the movement, and with those excellent persons at the head of King's College by whom the movement had been introduced, than from any hope that he could add by his advocacy to the acceptability of such a movement; because it seemed to him that the difficulty in the matter, was rather to find why there should be need of advocating the extension of education for women, than to find arguments in its favor.   The burden of proof lay on the other side. Why was the higher education not to be as much the privilege of women as of men?"

We may hope that this question will never need to be asked again.   The privilege is won; the door so long closed is open wide, and the ways and means of knowledge abundantly provided.   It remains only that women shall prove themselves worthy of the freedom they have gained; that they throw off the mental and moral defects contracted during long ages of irresponsible dependence; that they learn and practice the first lesson of true liberty —obedience to law voluntarily accepted, and make it their duty and glory to show that the most cultivated woman can be, and is, the most womanly in all the essential attributes and offices of womanliness.

III.—WOMEN IN MEDICINE.

BY FRANCES ELIZABETH HOGGAN, M.D.

[Frances Elizabeth Hoggan (*née* Morgan) was born at Brecon, in South Wales, on December 20, 1843, but a stone's throw from the house in which England's greatest actress, Mrs. Siddons, first saw the light. She commenced medical study in London in 1866, graduated at Zurich in 1870, established herself in private practice in London at the close of the same year, and was for six years and a half physician to St. Mary's Dispensary, and to the New Hospital for Women, in which the Dispensary became merged. She married, in 1874, Dr. George Hoggan, a staunch supporter of the equal rights of women, and a well known scientific investigator. She co-operated with Dr. Elizabeth Blackwell in founding the National Health Society, of which she was the first Honorary Secretary, and has taken an active interest in educational and social reforms, and in all movements for the improvement of the legal and social position of women. She became a Licentiate of the King's and Queen's College of Physicians, in Ireland, in 1877, and a Member in 1881. She is, jointly with her husband, Dr. George Hoggan, a regular contributor of scientific articles and reviews to English and foreign medical journals. They have published many researches into the minute anatomy of the lymphatic system and other subjects, and they are now engaged in investigating some important points in the nervous system both in health and disease.]

THE first qualified medical woman in England, as in America, was Dr. Elizabeth Blackwell, a native of Bristol, in the west of England, a graduate of Geneva, New York, and the first woman admitted to the English Medical Register. Curiously enough, she had a predecessor of the same name, a midwife, who in the last century wrote a much-esteemed treatise on botany; and among the English midwives of an earlier date there are not wanting many who clearly perceived and wrote on the importance to women of having medical advisers of their own sex. The heartburnings and recriminations between midwives and men-midwives, prior to the incorporation of the College of Surgeons in 1800, testify to the existence of a strong feeling on the part of women practicing midwifery, that men were tending unjustifiably to invade their domain; and a royal midwife of the eighteenth century (Mrs. Stephens, midwife to Queen Charlotte), did not hesitate to employ, in a book published by her, the following significant language, which many thoughtful persons at the present day might be found ready to indorse : " I cannot help thinking that so general a use of men in the business of a midwife, has introduced a far greater number of evils among society than it has prevented."

Old records tell of patents granted to women as well as men, for the practice of certain well-defined branches of the healing art ; and there is evidence that there existed in England in the seventeenth century, a vigorous and sturdy race of women practicing midwifery. It is noteworthy that as early as 1646, a petition was presented to Parliament, entitled " The midwives' just complaint, and divers other well-affected gentlewomen, both in city and country," which appears to be the first public protest ever made by Englishwomen in favor of peace and in condemnation of war. It is further to be noted that the most eminent of the midwives of that day, Mrs. Elizabeth Cellier, a woman of such strong character * that had she been a Protestant, or had she lived a century or two later, she

---

* Mrs. Cellier, on the occasion of her acquittal at her first trial for high treason, dauntlessly refused to pay the jurymen the guinea apiece which they demanded of her, promising, in her own quaint and forcible language, to serve their several ladies, " if you and they please, with no less fidelity in their deliveries, than you have done me justice in mine."—F. E. H.

would doubtless have become one of the imperishable heroines of history, drew up a scheme for the incorporation of a College of Midwives, which she submitted to James II., and to which he accorded a favorable reception. In spite, however, of his promise to unite the midwives into a corporation, by his royal charter, nothing was ever done by the king. It may be that his parsimonious nature took alarm at the proposed large expenditure ; it may be that the medical profession of the day, anxious as it appears to have been that midwives should be instructed in all subordinate branches of their art, were yet unprepared to allow them to take a position which would have placed them on a footing of complete equality with male practitioners of surgery and medicine. Good grounds for the presumption of some such feeling are afforded by the pamphlet published by Mrs. Cellier in 1687, which evinces much professional susceptibility, roused by the remarks and queries of at least one doctor. Viewed by the light of our nineteenth century experience, it would seem as if thus early the exclusiveness of medical men had crept in to mar the harmonious relations which ought to have existed, from the first, between men and women whose lives were alike devoted to the service of the sick and suffering.

Passing on to our own century, we find the name of Dr. Elizabeth Blackwell placed, in 1859, on the English Medical Register, where it remained solitary until 1865, in which year the name of Elizabeth Garrett was added to the Register. Dr. Blackwell, unfortunately for the cause of medical women in England, but no doubt fortunately for our sisters in America, was prevented, by force of circumstances, from carrying out her original intention of settling in London. Thus, though an English physi-

5

cian by the recognition of the register, Dr. Blackwell first practiced in New York. She returned to New York in 1859, and continued to practice there until 1869, when she came back to England, to leave it no more. After some years' practice, during which she took an active part in the solution of many of the social questions of the day, and especially in all bearing on the degradation of women, Dr. Blackwell founded, in 1871, the National Health Society, which has since done a great deal of useful sanitary work. She now lives at Hastings, a centre of bright, cheerful activity, both social and professional, and venerable, less from age than from the unselfish unwearied labors of a lifetime, spent not in personal aggrandizement, but in working for the public good. Dr. Elizabeth Blackwell has published several works on the healthy bringing up of children, and especially of girls, and her latest work, " On the Moral Education of the Young in Relation to Sex," which has been translated into the principal European languages, is a valuable contribution to the educational literature of the day, and a fearless exposition of the false morality which saps all true education, for which parents owe the pioneer medical woman of England and America a lasting debt of gratitude.

The early history of all social questions is more or less a history of the individuals who represent them. Thus a brief notice of two or three of Dr. Elizabeth Blackwell's more immediate successors must here be given. Elizabeth Garrett (now, through marriage, Elizabeth Garrett-Anderson), the first to follow in her steps, obtained official recognition, and the right to practice as a licentiate of the Society of Apothecaries, in 1865. The important achievement of having obtained an English registrable diploma, although of the lowest kind, cost Mrs. (now

Dr.) Garrett-Anderson more time, money, perseverance and patience than would have been needed by a man to obtain the highest honors in his profession. No school in Great Britain would admit her as a student. She had to take some of her classes and hospital practice as a pupil-midwife, or as a nurse, merely tolerated in the wards; and on one occasion she was dismissed because her answers to clinical questions put to the class were too good, and the students mutinied. In other subjects she paid away a small fortune in fees for private teaching from recognized lecturers at medical schools. Only in this way could she gain the certificates technically necessary to enable her to comply with the requirements of the Apothecaries' Society, the one medical licensing body in Great Britain which found itself precluded by its charter from refusing to examine women on the ground of sex, and which, therefore, however unwillingly, was at length obliged to let her slip through. When once on the Medical Register, she lost no time in establishing herself in practice in London. In the summer of 1866, a public dispensary for women and children was opened, for the purpose, as stated in the first yearly report of the committee, of affording to poor women the option of obtaining medical advice from a qualified woman. This dispensary was under the entire medical control of Dr. Garrett-Anderson for the first four years, when another qualified medical woman made her appearance on the scene.

Frances Elizabeth Morgan (now, by marriage, Frances Elizabeth Hoggan) began her medical studies in 1866, in company with two other ladies, both of whom were hindered by too early marriage from carrying out their studies to their legitimate end, under the then arduous conditions of work and life imposed on women students by the adverse verdict of the medical profession. It was almost impossible, in those early days, for a married student to hold on her course undaunted, when that course implied severance from home and country, studying in a foreign tongue, and pecuniary sacrifices, all to be undergone without any certainty of ultimately succeeding in winning a legal professional status in her native land. But although precluded by circumstances from persevering in their medical career, these two ladies proved themselves in every way worthy of the profession they had chosen, and they carried on the traditions of their student life by becoming the founders of two of the most flourishing hospitals for children in London.*

Dr. Frances E. Hoggan and her two friends, in commencing their medical studies, strictly conformed to the letter of the regulations laid down by the Apothecaries' Society, the only one of the nineteen licensing bodies of Great Britain from which there was at that time any prospect of obtaining a diploma. To satisfy its demands, expensive courses of lectures were secured from registered lecturers at medical schools, the fee paid for the anatomy course alone amounting to fifty guineas. Before, however, incurring such heavy expenses, they had ascertained, by direct inquiry at Apothecaries' Hall, that no new prohibitory regulations were in force ; yet, notwithstanding all their caution, no sooner had these three women passed successfully in January, 1867, the preliminary examination in Arts (one of them taking honors) † than the council of the Apothecaries' Society, realizing apparently for the first time that an invasion of the medical profession by

* The East London Hospital for Children, and the North Eastern Hospital for Children.—F. E. H.

† Mrs. Hoggan.—T. S.

women was imminent, held a meeting forthwith, and published, within a week, a resolution which in effect, although not in terms, excluded women thenceforward from any of the professional examinations.

Only one course was now open to the baffled students, that of seeking thorough medical training at some reputable foreign school. Zurich, at that time the leading University in Switzerland, true to its ancient traditions of liberality and liberty, had just distinguished itself by admitting, in the year 1867, its first woman student to matriculation and graduation, at the termination of the usual period of study, a period which had been spent by the worthy pioneer, Dr. Nadjesda Suslowa, in cheerless, conscientious, solitary work, hardly lightened by the hope which she sometimes ventured to think had been prophetically breathed into her own name of Nadjesda (the Russian for hope), that her labors would eventually be crowned with success. Before Nadjesda Suslowa went to Zurich, other ladies, as early as 1839, had been allowed to attend lectures at the University, but none had been allowed to matriculate. It is a notable fact, and one which contrasts brightly with many facts in the history of medical women in England, that no sooner was the justice of allowing women to matriculate recognized by the Medical Faculty of Zurich, than all trace of past injustice was at once swept away, and the necessary classes and hospital practice having been already taken by the applicant, permission was forthwith granted to Miss Suslowa to enter for her examinations and to graduate at the earliest possible date.

To Zurich, therefore, went Frances E. Hoggan (then Morgan), in the autumn of 1867, hoping there to breathe freer and purer air than seemed possible to her at that time in England, when the medical profession was heaping its anathemas, coupled with disgraceful epithets, on those women who chose the profession of medicine as a career.* The next few years, spent in serious study, and cheered by much professional kindness from both professors and students, form a bright spot in the life of one who began medical study under difficulties unknown to the present generation of students. Dr. N. Suslowa's graduation ceremony, in 1867, was memorable from being the first graduation of a woman that had occurred in Switzerland, and Dr. Frances Hoggan's, in 1870, was memorable for being the first and the last, in the annals of the University, which took place in the Aula, an adjournment thither from the room generally used on such occasions being rendered necessary by the great concourse of spectators, some attracted by curiosity, many drawn to the spot by kindlier feelings of sympathy and interest. On the wall of the Aula hangs the portrait of Charlemagne, the founder of the early Zurich school, and never had it looked down before on a more eagerly excited crowd than it did on that March morning in 1870, which so clearly placed beyond all doubt the interest which the question of medical women had called forth in the University and town of Zurich.

Armed with the Zurich diploma, and after having

---

* If any doubt the correctness of the above remark, a glance through the English medical journals from 1865 up to the present time, will convince them of its perfect accuracy. The language often used by members of the medical profession is so bad that it cannot even be quoted. A few generous men, it is true, held out the hand of fellowship, at the risk of incurring professional odium and loss, but the bulk of the medical men of the country raised angry protests against medical women, and the medical journals were inundated with letters and articles, alike false in substance and disgraceful in tone.—F. E. H.

visited many of the most esteemed foreign schools, Dr. Frances E. Hoggan returned to London toward the close of 1870, being the first Englishwoman in possession of any European degree of Doctor of Medicine, although shortly afterward, Mrs. Garrett-Anderson, added to her L.S.A., the title of M.D., of Paris.

Several Englishwomen followed Frances Hoggan almost immediately to Zurich, and after successful, and, in some cases, brilliant examinations, returned to practice in their own country. In the meantime, the solution of the question of medical study for women had been sought in England in another way. Miss Jex-Blake, a pupil of some of the earlier American physicians, applied to the University of Edinburgh, in the spring of 1869, for admission as a medical student. It was not thought advisable to make any special arrangement in the interests of one lady only ; and therefore, in June, 1869, having secured the co-operation of four more ladies, all intending students, Miss Jex-Blake wrote to the Rector of the University, inquiring whether arrangements would now be made for the instruction of herself and her companions. After much deliberation, the Edinburgh University decided to admit women tentatively to matriculation and to the study of medicine at the University, with provision for their instruction in separate classes.

Miss Jex-Blake and four other ladies matriculated in Edinburgh during the winter of 1869, and, to use her own words, "it seemed now as if smooth water had at length been reached, after seven months of almost incessant struggle." Had the same policy of unobtrusively working on, claiming no distinctions, and sedulously and quietly avoiding all occasions of rivalry between the sexes, which led to such marked success at Zurich with

Dr. N. Suslowa, and in Paris with Dr. Mary Putnam Jacobi, the able and judicious American physician, who opened to women the University of Paris, been now followed, the result of the Edinburgh experiment was assured, and years of struggle, heart-burnings, injustice and hope deferred might have been averted. But through want of tact or patience the regrettable incident occurred, which is here given in the words of one * who was throughout one of the ladies' warm friend and helpers.

"As one of the most devoted servants and supporters of the cause of medical women at that time in Edinburgh, I may describe what I, from personal knowledge, know to be the turning point at which the cause, which seemed to have a fair chance of success, was destroyed by the injudicious conduct of its leader. That point was the agitation connected with the Hope scholarship. In order to understand the question, a few preliminary words are necessary. In the first place, it was clearly understood that the ladies were admitted into the University of Edinburgh only on the basis of an experiment. There was no equality of rights granted to them with the regular students, but only certain privileges, which allowed them to receive instruction from some friendly professors, who had previously announced their willingness to teach them, provided that those professors who were opposed to the whole question should not be called upon to teach them against their will. At that time the professors in the University might be divided into two parties, those favorable to, and those opposed to the claims of the women students. Those opposed to the question did not wish to control their favorable colleagues in the matter, so long as their col-

* George Hoggan, M. B. Edin., husband of the author of this essay.— F. E. H.

leagues did not seek to control them; and thus, at the meeting of the Medical Faculty which decided to allow the experiment to be tried, we find several of the professors were hostile; Professors Laycock, Turner and Christison abstaining altogether from voting rather than oppose actively the wishes of their colleagues who had, on the other hand, consented that the hostile professors should not be called upon to teach the ladies if they objected to do so. It was on these terms only that the ladies were allowed to matriculate, and to receive instruction in special classes, apart from the regular classes of the University. At that time, Professor Crum Brown was the lecturer on chemistry, and a warm friend of the women's cause. He agreed to give the ladies the same course of lectures that he gave to his regular class, receiving, however, for the former a fee amounting only to about a thirtieth part of that which he received from his regular class, and giving, moreover, to the ladies certain privileges which his male students did not enjoy. He granted the women special class examinations, at which the same printed paper of questions was used as that for the men students at the competitions for the class medals, and for the scholarship bequeathed by a former professor, and named after him the Hope scholarship.* In doing so, he little imagined that he was forging a weapon that would be used against himself.

"An authority of the most absolute nature was exercised over the women students by the leader of the party, as she naturally imagined that for the ladies to show extraordinary capacity would at once enlist public sympathy,

---

* These scholarships were founded with the proceeds of some very successful lectures given to ladies, and it is hardly to be wondered at that the ladies should feel they had some special claim to compete for them.—F. E. H.

and force the University to admit them, as of right, to all the privileges of students. Miss Pechey, a student of great ability, was, therefore, provided with a good chemical laboratory and private tuition, in order that she might be enabled to pass the best chemistry examination.

"Professor Crum Brown not only used the same examination papers for both classes, but he also used the same valuation terms, and found that Miss Pechey's paper was the best of any male or female student's of her year, and that, had she been a member of the regular class, instead of *the private class* only, she would have become entitled to hold the Hope Scholarship, which had a nominal money value, but was actually given in the shape of three months' tuition in the University laboratory for analytical chemistry.

"A demand was made that the Hope Scholarship should be awarded to Miss Pechey. But even had her private examination entitled her to this, it was impossible to grant it to her, for, in order to enjoy it, either she would have had to study with the male students, who worked all day in the chemical laboratory, or the laboratory would have had to be reserved for her alone, by turning out all the men ; one of the most stringent regulations under which the female student experiment was conducted being that there should be no mixed classes permitted. She had, however, no legal right to the Hope Scholarship, which was a prize for the students of the regular class, and not for members of any irregular, exceptional, or experimental class which the professor might be allowed to form. * A long series of violent attacks was made by

* In Great Britain alone could such an anomaly exist as students allowed to matriculate and yet not legally admitted to the rights and privileges of University students.—F. E. H.

the press upon the University authorities in general, and upon Professor Crum Brown in particular, who, however, did all he could to pacify and satisfy the ladies. He gave the University (bronze) class medal to Miss Pechey, and even offered to add to this the actual money value of the scholarship out of his own pocket, as the rule against mixed classes prevented him from giving the educational equivalent in his laboratory, but this was refused, the entrance to a mixed class, and not the actual prize, being the point aimed at.

" It is difficult for any one not then present in Edinburgh to realize the excitement which prevailed in the local press and in the University. That excitement produced its natural and inevitable result. Those professors who had remained benevolently neutral, when they might have been actively antagonistic, and who had expressed themselves at the beginning as willing to give the experiment a fair chance, now thought that they had made a mistake, and determined to get rid of the rebellious element, which, in the guise of a few young ladies had determined to hold them up to public obloquy. The consequences were foreseen and foretold by many, including myself, to those most interested. Friendly professors became first neutral, next hostile. The ladies were driven out of the University and out of the medical school, and the question which, judiciously conducted, might have had a favorable solution within five years, was thrown back fifty years further in Edinburgh than in any other medical school of the three kingdoms.

" The same kind of injudicious action which initiated the exclusion of women from the University, had the same effect subsequently in excluding them from the independent school of medicine at the College of Surgeons, only that in the latter case it was the antipathy of the students which was roused, and it was the influence of the students which excluded them. The board of lecturers at the College of Surgeons was favorable to trying the experiment of teaching the ladies in mixed classes, and the experiment was first tried in the classes of anatomy and surgery. In the latter department, I had the honor of giving the ladies their first lesson in practical anatomy, besides delivering the winter course of lectures on regional anatomy to a mixed class of male and female students.

"The episode of the Hope Scholarship had just taken place, and the bitterness which it had aroused made it impossible that mixed classes, with competition for prizes, could be then and for some time afterward a success. One of the professors permitted this rivalry, however, and even showed a certain leaning toward the ladies while adjudicating the daily marks which ultimately determined the question of prizes. The anger of the students, thus called forth, knew no bounds. They organized an opposition, and on the next occasion of an examination in anatomy the first of that series of dastardly riots occurred which disgraced so deeply the Edinburgh Medical School.

"The history of these riots is a painful one, and exceedingly discreditable to medical students.* On the other hand it has been sought to show, as a set-off to their misconduct, that, stung by the disgrace of the riots, a body of the more respectable students formed a guard, who in turn defied and maltreated the rioters, and escorted the ladies home every night while the riots lasted. As the organizer

---

* Professor Blackie, an eminent professor of the Faculty of Arts, exclaimed on hearing of it : " Ye can say now that ye've fought with wild beasts at Ephesus ! "—F. E. H.

and leader of that escort, I regret to say that its constitution did not bear out the alleged facts. Of the whole guard, only four were medical students, not one of whom belonged properly to the extra-mural school. In fact, the main body of the escort was composed of Irish students, studying at the Royal Veterinary College, who were marshalled up each evening by their leader, brave and simple Micky O'Halloran, an Irish Bachelor of Arts, and an ex-trooper in the Confederate States' Army. These men, each armed with the national shillelah (anticipating by some years the act of justice to medical women which the Irish College of Physicians was the first to accomplish, by admitting women to examinations for the diploma of the college), soon showed the medical students that rioting was a hazardous game. When the riots proved a failure, the students almost unanimously signed and presented a memorial, asking that ladies should be ejected from the mixed classes; the effect of this being that the lecturers actually rescinded the permission given by them at the beginning of the session, and excluded the female students altogether from the school. That rivalry and jealousy were the great factors at the extra-mural school, was made evident by the fact that personal antipathy was shown by the male students to one lecturer only, the one in whose class the men and women contended for the same prizes. In Dr. Patrick Heron Watson's mixed class of surgery not the slightest sign of disturbance was ever shown ; but then, while the ladies had no better, more determined, and unselfish supporter than Dr. Watson, in Edinburgh, he refused to accede to their wish that the men and women of his class should be allowed to compete for the same class-prizes, choosing rather to give a second set of prizes to the women out of his own pocket."

Those were exciting days in the old city of Edinburgh. All the forces of society were arrayed on one side or the other. The daily papers took up the cudgels for or against the ladies, and letters and leaders couched in the strong language of the North, kept the question of medical women constantly before the Scotch public. The aid of one tribunal after another was invoked, * either by the ladies or their opponents ; but the contest between a handful of women and their supporters, on the one hand, and on the other a powerful University, backed by all the resources and traditions of the past, was too unequal for the result to be doubtful. That result was complete failure to obtain a footing for women medical students in Edinburgh, their exclusion from qualifying classes and examinations, and dispersion of the students, most of whom eventually completed their term of study and graduated at foreign schools.

During the time that Scotland was the theatre of such exciting scenes, the question of medical women was making quiet and comparatively uneventful progress in England. St. Mary's Dispensary grew into a Hospital for Women, which for many years was under the medical care of Dr. Garrett-Anderson, and Dr. Frances Hoggan. This hospital enlisted from the first the sympathies and practical help of those interested in the cause of medical women. It became gradually known, and appreciated by

---

* The women (now ten in number) tried the case, in 1872, by an action of declarator ; Lord Gifford (the Lord Ordinary) gave judgment in their favor. Had the University been desirous not to fail in honor, but to fulfill their obligations if they could, they might have rested upon this judicial decision. On the contrary, they appealed against it to the whole Court of Session, and, in June, 1873, by a bare majority of the Court, they obtained a reversal of Lord Gifford's judgment ; and the ladies were mulcted in the costs of both sides in both suits." Right Hon. James Stansfeld, M.P.—F. E. H.

women of the humbler classes, who willingly paid a small weekly sum in the Women's Hospital, although at most of the other Metropolitan Hospitals outdoor and indoor treatment was entirely gratuitous. The New Hospital for Women, Marylebone, has had the usual success of hospitals officered by women, as testified to by American experience; that is to say, it has been gratefully appreciated by patients, and generously supported by the public. Changes have from time to time taken place in the constitution of the medical staff. One of the original two medical officers has resigned, and Dr. E. Garrett-Anderson and a full staff of qualified women now carry on the medical work of the institution.

One by one, at the expiration of their term of study, medical women returned home from abroad, some with a Zurich, some with a Paris diploma. Some settled in London, others established themselves in the larger provincial towns, amongst which Birmingham early distinguished itself by appointing a lady as house-surgeon to the Midland Hospital for Women, a precedent which, up to the present day, has not been departed from.

In spite of the disabilities under which all unregistered foreign graduates labored, disabilities which are exactly paralleled at the present day in Prussia, and which were so serious as to make it doubtful whether the women could maintain their position at all; in spite, too, of open hostility and covert attack on the part of the medical profession, medical women have made fair, and in some cases, large practices. From the first they fixed their scale of remuneration as high as that of medical men, and therefore financial success may be accepted as a fair test of the value set by the public on their services.

Prior to 1876, several Bills for the purpose of relieving

medical women from the disadvantages under which they labored, and of enabling them to obtain that official recognition in their own country, hitherto denied them by the nineteen licensing bodies of the kingdom, were brought before Parliament. In that year, what is called an " Enabling Bill," was passed, the principal provision of which was as follows:

" The powers of every body entitled under the Medical Act to grant qualifications for registration, shall extend to the granting of any qualification for registration granted by such body to all persons without distinction of sex: provided always that nothing herein contained shall render compulsory the exercise of such powers, and that no person who but for this act would not have been entitled to be registered, shall, by reason of such registration, be entitled to take any part in the government, management, or proceedings of the Universities or corporations mentioned in the said Medical Act."

The first examining bodies which expressed their willingness to examine women, in accordance with the power thus conferred by " Russell Gurney's Act," were the King and Queen's College of Physicians, Ireland, and the Queen's University, Ireland. The friendly spirit thus shown at Dublin was due no doubt in part to the good impression produced on the minds of the professors by a quiet unassuming student, who had been steadily working at Stevens's Hospital for several years. I have it on good authority that, so long ago as 1873, many of the professors were avowedly favorable to medical women, but that the Edinburgh troubles made them uneasy, and they hesitated to open their school unreservedly, for fear of encountering similar difficulties. The good intentions of the Queen's University were frustrated by the refusal of the affiliated colleges to admit women students.*

Early in 1877, the first woman, Dr. Eliza W. Dunbar, a graduate of Zurich, was examined by the King and Queen's College of Physicians, and received their license, which enabled her to be placed on the Register; and her example was quickly followed by other ladies.

The London University next decided to throw open all its degrees to women. This liberal proceeding resulted indirectly from the opposition of the majority of the medical members of the University to the granting of medical degrees to women, so long as the other degrees of the University were refused to them, and it was carried by a majority of non-medical votes. Thus, after years of waiting,† of work and of quiet progress, a legal and professional

---

* The late Sir Dominic Corrigan wrote on May 1st, 1877:—"The Senate of the Queen's University, of which the Duke of Leinster is President, and of which I am Vice-President, passed a resolution that we would admit women to examination, on their complying with our regulations, that is, submitting to education and examination the same as men. Armed with this, twelve women presented themselves as students, as I have been informed, requiring only one session to perfect their course, and not even requiring medical courses. They were refused entrance by the Colleges both of Belfast and Galway, the Colleges thus setting the University at defiance; in short, the Colleges, by this act, setting themselves above the Senate of the University. The whole system must be overhauled. In the face of this, to my mind most improper arrogance on the part of the Colleges, their professors are now seeking an augmentation of salaries, without any promise of amendment in this or other particulars. . . . . . The Colleges never condescend to communicate their proceedings to the Senate, so that I only know of the refusal from conversation with some of the professors of the Colleges. Of Cork College I have no knowledge, but I believe it unites with the others."— F. E. H.

† The first Zurich graduate was seven years in practice in London before she was allowed to present herself for examination and subsequent registration.—F. E. H.

status was at length granted to medical women in England.

After many unavailing attempts had been made to obtain admission for women students at one or other of the existing medical schools, a school of medicine for women was opened in August, 1874, at 30 Henrietta street, Brunswick square, London. The initiative in this work was taken by Dr. Jex-Blake, and some of the late Edinburgh students. Dr. E. Garrett-Anderson joined in the scheme, and Dr. Elizabeth Blackwell was also one of the early co-operators and teachers. The school became connected with the Royal Free Hospital in 1877, and it is now a recognized place of medical instruction for women. It has some funded property, a regular curriculum, and a fair supply of students. In the year 1882 there were 44 students on the school and hospital books, and every year some of the students complete their medical course, and enter the profession as licentiates of the Irish College of Physicians. Sufficient time has not yet elapsed for any to have graduated at the University of London, but several women have passed successfully the earlier examinations, and have shown at all the examinations a very high average of attainments ;* and there can be no reasonable doubt that women will go on as they have begun, and graduate at the London University with credit and even with distinction.†

The position of medical women at the present day in

---

* Miss F. Helen Prideaux has taken the gold medal for anatomy at the first M. B., or intermediate examination in medicine, the highest distinction given at this examination, and other ladies have also taken honors in the medical examinations of the London University.—F. E. H.

† Since the above was written two women have graduated at the University of London, one in medicine only, the other with great distinction in medicine and surgery.—F. E. H.

England, may be briefly stated as follows : They have a school and hospital of their own, and they are admitted to no other school ; they can present themselves for examination at the University of London, and at the King and Queen's College of Physicians, Dublin ; they have a legal professional standing as duly qualified registered practitioners of medicine ; they have patients, and their popularity and influence are growing from year to year. All these advantages they have gained by the help of some earnest, generous members of the medical profession, and of many chivalrous, liberal-minded men outside the profession. The attitude of the general public has undergone a very marked change within the last ten or twelve years, and medical women may now be said to have firmly established their hold on the public mind. But with the male members of the medical profession their position is far from satisfactory. They are met in consultation, because it would be contrary to the established code of medical etiquette to refuse to meet a registered practitioner. The number of friendly medical men may perhaps be said to be increasing ; still most of the practice at the general and special hospitals is closed to them, and all the medical societies refuse them membership. Medical women thus miss all the sharpening of wit, and all the advantages of professional intercourse, which such societies afford.

No better illustration of the narrow spirit which still pervades the dealings of the medical profession in England with medical women, could be given than the vote of the English organizing committee of the International Medical Congress, held in London, in 1881, excluding women from all but " the social and ceremonial meetings of the Congress." This vote, it is well known, was mainly brought about by the influence exercised by Sir William Jenner, Physician in Ordinary to the Queen, and by a few others ; but it sufficiently indicates the animus still existing in the profession.

The exclusion of qualified medical women from medical societies and congresses is now, indeed, so much the order of the day, that it deserves more than a passing notice or brief reference, and it will no doubt prove of interest to pass in review some of the most notable instances of this arrogance of sex, both in our own, and in neighboring countries. Among the societies, the Obstetrical Society* stands forth prominent in its opposition to the claims of women. It met the application for membership of a registered medical woman by a resolution excluding women, as such, from all rights of membership. When, subsequently, a joint paper by a man and a woman † was presented to the Obstetrical Society, an abstract only of the paper was published in the Transactions of the Society, but with the woman's name carefully omitted. The abstract, however, having attracted the notice of an eminent foreigner, the paper was, at his request, sent over to him in Germany, and published in full in one of the first German medical journals.

Following on their exclusion from the Obstetrical Society of Great Britain, comes the exclusion of women from the British Medical Association. For some years previously, two women had been, after regular election, members of the Association. In 1875, they, for the first

---

* "It is curious to note how persistent hostility still finds its stronghold in the ranks of those practitioners who have devoted themselves to the special treatment of the diseases of women, and to the practice of midwifery. Can it be that they, more than others, tremble for their monopoly?"— "Medical Women," by Right Hon. James Stansfeld, M. P., July, 1877.— F. E. H.

† George and Frances Hoggan.—T. S.

time, attended the yearly meeting, joining in the discussions, and reading papers. Thereupon a determined set was made against the ladies, and counsel's opinion taken as to the possibility of getting rid of them. In the election of the first lady, Dr. Garrett-Anderson, no flaw could be made out. It was, however, discovered by the legal quibblers that a period had existed, prior to the incorporation of the British Medical Association, during which elections might be considered void if the Association so pleased. During that period Dr. Frances Hoggan, together with a large number of members of the male sex, was elected. Her election was duly notified to her, and her fees were regularly taken. Nevertheless, at the yearly meeting, in 1877, a vote was first passed declaring women ineligible for future election, and immediately afterward all the *soi-disant* irregularly elected members, with the one exception of Dr. Frances Hoggan, were re-elected. We leave to the appreciation of our readers the above novel and ingenious method of procedure which the British Medical Association, the largest and most influential body of medical men in the kingdom, thought fit to adopt against a medical woman whom they had duly elected a member and to whom it was expressly stated that they had no personal objection.

Next in chronological order, we have to note the exclusion of women from the Association of German Naturalists and Doctors, which took place in 1879, under the following circumstances. The same lady who experienced such scant courtesy at the hands of the British Medical Association, was also a member of the above-named German society. In 1878, a resolution was brought forward, proposing the exclusion of women as members. The originator of the resolution appealed to his countrymen to support him, urging them in the most moving terms to emulate their English brethren, who had recently " purged the British Medical Association of the presence of women." The vote was not taken until the following year, but when taken it was adverse. Women were excluded from membership of the Association of German Naturalists and Doctors, and a protest which had been forwarded by the excluded member, with a request that it might be read at a general meeting of the Association before the resolution was put, was neither read, nor its receipt in any way acknowledged.

A similar reception was accorded to the protest of medical women excluded, for the first time, by the vote of the English Organizing Committee, from the International Medical Congress recently held in London. In fact, a curious resemblance in points of detail characterizes the exclusion of women from medical societies, in all its various phases ; and the reference of the German doctor to the superior wisdom of the British Medical Association in " purging " their society of women, is highly suggestive, and clearly indicates the influence which extends from England to Germany, strengthening the strong class feeling which still prevents medical men from treating their colleagues of the opposite sex with fairness ; which enables them to see no unfairness, for instance, in excluding from the advantages of a great international scientific gathering, by the vote of none but recent members, women * who had long preceded them in the Association as members of former Congresses.† To the thoughtful mind it is painful to see the medical profession in the two

---

* Dr. Frances Hoggan and Dr. Aletta Henriette Jacobs, of Amsterdam, referred to at some length in the chapter on Holland.—T. S.

† One by four years, another by two years.—F. E. H.

greatest Teutonic nations, England and Germany, thus leagued together against the professional interests of medical women, and, regardless of the strongly expressed desire of other women to have physicians of their own sex, refusing to them those precious opportunities of scientific intercourse and culture which are the necessary complement of the right, now conceded to them in England, but still contested in Germany, to study and practice medicine, on equal terms with men. The lovers of fair play must, alas, look beyond the Teutonic to the Latin race, to find that fine sense of justice and feeling of true chivalry, which has never yet excluded a colleague from a medical society or congress on the ground of sex.*

---

* Some of the great English scientific societies seem to be pervaded by a more liberal spirit than those of the medical profession, as is shown by the following extracts from an interesting letter by Miss Eleanor A. Ormerod, Consulting Entomologist of the Royal Agricultural Society, dated Dunster Lodge, Isleworth, England, October 30, 1882. "I was the youngest child," Miss Ormerod writes me, "of the well-known genealogist and historian of Cheshire, George Ormerod, and was educated at home (without help from schools, governesses or the lectures we hear so much of at the present day), by my mother, a woman of great information, accomplishment and solid piety. Her principal rule was that everything learnt must be thoroughly mastered, and she instilled into me a lively interest in all natural objects, plant, animal and mineral. This was my beginning, on a basis of intense love, of any pursuit which took me into the open air. Later I suffered much from ill health, and in a succession of long illnesses I beguiled pain and weariness by study of my favorite subject. About 1868, when the Collection of Economic Entomology now at the Bethnal Green Museum (London), was commenced, I wrote and offered to contribute, and from that time until the decease, in 1878, of Mr. Murray, the curator, I contributed not only by constantly collecting, drawing, modelling, etc., but also by working out life histories when requested. Thus I laid the foundation of a good deal of knowledge as to the feelings of, and the great amount of information possessed by, field-laborers, farmers, gardeners, foresters, etc., on these subjects, and about the beginning of 1877, I invited, by a circular, contributions from those who would give me information, for publication in reports, as to means

Public opinion in England, on the question of medical women, is in advance of the general opinion of the medical profession, notwithstanding the generous help which some members of that profession have always held out to their professional sisters, often to their own great personal detriment.*

That the tide of public feeling has turned is sufficiently proved by the increasing numbers of medical women. In February, 1882, there were 26 women on the medical register, and other names have since been added. At Birmingham, a lady, Dr. A. Barker, has been appointed Honorary Acting Physician to the Midland Hospital for Women. Last year there were three dispensaries officered by women in London, one at Bristol, one at Leeds, and one at Manchester. Several qualified women have gone out to the East as Missionary Physicians, and the question of an adequate supply of Medical Women for India has become one of general interest, in which the Queen and country alike share. Women are also beginning to contribute their share to medical literature, and to scientific research. In

---

found practically serviceable for prevention of injury to oaks by insects. In this way and by constant study I have become possessed of some knowledge on the subject. In the spring of this year I had the great honor of being asked to become Consulting Entomologist of the Royal Agricultural Society of England. The post is, I am happy to say, no sinecure. Since then I have had the further honor of being appointed the Special Lecturer on Economic Entomology at the Royal Agricultural College, Cirencester, a very important post, in which I try to do my duty."—T. S.

* In 1880, Dr. Allen Sturge, now of Nice, was refused a hospital appointment, for which he was admittedly the most fitting candidate, and for which he had worked for years, at a hospital *founded by a woman*, because the committee could not get over the difficulty that he was married to a lady-doctor. Another friend of the movement was, some years ago, offered an independent teaching post, if he would give up his advocacy of the medical women's cause, an offer which he at once declined.—F. E. H.

short, the future looks fair, in spite of the disadvantages under which they still labor ; and it may be confidently predicted that complete success is now but a matter of time, and that the next quarter of a century will have to record fresh achievements and much valuable work accomplished by medical women, in the practice of their profession, in the field of science, and in the direction of much-needed social reform.

IV.—THE INDUSTRIAL MOVEMENT.

BY JESSIE BOUCHERETT.

[The Boucherett family, which is of French Protestant origin, settled at North Willingham, in Lincolnshire, where they still reside, more than two hundred years ago. Emilia* Jessie Bouchreett was born in 1825. From early youth she felt an especial interest in the condition of women, who, she thought, had to endure more than their fair share of the hardships of life. Of their various grievances, the most widely felt, and at the same time the least difficult to remedy, seemed to her to be their exclusion from the means of earning a good livelihood. It was, therefore, in this direction that, when the opportunity for acting offered itself, Miss Boucherett turned her efforts, and, in conjunction with some friends, she succeeded in founding the Society for Promoting the Employment of Women, an account of which is given in the following pages. Miss Jessie Boucherett is the author of a little book called "Hints on Self Help for Young Women," published nearly twenty years ago, which is now out of print and out of date, the information contained in it being old, but which at the time had some effect on the class it was intended to assist. She has also written numerous tracts, pamphlets and articles, the most important of which, on the "Condition of Women in France," appeared in the *Contemporary Review*. This essay showed how women had gradually been excluded from many well-paid trades into which they had been freely admitted before working-men obtained the electoral franchise. Mrs. Josephine E. Butler's "Woman's Work and Woman's Culture," contains an essay by Miss Boucherett on "How to Provide for Superfluous Women." Miss Boucherett was one of the earliest promoters of the movement for obtaining the Parliamentary franchise for women householders and was a supporter of the Married Women's Property Bill, which happily became law in January, 1883. She is now anxious to persuade poor

---

* Until she had occasion to consult the parish register, at the age of thirty-five, Miss Boucherett was under the impression that "Jessie" was her first name, having always been so called. She considered it too late to make a change and has therefore continued to omit "Emilia."

ladies to turn their attention to pig and poultry farming, for she believes that a clever, active woman could add considerably to her income by so doing.]

IN 1845, Thomas Hood, shortly before his death, wrote the well-known " Song of the Shirt." It is probable that some special circumstance or tale of sorrow had at that time called the attention of kind-hearted people to the condition of the London seamstress. The pathos of the " Song " roused public sympathy strongly, and an impression became general that the condition of working women of the lower class was not what it ought to be, and that it would be well if something could be done to raise their wages. This impression, though vague and impracticable, was of great use, for it not only turned the minds of philanthropists toward the subject, but it prepared the way for any efforts that might be made to introduce women into new occupations; the evident plea of necessity diminishing the dislike with which such efforts were sure to be regarded at first.

From another quarter, about the same time, attention was called to the distress existing amongst educated gentlewomen. The Governesses' Benevolent Institution was started in 1841, but it was not completely organized till two years later, when the Rev. David Laing undertook the office of Honorary Secretary. It had for its object to give pensions to worn-out governesses. The amount of actual destitution amongst educated women which came to the ears of the committee was appalling. When the sum of £500 had been raised, and was invested so as to create a perpetual annuity of £15, there at once appeared thirty candidates for this small income, a large proportion of whom were entirely destitute. A little later, when the institution had grown richer, there were one hundred and twenty candidates for three annuities of £20 each. Here was a revelation of misery, undeserved and unsuspected! The Governesses' Benevolent Institution is now one of the largest charities in London, and gives pensions to 243 aged governesses, besides affording other relief. Useful as this institution has been, and still is, in relieving distress, I believe that it has been indirectly even more useful in making the distress known.

A considerable number of people having thus become impressed with the unhappy condition of women who had to earn their bread, whether as teachers, or needlewomen, some efforts were made to relieve their distress by introducing them into new occupations. The Female School of Art, which was started in Gower Street, and thence removed to 43 Queen's Square, dates from this period. The annual exhibition of paintings by women artists was opened not long afterward, and has been continued with increasing success up to the present time. Other schemes then started failed, but a part of one of them—the teaching of women to paint on glass for windows—was less unfortunate, and a few women have been thus employed ever since.

A most successful effort was made by Mr. Ricardo, M. P., to introduce women into the telegraph service, as is shown in the following extract from the *Englishwoman's Journal* of December, 1859: "It appears that about six years ago Mr. Ricardo, M. P., the then chairman of the International and Electric Telegraph Company, heard of a young girl, the daughter of one of the railway stationmasters, who had for three years carried on day by day the whole of the electric telegraph business for her father, and that too with great intelligence and correctness. The idea then suggested itself of training and employing women as clerks for the telegraph company, and on its being proposed to the committee, the proposition was warmly advocated by General Wyld, who has proved a most untiring friend of the cause. Opposition was of course naturally enough shown by the clerks of the establishment, but the experiment was permitted to proceed, and Mrs. Craig, the present intelligent matron, appointed to instruct in her own room eight pupils on two instruments. At first the instruments in one room were worked by young men, and the instruments in the other by young women, and it seemed as though the directors were pitting them against each other, establishing a kind of industrial tournament, to see which description of laborer was worthiest. With what tact, perseverance and success Mrs. Craig and her pupils worked may be gathered from the fact that, at Founder's Court alone, upward of ninety young women are now (1859) in active employment, the whole of the actual working of the instruments having fallen into their hands. The committee are now perfectly satisfied that girls are not only more teachable, more attentive and quicker eyed than the men clerks formerly employed, but have also pronounced them more trustworthy, more easily managed, and, we may add, more easily satisfied with lower wages. So well pleased are they, indeed, with the result of their experiment, that about thirty more women are now employed at the branch offices, viz., eight at Charing Cross, two at Fleet Street, two at Knight's, etc., and eventually there is no doubt they will fill posts in all the branch offices in England."

The success thus foretold has been far more than attained. The government took possession in 1870 of the electric telegraphs of the country, and the staff employed by the companies passed into the hands of the Postmaster General.

By good fortune, or more correctly speaking, by the mercy of Providence, Mr. Scudamore, whose official duty it was to regulate the telegraphs, was favorable to the employment of women. He retained the women clerks whom the company had employed and even added to their number. Before that time, women had often been employed by local postmasters in country towns as assistants, but they had never been employed by the government. Under Mr. Scudamore women were employed in London as post-office counter-women as well as telegraphists ; they gave satisfaction by their conduct, and their numbers increased. The success which attended the employment of women in the minor duties of postal work, encouraged Mr. Scudamore, in conjunction with Mr. Chetwynd, to make the experiment of employing women of higher education as clerks in the discharge of work of a superior sort. The following history is taken from the London *Times* of January 3, 1882 : " In 1871 it was decided to institute a department check, with a view to discover, without waiting for complaints from the public, whether the various officers employed throughout the country upon telegraph work were doing it ill or well, since it seemed desirable to Mr. Scudamore that something should be done for those long-suffering people who ' sit down calmly under their grievances and never let the department know what they have suffered.' And it was for this purpose that the Telegraph Clearing-House Check Branch was established, with a staff composed wholly of female clerks. In the early days of the government telegraph system such a check seemed, indeed, very necessary, and the work which it involved was well within the capacity of a female staff, since, as Mr. Scudamore naïvely put it, ' it consisted chiefly in fault finding.' * * * * The test of female ability to perform clerk work having been thus satisfactorily applied, more important duties—such as telegraph account work—were intrusted to the young ladies in question, and it is now by them that the accounts are prepared and rendered to the various newspapers, etc., with which the telegraph department has to deal. It is only necessary to state that the Post Office receives annually from newspapers, press associations and agencies, clubs, hotels, etc., a sum of considerably over £50,000, in order to show the important and responsible nature of the work performed by the female staff of the Clearing-House Branch, who have also, it should be added, to check the claims against the Post Office by the railway companies in respect to the telegraphic work done by them at their various stations on behalf of the government. It was no doubt owing to the very successful results of the experiment, as regards the Telegraph Clearing-House, of employing female clerks that Lord John Manners, whose warm sympathy and co-operation the movement appears ever to have received, was induced to recruit certain branches of the savings bank department with ladies, intrusting to them that simpler kind of work which hitherto had for the most part been allotted to boy clerks. And, so far as can be learnt, there has been no cause to regret the step taken in this direction. The employment of females has also been tried since 1873 in the Returned Letter office, where they have been engaged upon what is described as ' returning work ; ' which consists in returning the ordinary correspondence that the Post Office has not been able to deliver. No better proof of the capacity of females for certain kinds of clerk work could be afforded than the emphatic testimony in this report tendered before the Playfair Commission by the Controller of the Returned Letter office, who stated that their employment in that office had been a ' perfect success.' They have, he continues, ' completely surpassed my expectations. They are very accurate, and do a fair quantity of work; more so, in fact, than many of the males who have been employed in the same duty.' When the new system of postal orders was introduced at the commencement of last year, it was not unnatural that Mr. Chetwynd, profiting by the experience of the Telegraph Clearing House under his control, should desire to intrust to young ladies the simpler portions of the work connected with the system—those duties probably which would have been performed by boy clerks. As a matter of fact, however, Mr. Fawcett has told us that the whole of the clerical work connected with postal orders is performed by a staff of female clerks and is done in a very satisfactory manner. Some slight idea may, perhaps, be formed of the extent and importance of the work thus involved when it is mentioned that postal orders are being issued at the present time at the rate of 4,000,000 a year, for the value of about £1,350,000."

The number of clerks employed is 337, who receive salaries from £65 a year to £300. There are forty-five returners of letters, who earn from fourteen to fifty shillings a week, and 1,060 counter-women and telegraphists who earn from ten shillings a week up to £180 a year. The number of assistants in post-offices employed in the country by local postmasters cannot be known until the publication of the census of 1881.

Having thus traced up to the present time the experiment commenced by Mr. Ricardo in 1853, let us now return to the earlier period and trace the course of other efforts to find suitable employment for women.

In 1855 a pamphlet appeared entitled, " Women and

Work," written by Miss Leigh Smith, now Madame Bodichon. This work gained some attention, and in 1857 a small monthly publication called the *Englishwoman's Journal*, was established by Madame Bodichon and others interested in the condition of women. Miss Bessie Parkes was the editor of the new periodical, around which gathered a small but earnest circle of sympathizers. A reading-room for women was opened in the house which contained the office of the *Journal*, and from this small office and humble reading-room have grown almost all the great women's movements of the present day. They have long passed into other hands and become a shop, but I shall always regard the place as classic ground.

In April, 1859, an article was published in the *Edinburgh Review* on the industrial position of women. It must have had a wide effect, and inspired many with a desire to assist women to earn their livelihood. It gave me the idea of establishing a society, the object of which should be to introduce women into new employments. I had seen the *Englishwoman's Journal*, and I applied to the editor for advice and assistance, and by her was introduced to the reading-room, where I was made acquainted with Miss Adelaide Proctor, the poet, who became my coadjutor. As she had many friends in London and considerable influence, we succeeded in drawing a few people together, and opened, in 1859, a very humble room over a shop, as the office of the Society for Promoting the Employment of Women. It was shortly afterward removed to 19 Langham Place, where the *Journal* office and reading-room had already been established. The Association for the Promotion of Social Science, of which Mr. George Hastings was secretary, gave us its support; the Earl of Shaftesbury, whose name was a tower of strength, became

7

our president, and, with a committee of twenty-two members, we made a beginning. The first trade we thought of was printing, but thinking it probable that such an undertaking would succeed better in private hands, we apprenticed five girls to Miss Emily Faithfull, who started the Victoria Press. This undertaking did not, I believe, become a commercial success, but it completely proved that women were good type-setters. Many women were taught the trade, and several printing offices now employ women as type-setters. The number of women printers returned in the census of 1871 was 741, and is probably considerably larger at the present time. A women's printing office is now established at number 21*a* Great College Street, Westminster, of which Mrs. Paterson is the manager. The women are not merely type-setters, but they work at the higher branches of the trade as well.

The next trade into which we endeavored to introduce women, was that of copying of law papers. We hired a house at number 12 Portugal Street, W. C., and engaged a lady superintendent and an invalided law-stationer's clerk as teacher. Unfortunately, before the girls who came to learn had attained to the highest mysteries of the art, the superintendent and the teacher had a dispute, and we parted with the latter. It is to this cause that I attribute the fact that only partial success has attended this undertaking. However women are still employed at the same place, and in this office, which long ago passed into private hands, a considerable number of women have received instruction.

The society was always desirous of teaching girls to become commercial clerks and book-keepers. This was very difficult to manage, and when at last a few girls had been well taught, it was not possible to obtain situations for them until such a length of time had elapsed that they had grown tired of waiting and engaged in something else; so that, when employers came forward, there was no one to take the situations offered. At last, however, owing to the steady perseverance of our secretaries, Miss King and Miss Lewin, a few girls were fitted into situations. They gave satisfaction and other employers were encouraged to apply. As soon as it was found that instructed women were capable of doing the work, several employers taught their own daughters, nieces or other dependents, how to keep their accounts. Sometimes an employer who had engaged one of our clerks would take other girls and have her to teach them the business. In this way the number of women clerks and book-keepers has increased with great rapidity, and to-day there is almost an unlimited field of employment for women in this direction. A girl, who is a good arithmetician, writes a good hand, and obtains a certificate for double entry, is sure of a situation, and if in addition she learns to write short-hand, she may aspire to a superior position. Ordinary book-keepers (not short-hand writers) receive at first about fifteen shillings a week without board and lodging; at the end of each year their wages are generally raised two or three shillings a week till they reach twenty-five shillings, while some experienced accountants receive thirty or thirty-five shillings a week. The number of women commercial clerks increased between the years 1861 and 1871 from 404 to 1,755, and it is now probably much larger.

In 1876, Miss Crosby, now Mrs. Müller, opened an office under the auspices of the Society for the Employment of Women for tracing plans for engineers and architects. Ladies are found to do the work well and they earn on an average seven pence an hour. The office is now very successfully carried on by Miss Long, at 8 Great Queen Street, Westminster.

It was at one time hoped that glass engraving would have been a great success, for good and elegant work was executed by the girls who were taught at the society's expense, but trades unions made it impossible for them to obtain employment.

The society has started women in various other trades which it would be wearisome to enumerate. A register is kept at the office, 22 Berners Street, from which competent women can be obtained in the following capacities: secretaries, readers, clerks, book-keepers, copyists, canvassers, wood engravers and carvers, art decorators, proofreaders, printers, lithographers, law writers, upholsterers, hair-dressers, waitresses, gilders, lace-cleaners, linen markers, and needle-women. Her Majesty the Queen became patron of our society in 1869, and at the same time H. R. H. the Crown Princess of Germany and the Princess Louise, Marchioness of Lorne. The society was incorporated in 1879, which gives it a legal status and enables the City Guilds to act in conjunction with it.

It is not intended in this paper to enumerate all the efforts which have been made of late years to assist women to earn a better livelihood. Of some schemes I have probably not heard, and of others I know so little that I will not venture to write upon them. For instance, the great subject of sisterhoods and nursing institutions is altogether omitted, although the number of poor ladies who are earning their livelihood in a noble and useful manner in these establishments must be very large. However, I will give a brief account of some of the trades open to women which have not already been mentioned.

Wood-engraving, it is said, is not a favourite employment with Egnlishmen, and the best work is done by foreigners, who reside in England for the purpose of illustrating our newspapers and books. Three years ago the City of London Guilds opened a wood-engraving school, at 122 Kennington Park Road, to which girls as well as boys are admitted. Few boys attend, but there are twelve girls, who like the work and have aptitude for it. Some are already skilled enough to earn money. It is said to take five years to become proficient in the art, and when that time is elapsed it is hoped that they will earn at least £2 a week. Mr. Paterson, of East Temple Chambers, Whitefriars Street, gives excellent instruction to women in this art, and some of his former pupils are already working independently with success.

The Society of Arts has established a wood-carving class at the Albert Hall, where girls are taught the art under an Italian master. The work done is very beautiful.

In the article already referred to, which appeared in the *Edinburgh Review* in 1859, mention was made of the oppression of the women engaged in china-painting in Worcestershire, who were forbidden by their fellow-workmen to use hand-rests in painting, lest they should be able to rival men in skill of execution. This statement has often been vehemently denied, and equally often reasserted. It appears, however, to have been true, and I am by no means certain that the abuse has even now been put an end to in the great factories in Staffordshire and Worcestershire. In London, however, means have been found of evading the difficulty. Mr. Minton set up a workshop where women were taught china-painting and received employment if they proved skilful. His work-

shop some years ago was burnt down and not rebuilt, but
many women had meanwhile learnt the art and furnaces
had been erected for baking their wares.   A large number
of women are now engaged in the trade ; some have studios
and sale-rooms of their own, while some paint for Mr.
Mortlock, Messrs. Howell and James, and other establishments.   The amounts earned by china-painters vary very
much.   A fairly skilful one told me that she earned at
least nine pence an hour.   Very superior artists would
earn more and inferior ones probably much less.   At
Mr. Doulton's factory of pottery in Lambeth, one woman
was employed as an experiment in 1871 ; at the present
time (1882) more than two hundred are employed there.

About the year 1871 the Hon. Lady Welby conceived
the happy thought that employment might be afforded to
gentlewomen in distressed circumstances by reviving the
curious and beautiful forms of art needle-work, as practiced
by our ancestresses, and applying the art to decorative
purposes on a large scale.   A humble room over a bonnet
shop was opened in Sloane Street, in which to teach the
art to poor ladies, and in spite of many difficulties the
work commenced.   From the first Her Majesty the Queen
approved of the scheme, and H.R.H. the Princess Christian
spent much thought and time in carrying it out.   Lady
Marian Alford and several other ladies took deep interest
in it and gave valuable assistance.   Success attended the
effort, and the school was removed to its present quarters in
South Kensington.   The beauty of the work speaks for
itself and needs no recommendation.   Employment of a
sort eminently suitable for gentlewomen is thus afforded to
a considerable number of ladies, who are enabled to earn a
tolerable livelihood by eight hours of daily work.   A new
kind of employment has thus been created, so that it is

not only those who are in the School of Art Needle-work who owe gratitude to the memory of Lady Welby, but all who are engaged in art needle-work wherever they may be.

The Working Ladies' Guild, established by Lady Mary Feilding in 1876, set up a work-room for art needle-work under the special superintendence of Lady Eden. Specimens of the work may be seen at 3 Lower Grosvenor Place, S. W. About thirty-eight ladies obtain employment in this manner through the Guild, eleven of whom derive their livelihood from it, and earn, it is calculated, from five to six pence an hour.

A good many shops now sell art needle-work and employ women to do it, but the work done for shops is not as good as that done at the establishments mentioned above, and the wages earned are inferior.

Several years ago the Misses Garrett * set up as house-decorators and have met with great success. Some other ladies have followed their example. It is a trade well suited to women who possess taste, business capacity and capital.

A few educated women are now being taught how to dispense medicines, and Miss Clarke keeps a chemist shop in London.

The subjoined table, taken from the former censuses, will be found of some interest.†

---

* Miss Agnes Garrett is a sister of Mrs. Fawcett and Dr. Garrett-Anderson, and Miss Rhoda Garrett, a cousin, who died in November, 1882, was, Miss Caroline A. Biggs informs me, " an accomplished speaker for women's suffrage."—T. S.

† A circumstance which has the effect of making this paper less satisfactory than it otherwise might have been is that the new census will not be published till 1883, for it is only by means of the census taken every ten years that the increase of women in any employment can be definitely

Comparison of the census of 1861 with that of 1871, as regards the employment of women in various branches of industry in England and Wales.

OCCUPATION.	NUMBER IN 1861.	NUMBER IN 1871.
Civil Service.....................	1,931	3,314
Law stationers...................	21	51
Painters and artists..............	853	1,069
Photographers, including assistants...	168	694
Commercial clerks, accountants, etc.	404	1,755
Saleswomen (not otherwise described).	1,055	1,721
Drapers and assistants.............	11,993	19,112
Hosiers and haberdashers...........	2,126	4,147
Shopwomen (in undefined branches).	4,520	8,333
Apprentices (in undefined branches)..	185	743
Stationers.......................	1,752	3,004
Booksellers and publishers..........	952	1,077
Printers.........................	419	741
Hair-dressers and wigmakers........	501	1,240
Gilders..........................	74	234

It will perhaps be asked whether what has been done has had any perceptible effect in lessening the distress among women. As far as regards women of the higher classes who are obliged to earn their bread, I confess that in my opinion no improvement has taken place in their condition, but rather the contrary. The number of ap-

ascertained. We may know by other means that so many women have been trained for certain employments and have been successful in their profession, but the effect which their success may have had in encouraging others to follow their example, or in inducing employers to engage them, can only be known through the census; therefore it is to be regretted that this paper must be prepared before the publication of the new census, as much more exact information could be furnished in another twelve-month.— J. B.

plicants for pensions at the Governesses' Benevolent
Institution still far exceeds the number of pensions, and
every charitable effort to give assistance to ladies brings
to light an innumerable host of helpless women, chiefly
composed, as far as England is concerned, of the widows
and daughters of officers, clergymen and professional men
who are left destitute or nearly so. The explanation of
the anomaly is that the efforts made to obtain increased
employment for ladies have been more than counteracted
by other causes. The excellent day-schools which have
been established in London and other great towns have
almost put an end to the occupation of the daily governess,
and have greatly diminished the demand for resident
governesses. At the same time a great increase has been
made in the number of ladies seeking employment by the
political troubles in Ireland. The widows and daughters of many landed proprietors there have lost the
incomes which were supposed to be secured to them on
the rentals of the estates. The rents not being paid, the
income naturally stops, and some of these ladies have been
reduced to such poverty as to have been compelled to
take refuge in the work-house. Those who are capable of
teaching seek for situations as governesses, and thus the
profession of the teacher becomes more overcrowded than
ever. Gentlewomen are also now exposed to competition
from the ex-pupil teachers in board-schools, who often
become nursery governesses. Hence the salaries of
ordinary governesses have fallen, and it is only highly
superior, accomplished or musical governesses who are
still able to obtain good salaries. I may here remark
that the competition would have been even keener if the
industry of a large number of ladies had not been turned
into other channels. The position of poor gentlewomen,

bad as it is, would have been still worse if no efforts had
been made to assist them.

It is sometimes said that women have nothing to do
with politics, but the case of the Irish ladies shows that
politics have a good deal to do with women. When
adversity falls upon a nation or a class, it is always the
women who suffer first and suffer most, and as adversity
is sometimes caused by injudicious public measures,
women have in reality at least as much concern in politics
as men have. One sign of the times is very satisfactory.
A society of young ladies has been formed, called the
Emergency Society, each member of which binds herself
to learn some one thing, whether art, profession, or trade
so thoroughly, that if misfortune comes she will be able to
maintain herself by its exercise. I sincerely hope that
this society will spread, and the principles of self-help,
which it inculcates, will become general.

With regard to the women of the working classes, it
appears to me that their condition has improved of late
years. The great number of women who earn their livelihood in shops and factories has caused the wages of servants and needle-women to rise. The pay for plain sewing
is still too low, and sad stories of destitute needle-women
sometimes appear, but I believe that they are rarer than
they used to be. The women who are engaged in
the government army-clothing establishment earn from
seven to eight shillings a week for ten hours a day work,
and they can add a trifle to their earnings by working at
home after hours. If two or three girls club together to
share the same room, they can pay their rent and live
tolerably well. The pay of the women who do needle-
work for shops seems to be nearly the same.

The class which was formerly the most wretched next

to needle-women was that of "lodging-house slave." But here there is a decided improvement. Twenty-five years ago a lodging-house servant would be kept up till any hour at night to bring the lodgers their supper, and would rarely get a holiday; now the usual stipulation made by a girl, when engaging herself, is that she shall not be expected to answer the bell after ten o'clock at night, or be required to rise until six o'clock in the morning, and that she shall have alternate Sunday afternoons at her own disposal. The poor girl's life is thus rendered endurable. The cause of this improvement is that there is less competition for employment among women of the working classes than was formerly the case, and this enables them to make better terms for themselves. There being less competition is probably due partly to the opening of new occupations to women and partly to emigration. Many men emigrate rather than submit to low wages, and employers prefer to accept women at lower wages in numerous easy occupations. This emigration is most beneficial. The emigrant himself is far happier engaged in some manly out-of-door pursuit in the colonies than he could have been while following a sedentary feminine trade in England. He probably marries, and thus three individuals are directly benefited by his emigration—the emigrant himself, his wife, and the woman who has taken his place in the old country. More remotely benefit is conferred on those women who are relieved from the competition of the woman who is engaged in the man's former trade. Women in England owe much to the high spirit of the men who so bravely go forth to spread wider the area of civilization, thus taking on themselves the rough work of the world, and leaving space for their sisters to follow less laborious occupations at home.

V.—WOMEN AS PHILANTHROPISTS.

BY HENRIETTA O. BARNETT.

[Henrietta Rowland was born in 1851, and in 1873 became the wife of the Rev. S. A. Barnett, who had just been appointed Vicar of St. Judes, Whitechapel, London.   Since that date they have lived in Whitechapel and Mrs. Barnett has been especially engaged in work for the help of girls and young women.   She has written, for magazines, " The Young Women in our Work-houses," " The Work of Lady Visitors," " At Home to the Poor," " Passionless Reformers," and " Pictures for the People."   " Mrs. Barnett occupies an honorable place," Mrs. Fanny Hertz, of London, writes me, " among the band of devoted women who are applying their intelligence, their energy, and their sympathy to the solution of some of the most difficult and urgent problems wherewith the social reformers of the time have to deal.   Her life has for many years been mainly given up to the amelioration of the lives of the people about her in the East-end of London."]

THE task given to me is a great one.   I have been asked to tell something about the work of women as philanthropists.   But the space assigned me is limited, so I must pass over the work of which I have the least personal knowledge, or which has been already much and well described.   I must pass over the noble work done by women for the sick; work which, whether voluntary or paid, has been in truth inspired by love; a kindred love, if it be in the breast of the well-born Florence Nightingale, or sheltered under the blue ill-fitting gown of the pauper nurse.

The sick have not been sufferers in vain (unless the development of good is vanity), for their needs have called forth great acts from women of all classes.   Ladies delicately nurtured, and rejoicing in the cultured retirement natural to the refined, have emerged therefrom to take the control of hospitals and pauper asylums ; or, when administrative power was denied them, to dress with deft fingers ill-gotten wounds, and soothe with gentle tones and kind words weariness (born of hard work and rough usage) such as too often no tonics can cure. But on this subject there is no need to linger ; the language with which the sick appeal to women is universal. It is "the language of a cry" heard and surely responded to by the mother sex in every nation alike.

I must also pass over teaching, which was for many years looked upon as the only bread-winning resource for poor ladies ; but is now, happily, considered as a noble profession, not beneath the acceptance of any. It is work which for its highest ends demands that its workers should be philanthropists, whether it be undertaken in ladies' colleges and high schools, within ear-shot of the bells which have sounded through the generations, in the great sister universities of England, or carried on in underground cellars in back courts for the good of cinder-sifters and rough scavenger lads.

The want of space, too, forbids me to discuss temperance work, which has enlisted in its cause an army of earnest women, who bravely, whether by wise or unwise methods, fight the devil of drink and his evil brood. Space forbids me also to give the details of much good work that has been done by women in the cause of health, in societies such as the National Health Society, or Ladies' Sanitary Association, as lecturers and organizers. Nor can I stop to describe the enthusiasm which has sent so many women to the laborious tasks of district visitors or tract distributors ; to serve as workwomen at dull suburban afternoon sewing parties ; as superintendents of mothers' meetings; as librarians of parish libraries; as relief agents; as guardians; as schoolboard members. In these and countless other ways women have done and are doing good work—work owing its birth to love and to the pity which is akin to it. But of none of these do I now wish to write. Not because during ten years, living side by side with the poor, I have not seen the good results of such work—results which, like the quality of mercy, are twice blessed, both to him who gives and him who takes—but because I would rather here tell of work not so generally known, or so universally approved, and yet perhaps based on a surer foundation, and destined to an even greater future. The key-note of these labors is, that not only should the needs of the times be taken into consideration, but the deeper truth that it is only friendship, the care of one individual for another—love—which can enable human beings harmlessly to receive help from one another.

One of the things which, in London, is most striking, even to casual observers, is the way in which the poor are housed. In the West-end, ever and anon, as the well-horsed, richly-appointed carriages roll along the broad streets, where across the shops is written, in various characters, the same word "wealth," the luxurious riders can, if they will, catch a glimpse of the homes of the poor. They are described thus by the Medical Officer of Health for Marylebone, one of the richest districts in London, in the year (though it seems almost irony to say it) of our Lord 1868: " In Edwards Place there are ten six-roomed houses which are occupied by 84 families, in all 277 persons. The houses are very dilapidated, many of them unfit for habitation, the closets are filthy in the extreme, the yards badly paved, and the drains constantly out of repair. Orders for sanitary work are continually being sent out by the vestry to the owner of the wretched property. A rental of £10 per annum would be an extravagant sum to pay for either of these miserable dwellings, and yet more than three times that amount is exacted from the destitute and indigent people who inhabit them."

Does it need much imagination, if this is the outward condition of things, to picture the lives and characters of the inhabitants? Imagine the feelings of the widowed mother whose large family and small earnings have brought her to one room in such a court. Imagine her at weary work all the day long, her well-earned sleep broken by the drunkard's home-coming, while she shudders at his ribald song, or trembles in fear that her children should hear or understand his coarse jokes. The children cannot long retain that innocence which is their only effective deafness if they continue in such a moral atmosphere.

This description speaks of the West-end, the wealthy quarter of our great metropolis. In the East-end, the home of the poor, the prospect is not much more cheering. A report made by the Medical Officer of Health to the Whitechapel Board of Works in 1873, states: " Castle Alley is a very narrow thoroughfare leading from Whitechapel, High Street, which is entered by a covered way several feet in length and only about three feet in width. Owing to the frequent deposit of filth in this narrow passage, and from its defective ventilation, it is generally in an offensive condition. The alley contains an area, including the space on which the houses stand, of about 1,496 square yards, and has a population of 347, consisting of the very poorest class, each person having an average space of only four square yards. The eight houses on the west side of the court are very old. The walls and flooring of the cellars are wet, and a most unwholesome smell comes through the lower rooms, which renders such rooms unfit for habitation. The privy of each house is in the cellars, the nuisance from which— there being no other means for its escape—ascends by the staircase and makes its way into every room of the house. It is almost impossible for the tenants of these houses to keep the rooms clean, for the houses are three stories high, the privies are in the cellars, which are difficult of access, and the water supply is in the court. As there are no sinks in the houses, all the dirty water must be carried down four flights of stairs to the privy or thrown into the open court."

And this is not the sole evil. In another report to the same body we read: " The great evil of the overcrowding of the tenements of the poor prevails very extensively." Of one visit the inspector writes: " In the front room of the first floor of one house, which has a cubic space of 1,408 feet, there were four men, one woman, and a child, and in the room above there were eight persons, viz., four men, three women, and a child." In another house, in one room on the second floor they discovered " three women, two men, and a child ;" in another, " three men and three women." " The smell of the rooms inspected on these occasions was most offensive and overpowering." After another visit the inspector reports: " In room No. 2, which is regis- tered for the occupation of four persons only, six were found, viz., two men and one woman, who were in bed to- gether, and three children lying on the floor. In room No. 5, registered for the occupation of three, there were seven persons, viz., three women, one man, and three chil- dren ; and in room No. 8, which is also registered for three persons, there were two men, one woman, and five children."

And here again the moral corruption keeps pace with the physical. Such property, let in single rooms, is difficult to manage. The rich owners, experiencing this, and not recognizing their responsibility, let or sell their small house property, which frequently falls into the hands of a class of men who, themselves living on the spot, can make it pay by letting the rooms, alas! too often for the worst purposes, while keeping within the limits of the law. Many of the rooms are what is called "furnished"; that is to say, that the landlord has "put in a sack of straw to be used as a bed, some rugs for bed-clothes, a table and a chair, with some crockery, more or less broken. This so-called furnished room he had let for 8d. a night." This plan is both remunerative to the landlord and convenient to his tenant. To the thief, to the ne'er-do-well, to those who earn their livelihood by vice, what is more convenient than to have a home for one or two nights, a home from which they can flit at a moment's notice, should the police become dangerously inquisitive, or should the neighbors' tongues be uncomfortably communicative? What more convenient? Dangerous, tragically convenient, and one was helped to realize all its possible terrors by a poor mother, who had lost her girl, saying, "I can never hope to find her, when there's so many furnished rooms about."

It needed not a prophet to see nor a statesman to cure such evils, but it needed a brave and noble-hearted woman, and Octavia Hill, with sympathetic eyes, large heart, and clear brain, came forward to solve the problem. She did not come forward backed by a committee, nor supported by influential names and abundant money.

She did not come forward with schemes carefully drawn on paper, with plans cut and dried, and rules framed and printed. She began, supported by the belief of one friend, a man whose name is known wherever the language of art has penetrated, John Ruskin, who so far believed in her, young as she then was, as to buy a number of small houses (technically called a " court "), and put them under her charge, to manage according to her ideas, because he " trusted her with his poor." She did not, in those days, come publicly forward at all, but since then her work has, and it is good. It has borne the crucial test of successful working by other hands than hers, and during many years' experience it has been weighed in the scales of usefulness, and has not been found wanting.

Briefly, the plan is to bring together owners of property, and those ladies who care to visit the poor, the latter to act as the rent collectors and to be the link between the landlord and tenants. The plan has many recommendations. Without it, those who, having advantages of education, or the superior cultivation which leisure permits; or who, having the brightness of nature born of happiness and kinder circumstances ; or the lessons to teach, which have grown like flowers from a dead-leaf soil, enriched by sorrow and pain; without it, the many who, for varied reasons, wish to know and help the poor, have to make excuses to visit them, or to force an entrance, which every Englishman, considering his house (or room) his castle, rightly resents. By going to collect the rent, a natural introduction of landlord and tenant is effected, and the introduction once made, it depends on the will and wishes of the collector and tenant whether the connection shall remain merely a business one, or whether it shall ripen into the priceless relation of friendship.

The rent must be obtained. That is an initial element of Miss Hill's scheme, though, as any one who has had the privilege, as I have had, of working with her, must soon perceive, it is by no means the end. The rent must be obtained, and even the services of the broker (or "bailiff") used if it be not forthcoming. But there are many steps before this one is reached. If the money is not ready because the public-house has swallowed all except what the children's cries helped to save for bread, the rent collector, in friendliness and with all delicacy, has the right to speak of the defalcation and its cause. If work for the man is scarce, there are little jobs about the building to be done, a room to be color-washed, a message to be sent; or the wider outlook which education gives can be utilized to meet his need. The small sums necessary to enable the journey in search for work to be taken can be lent; the advertisement pages may be sympathetically searched; thousand are the means which friendship may dictate to combat the difficulty. The rent must be collected, for on that depend the pecuniary success and the consequent growth of the plan.

And the business side of the scheme will stand examination. In one large block of buildings, the capital being £30,700, the number of families 130, the volunteer workers 5, the paid workers 2, the net profit was £1,525, which, after allowing £300 toward a reserve fund, enabled the directors to pay a dividend of 4 per cent. In this parish, where there dwell some two hundred or two hundred and fifty families, whose rents are collected and whose dwellings are managed by ladies, the net profit, after all expenses are paid, averages 4½ per cent.; and this is on property a considerable portion of which is old, and for which the repairing expenses are very heavy. The yearly interest is 5 per cent. (besides the annual sinking fund) paid on a large block in Marylebone, built by the influence of Miss Hill, who herself tells the story of how she took under her care some dirty houses, dilapidated as they were, with their human inhabitants, their sorrows and their sins, one winter's evening in 1870.*

But, necessary and important as the business portion of the scheme is, it bears but the same relation to the whole as the skeleton does to the character of the child in the far-sighted eyes of a responsible mother. The business part is necessary: it gives the introduction, insures the regular visit ; but it is mainly valuable inasmuch as it supplies the means of communication, and gives the possibilities of helpfulness. Friendship—the friendship between the member of one class and another, the care of one woman whose heart is sorry because of the pain of another woman, the strength-giving link between two human beings, one of whom education and past life have perhaps helped to turn more readily towards the Sun of Righteousness, sometimes obscured to her less happy sister by the clouds of sin and suffering which encompass her life : to form such friendship, to give scope to such care, to forge such links, is the object, indeed the whole use, of the work.

The relationship once established, the means of mutual usefulness rapidly offer themselves ; the chance meeting of the few elder girls may soon develop into a regular gathering for sewing or the learning of singing ; the desire for hearing about other people, easily degenerating into gossip, may be guided until the meeting becomes an

---

* See "Homes of the London Poor," by Octavia Hill, to be bought at 52 East 20th Street, New York, and 146 Marylebone Road, London N.W. Price one shilling.—H. O. B.

opportunity of learning about other classes, or concerning those great lives examples of which can be found in all ranks alike. The talks about books and public events might stimulate book-lending, and books, in themselves friends worth having, will yet create more living friendship. "Yes, ma'am, we have real pleasant reading evenings sometimes, but the worst of it is, if she's cross, or if anything puts her out, she'll stop in *just* the most interesting part, and nothing will move her, whatever we say." A trying stoppage, all story lovers will agree, when it is taken into consideration that the "she" is the only member of the party who can read. The sight of the high-spirited rough lads, during an evening's visit to the court or building (which is sometimes necessary to enable the landlady to see her out-all-day tenants, or to assure herself that all goes well) will suggest the advisability of some place of rendezvous out of the street temptations and the mischief which lurks in corners for hangers about. A story-telling evening, if it be but once a week, will keep them together until time and personal influence can weld them into an associated body, likely to be all the stronger and longer-lived if self-governed, by "own pennies" supported.

The large-hearted landlady will not only be content to give her own friendship; valuing friendship, she will be anxious that it should exist between her tenants. She will aim at bringing the men together and binding them in some form of corporate life; she will suggest little ways in which one family can help another. She will kill the germ of discord, which cannot live in the atmosphere of mutual helpfulness. Valuing friendship, she will wish her older and richer friends to know her newer and poorer ones, that they in their turn may give and get all that she finds priceless. And many are the ways of happiness that will open out from the friendship-paved road. The rich country friend can find a spare room for the smoke-paled child, or perhaps arrangements can be made so that one of the village cottagers can receive as guest the tired mother, weakly from her last confinement, and weary with life's struggle amid the noise and dirt. The hushed country noises sounding in her dinned ears may be for her " God's voice at eventide." The offer of help, such as hospital letters, loans, or even the gift of money, will come from the landlady friend followed by no sense of degradation. For cannot presents be reciprocal between friends ? " My reward is greater than I can bear " was the ungrateful sentence of one of the lady collectors, as she displayed to me her gifts received on that day's round. And it must be confessed that a haddock, a bunch of wall-flowers, a tin toasting-fork, a perforated card book-mark, and a bundle of rhubarb are incongruous elements to tidily pack, and somewhat difficult to transport on the journey by omnibus or train which the three to six miles dividing the rich and the poor ends of our big London unfortunately makes necessary.

Only friendship can bridge it, but friendship is powerful enough to break down all barriers, social or educational, powerful enough to lighten cloud-darkened lives. " Dull! why it wouldn't be half living without our weekly ladies" might itself stand as a testimonial for the value of this branch of women's work ; or the sentence "Wherever I go, I shall try and keep under the ladies," uttered lowly by a poor woman (who, good soul though she was, had got hardly used in the fight for life, having to finally turn out of her larger first-floor room, and take a cheaper, smaller one), might be an encouragement, almost a banner-motto, to lead on workers dispirited by the laborious routine and the often wearying details, on the punctual fulfilment of which depends so largely the successful working of the scheme.

I have delayed the longer on the story of this kind of woman's work, in London, because in it lies the germ, already ripening and vigorously growing, of a great social change—perhaps almost a social revolution—in the best sense. It is no longer the work of one woman, and her friends and followers, or of one set of women, but has already spread itself through London, so that, at this time, over one thousand families live under it, and by it are helped to their place in life and society. This method has commended itself to other workers in the great cities of England, and I believe also of America. In the growth of large cities, and the constant tendency to the creation of poorer quarters, and the separation of rich and poor, by the conditions of city life, such a plan as this seems to offer the most hopeful method of restoring the kindlier relations of landlord and tenant, which in rural districts still help to bind classes together. In great cities these relations had ceased, and were replaced only by the mechanical call of the rent-gatherer, whose only object was money-getting, often divorced from any sense of reciprocal duty, and far removed from the pale of loving-kindness, on which alone the social world can safely turn. There is another relation of this work, which has already shown itself, and which promises to be as far-reaching in its good effect as the work itself. On this I can only say a word, for it would lead too far. The ladies who act as rent-collectors and friends of their tenants acquire knowledge of circumstances and character which makes them the fittest people to afford such information as poor-law officers need; and should be the essential basis of any system of public, or, as we call it, poor-law relief: hence, such ladies may become either the agents or the collaborators of those who are now seeking to supplement State relief, or to substitute it by the organization of charity.

Of what is meant by the organization of charity, most transatlantic as well as British readers are already sufficiently well-informed; and to those who are not, it would be hopeless to attempt in any few words to map out the relative places which committees of charity, lady rent-collectors, and poor-law officers should occupy, and are beginning to occupy, towards one another. This, however, will, I am sure be clear, that in the work of the lady rent-collectors lies a germ of usefulness which, wherever and whenever thoroughly developed, will substitute (as it has already largely substituted) the relation of rich owner and poor tenant, of well-to-do master with laborer, artisan, or invalid.

I pass to another subject. In all ages, in all nations, in all ranks the work and privilege of women has been largely that of pleasure-givers. As hostess she has exerted herself to please. For her friends, her neighbors, her children, her aim has been to give pleasure, or to provide for them recreative rest. And it is work which bears no mean relation to the rest of life. Without it, life would seem grimly bare, hopelessly flat, sin-suggestively insipid. Pleasure is as essential to right human life as sunshine to a healthy physical condition. Women have already counted it one of their duties in life to give pleasure, or to arrange rest for their relations and friends; (how many fathers, brothers, and husbands have not had the seed of selfishness sown and cultivated in such generous soil?) but they have, as yet, rarely recognized it as a duty to give rest and pleasure to the poor. To feed, to clothe, to educate, to improve, to help the classes below them, are duties for which many a thousand women have sacrificed and striven to perform. To rest them, to recreate them (and pleasure in the highest form must include these two elements, indeed the Christian name for pleasure might be "recreative-rest") has been left out, and yet it is a gift of which the wealthy and the leisurely classes have the monopoly, and which they alone can offer. The poor cannot get it themselves.

In the one room where lives the whole family, father and mother, children of all ages, with occasionally the old grand-parent or the "lone woman" as a lodger, there is no accommodation for pleasure, there is not a possibility of sufficient pause in the ceaseless round of work to permit of recreative rest. The wages have to go for necessaries of life; there is but little margin left for books, concerts, picture-galleries, theatres, country visits, while social pleasure, the re-union where the enjoyment consists in mutual intercourse, the meeting of friends and the interchange of ideas on topics of common interest are prohibited, because practically impossible. Where is the room? where is the money?

But just as the women have made it their duty to give help to the poor, so now let them make it their duty to give them pleasure. When the idea is accepted that pleasure is a good and desirable gift, the ways and means will open. And the unusual and dreaded duty once performed, it becomes transformed into a delightful joy. "It is more blessed to give than to receive" will come home almost with the force of a self-discovered truth by those who have seen, as I have, the joy of the people at a country party. I do not mean a "treat," where they are taken down in hundreds to the country, turned into a

6

field or on a common, where the crowds engender noise and excitement, and only the scene, not the nature, of the daily life is changed; but at a party where the hostess entertains her guests as the friends of the person, the district-visitor, or the rent-collector where she receives and welcomes them individually; where she opens her garden, her conservatories, and maybe her house, for their reception; where she provides them with food not contracted for at so much a head, but cooked in her own kitchen and served by her own servants.

The pleasure given by such a party is touching to witness, a holy privilege to be allowed to create; and even simpler efforts give unspoken joy. The evening devoted to the ten or twelve girls—what is it but one evening and a little thought for the hostess? but the well-appointed tea-table, the merry-making games, the interesting portfolio, the suggestive talk, the soul-speaking music—what are they *not* to the ten or twelve guests amid their pleasure-barren life? "I did not think I could enjoy myself so much in ONE evening" made our breakfast-table look bright, in spite of yellow fog, as I read aloud our guest's letter one day not long after such a little party. It is good and gladdening to be the hostess where the care-worn face brightens at some harmless joke, to see the rough woman (withal a sister) lose herself and her sorrows in enjoyment of a simple play, to feel the sense of pleasure (unfortunately still too much mixed with surprise) with which some ordinary courtesy is received and accepted. "If we had been ladies born we couldn't have had better" finished up the lengthy description of one of such parties, as told by a guest to her neighbor; and methinks it would have been, if the hostess could have seen the radiant face, an ample repayment for her trouble, and worth more than all the murmured conventional politenesses about " having passed such a pleasant evening " which usually reward the tired hostess.

But besides the gift of pleasure, such parties may do more. At them introductions can be effected, introductions between people of different classes, with different manners, and different ideas on many matters, making it none the less important that they should be introduced. Deep human insight is shown in the old story of the man who emphatically stated, the conversation having turned on a neighbor, " Oh, I hate the fellow." " Hate him ! " replied his friend, " why I didn't know you knew him." " No, I don't," returned the hater ; " if I did, how could I hate him ? " and this, maybe, might go a long way to explain the reason of class hatreds and misunderstandings. Woman, if she accepts among her duties the blessed one of giving recreative rest to the poor, might, unknowingly, do yet greater work, attain a yet higher aim. She might bring nearer the good time, promised so many hundred years ago, yet seemingly still so distant ; she might, by bridging over class differences, put some living meaning into the now all but dead words, " There shall be one fold, under one Shepherd." " The next war will not be a religious war, nor a national war ; it will be a class war," has been declared by a wise seer. By such links as are easily forged, by friendly entertainments, might not women make a strong chain, strong enough even to bind men's evil passions ? By the gift of pleasure might they not earn the blessing promised to peace-makers?

I do not advocate an untried theory. In our parish, during the last ten years, we have given, or planned, and always ourselves accompanied, over three hundred such parties. Anxious days, tiring evenings have we often thus passed, but bright happy ones, too, with a reflective brightness, for who could help rejoicing when pleasure so real and simple was all around? Great care has been taken that the guests, whether received in our drawing-room or school-room, or at the houses of town or country friends, should not be more numerous than could be personally entertained as individuals, but with this simple rule, and perhaps a slight additional provision for entertainment in the shape of pictures to look at, or songs or recitations, the parties have been in all essential respects exactly similar to those to which the friends of one's own class are invited.

As I write, it strikes me as sadly strange that there is not a larger and more universal experience to record concerning this form of woman's love-inspired work; all the stranger because it is no new idea, being as old as their common name of Christian. The Master himself suggested the idea, painting the picture of a possible host, and possible guests, who could not " bid him again." Can it be true that mere fastidiousness and dislike to come into contact with suualor and dirt have been strong enough to render a prophet's words of none effect?

But there are, besides social gatherings, other means for recreative rest. The pictures by the great artists might, so far as their immediate effect is concerned, hardly have been painted for all the use they are to the poor. Pictures whose fame is spread over the whole world, which are the study books of the most interesting of all histories, the history of human thought and feeling, are to them as if written in a dead language. In London the galleries are some distance from the poor part of the town, and why should the poor spend their hardly earned pence in

taking the journey to see treasures the beauty of which
they do not hàlf understand, having never been educated
to see and appreciate them? But if women will, following
the example of the few* who have cared to "bring beauty
home to the lives of the poor," and if they will adopt it
as a duty to make the places where the poor meet more
recreatively restful, they will find a field of work but yet
little trodden, a wealth of flower-rewards only waiting to
be plucked. By turning to account in tile or panel painting the various accomplishments which so many women
possess, beauty might be brought to the homes and meet-
ing-places of the poor; by the gift or loan of pictures
(and who misses one picture from the drawing-room wall
for a few months?), by decoration, by beauty in all its
forms, pleasure is given, pleasure often silently received,
but fulfilling our two tests as to the requirements of holy
pleasure, viz., being both recreative and restful. Here, for
woman (the pleasure-giver) has a new opportunity of
giving pleasure opened out of late years. She may plan
to take little groups of her poor friends to see galleries or
exhibitions. The sixpence or the shilling for the fares
and admission will not, in most cases, make a large dimi-
nution in her pin-money; or, if so, there are our national
galleries free, unbarred even to the poorest, and yet by
them but little used—with the lady friend as cicerone, how
different the pictures look! The homely explanation offered, the simple story told, the artist's history sketched,
lend to them living interest. " She makes the pictures
speak and walk," was a compliment, by no means empty,
given to one explainer; and neither did it imply miracu-

* Particularly the Misses Harrison, who, while supporting themselves, yet
find time and opportunity to leave many a public hospital and poor people's
building lovelier than they found it.—H. O. B.

lous powers in the direction of picture explaining. She had but told them what she saw with her more practiced eye, cultivated by the long looking at pictures; but for her poor friends it was all fresh, and came to them with the force of originality. "Don't look at me, dear friends; look at the pictures," exclaimed one lady to her party of picture-seers, who were standing gazing, with varied expressions, at her as she expounded, and not at the pictures. "Yes, to be sure," apologized one woman, "but I was only looking to see where it all came from."

Never ending is the pleasure gained and given by introducing beauty into the lives and thoughts of those sad pleasure-barren livers. In the last two years we, aided by a large committee, have succeeded in getting up a loan exhibition of pictures. In all kindliness was our request responded to, and we have been able, each year, to show one hundred and sixty to one hundred and seventy pictures to our neighbors. Pictures not of the oleograph, and colored print description, but some of the finest works of Sir Frederick Leighton, Watts, Millais, Breton, Rivière, J. Israel, Munckasy, Bret, Ouless, Faed, Davis, Richmond, Holman Hunt, Lewis, Long, Herkomer and Goodall—pictures containing the highest thoughts nobly expressed. The exhibition, held in our parish school-rooms, themselves not well placed for advertisement purposes, was opened in April, 1881, for nine days, and attracted, in spite of the payment of threepence, for seven days, 9,258 people. In 1882, it was open thirteen days, Sundays included, and no less than 25,776 persons came to see it. The figures are the best answer to the argument that the poor do not care for art. If they do not care as they might, if they do not gain from it all the help that is possible, if they do not learn from these poet teachers all they can teach, it is yet open to women (the pleasure-givers) to get and give to them this joy, a joy by which reverence grows, and by which the greatest lessons might be taught; for are not pictures the parable language of our day?

One other development of woman's work is in connection with music for the people.

> " Music is an angel of holy thoughts,
> Inspiring to noble deeds,"

is the heading of the report* of a society whose work is, in their own words, "to give good music to the working people;" "to call a fractional percentage of the working multitudes of London to a sense of joy, to the feelings and suggestions of higher and more delicate delights than commonly fall to the lot of those who are, for the most part, condemned to lead a dreary, monotonous life of almost unceasing toil, with rare occasions and lower kinds of pleasure." And then the report further explains the large hope, necessarily large to bear the burden of the small details and many disappointments contingent on the work: " Even small seeds of good are apt to germinate and produce noble and delightful fruit; a little leaven leaveneth the whole, and to bring to masses of people whose lives are dull, hard-working, and commonplace, and whose minds are uncultured and too often vacant, those pure sources of delight and elevating elements of joy, and those reachings after higher thoughts, of which music, with its beneficent influence, is acknowledged to be a perennial fountain, is at least a labor of love preg-

---

* " A Statement of the Aims and Work of the Popular Ballad and Concert Committee, 1883." Printers: Hazell & Viney, Kirby Street, London.

—H. O. B.

nant with good." And fruitful of as well as pregnant
with good, all must for truth witness who have seen the
effect of music on the poor. It is both rest and recre-
ation; speaking for them the things they feel; explaining to them what they are and cannot say. It is not, I
think, often taken into consideration what the poor suffer
from their dumbness. Education unlooses tongues. Men
find in a knowledge of literature the expression of their
thoughts. The ignorant are still left with this pain.

> " Music, which is earnest of a Heaven,
>   Seeing we know emotions strange by it,
>   Not else to be revealed, is a *voice*."

says Robert Browning; while George Eliot, our woman
poet, tells us

> " Music is melted speech
>   .   .   .   .   that can reach
>   More quickly through our frame's deep-winding night,
>   And, without thought, raise thought's best fruit—delight."

In London there are three associations actively engaged in similar work to the one whose report I have
quoted, giving freely (or what is perhaps better, bringing
within their reach) good music to the people. In all
three the work of women is the mainspring of the enter-
prises; and all largely avail themselves of the musical
gifts of lady amateurs. It would be easy and interesting to write folios of their experience; but I will content
myself with one quotation from the same report* which
I have especially chosen to illustrate a point which, after
long intimacy with the poor, I feel strongly. After
speaking of the music selected for the programme, the report goes on to say: " Perhaps among all the pieces given

---

* " A Statement of the Aims and Work of the Popular Ballad and Concert
Committee, 1883."—H. O.B.

at these concerts nothing has evoked greater enthusiasm than Beethoven's 'Creation's Hymn' and Handel's 'Rejoice Greatly.' The audience, composed of the genuine working classes, has received with enthusiasm the best performances and the best music, while, at the same time, their uniform courtesy, and thoughtful attention, and their just discrimination of the relative merits of music provided, and of the power and skill of the artists who appeared, have shown that they not only ardently enjoy good music, but that they judge with kindly but singularly accurate tastes the qualities of the music, and the art and talents of its interpreters." And of the very poor, the classes lower than this society reaches, the same can be said. There is a response to the highest kind of music not accorded to the lighter and more popular. After a musical evening, given at a club in one of the lowest courts in the quarter of the town where the criminals congregate, a listener remarked, " Why, the fiddler says what I've all along wanted to." The dumb being, by his dumbness, made more animal, had received the gift of speech. It was Luther who said that "Music is one of the most magnificent and delightful presents God has given us." Women, always anxious, and rightly so, to gather into their homes every care-soothing charm, cultivate music. But if it is true what Mrs. Browning says, that

> " If we say a true word, instantly
> We feel 'tis God's, not ours, and pass it on
> Like bread at sacrament: we taste and pass,
> Nor handle for a moment, as indeed
> We dared to set up any claim to such ; "

then surely it must with equal truth relate to our duty concerning the "melted speech," the "earnest of a Heaven."

At a people's party, such a one as those described, there
6*

met one winter evening in 1871 a man and a woman, both troubled by the questions affecting the large class of girl children whom poverty had compelled the State to support. The man was the Right Honorable J. Stansfeld; the woman, Mrs. Nassau-Senior, whose work has decreed that "all generations shall call her blessed." From that almost chance-made acquaintance there was developed a much needed work.

There were then in London at least thousands of State-supported children. They had been (thanks to the earnest work of previous social reformers) removed from the evil influences of the workhouses, where the elder paupers and the criminal class congregate, and had been housed in schools in the country or suburbs. The schools, fitted with every appliance which thought or money could suggest, were large; the children sheltered in each being rarely fewer than five hundred, sometimes more than eight hundred.

Mr. Stansfeld had, as Mrs. Nassau-Senior says in her report (published in the Blue Book of 1873–4, of the Local Government Board), "expressed his wish to have a woman's view as to the effect on girls of the system of education at the pauper schools," which wish he was able to further by appointing her an Inspector of the Workhouse Schools. She set to work, visiting carefully every pauper school, spending hours with the officers and children so as to get a right and fair judgment concerning the questions which affected both. She traced, laboriously, the after careers of the girls, and in conclusion wrote a report, one of the results of which has been the growth of a woman's society called the Metropolitan Association for Befriending Young Servants. It is an army of kindly ladies fighting sin and sadness, their chief weapon being friendship.

After many wise and womanly suggestions concerning the care and education of the girls while in the schools, where some of them live from their earliest infancy, Mrs. Senior turns her attention to their first start in life. They are sent out, she says, to service, "an unusually difficult life at an age (fourteen or fifteen, sometimes younger) when other children, whose previous advantages have far exceeded their own, are still under guidance and protection." The faults she finds most common among them are "bad temper, untruthfulness and apathy," while "their ignorance of the cost of clothes, and consequent carelessness about keeping them tidily mended," their ignorance, "difficult," she says, "to realize, about things that are familiar to most children of a few years old," do not make them the most handy or desirable servants. Not a very hopeful account of the material to be dealt with, but still the material, dubbed, as it often is, pauper, or low class, or hopeless, is, when subdivided, just a girl! a creature of the "mother sex," having in her possibilities of infinite good, capabilities of destroying evil. And the future of this material—what is it?

In tracing this, Mrs. Senior's experience was not without its sadness, and her sweet eyes were often tear-bedimmed, as she told of some poor girl so absolutely friendless in the world that even the arrival of a strange "some one" to question the mistress about her, was hailed with a joy only begotten by loneliness. And this loneliness is perhaps the feature which is the most surprising to her disciples who have followed on the lines that Mrs. Senior indicated. "Why do you cry, dear?" one girl was asked. "No one ever looked at me to make me feel that way before," was the answer; and it was no wonder she wept—her way of taking off her shoes—for she had seen a vision of the angel of Friendship, and she felt she trod on holy ground. And the poor child was so altogether lonely! After years in the school, she had been sent to her first place, which she soon left. "When a girl leaves her first place, no matter how young she is, even this small amount of legal protection ceases," writes Mrs. Senior, the "small amount" referred to being "that the relieving officer should visit girls up to the age of sixteen."

She was but fourteen, but, her first place left, there was no one to turn to, and she hired herself out to any one who would take her. The place was not all it might have been. It was not a den of infamy; it was *only* the home of cruelty: but from it the child at last, her youthfulness gone, her frame worn, her growth stunted, ran away, and it was only the direction of a kindly policeman which helped her to find a friend at last.

Sad as such cases are—but there are not many now, or else the work of Mrs. Senior had not accomplished all it might—they are not perhaps so hopelessly sad as those of girls whose relations, to quote again from the report, are "as might be expected often of the worst class, fathers from prison, drunken mothers, worthless aunts." "The girls thus tempted" (by their relations) "were often well-beloved, promising children while in school, and I am inclined to believe that the warm-hearted, generous natures are just those who are the most exposed to this danger." And, as I write, they rise before me, just such girls as Mrs. Senior speaks of. I see them troop past, some of them ruined by the bad influence, strengthened by the relationship, some saved by what Mrs. Senior proposed, "a strong counter-influence in the right direction."

There goes E. B., such a naughty, dear child, with a bad

mother and a number of brothers and sisters leading lives
that don't bear looking into. She is so far safe, a bright,
happy, naughty, wayward dairy-maid, her work with milk
and butter in her sweet-smelling workshop in kindly contrast with the work and surroundings her mother would
have had her come to. Here lumbers along (for her gait
still bears testimony to the heaviness and bad fit of the
workhouse-made shoes) M. T. She comes to show a
warm tippet, the gift of her mistress, but to say, too, that
the elder sister won't give up the old bad life, and is
always "at her" to come too; and to ask for some of her
savings to help pay for the confinement of an unmarried
sister. There will be work for the lady friend here; there
will be a hard tussle for that girl's soul—on which side
will the victory be declared?

Here comes D. M., puffed up with importance, for "My
aunt says she will keep me like a lady, and there is no
need that I should work no more." A big bait this to
an idle, vain novel-reading girl; but the friend has
made herself trusted. She promises to see the aunt, and
the girl agrees, after some difficulty, not to "give notice"
until the friend writes or sees her again. And here is J.W.,
in tears too. The usually sunny giggling Jane. "What
is the matter, childie?" "My mistress gave me notice
because I was not 'ome right time that day I came to see
you." "Not home! why you left me directly we left the
Zoological Gardens. What came to you?" Then, tear-
choked, it comes out. A big never-before-seen brother
had told their aunt (a decent hard-working woman) that
he wanted to see his sister, as he was "in trouble." The
child tramped for hours seeking him, and when found he
only wanted a shilling or two. To take her wages, to make
her lose her place, was the help that manly brother gave.

The experience of the three hundred and twenty ladies —now working with the Metropolitan Association for Befriending Young Servants, working because Mrs. Senior worked, protecting from the evils which the feeling for these girls the motherly tenderness of a rich nature feared for them—the experience of the three hundred and twenty ladies will support Mrs. Senior when she says : " It not unfrequently happens that a girl who would otherwise do well is unsettled by her relations."

And Mrs. Senior foresaw yet other dangers for the friendless, or worse than friendless, girls. She writes in 1873 : " The importance of a girl's keeping her first place is greater on account of the difficulty of providing suitable protection for her when she is out of place. She has a right to return to the work-house, but all agree that this is about the worst thing she can do." It needs no further argument to prove this last point, when it is remembered that the work-house houses the human refuse, a contaminating influence for a girl who has perhaps only failed in temper or health, not fallen in character.

And the number of times a girl will change her place, particularly the first two years of her service life, is almost incredible. C. L. had nine places in eleven months. She always liked them " so much " for the first week ; the mistress was a "dear lady," and the children (if there were any) were " quite pets," but the song dropped into the minor key during the second or third week, generally to a doleful duet, for the lady usually joined in also. What would have become of this girl if it had not been for the friendship, for her and those like her, which Mrs. Senior had awakened in the breasts of the other women? The Befriending Society had provided the girl with a friend, who saw she was safely housed between her places, though, poor child! few were her gowns and hats, for most of the wages had to go in paying for lodging "between places."

"Yes, ma'am, the missus do like me very much, she does. She's quite pleased with me. Still she thinks I'd better leave," came from a pretty, high-spirited girl, a contradictory sentence and not a hopeful sign that there would be a future effort to please the new "missus." And the speaker failed again and again until, at last, aided by her friend, she was able to trace the fault to herself, and out of her humility grew hope. "Pride goeth before destruction, and a haughty spirit before a fall," might have been true of her, had it not been for befriending care ; for to such a girl, the dangers of often being out of place are known to all dwellers in cities, and need not be dwelt on here.

And there is yet another side to the character of these friend-needing children. In Mrs. Senior's report we read :* "All without exception were curiously apathetic in temperament, described as 'not caring for anything,' 'taking no interest,' 'not enjoying,' 'seeming like old people,' etc." A curious description of the characters of young people under twenty; and one in which I cannot but concur with the writer. "The system of training must be in great measure responsible," and this apathy, this self-indifference (a wholly different quality to unselfishness) opens out other dangers to these unfriended girls. They have no consciousness of rights, often not even the right to their own person. Never having possessed anything, they know not how to guard themselves, nor to "possess their own souls." And in

* Quoted from a letter written to Mrs. Senior by a friend who had made inquiries about the girls who had been sent to service.—H. O. B.

the endeavor to cure this evil, perhaps more has been done by her women-followers than Mrs. Senior herself anticipated.

The lady friend introduced by the Association to the girl, on her leaving school, becomes the somebody " to care for." And it is part of her work to see that her child-friend has something in which to " take an interest." The lady friend's house, the lady's pleasures, her jour-neys out, her home-comings, her health, her relatives, her dresses, her ordinary life, in fact, if she be admitted sympathetically into it, is in itself an interest to the girl; and to this the wise woman friend will add other and more personal interests for the girl herself. The monthly periodical, the occasional letter, the thought-suggested gift, the carefully planned holiday, are trifling things to do, but without which there is no opportunity for " en-joying " in the gray lives of these children servants. And their wealth of gratitude and love is worth harvesting. For such a little outlay of trouble given, there is such a liberal repayment of affection received. Instead of sor-rowing over wasted pains, I often feel with Wordsworth:

> " Alas, the gratitude of men
> Hath oftener left me mourning."

" I am never able to say much, but I do feel a great deal about you," wrote a girl, pronounced " hopelessly unimpressionable " by the school official; and " I will do it if *you* wish me to," I have heard more than once from the lips of girls who would find the " it " no easy matter. And it is no easy matter to apologize to a harsh, rough-speaking (or, as they would describe her, a " jawing ") mistress. It is no easy matter to give up the lover who is " really very kind." It is no easy matter to go on wearily drudging at unlovely work when the sun shines, when outside life looks bright, and there is only one step to be taken to make it their own. The friend, by her love, may become a saviour. Love is stronger than evil; God than the devil.

Mrs. Senior's loving wisdom has had many children. In the Report of 1882 of the Metropolitan Association for Befriending Young Servants, the society which is the more immediate outgrowth of her work (though indirectly the Girls' Friendly Society, and kindred societies, might be said to result from the same spirit), we read that there are now (1883) fourteen branches, each with its organization, its free registry office, clothing club, savings bank, means of safely housing girls, etc., connected with those branches no less than 320 ladies, and the Association has not reached a full stop yet. Under the able captaincy of Miss Anne Townshend (who, herself a friend of Mrs. Senior, took from her the germ of the idea), the society still hopes to grow until it extends its influence all over the metropolitan area; until it has its office in each poor-law division, its volunteer workers aiding and suplementing the work of the State-paid almoners; until it imbue with its spirit, and modify the mechanical, and therefore often harsh, action of the legal overseers of the poor.

And of this work the keynote is friendship, the same keynote which is struck in the other two kinds of women's charitable work which I have tried to tell about. It is only the gift of friendship, of love, which can help the world. It is only the care of one individual for another that can elevate a soul. It has been woman's work to teach love. To her child she teaches:

> " Love's holy earnest in a pretty play,
> By tying sashes, fitting baby shoes,
> And kissing full sense into empty words."

For the world she keeps it alive and warm. By it the two great women I have spoken of were guided to see the needs and think out some of the remedies for the sufferers with whom they come in contact. By love, not love in the abstract, but by loving and serving one needing individual, each woman can bring a stone towards building a harbor of refuge for the sorrowful, the sinful, the suffering.

> The world waits
> For help.   *   *   Let us love so well,
> Our work shall still be better for our love,
> And still our love be sweeter for our work.

CHAPTER II.

GERMANY.

I. A GENERAL REVIEW OF THE WOMEN'S MOVEMENT IN GERMANY.

BY ANNA SCHEPELER-LETTE AND JENNY HIRSCH.

[Mrs. Anna Schepeler-Lette was born December 19, 1829, at Soldin, Germany, and was the eldest daughter of Dr. Lette—mentioned in the following pages—whom she accompanied, in 1848, to Frankfort-on-the-Main, whither he went as a member of the German Parliament. In 1866 she joined her father at Berlin, and was initiated into the work of the Lette Society, to which admirable organization she has ever since devoted all her time and energy. Mrs. Schepeler-Lette went to America in 1876, and visited the Centennial Exhibition, and many of the principal cities of the United States, where she carefully examined various institutions whose aims were similar to those of the Lette Society.

Miss Jenny Hirsch, born November 25, 1829, at Zerbst, Germany, was brought up as a child by very strictly orthodox Jewish parents, but, although she had many narrow prejudices to contend against, secured by her own efforts a good education. In 1860 Miss Hirsch went to Berlin, became interested in a fashion paper, and accumulated in four years sufficient money to enable her to devote herself entirely to literary work. At this epoch she published numerous essays and criticisms, and many translations from the French, English, and Swedish, among others John Stuart Mill's " Subjection of Women." Since the spring of 1866 Miss Hirsch has been the secretary of the Lette Society and editor of the *German Women's Advocate* (*Deutscher Frauen-Anwalt*), which is devoted to the industrial and general education of women.]

THE woman question, like several other ideas thrust

upon the attention of the world by the French Revolution, was not hastily accepted by the German mind. Many excellent reforms have encountered a long and obstinate resistance on this side of the Rhine simply because they were said to be a product of the upheaval of 1789, and the women's movement, in addition to its unfortunate origin, was brought into disrepute as the "Emancipation of Women." The greatest stumbling-block in our way has been the signification given to this term, and we tacitly agreed to avoid its use, although it was impossible to find one which could exactly replace it.

The year 1848 was the signal for the setting free of forces until then held in check, and new truths were propagated of which the masses had scarcely a presentiment a few days before. It was the early spring time in the life of nations. It produced a forced and quick growth, and its effect was felt even by women. Mrs. Louise Otto-Peters, of Leipsic, who has since become well-known, caught the spirit of the times, proclaimed the principle of women's progress, and devoted her great energies and talents to the young cause.

The brilliant beginnings and lofty hopes of 1848 were immediately followed by a sombre and troubled period. The liberty trees were planted in a soil so poor and badly prepared that they could not take root. They soon perished under the influence of the reaction which set in, and all that had been accomplished for good or for evil in that short season was indiscriminately destroyed. What had been done for the amelioration of the condition of women shared the common fate. For the moment these questions were forgotten ; they were pushed aside, repressed, but they could not be extirpated. Political and social life could no longer be confined within the narrow limits which had existed previous to the Revolution of 1848. The woman question also came to the surface again, and in 1865 we find it once more before the public, when it took on the form by which it has since been known, marching on, year after year, from victory to victory.

The most striking proof of the vitality and the necessity of the reformation lay in the fact that it was demanded at the same time in various places, so that its advocates, ignorant of each other, differed on minor points. The woman question in Germany has this same argument in its favor; it sprang up simultaneously in several parts of the country, and especially at Leipsic and Berlin.

The Leipsic movement had its origin in a women's meeting—to which men, however, were admitted—held in that city in October, 1865, and due to the efforts of Mrs. Louise Otto-Peters, of whom we have already spoken. The Berlin movement dates from a gathering of both sexes at the capital in December of the same year, under the presidency of Dr. Adolf Lette, one of the most eminent philanthropists Germany has produced. At Leipsic, where the feminine element predominated, the question was regarded rather from the standpoint of sentiment, while at Berlin, where business men took part, more practical measures were adopted. In both places, however, good sense prevailed, and all felt that in order to construct a solid and durable edifice the foundation must be made before the roof, that slow and conservative, rather than hasty and radical, steps would be better in the end.

The first meeting in Berlin was followed in February of the next year, 1866, by the foundation of the Society for the Promotion of the Employment of Women (*Verein zur*

Förderung der Erwerbsfähigkeit des weiblichen Geschlechts). The new organization was placed under the patronage of the Crown Princess, and in 1869 its name was changed to the Lette Society (*Lette-Verein*) in honor of its founder, who died December 3, 1868.

Fault is sometimes found because the movement has been separated into two currents ever since its beginning. There is unquestionably much ground for this criticism, and we do not deny that our efforts would have produced more fruit if both organizations had worked together. But here comes into play a peculiarity of the German character which has considerably modified the evil. The two associations, although occasionally at variance, have not acted to the detriment of the common cause, but, on the contrary, they have displayed greater zeal, and have more quickly discovered and corrected errors, because of their independent positions.

The chief aim of the Leipsic reformers, the National Association of German Women (*Der allgemeine deutsche Frauen-Verein*), was to produce a broad and thorough agitation of the general question of women's rights, while in Berlin the object in view was more immediate, precise and limited. The former strove to disseminate the new ideas, and, for this purpose, annual congresses or conventions were held in different parts of the country, where eloquent addresses were delivered by these pioneers, and local societies established.*

Although the Lette Society was not founded for the purpose of propagandism, this important agency is not excluded from its plan of work. The scope of the organization was clearly set forth in an essay, read by Dr. Lette before the Central Society for the Improvement of the Working

---

* A fuller account of the Leipsic movement follows this essay.—T. S.

Classes of Prussia (*Central-Verein für das Wohl der arbei-tenden Klassen in Preussen*), in which he proved, by the aid of statistics, that a large body of women were forced to earn their own livelihood, and that marriage—since fe-males outnumbered males in Prussia, and also because of certain economic reasons—was not always possible. He called attention to the precarious situation of the daughters of poor government employés when, on the death of their father, they are thrown upon the world wholly unprepared for the struggle of life. He spoke of the few pursuits open to women, of the over-crowding of those not shut against them, and of the low pay resulting from this state of things; and, in conclusion, he predicted fatal results if the sphere of their activity was not enlarged and em-ployments which were once theirs were not restored to them.

These ideas formed the basis of the Lette Society, whose organization was substantially that of the London Society for Promoting the Employment of Women.* We did not, however, servilely follow the English model, but while we utilized the experiences of the London Society, we did not hesitate to introduce modifications demanded by the peculiarities of the German character. The essen-tial principles and aims of the Lette Society have been, from the beginning, to discover new occupations fitted for women, to protect their interests in those where they al-ready have a footing, and to educate them for more im-portant and profitable employments.

Notwithstanding the many difficulties which the society has encountered during its long period of activity, it has, on the whole, remained faithful to its origin. It is true that we have found it more and more necessary to devote

---

* For an account of this Society, see page 97.—T. S.

attention to practical instruction, for it was soon discovered that most women did not know how to work carefully, conscientiously, and accurately. This is not due, however, to any innate and fundamental defect in the sex, but is rather a result of bad education and habits, which, as experience has shown, quickly disappear, and are replaced by remarkable aptitude as soon as irregular employment gives place to methodical work preceded by a rational preparation.

After the death of its founder and first president, the Lette Society was directed for several years by Dr. von Holtzendorf, professor at the University of Berlin, until Mrs. Schepeler-Lette succeeded to the post in 1872, where she has ever since remained.

The society supports at this moment, at its rooms in Königgrätzer Strasse, Berlin, a commercial school, a drawing and modeling school, and a cooking school, while it also gives instruction in washing, ironing, cutting, dressmaking, hand and machine sewing, the manufacture of artificial flowers, and many other kinds of manual and art work. The pupils of these various schools are prepared for the State examinations for drawing teachers and instructors in mechanic arts, and subsequently find employment in boarding, private, and girls' grammar schools. In another building is a printing office, where women are taught to set type. The society also conducts a boarding-house for women (*Das Victoriastift*), and in connection with it a women's restaurant. A shop for the sale of female handiwork, known as the Victoria Bazaar, a free intelligence office, and a bank where women may make on easy terms small loans, with which to commence or enlarge their business, or to buy sewing machines, are some of the other admirable features of the Lette Society.

The number of those who have been benefited by this institution can be counted by the thousands, so that a great and good work has been accomplished with proportionally very small means. Nor has its usefulness been limited to the capital alone. The reputation of the society has spread throughout the country, and similar organizations have been established in Bremen, Hamburg, Breslau, Brunswick, Rostock, Stettin, and Potsdam. At Darmstadt is the Alice Society (*Alice-Verein*), devoted to the industrial and general instruction of women, and whose patroness was Alice, the late Grand Duchess of Hesse. There are like institutions at Dusseldorf, Cologne, Elberfeld, Weisbaden, Königsberg, Dantsic, and other cities, all modeled after the Lette Society, whence are drawn their corps of teachers. The societies founded by the National Association of German Women, as well as those which have sprung up independently of both organizations, are all working in the same field, have a similar aim in view, and are animated by that spirit of moderation which has done so much for the success of the common cause.

It cannot be said of this movement that it purposes to overthrow existing institutions, that it desires to estrange women from their peculiar vocation in the family, State, and society. This conservative character of the German reformers has been criticised. They have been found too timid, too considerate of old prejudices, too slow, too circumspect. The stricture arises mainly, however, from an imperfect understanding of the situation in this country. Because of the excellent system of compulsory education which exists in Germany, we had not to begin so low down as in some other parts of Europe. All German girls were furnished with, at least, the foundation of an education. And yet the women's movement has accomplished admirable reforms in this very field. To it is due the introduction into the girls' primary schools (*Volksschule*) of compulsory and systematic instruction in sewing and similar handiwork, and the persevering and finally successful efforts to enlarge the scope of the girls' grammar schools (*Töchterschule*), efforts which have met with the approval of competent persons and which have not passed unnoticed by the government itself. Still greater progress might be made in this direction, if only the proper laws were enacted. All attempts to bring about the establishment by the municipalities or the government of girls' high schools have failed, but it is almost beyond doubt that this worthy object will be accomplished sooner or later. When it is, women will be able to obtain a training similar to that furnished at the boys' gymnasiums, so that, provided with a diploma (*Abiturientenzeugniss*) they may enter the universities and receive a degree.

German women who would secure a higher education must study in private, for their admission into the lecture-rooms of any of our universities is very difficult. Female students, to our knowledge, have been admitted only at Heidelberg and Leipsic, and even in these two institutions they have not been suffered to pass the examinations. It is at foreign universities that our women are forced to pursue their studies and take their degrees. The two female physicians at Berlin, Dr. Franziska Tiburtius, and Dr. Emilie Lehmus, are graduates of Zurich, and Lina Beger, Ph. D., who began her career as a teacher at the capital, received her degree at Bern. The two Berlin dentists, Mrs. Dr. Tiburtius Hirschfeldt, and Miss Carsten, studied at Philadelphia.

In its treatment of the great question of the higher education of women, Germany is outstripped, not only by the republics of Switzerland, America and France, but lags behind the monarchies of England, Sweden, Italy, and Russia, which, after an obstinate resistance, have finally opened their universities to women and graduated them with full academic honors. We are convinced that Germany must soon follow their example, either by the foundation of special institutions or by throwing wide the doors of the existing universities. But we fear that the struggle will be longer and harder here than in other countries, for our universities, venerable by their antiquity and conservative by their organization, are immutable for good or evil. The same thing is seen in England, where the London University, which is of recent origin, long ago conferred its advantages on women, while ancient Cambridge and Oxford, although they have made some concessions, still hold back.*

Until that day arrives, we must be contented with those excellent institutions which have sprung up in many cities under the name of lyceums (*Lyceen*) and which afford our girls admirable instruction.† The oldest and best known

---

* The United States presents similar examples. While Cornell, Michigan, and other young universities are not afraid of women, venerable Harvard, Yale and Columbia, the latter in spite of the repeated efforts of President Barnard in favor of the reform, tremble for their future if co-education be adopted.—T. S.

† The prospectus of the Victoria Lyceum at Cologne, of which Mrs. Lina Schneider, a lady of wide culture, is the principal, gives a fair idea of the scope of these institutions. "The instruction comprises," says this prospectus, "thorough English in all its branches, German, French, Italian (taught respectively by native professors), Latin and Greek classics, mathematics, shorthand-writing, history, literature, and other sciences, music, drawing, painting, calisthenics, and all female accomplishments. * * *

of these educational establishments is the Victoria Lyceum, in Berlin, founded and directed by Miss Archer. It contains the nuclei of what could be developed on the one hand into a gymnasium, and on the other into a university. The Alice Lyceum, established at Darmstadt by Louise Büchner, would have attained an equally high position if its growth had not been suddenly checked by the death of its founder, who, as Vice-president of the Alice Society, and as a writer on the woman question, showed marked ability and accomplished much good work. Lyceums patterned after these two have been organized at Breslau, Karlsruhe, Dresden, Cologne, and Leipsic.

Closely connected with this movement in favor of the higher education of women and of the amelioration of their position in the field of labor, is the effort to spread the Fröbel system. Many of the industrial societies (*Erwerbvereine*) already mentioned have accepted Fröbel's ideas, and have opened kindergarten schools, courses for the instruction of teachers for such schools, and courses for the preparation of children's nurses. Nobody interested in the general progress of women can underrate this important work, and Mrs. Johanna Goldschmidt, of Hamburg, a pioneer of the Fröbel system, will always occupy an honorable place among those who have labored in this field.

Women's domestic duties are not excluded from the programme of our movement. Hygiene, the care of chil-

---

There are also opportunities for learning dancing, swimming, skating, and riding." It appears that the lyceum can prepare (the prospectus from which I quote is addressed to the English public) " with special facility and success for the Oxford and Cambridge local, the Irish intermediate, the University or other examinations."—T. S.

dren and rational housekeeping are essential parts of any plan of female education. Furthermore, women should know how to care for the sick of their own household, and should even be taught professional nursing. There may be a question as to whether they should be physicians, but as regards the training of women as nurses there can be but one opinion. The Catholic and Protestant Churches have long had training schools for nurses, and similar institutions have sprung up all over the country during the past fifteen years. The oldest of them is the Baden Women's Society (*Badischer Frauen-Verein*), under the protection of the Grand Duchess Louise, which has many branches, and which, besides the instruction of nurses, succors the poor and aids working women.

The Women's Patriotic Society (*Vaterländischer Frauen-Verein*), patronized by the Empress, besides doing a work similar to that of the last mentioned organization, in time of war takes care of the families of militiamen (*Landwehr*) in service, establishes hospitals, nurses the wounded, etc. The same ground is covered by the Albert Society (*Albert-Verein*) in Saxony, to which the regretted Marie Simon devoted her life; the Olga Society (*Olga-Verein*) in Würtemberg, which is patronized by the good Queen Olga, and by like bodies in Bavaria, Saxe-Weimar, Mecklenburg, etc.

Three groups of women's associations still remain to be mentioned. The German Teachers' and Governesses' Society (*Verein deutscher Lehrerinenen und Erzieherinenen*), which, with its branches, looks after the intellectual and material interests of teachers, possesses in the neighborhood of Berlin a retreat for aged and invalid members of the profession. It has also organized boarding houses and clubs, where male and female teachers meet to discuss subjects which interest them. The second group consists of Housekeepers' Societies (*Hausfrauen-Vereine*), which owe their origin to Mrs. Lina Morgenstern, to whom is also due the Soup-kitchens (*Volksküchen*), where the poor are fed at a very moderate price. All the important questions pertaining to domestic economy, come within the scope of these excellent associations. The third and last group are Societies of Art Students (*Vereine der Künstlerinnen*), which, as is the case at Berlin, have established schools where women may study painting and sculpture; it being difficult, if not absolutely impossible, for them to obtain admission to the School of Fine Arts. There are similar institutions for women at Weimar and Munich, though the school in the latter city is more especially devoted to industrial art, while many pursue their studies in the studios of eminent artists.

Our women have proved by their productions that they have richly profited by these advantages. The last two exhibitions of fine arts at Berlin, and the international exhibition at Munich, in 1879, contained specimens of female talent which received the highest praise from impartial critics. It is no exaggeration to say that women contribute in no small degree to the art industry of Germany. With the needle, the pencil, the brush, they produce magnificent ornamental work. The schools of art and design established by the Berlin Industrial Museum (*Gewerbe-Museum*) and the Lette Society, and the similar institutions in Munich, Reutlingen, Karlsruhe, Dresden, and other cities, have turned out many trained women who have become teachers or artificers of fine needle-work, designers, pattern-makers, and the like.

German unity, so long desired and so heartily welcomed, has been prejudicial, we are sorry to say, to the employment of women, as in Austria, in the railroad, postal, and telegraphic service. While the States of South and Central Germany have long availed themselves of females for these positions, Prussia and the countries united with her in the postal and telegraphic union have taken the opposite course. When, on the formation of the Empire, the government assumed control of the post-office and telegraph, it looked for a moment as if all the female employés would be dismissed. A petition, however, was sent to the Imperial Parliament (*Reichstag*) in 1872, which not only checked this tendency, but secured the admission of women into the telegraphic and postal service of Prussia itself. But, as the Postmaster General of Germany, Mr. Stephan, is opposed to the employment of women in his department, everything has been done to defeat the measure, so that we are forced to admit that in this matter our country has taken a step backward.*

But, on the whole, the agitation begun at Leipsic and Berlin, has accomplished a great deal during the past eighteen years. We have been able to give here only an incomplete outline of its history. What has been written in Germany, for and against the woman question, would form a large library. A number of periodicals are exclusively devoted to this subject. Besides the *New Paths* (*Neue Bahnen*), the organ of the Leipsic movement, we may cite housekeepers' journals published at Berlin and Cologne, also a paper which represents the interests of

---

* Mr. Stephan's course is strongly contrasted by that of the English Post-master General, and is a striking example of how much the success of laws, even under the modern parliamentary *régime*, depends upon the personal opinions of those who execute them. For an account of what Mr. Fawcett and others have done in England in connection with this subject, see page 93.—T. S.

girls' high schools, and the *German Women's Advocate* (*Deutscher Frauen-Anwalt*), organ of the United Societies for the Education and Employment of Women (*Verband des deutscher Frauenbildungs und Erwerbvereine*).

The last named organization was formed in November, 1869, at a meeting in Berlin of delegates from all parts of Germany, and embraces a large number of women's industrial, educational, house-keeping and Fröbel societies, and training schools for nurses. It holds general meetings at irregular intervals. Such assemblies have occurred at Darmstadt, Hamburg, Weisbaden, and at Berlin, in the autumn of 1879, where delegates were present from the Leipsic National Society. At these congresses all the various themes relating to women are discussed; resolutions are passed, subjects for prize-essays announced, and petitions sent to the Government. At the Berlin Congress petitions were drawn up praying for the admission of women into the pharmaceutical profession, for the providing of means for their higher education, for their employment in the postal and telegraphic service, and for the modification of certain regulations which check their participation in business and trade.

More radical demands than these have not been seriously made in Germany. The opening of politics to women has not been pressed. Contrary to the course pursued by the American and English reformers, who hold that the only way to emancipate the sex is by means of the electoral franchise, and who consequently make suffrage the chief aim of all their efforts, we Germans believe that the lever is found in education. In working for the present generation, and in helping women already half through the journey of life to earn their daily bread, we are sowing seed which will bear a rich fruitage in the future. Thanks to our untiring labors the conviction is spreading that every woman, rich or poor, high or low, ought to have an education such as will make her, in the highest and best sense, the helpmate and companion of man—wife, mother, and teacher. The German movement aims to elevate the whole female sex, and to render women capable of serving themselves, the family, society, the State, and humanity. Our object is to lift women out of their insignificance, frivolity, poverty, misery, and shame, and train them for work which will render themselves and others happy, and thus advance the general interests of civilization.

II. THE NATIONAL ASSOCIATION OF GERMAN WOMEN.

BY MARIE CALM.

[Miss Marie Calm was born at Arolsen (where her father was burgomaster or mayor), in the Principality of Waldeck, on April 3, 1832. She was sent to a private school in her native town and finished her education at a well-known boarding school in Geneva, where she made great progress in the English and French languages. Afterward Miss Calm spent three years in England and two years in Russia, returning to Germany to take charge of a girls' high school in the Rhenish Provinces. Her first appearance in literature was as a story writer in the noted *Illustrated World* (*Illustrirte Welt*) of Stuttgart. In 1865 she heard of the movement in Leipsic in favor of women—which she describes in the following pages, put herself in communication with the leaders of the new agitation and was invited by them to take part in their next congress. She accepted this invitation in 1867, and has ever since been one of the most zealous advocates of women's rights in Germany. At Cassel, where she now resides, Miss Calm has done much for the education of girls by opening, in conjunction with some other ladies, an industrial school which has proved most successful. Since 1869 she has lectured all over Germany on educational subjects, has founded girls' schools similar to that at Cassel and organized women's societies auxiliary to the National

Association. Miss Calm is the author of stories, poems, works on pedagogics, and " Leo," a novel in three volumes, "which fastens the reader's
attention with the first page," says an American writer, " and holds it un-
waveringly to the closing paragraph." I had the pleasure of making Miss
Calm's acquaintance at Paris in 1881, and was struck not only by her excellent command of English and French, both of which languages she speaks
and writes with great ease, but also by her agreeable presence, her enthusiasm and her liberalism.]

THE National Association of German Women (*Der
allgemeine deutsche Frauen-Verein*), was founded at Leipsic in October, 1865, and was the first organized movement in Germany in favor of what is now known as the
Woman Question (*Frauenfrage*). I do not wish to say
that previous to this date many noble minds had not examined the great subject of women's needs and women's
position, but what I do mean is that until the autumn of
1865 this work had been isolated, unorganized and consequently barren of practical results. Again, the few wom-
en who, about fifty years ago, tried to cut free from the
restraints imposed upon their sex and to gain the liberty
denied them by society, overstepped the limits of what is
considered womanly by imitating the other sex in dress, in
smoking, etc., so that the word *emancipation*, originally
applied to their agitation, has ever since retained an
odious meaning and is therefore carefully discarded by
the leaders of the present movement.

This latter movement is indeed quite different in its
origin, its aims and its means from the generous, but
rather sentimental, outburst of 1830. The English census
of 1856 had brought to light the fact that two millions of
women in that country were dependent upon their own
labor for their livelihood, and that most of them knew
not how to work, or were so poorly paid that, as the German saying goes, they had too much to die, too little to

live. About this time Hood's " Song of the Shirt " appeared in all our newspapers, rousing the public to indignation at the neglected condition of working women and
filling it with pity for the unhappy creature of whom the
poet sang. A census in Prussia shortly afterward proved
that there was about the same number of women in that
country who were unprovided for, and drew attention to
the crying necessity of giving them the means of earning
their daily bread. Some philanthropists wrote and spoke
on the subject, and Dr. Adolph Lette, a man of eminent
merit, gave permanent form to this new public sentiment
by establishing what afterward became the admirable
Lette Society.*

Among the women who, not only then but long before,
had shown a deep interest in the amelioration of the condition of her sex, stands in the front rank, Mrs. Louise
Otto-Peters. In her novels, most of which treat social
questions, she has always pleaded for the oppressed, and
when, after the publication of her " Castle and Factory "
(*Schloss und Fabrik*), a deputation of Leipsic workmen
invited her to contribute to their newspaper, she replied
that she would gladly do so if allowed to defend the
cause of work-women in its columns. She also took a
very active part in the political movement of 1848, and
founded in that year the first women's paper, to my knowledge, in Germany, which bore the motto " I enlist women
in the cause of liberty " (*Dem Reich der Freiheit werb'
ich Bürgerinnen*). The reactionary period which followed
put an end to the paper, but Louise Otto continued fear-
lessly devoted to woman and liberty.

It was very natural, therefore, that she should become

---

* For a more complete account of the work of the Lette Society, see the
preceding essay.—T. S

the centre of a movement for promoting the welfare of her sex. In October, 1865, a few men and women met in Leipsic to consider the subject, and the conference ended, as has already been said, in the foundation of the National Association of German Women. The name was rather ambitious when we consider the small number of persons who were present at the birth of the organization. But they looked far into the future, and ardently trusted that in the course of time the title of their young creation would be no misnomer. The Association set itself the task of elevating the educational and social position of one half of the nation. It declared work to be the right, the duty and the honor of women as well as of men, and denounced all those obstacles which hinder the former from a free participation in every employment and profession for which they are fitted by nature. In order to propagate these ideas it was resolved to establish a newspaper and to hold annual conventions in different parts of Germany.

The organ of the Association, a bi-monthly, which treats all aspects of the woman question, both in Europe and America, was named *New Paths* (*Neue Bahnen*), and has been edited from the beginning by Mrs. Louise Otto Peters and her friend, Miss Auguste Schmidt. But reforms are not accomplished by the pen alone. Our articles are read chiefly by those already friendly to our views, not by our opponents, and least of all by the great mass of the indifferent. It therefore appeared necessary for the complete success of the cause to propagate it by word of mouth. Never had women assembled in Germany to discuss their own position in society; never had they been seen on the platform addressing an audience with eloquence and logic. These were prerogatives of the masculine sex alone. The National Association of German Women was first to show that the other sex, too, was capable and ready to present its claims before the public. But our aim was not simply to be heard, but to convince ; and this object has always been attained. Wherever our congresses have been held, we have met with success, as witness those of Leipsic (1867 and 1871), that of Brunswick (1868), Cassel (1869), Eisenach (1872), Stuttgart (1873), Gotha (1875), Frankfort-on-the-Main (1876), Hanover (1877), Heidelberg (1879) and Lübeck (1881). * These meetings have, of course, encountered strong prejudices. People were curious to hear what women had to say ; they wished only to be amused, but many became interested, convinced, and often before the close of the sessions were enthusiastic supporters of the cause.

In these congresses addresses are delivered on all subjects connected with the woman question, and reports are read by delegates of the work accomplished by the auxiliary societies, so that the audience obtains a pretty good idea of the operations of the National Association since the previous meeting.† At the end of each congress an

---

* In a recent letter from Miss Calm, she says : " There has not been any congress this (1882) year, owing to the Berlin Society being rather loath to undertake the trouble and cost of these meetings. It was their turn and they postponed it. I am going to Leipsic next week in order to arrange with my colleagues about next year's congress."—T. S.

† The following programme of the last congress, will give the best idea of the nature of these assemblages, and of the scope of the National Association.

THE ELEVENTH CONGRESS OF THE NATIONAL ASSOCIATION

OF GERMAN WOMEN,

HELD AT LÜBECK FROM THE 5TH TO THE 6TH OF OCTOBER, 1881.

Wednesday, Oct. 5th, 10 A.M.—Business meeting. Election of officers, etc. 7 P.M.—First public session. Reception of the delegates by the local committee. Preliminary addresses by Miss Auguste Schmidt, of Leipsic.

effort is made to found a local auxiliary society (*Lokal-Verein*), which accepts the plan of the National Association and endeavors to embody its aims in some useful institution. Organizations of this kind have thus been established in all the above-mentioned cities with one exception, and in several other places through the efforts of individuals. They have created girls' industrial or professional schools, mercantile institutes and lyceums. In some instances the members of these societies arrange courses of lectures and hold monthly gatherings, where women of all classes meet on a common footing, either to listen to an essay, to discuss subjects of mutual interest, or to be diverted by music and declamation. Similar entertainments are sometimes offered to working-women, who thus enjoy simple and innocent amusements.

Since the year 1876 an agreement has existed between the National Association and the United Societies, at the head of which stands the Lette Society, for calling these congresses alternately, and for sending delegates from the one organization to the congress held under the auspices of the other. But the spirit of active propagandism and

---

Thursday, Oct. 6th, 10 A.M.—Business meeting. Treasurer's report, etc. 3 P.M. to 5 P.M.—Visit to the churches and other celebrated monuments of the city. 6 P.M.—Second public session. Opening of the Congress by Mrs. Louise Otto‑Peters, of Leipsic. Address by Miss Marie Calm, of Cassel, on " The Women's Movement in its Principal Localities from a Historical Point of View." Reports of delegates. Address by Miss Willborn, of Schwerin, on " The Scientific Education of Female Teachers." Social reunion. Friday, Oct. 7th, 9 A.M.—Third session. Address by Miss Menzzer, of Dresden, on " The Compensation of Women's Labor." Reports. Address by Miss Assmann, of Hanover, on " The Citizenship of Women." 3 P.M.—Address by Mrs. Füllgraff, M.D., of Hamburg, on " Women's Position in America." Reports. Address by Mrs. Lina Morgenstern, of Berlin, on " The Food Question." 7 P.M.—Banquet.—M. C.

the foundation of new societies appear to be alone peculiar to the congresses of the National Association.

In 1877 the executive committee of the Association sent to the Imperial Parliament (*Reichstag*) a petition signed by a great number of women, praying for certain of their civil rights, for the amelioration of their condition as wives and mothers, and for the abrogation of those laws which treat them as minors. This petition was accompanied by a memorial, drawn up by Louise Otto-Peters, which contained all the laws concerning women as found in the different statute books of Germany, for it must be borne in mind that every State, and even a great many towns, of the Empire has a code of its own. The answer of Parliament to this petition was that a code common to all Germany was soon to be prepared, and that then our demands should be considered.*

The above-mentioned executive committee consists of Mrs. Louise Otto-Peters, Miss Auguste Schmidt, the associate editor of the *Neue Bahnen* and one of the ablest speakers in our congresses; and Mrs. Henriette Gold-

---

* I select a few paragraphs from the Prussian and Bavarian codes. *Ex uno disce omnes.* Here is the law of Prussia : Children may not marry without the consent of the father.—§45. (So the mother is of no account when it comes to giving up her daughter!) By marriage the husband obtains control of the wife's fortune.—§205. Whatever the wife earns during her marriage belongs to the husband.—§211. The wife may not contract any debts on the fortune she has brought to the husband.—§§318 and 319. (He has the right to squander the whole of it, but she may not spend a farthing of what was once her own!) In regard to divorce : Bodily ill treatment may be a cause of divorce, if it endangers the health or life of the wife (!).—§685. Here are a few specimens from the Bavarian statute-book : By marriage the wife comes under the authority of the husband and the law (*Gewalt*) allows him to chastise her moderately (!).—§2. Women, with the exception of the mother and grandmother, are unfit to be guardians.—§90. (So are minors, lunatics, and spendthrifts!)—M. C.

schmidt, a leading promoter of the Fröbel system in Germany, who has formed a society in Leipsic for popular education and a girls' lyceum, and who, by her eloquence and her lectures in different parts of the country, has done a great deal to keep alive public interest in the various phases of the woman question. These three ladies and Mrs. Winter, treasurer of the Association, live in Leipsic. Another member of the committee, Miss Menzzer, is at the head of a Women's Educational Society (*Frauenbildungs Verein*) at Dresden ; a sixth, Mrs. Lina Morgenstern, is a lady of great talent and activity ; and, lastly, the writer of this sketch, who is president of the Women's Educational Society of Cassel.

This brief account shows that the National Association of German Women has not been unsuccessful in its efforts to raise the level of instruction and thereby to improve the general condition of the sex. It is to be hoped that the interest in this question may spread wider and wider —and it was for the accomplishment of this end that our Association was founded—until the victory is complete, and women secure in the family and in the State the position to which they are entitled, but which customs and laws so often deny them.

CHAPTER III.

HOLLAND.

BY ELISE VAN CALCAR.

[Mrs. Elise van Calcar was born at Amsterdam, in 1822. Her first liter-ary production was " Hermine," a domestic novel, which championed the elevation of women and strongly protested against the impediments thrown in the way of their progress by Calvinistic orthodoxy. It proved an unex-pected success and was followed by many other works, one of which, " Evangeline," was exclusively devoted to a consideration of woman's life and destiny. Later, appeared a treatise on the influence of women in improving the condition of sewing girls, which carried off the gold prize medal of the Universal Benevolent Society (*Maatschappy tot nut van 't algemeen*), the first time such an honor was conferred upon a woman in Hol-land. Some time ago the Industrial Society (*Maatschappy voor industrie*) offered a gold medal for the best essay on the following subject : " How must a girl be educated in order to gain her own livelihood without unfit-ting herself for domestic life, in case she should marry?" She was here, also, the successful competitor. Mrs. van Calcar has taken an active part in the movement to improve women's education. She founded a kindergarten and lectured on the subject of infant schools throughout Holland ; she was appointed by the Government to inspect these institutions, and a radical change followed her report ; and she established a seminary for the instruc-tion of teachers in the Fröbel system, which remained under her direction for ten years. Mrs. van Calcar next turned her attention to spiritualism and magnetism, and published a novel in three volumes entitled "Children of the Century" (*Kindren der Eeuw*), with the object of popularizing these new phenomena. She is now conducting at The Hague a spiritualistic monthly, *On the Banks of Two Worlds* (*Op de Grenzen van Twee Werelden*). Besides the works already mentioned, Mrs. van Calcar is the author of many other books, articles in reviews and newspapers on various social, religious and literary topics. Her last production is a life and defence of Swedenborg.]

WHEN the report of a movement in favor of women's rights first spread from America to these shores, our women were offended that one dared apply the word emancipation to their condition. Are we, then, slaves who need deliverance? they said, just as a cage-born bird would ask, What happiness is there outside these wires? May I not do everything I wish: jump from one perch to the other? The Dutch woman is proud of her origin. She remembers that she first saw light on a soil redeemed from tyranny by the blood of her forefathers, and, like a true child of the Reformation, looks with contempt upon her Catholic sisters, condemned to ignorance and bred up in narrow-mindedness and superstition in the convents. To contend for the rights of women seemed to this class quite useless, and men in particular strongly objected to the term emancipation. The idea of a possible equality of man and woman appeared to them to be as dangerous as ridiculous, and, in all newspapers and public utterances, emancipation was branded as a mental alienation, and ranked among the symptoms of the disease of the century, which had to be kept carefully at a distance like a deadly epidemic. However, even in Holland, so very conservative in many respects, there were a few earnest thinkers who took a broader view of the question, and some highly gifted women whose talents were too brilliant to remain buried in the kitchen, or to find in the petty duties of the family, a field large enough for their aspirations. It was, for a long time, an open question whether woman really possessed the necessary mental capacity to place her on a level with man, and to make her the spiritual companion of his life. Most men were afraid to solve the problem. In the meanwhile, many women effectually proved the superior quality of their intellectual gifts, in spite of the adverse circumstances in which their powers were developed.

The only field of labor, except the care of husband and children, which has never been contested to women, is charity.* They made an ample use of this liberty, and thus became conscious of their imperfect training, often discovering that even for this work, they had not received the proper preparation. Charitable institutions were founded on every hand. Asylums for fallen women and homeless children were opened, hospitals were established, and many women found employment as nurses in Amsterdam, Rotterdam, Utrecht, The Hague and Leeuwarden. Sewing and knitting schools also sprang up in great numbers. But whoever, twenty years ago, advocated the admission of women to other callings received no hearing.

Yet we possessed an author, Mrs. Geertruida Bosboom Toussaint, who, by a series of able novels, usually drawn from our national history, evinced what talent and learning a woman could possess.† She was soon followed by

---

* Miss Elise A. Haighton, of Amsterdam, who enjoys a high reputation in her country as an author, and whose writings on social questions are widely known, has been kind enough to furnish me notes, which will be found scattered through this chapter. "Our women of the upper classes are much interested in charity," she says, "but as they are generally orthodox, a good deal of unhealthy religiousness mingles with their acts. In Holland, a great deal is done for the women who fall, but nothing to prevent them from falling."—T. S.

† The seventieth anniversary of her birth was celebrated with the greatest enthusiasm, on September 16, 1882, by the literary world of Holland.— E. van C. Miss Frederica van Uildriks, an intelligent teacher, of Groningen, Holland, whose notes, chiefly on educational matters, I shall have occasion to cite in other parts of this chapter, writes me that "the *Revue des Deux Mondes* has published some of Mrs. Bosboom Toussaint's novels, and that others have appeared in German translations."—T. S.

some young female writers who, though not her equal in mental vigor and erudition, have, nevertheless, powerfully helped to combat the prejudice which would deny to woman the development of all her intellectual faculties.

In 1856, Bertha von Marenholz, Countess of Bulow, a noble and highly gifted soul, visited these parts to acquaint us with the kindergarten system. She exhorted us to be not only the physical, but also the moral and intellectual, mothers of our offspring, so that, while pleading for children's rights, she sowed seed for women's rights. The advent of Bertha von Marenholz was an epoch in the women's movement in Holland. A female lecturer was a wonder in the Netherlands, and she spoke so well that she commanded attention and disarmed prejudice. Her eloquence, simplicity and earnestness beat a breach in the thick walls of old Dutch conservatism concerning the higher education of women. Blessed be her glorious name among all those of our sex who desire our real progress, and who seek its accomplishment in the right way !

When this wise and lovable reformer left our country, I felt that her prophet's mantle had fallen upon my shoulders, and that I had henceforth to walk in her footsteps. I accepted the apostleship, and devoted myself to the educational work which she had initiated. I was therefore the first Dutch woman to mount the public platform. I lectured in our principal cities, and called upon women to improve themselves for their own and their children's sakes. I projected a plan of a college for the higher training of girls, which was laid before Queen Sophia, the Premier, Thorbecke, and other eminent personages. I applied for aid in vain to all sorts of moneyed organizations. But nobody seemed to share my enthusiasm. I began to fear that my project would never be realized, when the Universal Benevolent Society opened at Arnheim the first girls' normal school. Although the new institution fell far short of my own design, I felt that it was a good beginning.

In the meantime, Mrs. Storm, a clergyman's widow, who had spent several years in America, returned to us with brilliant reports of the excellent education provided for girls in the United States. She also delivered lectures, telling what she had seen in the New World; and, although neither the first nor only person to describe to us the schools of New York, she addressed herself more to women and the general public than others who had written on the same subject. Mrs. Storm urged us to follow the example set by the United States and to found industrial and high schools. We now have several industrial schools for girls, weak institutions as yet, it is true, and very inferior to those of America; but the experiment has been tried, and that is something.

Twenty years ago nobody would have believed that women could ever be apothecaries, watchmakers, clerks in the post, railroad and the telegraph offices, and above all physicians, and yet, to-day, they are found in rapidly increasing numbers in all these callings. For the time being we have but one female physician, Miss Aletta Henriette Jacobs, who is practicing in Amsterdam, but, as she is meeting with marked success, others will soon follow her example. * Several years ago the National

---

* The following extract from a letter which I received from Dr. Jacobs in October, 1882, will be read with interest: "As my father was a physician, medicine always had a strong attraction for me. In 1871, at the age of seventeen, I began my studies at the University of Groningen, after obtaining the necessary permission from the Prime Minister, Mr. Thorbecke,

School of Fine Arts was thrown open to both sexes, in compliance with a request made to the Government by some women. The male students were at first discontented at the innovation, but to-day girls attend lectures and work after living models in the studios of sculpture

---

who, by the way, added that this was only an experiment, so that, if I had failed, it is probable that the four Dutch universities would be still shut against women, and not frequented by female students pursuing various branches, as is the case to-day. To tell the truth, it was a long time after I took the first step in my present career, before I reflected upon its importance to other women. I attended the lectures without ever experiencing any annoyance from either professors or students. In 1872 I passed my *propædentisch-examen*, embracing physics, chemistry, botany, zoology, and mathematics. Two years later, in April, I did the same for my *candidaats-examen*,—physiology, anatomy, pathology, etc., and in October, 1876, for my *doctorraal-examen*, which was of an almost totally theoretical nature. I then went to Amsterdam, which, being a larger city, was preferable for the practical part of my medical studies. In April, 1878, came my *arts-examen* (conducted by a board of examiners appointed by Government), which confers the privilege of practicing medicine, surgery and obstetrics. There now remained but one more degree for me to take, that of doctor, which is given by the universities, and which was the only medical degree in Holland prior to 1867. I returned to Groningen, and in ten months' time had accomplished my object by successfully defending my thesis, "On the Localization of Physiological and Pathological Symptoms in the Cerebrum" (*Over Localisatie van Physiologische en Pathologische Verschijnselen in de Groote Hersenen*). I immediately left for London, and visited daily, during several months, the different gynecological and children's hospitals. On September 15, 1879, I established myself at Amsterdam for the treatment of the diseases of women and children. I have no fault to find with my success, nor, if the inevitable professional jealousy be excepted, with the conduct of my *confrères*. I have been admitted with the greatest complaisance to the Medical Society and participate in all its meetings. The State and municipality accord me the same rights and impose upon me the same duties as in the case of my fellow practitioners, and yet this same State and municipality treat me, as in fact they do all women, as a minor ! Public opinion, it will be observed, throws no obstacles in the way of my professional success, so that in this respect my own land is in advance of every other European country. Great progress in favor of bettering the position of women in State and

and drawing, with as great freedom as the young men. Among other signs of progress, I may mention that a few years ago an exhibition of female industry and art was held at Leeuwarden, while reading-rooms for women have been opened in Amsterdam and Rotterdam. *

The press being always hostile to our movement, women determined to have an organ of their own. Miss Betsy Perk therefore founded and edited for two years the *Our Vocation* (*Onze Roeping*), a weekly journal which was, however, overshadowed by another periodical in favor of women, *Our Striving* (*Ons Streven*), supported by

---

society has been especially noticeable in Holland during the past two or three years." " Although the law now allows women to be apothecaries and assistant apothecaries," says Miss Uildriks, " Miss A. M. Tobbe was refused admission to the examination in 1865. In the following year this calling was opened to women, and at the end of 1881 two hundred and sixteen had passed the assistant apothecaries' examinations. The results of these tests during the past two years prove that the female, are far superior to the male, aspirants. The first and only woman up to the present date (October, 1882), to take the apothecary's degree, is Miss Charlotte Jacobs, one of the sisters of our first physician. This occurred in 1880."—T. S.

* It is only within a short time that the prejudice against women appearing alone in public has begun to pass away. How was this change brought about? By women simply doing, while strictly adhering to propriety and decorum, what society had been pleased to call improper. Their conduct immediately received the approbation of our best men, who, by the way, are not to blame if our sex does not enjoy in Holland all the liberty it deserves. The definition of the term *womanly* broadens every day, and when society hesitates to give us what it is our right to have, our women associate and establish for themselves organizations similar to those from which they are excluded. This is the origin of the women's reading-room at Amsterdam. To-day we may travel alone, may, if business requires it, take rooms and receive our friends, dine at a restaurant or *table d'hôte*, etc., without running the risk of losing our reputation. Our authoresses may now take up any subject they please, although formerly moral themes and fiction— even novel writing was considered eccentric—were alone thought proper for a feminine pen.—E. A. H.

some clergymen. But both were too timid to live for any length of time. Although Miss Perk's paper soon died, it left behind an admirable creation, a women's society, whose motto was "Work Ennobles" (*Arbeid adelt*), and whose aim was the providing of poor gentlewomen with home work; which was afterward sold in shops established for the purpose. This beneficent institution is still in existence. A third journal, *The Housewife* (*De Huisvrouw*), edited by Mrs. Van Amstel, is, as its name indicates, devoted more to domestic matters than to the general question of women's rights, while Miss Alberdingh Thym, a young author of considerable talent, has just begun, at Rotterdam, the publication of a periodical which addresses itself to our girls. Although these papers are not in every respect all that one could wish, still it is a good sign that we ourselves are creating our own mouthpieces in the journalistic world. I should prefer to see them deal with broader questions, and to have them more exclusively the work of women, which could be easily the case, as the number of female writers has greatly increased of late, and their united efforts would be sufficient to carry on a solid journal.

Some authors deserve a place in this essay. Miss Catharina van Rees, for example, is distinguished not only for her literary productions, but also for her highly developed musical talent. She has sketched the lives of several great composers, in the form of novels, which deserve a wider recognition than they can obtain in the original language, and has written many admirable pieces of music. Miss van Rees has also published important articles on art, and is the editor of a Collection of Dutch Authoresses which brings out clearly the gifts of many of our rising female writers. Among the latter is a young woman who commenced her literary career at twenty, and who, if she continues as she began, promises to take a very honorable place in our literature. She is known in letters by the pseudonym of A. S. C. Wallis, but it would be no disgrace to her father, who is a professor of philosophy at Utrecht, if she were to write under her own name. Miss Emy de Leeuw is remarkable for her knowledge of botany and her skill in rendering that science enjoyable to women, which she has done in a very clever book entitled " Letters of a Country Girl " (*Brieven van een Landmeisje*). She is now the editor of a popular weekly, *The Swallow* (*De Zwaluw*). But however rich in intellectual women our country may be, their efforts are not as yet sufficiently bent on universal interests and the important demands of the hour.

The tendency toward teaching has not only very much increased among girls, especially since the establishment of normal schools, but it has developed into a veritable mania, which is encouraged with an almost superstitious zeal by the parents, who seem to look upon pedagogy as a sort of life insurance. But this notion is based on an error. All women have neither the taste nor the ability necessary to become good teachers, even if they succeed in passing the very difficult examinations required by the State. And furthermore the training is very one-sided : the cramming of manuals, rather than a rational development of all the mental faculties.

It was a long time before public opinion could be brought to give girls the educational advantages enjoyed by boys. But now the intermediate schools for girls are increasing in our chief towns and we shall soon have a population of educated women. Their instruction, however, will be imperfect, because to my mind too little attention is paid to the peculiarities of female character and destiny. The course of studies is the same for both sexes, but too much time is devoted to our three neighboring languages, French, German and English, so that Greek and Latin are neglected. In my whole life I have met only three or four Dutch women who understood the ancient classics. But I shall not be hypercritical: let us rather be contented that at last a somewhat broader field of culture has been opened to our sex.*

---

* In 1864 higher elementary instruction (*middelbaar onderwys*), was established in Holland, and in 1876 there were in existence fifty-two higher elementary schools (*middelbare scholen*), for boys, and, although several similar ones have been opened for girls, not one of the latter is supported by Government. There was great opposition to these girls' schools among the general public, and in the Lower House (*Tweede Kamer*) many members predicted that grave evils would result from this conferring on women more than an elementary education. Eighteen hundred and seventy is an important date in this movement. In this year a majority of the municipal council of Amsterdam refused to have a girls' *middelbare* school in their town, and the Dutch press teemed with essays, pamphlets and newspaper articles on the subject of the education of women. Dr. Vitringa, rector of the gymnasium of Deventer; Dr. J. P. de Keyser, a clergyman of Arnheim ; Marie Delsey, who wrote "Instruction, Education and Emancipation of Women" (*Onderwys, Opvoeding en Emancipatie der Vrouw*); Dr. D. J. Steyn Parvé, inspector of *middelbare* schools and perhaps the most earnest champion of the measure ; and Dr. B. H. C. K. van der Wyck, professor of philosophy at the University of Groningen, are a few names selected from a long list of men and women who spoke out in favor of the innovation. "If man and woman are mentally equal," says the last writer in his "The Education of Women" (*De Opvoeding der Vrouw*), "then we continually lose funds of immense value by not utilizing the faculties of the female sex." The question of opening boys' *middelbare* schools to girls in towns where no such schools exist for the latter is being agitated, and meets with the approval, among others, of Dr. Vitringa and Dr. S. A. Naber, professor at the University of Amsterdam. It was one of the subjects discussed at the meeting of the Society of *Middelbare* Teachers held in August, 1881. This discussion brought out the fact that since 1871 one hundred and fifty-five girls have attended twenty-one of the fifty-four boys'

Dutch women have shown a considerable talent for the fine arts. In painting I may mention the names of Vos, Haanen, Schwartze, Bisschop, Rooseboom, van der Sande Bakhuyzen, van Bosse, etc., and in music, while I say nothing of the professional artists, I must devote at least a word to an amateur, Mrs. Amersfoort, who has distinguished herself by the composition of an oratorio and some other fine works.*

The legal condition of women is the same in Holland as in France: we are still subject to the evils of the Napoleonic code.† The idea of women enjoying the same political rights

---

middelbare schools with none but the best results. The meeting decided in favor of the proposition. Although some of the female teachers in these schools are members of this society they rarely participate in its proceedings, so that the example set by four of their number from Groningen, who attended the assembly of 1881, might well be followed by all. At the beginning of this note I gave an example of the half-hearted way in which the Government aids the cause of girls' education. Here is one of many instances of this same spirit in its treatment of female teachers : Article 25th, of the law of 1878, concerning elementary instruction, states that women are preferable to men in the lower classes of primary schools, and yet but one governmental normal school, that at Nymegen, has as yet been established for their training.—F. van U. Miss Haighton also pronounces co-education in Holland a success. "Female scholars are admitted to our gymnasia," she says, "and I am told by some of the teachers that their presence has a good effect on the behavior and industry of the boys." Thus, one of the chief arguments used in America by the friends of co-education finds its confirmation among the intelligent people of the Low Countries.—T. S.

* The School of Dramatic Art (*Tooneelschool*), established not long ago at Amsterdam, is doing a good work in preparing women for the stage. Mrs. Kleine, one of our best actresses, teaches at this institution, and among its graduates who to-day occupy a high position in the theatrical world may be mentioned Miss de Groot, Miss Poolman, and Miss Sablairolles. Some of our other distinguished actresses are Miss Beersmans, Mrs. Albregt, Mrs. de Vries, Miss van Biene, Mrs. de Graeff Verstraete, Miss van Ryk and Mrs. van Offel-Kley.—F. van U.

† The most noticeable example of legal progress we have to record is,

as men is as yet accepted by a very small number of persons. Our great female landed proprietors especially feel their undignified position, for they signify less in the sight of the law than the very peasants on their farms, who exercise the elective franchise, from which they are excluded. They often think the distinction wrong and absurd, but still lack the courage to demand a reform. Our women are so little conscious of their gifts and powers that they dare not form a society or found a philanthropic institution, without always choosing a man as president, secretary or trustee. *

---

without doubt, the adoption of a new penal code by which adultery of any kind on the part of the husband is sufficient ground for giving the wife a legal divorce.—E. A. H.

* If Dutch women do not vote it is probably due in the main to the fact that they have never earnestly asked for the right, for it is by no means sure that female taxpayers might not vote under the present law. Every 45,000 inhabitants, which includes women, are entitled to a representative in the Lower House. A few of our women do not hesitate to participate actively in politics and social questions in so far as this is possible. The Union (*Unie*), a society which aims to promote popular interest in politics by meetings, discussions, tracts, etc. ; the Daybreak (*Dageraad*), a radical association which holds very ultra opinions on politics, religion and science, and supports a magazine to which many scientific men contribute ; and the New Malthusian Bond, an organization sufficiently explained by its name, all count several women among their members.—E. A. H. In 1870 there appeared at Leeuwarden an essay entitled " Equal Rights for All, by a Lady " (*Gelyk Recht voor Allen door eene Vrouw*), which claims for women not only better instruction, but more social freedom and the amelioration of her legal *status*. " The law seems to take it for granted," we read on page five, " that women have no interest whatsoever in the political affairs of their country, that they are indifferent as to the manner of raising the taxes, how the public moneys are spent, what measures are taken to defend the honor of the nation, or for the instruction of their children. The laws, therefore, shut against them all the paths which lead to public life and do not suffer them to have any voice in the election of their rulers." But, as Dr. B. D. H. Tellegen, professor at the University of Groningen, has well remarked " our customs are better than our laws."—F. van U.

A tremendous obstacle to progress in Holland is the strange perversity of the upper classes to cling to the old traditions and customs. Instruction has made great advances during the last twenty years, and our schools can now vie with those of any country. But who are benefited by them ? The middle classes alone. The higher, as well as the lower and poorer classes, use them but very little. So long as education is not compulsory, there will remain at the bottom of the social ladder a motley mass of proletaries still groveling in darkness and ignorance, while at the top, will be found a group of refined aristocrats who take quite as little advantage of this State instruction—young ladies even less than young gentlemen. The children of our best families are not sent to school, nor are they taught at home by well-trained Dutch tutors, but, for the sake of a proper pronunciation of the modern languages, they are confided to the care of foreigners, in many instances mere adventurers ; to French, German, English and Swiss governesses, with whom Holland is plentifully stocked, and who finish the education of the daughters of our oldest houses. Hence it is that the most fanatical religious and political convictions prevail in this stratum of society, for the aristocracy, with some exceptions, are as bigoted to-day as in the past, and hold fast to all sorts of clerical and social prejudices. As soon as the new instruction penetrates into this narrow circle, we shall hope to find there powerful friends of the women's movement, but until that day arrives, all solid work, intellectual light and progress, will continue to issue from the more liberal middle classes.*

* Holland is considered to be a Protestant country, although one-third of the population is Roman Catholic. The aristocracy and the lower classes are orthodox, while the middle classes, though liberal, still profess a belief.

I am sorry to have to confess that, as regards the general emancipation of women, we have accomplished but very little.* Our work is indirect: we can only proclaim the injustice of our position. This has been done in an admirable way by our gifted writer, Catharina van Rees, who, in the striking scenes of her novel, "From the South" (*Uit het Suiden*), shows the unfairness of the laws and public opinion in judging the moral transgressions of the two sexes; how heavy the punishment inflicted on the sinning woman, and how the equally sinning man escapes without even a reprimand. Our hopes are fixed on the coming generation, the fresh troops who will carry on the old battle to victory. We claim only our good right, our legitimate place in the world, free scope for the complete development of all our faculties. We wish to become cleverer, wiser and better, in order to be able to respond more fully to our vocation and destiny, so that, coming into a nobler and purer relation with the other sex, man and woman may the more successfully strive together to attain the ideal of a perfect humanity.

Irreligiousness, however, is increasing daily, and great is the number of men and women who never go to church. Our cleverest women become more and more of the opinion that Calvinism is their worst enemy,—that Calvinism which orders them to be weak and to submit absolutely to men. They are discarding the old motto, " My weakness is my strength," and are accepting the opinion that the best people are those who possess moral and intellectural force.—E. A. H.

* Among the members chosen by the Government to act on the jury on painting at the International Exhibition of 1883, was Miss Schwartze, of Amsterdam, who is mentioned on page 185. " Miss Schwartze is, we believe," writes Mme. Henry Gréville, " the first woman to form part of an art jury in Europe."—T. S.

CHAPTER IV.

AUSTRIA.

BY JOHANNA LEITENBERGER.

[Mrs. Johanna Leitenberger was born at Prague, Bohemia, in 1818. She published, at an early age, some lyric poems and prose essays which met with a favorable reception. After her marriage, separate volumes in prose and poetry began to appear, and an historical tragedy (*Veronika von Tesch-enitz*) was played with great success at the two theatres of Gratz. Mrs. Leitenberger edited the *Women's Journal* (*Frauenblätter*), devoted to the progress and instruction of women, which was published for a year and a half in this same city. In 1873 Mrs. Leitenberger traveled in Northern Italy and Southern France, and gave in several newspapers an account of what she saw. The next year she established herself at Salzburg, where she still resides, and where were written a collection of tales (*Lichtstralen*) and some religious poems (*Schneeglöckchen*). Mrs. Leitenberger is a contributor to many journals in both Austria and Germany.]

AUSTRIA-HUNGARY is composed of so many peoples of different language and origin, that, although they are all under one government, it is very difficult to give a precise account of this whole vast and varied agglomeration. Prince Gortchakoff's famous remark, that Austria is not a state but a government, is, perhaps, not wholly devoid of truth. But the other races of the Empire are grouped around the old German stock, which, in many respects, stands at the head of civilization and progress. This sketch, therefore, will have to do chiefly with the German women of Austria, for the women of the other parts of the Empire, and especially those of Hungary, have generally followed the lead of their German sisters in all movements for the amelioration of woman's condition. This preponderance of the Teutonic influence in our society is brought out still more strongly by the fact, that the position of the sex in state and family, and the conduct of the government in regard to our interests and rights, is, in all essential particulars, the same in the Austrian Empire as in the German Empire.*

The women's movement in Austria has had two phases: the economic and the educational. It is astonishing what opposition the latter question has called forth, especially among men. They have brought forward every argument the most careful research could produce, with which to combat the proposition to instruct women and to prepare them for callings monopolized by the other sex. Learned professors have not hesitated to assert the intellectual inferiority of women and to expatiate on the weight and quality of their brains. But, notwithstanding this resistance, great progress has been made in the industrial and professional education of women. Institutions for the preparation of women for active employments are continually appearing everywhere in Austria. In the front rank stands the Women's Industrial Society (*Frauen-Erwerb-Verein*), which was founded at Vienna in 1866, and which has grown every year in usefulness and importance. In 1874 the Society opened its school for the industrial training of women, and workshops, art studios, schools of design, etc., soon

---

* Mrs. Schepeler-Lette, of Berlin, writes me : " Austria, although politically separated from Germany, is so closely bound to her by the ties of a common ancestry, that the history of the development of the women's movement in the latter country would be incomplete, if the history of the same movement in the former country were neglected."—T. S.

followed. A class in lace-making is connected with the school, and the children of the poor lace-makers of the Erzgebirge, of Bohemia, are here taught gratuitously. But the aim of the Society is not simply to train the hand : it would also develop the intelligence of its pupils. It has, therefore, established a commercial school, formed classes in the French and English languages, and during the winter season courses of lectures on various artistic and scientific subjects are delivered under its auspices by competent professors and scholars. Far more than a thousand women have, during the past few years, enjoyed the privileges of this admirable institution, of which Mrs. Jeannette von Eitelberger is the president. Many of the other principal cities of the Empire possess similar societies.

The State participates in the good work and confers honors on the friends of the movement. In 1875, for example, the government founded at Salzburg a school of trades, which contains a department for women who wish to study certain of the arts applied to industry. Orders of merit have been bestowed on Mrs. Jeannette von Eitelberger, whom I have just mentioned ; Mrs. Emilie Bach, who is at the head of the Vienna school of art embroidery ; and Mrs. Johanna Bischiz, president of the united women's societies of Buda-Pesth.

If now we turn to the general education of women, we find that great progress has been made during the past ten years, especially in Austria. The public and private schools for girls are infinitely improved. The establishment of girls' lyceums (*Lyceen*), which aim at the higher and broader education of women and which cover almost the same ground as the boys' gymnasiums, was a great step in advance, although they are far from meeting all the de-

12

mands of the new era. Gratz has an excellent lyceum, and the mayor's wife took an active part in its creation. The normal schools for the training of female teachers are of a superior order in many of the Austrian cities. But they have turned out so large a number of pupils during the past few years, that many young teachers, after long months of waiting, are finally compelled to seek employment in private families.

Hungary also offers many signs of progress. The country possesses some four hundred organizations whose aim is the improvement of women's condition. A teacher of South Hungary writes me: " Here, too, the women's movement is a movement in advance, especially in the department of industrial pursuits or employments. Presburg, for example, has a society to encourage the employment of women. Many young girls of good family prepare themselves for teachers, although there is an oversupply in this profession, on account of the large number of Catholic sisters, who have of late invaded our school-rooms. These ecclesiastic teachers have gained possession of the girls' schools and kindergartens in every city and important town of South Hungary. Many young women, however, study the Fröbel system in the institutions for the training of kindergarten teachers at Buda-Pesth, Klausenburg and other places. Females also find employment in the telegraphic and postal service and in other departments of government. It is here that we find the most marked progress in the amelioration of the condition of Hungarian women."

If we approach South Austria, we meet with a goodly number of institutions for girls, as for instance at Laybach, in Carniola, where females are not only employed in the telegraphic and postal service, but are furnished the instruction necessary to fill these posts.* Girls may obtain private instruction in the commercial school of this same city. At Triest is a normal school which has been recently converted into a girls' lyceum. Primary schools for girls are found at Görtz, Fiume, and other cities in the south. Institutions of a higher grade for the instruction of women do not exist either in the maritime countries or in Dalmatia.

The Society of Austrian Teachers and Governesses (*Verein der Lehrerinen und Erzieherinen in Oesterreich*), founded in 1870, takes care of the intellectual and material interests of its members. Its work may be classed under three heads: 1. Normal school and scientific instruction. 2. The spreading of rational ideas on female education. 3. The aiding of needy members. These objects are accomplished by lectures and discussions on pedagogic and scientific themes, by the use of a library and reading-room, by participation in teachers' meetings and congresses, by the publication of the proceedings of the society in the newspapers, by gratuitous information to those seeking situations, by the setting apart of a fund for the sick, etc., etc. The Society supports a Home, which can at present accommodate eleven persons, and offers to teachers and governesses, during their sojourn at Vienna, a good, healthy, cheap boarding-house. The Society organizes lotteries from time to time, the prizes being various kinds of women's work. The net proceeds of the lottery of 1881 were turned over to the Home. This admirable organization is

---

* A recent law has, unfortunately, prohibited the further employment of women in this field. Those already in the service may, however, remain. The reason given for this unjust change is that the male telegraphists complained that the females worked for too low wages !—J. L.

under the able management of Mrs. Louise von Stahl-Almásy.

There are many women's charitable societies at Vienna and in the other Austrian cities. Among those at the capital may be mentioned a society for the maintenance of the widows and orphans of musicians (the *Haydn*), which was founded some twelve years ago ; an asylum for homeless women (the *Elizabethinum*), under the protection of the Empress, which, in the single month of February, 1882, came to the aid of 1,496 women and 407 children ; an aid society whose aim is to instruct and train Jewish girls for some trade; an asylum (*Töchterheim*) for the orphan daughters of Government officials; a retreat for poor and friendless women and girls (*Frauenheim*), which was established in 1882; the Housekeepers' Society (*Hausfrauen-Verein*), which has an intelligence office and a shop for the sale of women's work; a society (*Gisela-Verein*) under the patronage of the Archduchess Gisela, eldest daughter of the Emperor, which gives a dowry to poor marriageable young girls ; and a women's society for the training of domestics. The Vienna Women's Charitable Society (*Frauen-Woltätigkeits-Verein*) has brought about the creation of similar institutions in many other Austrian cities. The Rudolph Society (*Rudolf-Verein*) has established at Vienna a school for the training of female nurses, and in 1881 its students were admitted to the clinics of the celebrated surgeon, Professor Billroth.*

* The Baroness Kathinka von Rosen, a zealous friend of this school, published in the autumn of 1881 a " Guide for Nurses of the Sick " (*Leitfaden für Krankenpflegerinen*), which is rich in personal experiences in English hospitals and in the military hospitals during the recent troubles between Servia and Turkey, and Russia and Turkey.—J. L.

The statistical report for 1881 furnishes the following interesting information concerning the female population of Vienna, and may be taken as a fair sample of the condition of women throughout the empire generally:

Government employées	20
Teachers	2,790
Authors and editors	25
Actresses and musicians	739
Painters and sculptors	53
Employées of the Board of Health	5
Health officers	870
Innkeepers	133
Farmers	4
Miners	2
In industrial pursuits	4,855
In business	4,448
In banks	14
Messengers	116
Living on their incomes	9,460
Living on pensions, and the like	5,154
Heads of educational establishments	32
Heads of charitable institutions	19
In undefined callings	31,518
Clerks	2,378
Day laborers	49,376
Domestics	75,238

That is, 187,249 women, out of 373,156—the female population of Vienna—do something toward their own support.

Although the doors of our universities are closed to females, we possess many women who have pursued their studies abroad and who have acquired a reputation for their learning. Miss Rosa Welt, of Vienna, for example, is a graduate of Bern. During the summer semester of 1879, she attended the lectures on ophthalmy of Professor Mauthner, of Vienna, was admitted to the Rothschild hospital, directed by Dr. Oser, and was at one time mentioned as likely to become the assistant of Professor Pflüger, of Bern, on diseases of the eye. The wife of Dr. Kerschbaumer, who has an institute at Salzburg for the cure of diseases of the eye, studied medicine at Vienna, became her husband's assistant, and now aids him in all operations and sometimes performs them herself. The orientalist, Mrs. Camilla Ruzicka-Ostoic, who has spent six years at the Imperial Academy of Oriental Languages in Vienna, and has passed brilliant examinations in Turkish, Russian and Arabic, received from the Emperor a gold medal for her dictionary of Turkish-German transcriptions, and from the King of Bavaria the Ludwig's gold medal for art and science. In 1881 she established at Vienna a private school for instruction in the Oriental tongues and gave free courses of lectures to ladies on the Turkish language. Miss Sofie von Torma has done some very good work recently in the investigation of antiquities at Siebenbürgen. She has a book almost ready for publication in French and German, and has lectured on her discoveries. Professor A. H. Sayce, of Oxford, and Dr. Schliemann, have both spoken in high terms of Miss von Torma's excavations.* Miss Emilie Hörschelmann has lectured with success to women in Vienna on the history of art. Miss Amalie

---

* In a letter from Athens, which I received in October, 1882, Dr. Schliemann says : " In commenting on my Trojan antiquities in ' Ilios,' I have continually pointed out the great similarity which exists between many of them as compared to the antiquities found in Hungary, and in my mind there can hardly be a doubt that in a remote prehistoric time Hungary was peopled by a Thracian race, which, as it would appear by the signs brought to light by Miss von Torma, also extended over Siebenbürgen. A lady who excavates is a very rare thing, and such efforts as hers ought to be encouraged and applauded by every archæologist. I twice mentioned her important excavations on page 350 of my ' Ilios.' "—T. S.

Thilo, principal of an important girls' institute at the capital, is well known for her lectures on pedagogics, that on the great names in the history of education being specially worthy of mention. In 1881 Miss Helene Druskovich, Ph.D., spoke before a large audience under the auspices of a Viennese society, and showed a large acquaintance with the Italian and other foreign literatures. Miss Susanna Rubinstein, Ph.D., has made a name both at home and abroad by her lectures and philosophical works. These are a few names selected from a long list of women who have proved that intellectual power is independent of sex.*

---

* The number of women who have shown real talent in special studies is much larger than is generally supposed. Every country furnishes examples similar to those given in the text. The London *Times* (weekly edition, January, 19, 1883) in a review of the " Dictionary of Christian Biography," refers in these terms to the female contributors : "One, Miss Dunbar, of Duffus, has very appropriately been intrusted with the account of a few saintly women. The other, Mrs. Humphry Ward, has contributed a series of learned and interesting articles on a subject which few scholars would have been competent to treat. * * * It will be only necessary to refer to her article on Leovigild to see that she holds a distinguished place among the contributors, not only in respect of her command of the learning connected with her subject, but in point of independent judgment and literary ability. * * *" Here is another example which I find in the *Journal des Débats*, September 26, 1880 : In the sitting of Friday, September 24, 1880, of the Academy of Inscriptions and Belles-Lettres, M. Le Blant presented to the learned body, in the name of the Countess Lovatelli, a notice on a marble crater found in 1875 in the vineyard of the old monastery of St. Anthony on the Esquiline. "The author describes and interprets the figures which ornament this monument," said M. Le Blant, "and shows that she is perfectly well acquainted with the monuments of art and with Greek literature, whose original texts are familiar to her." At the German Anthropological Congress, held at Berlin in 1880, two or three women took seats as members along side of such savants as Virchow and Schliemann. Miss J. Mestorf and Professor Virchow served together on one of the committees.—T. S.

I shall next take up the part which women play in the fine arts in Austria. The theatre, especially during the past few years, has become a veritable magnet for every girl who feels that she possesses a particle of dramatic talent. A large number of our actresses and singers are famous abroad as well as at home. I may mention, for example, Mrs. Amalie Friedrich Materna, the daughter of a humble schoolmaster of Styria, who is to-day one of the most renowned prima-donnas of Austria and Germany; Mrs. Marie Wilt, Mrs. Ehnn, Miss Bianchi, etc. From the Imperial Theatre of Vienna I select the names of Wolter, Hartman, Wessely and Hohenfels. Outside of the theatres, a large number of women devote themselves to vocal and instrumental music, a taste which is greatly encouraged by the many musical societies scattered all over the country. Women generally prefer the piano, but the harp, zithern, the violin and harmonium have their votaries. The number of female composers is as yet small. In painting our women have made great progress during the past few years, as is evidenced by the art exhibitions which have occurred in various parts of the country. There are very few female sculptors.

Many of our women devote themselves to scientific literature and belles-lettres. Besides those already mentioned, I may cite Aglaja von Enderes, who has written on natural history; Eufemia von Koudriaffsky, who died in 1881, and who has often treated scientific subjects in her essays; Mrs. Elise Last, who published a few years ago "More Light" (*Mehr Licht*), an admirable exposition of the teachings of Kant and Schopenhauer; and Mrs. Charlotte Edle von Schickh, who also writes on philosophical subjects. Educational questions occupy the attention of many female authors. Austria has a large number of poetesses. Betty Paoli, the *nom de plume* of Elisabeth Glück, is distinguished for the strength and beauty of her verse; the poetry of Margarethe Halm (Berta Maytner) is full of originality; and Ada Christen (Christine Frederick) has published poems, dramas and novels. In lyric and epic poetry are found the names of the Countess Wilhelmine von Wickenburg-Almásy, Marie von Najmájer, a Hungarian by birth; Caroline Bruch-Sinn, the Baroness von Kapri, the Baroness Josefine von Knorr, Angelika von Hörman, Herma Cziglér von Eny-Vecse, and Constanze Monter (Rosa Pontini). Among our novelists are the Baroness von Ebner Eschenbach, Therese von Hansgirg, Hermine Proschko, Mrs. von Weissenthurn, and Louise Lecher. Ida Pfeiffer is a well-known writer on travels. She twice circumnavigated the globe, visited the countries of the north, Jerusalem and the island of Madagascar, and described her voyages in a simple, clear, and interesting manner. She died in 1858. Rosa von Gerold has recently published a fascinating account of an autumnal journey in Spain. Several very able works on spiritualism are due to the pen of the Baroness Adelma von Vay, *née* Countess Wurmbrand. Hedwig von Radics-Kaltenbrunner and Harriet Grünewald have written sketches, essays, etc., for different periodicals. Many women have treated the various aspects of the woman question. The poets, Rosa Barach and Henriette Auegg, have written on this subject. The essays and poems of Margarethe Halm are pervaded by a bold reformatory spirit. The Hungarian author, Ida von Troll-Borostyáni, published a volume on this question a short time ago, and Franzeska von Kapff-Essenther has handled the same theme in a novel.*

---

* Heinrich Gross, professor of German literature in the German State

Several newspapers are devoted to the different phases of the women's movement in Austria. Some years ago an ex-officer, Captain A. D. Korn, who, if I am not mistaken, had passed some time in England and America, founded the *Universal Women's Journal* (*Allgemeine Frauen Zeitung*). This newspaper was wholly devoted to women's interests, but it soon died. The same thing is true of the *Women's Journal* (*Frauenblätter*) of Gratz, which appeared for a short time under the editorship of the writer of this sketch. Mr. Karl Weiss (Karl Schrattenthal), who is professor of German literature in the State college at Deva, recently established at Vienna a paper bearing a similar title (*Frauenblätter*), which suspended publication after the third or fourth number.

On the 9th, 10th, and 11th of October, 1872, the third German Women's Convention (*Deutsche Frauenkonferenz*) was held at Vienna, under the auspices of the General Society for Popular Education and the Amelioration of Women's Condition (*Allgemeine Verein für Volkserziehung und Verbesserung des Frauenloses*). The other two meetings of this society had been held at Leipsic and Stuttgart. The soul of this new movement was Captain Korn, whom I have already mentioned. His study of the woman question in the United States may have prompted him to awaken a similar agitation among the women of the Austrian Empire.* Addresses were delivered at this convention by ladies from Vienna, Hungary, Bohemia and Styria, and

---

school at Triest, published in 1882 a work on German female poets and authors. He is now (1883) engaged on an anthology of the female poets of Germany.—J. L.

* Several years ago Captain Korn and his wife, who took an active part in this convention, returned to Hungary, his native land, and I have never heard of him since. I do not even know whether he is still living.—J. L.

all the various interests of women were discussed. The author of this sketch read two essays—one on women's work and wages, the other on the education of women. The convention decided to petition for certain reforms. A resolution was adopted, amidst general applause, that monuments ought to be erected at Vienna and Presburg to the memory of the great Empress, Maria Theresa. Another resolution called for the enactment of a law which should assure women the same pay as men for the same work. The proceedings of the convention attracted considerable attention, and produced a favorable impression on the audience, which was recruited from the better classes of the population. But the newspapers of Vienna ridiculed the young movement, its friends grew lukewarm, and every trace was soon lost of this first and last Austrian Women's Rights Convention.

The legal position of women in Austria does not differ essentially from what it is generally among Teutonic and Latin nations. They are subordinated to men. A woman of the nobility loses her title on marrying a commoner, and her children cannot inherit it. If a woman lives five years outside of her country without an official permit, she becomes a foreigner. The married woman who has the right to vote, must exercise the privilege through her husband, but the widow and single woman may delegate any man to represent them at the polls.*

To sum up the situation, we find that in the field of labor the most crying need is the prompt and better sale of women's handiwork. Although bazaars and lotteries have been constantly employed for the purpose, there

---

* The subject of women's legal and political rights in the Empire is treated at greater length in the chapter on Bohemia, in this work.—T. S.

still remains much to be done in this direction. Radical innovations are needed in the system of women's instruction. The gymnasiums and universities should be opened to them. But as a vast majority of men, public opinion and a large number of women themselves are opposed, or at least indifferent, to this question, much time, agitation and popular enlightenment will be necessary to bring about this very desirable reform. But the future is not all darkness. I. H. von Kirchmann, the distinguished author, in his recently published work entitled, " Questions and Dangers of the Hour" (*Zeitfragen und Abenteuer*), devotes a division of his volume to " Women in the Past and Future," where he shows that the female sex has been gradually gaining its freedom, and predicts that the day is approaching when women will obtain their complete independence and will compete with men in every department of life, not excepting politics. Among our educated women great interest is shown in this question, but the female sex in general has never thought on it. It is a great impediment to progress and reform that Austria is composed of so many separate races, speaking different languages and having dissimilar customs and aims. The German, Hungarian, Slavonic and Italian peoples, which make up the Empire, do not all think alike and do not all work in unison. Thus, lack of interest on the part of the great mass of our women, and want of national unity in the Empire, are immense obstacles to the triumph of our movement. But I feel convinced that the day will come, when these races will unite in their efforts to ameliorate woman's lot, however much the ways and means employed to attain this end may vary, according to the different qualities and characteristics of these nations.

CHAPTER V.

NORWAY.*

BY CAMILLA COLLETT.

[Mrs. Camilla Collett is the sister of the great Norwegian poet, Henrik Wergeland, and is herself one of the best known of Scandinavian writers. Her principal theme has been the woman question, and she has treated it with force, elevation, and, at the same time, with moderation. "As a poet," says Professor Dietrichson, of the University of Christiania, "she has many charms and lofty ideas, and as a thinker her judgment is profound, clear, and rich in penetrating analysis." "The Bailiff's Daughters," a novel which appeared in 1859, had a marked success, and has been translated into Swedish and German. Mrs. Collett has also published many books of travel, literary criticisms, stories, poetry, etc. She is a member of the order of *Lettris et Artibus*, one of the few women on whom this honor has been conferred. I had the pleasure of meeting Mrs. Collett personally during her sojourn at Paris in the winter of 1881–2, and her tall figure—now bending under the weight of advancing years—and stately presence left an impression which will not soon be effaced.]

IT is almost incredible how imperfectly this woman question is grasped, not only by the general public, but even by many of the leaders of thought and culture. If we consider the European women's movement, we will readily perceive that the north lags the furthest behind. In initiative measures the nations of the south are in-

---

* Norway is placed before the other two Scandinavian countries because of the comparative estimate of the triad with which the sketch begins. If they were to be arranged according to the progress made in the emancipation of women, Norway would fall to the rear and Sweden stand first, followed by Denmark.—T. S.

variably in advance of us, and positive results are there more easily observed. I venture to assert, however, that while the northern, the Teutonic, mode of treating this question is characteristic, and differs strongly from the course pursued in the south among the Latin races, it insures a solution which, if more tardy, will be more truthful, more in harmony with the fundamental principles of the subject. This question of women's rights is inextricably intertwined with the moral history of mankind, and strikes down into the very soul of social life. In these depths we must fathom for its *raison d'être*, therein we find the source of a world-wide wrong, thereon we must base our claims, there seek the means for redress. This moral victory won, the more material immunities will follow of themselves.

An examination of the three Scandinavian peoples presents many very striking differences.

Denmark, because of her more central position, is in a much better way to obtain a happy and speedy solution of this woman question. Her population is more closely massed, she has more life, more of that mobility found in southern nations, and further, she is blest with Grundtvigianism,* that "lucid and joyous, Christianity" which does not throw obstacles in the way of progress, but is rather auxiliary thereto.

But it is our neighbor Sweden which, although not enjoying the advantages just mentioned, stands first among northern states in the movement for the elevation of

---

* Nicolai Grundtvig, a man of high repute as poet and preacher, was the founder of Grundtvigianism, which is essentially nothing else than pure Protestantism, and is much too extensively diffused to be designated a mere sect.—C. C. See the chapter on Denmark for further reference to this school.—T. S.

women. She early outstripped them in a more lively and general interest in women's rights, and the result is that to-day the country is blessed with many noble reforms in this direction. This striking fact is unquestionably due to the liberal sentiments which Swedish men entertain for women themselves, as well as for the cause which these women advocate. From early times the men of Sweden have been considered to represent the specifically chivalrous virtues of our northern climes, and if the daughters of the land have not yet reaped the full benefit of this inestimable national trait, now assuredly has the harvest time come.

Norway remains to be treated—Norway of which I have as yet not spoken, and of which it is so difficult to say anything, for the simple reason that there is so little to say. But what I do state shall be candid and true.

One step in advance has been the partial opening of the university to women—the best thing that can be said of Norway.* The right of married women to

---

* Miss Cecilie Thoresen, the first female student to matriculate at Christiania University, writing to me from Eidsvold, Norway, under date of December 29, 1882, says that it was in 1880 that she decided to try and take an academic degree. Her father, therefore, applied to the Minister of Public Instruction for the necessary authorization ; the latter referred the application to the University authorities, who, in their turn, submitted the portentous question to the Faculty of the Law School. In due season Miss Thoresen received this rather unsatisfactory response : " The admission of women to the University is denied, but we recognize the necessity of changing the law on this subject." Thereupon, Mr. H. E. Berner, a prominent Radical member of the Storthing, or Norwegian Parliament, introduced a bill permitting women to pursue studies in the University leading to the degrees of arts and philosophy (*examen artium* and *examen philosophicum*). The Committee reported unanimously in favor of the bill ; on March 30, 1882, it passed without debate the Odelsthing, one of the two chambers of the Storthing, with but one dissenting voice—that of a clergyman ; on April 21,

control their own property, for which both Danish
and Swedish women have so bravely battled, has
been denied us. The laws of inheritance, which
dated from the time of Christian V. (1646–1699),
and which cut daughters off with half as much as

1882, it received the unanimous vote of the other house, the Lagthing ; and
it became a law on June 15, 1882. A London illustrated paper, which
gives a picture representing Miss Thoresen's matriculation, describes the ceremony in these terms : " On the 8th of September last (1882) the hall of the
University was crowded to excess, when 260 students and their first female
colleague, who had passed a most successful examination, were present to
receive their matriculation.   The body of the hall was occupied by the students of 1832 and 1857, who were assembled in Christiania to celebrate
their fiftieth and twenty-fifth anniversary. The gallery was principally filled
with ladies, no doubt anxious to see this new champion of their sex on the
high road to learning and academical honors. The proceedings were opened
by a fine quartette, sung by a choir of senior students. After the inaugural
address by Professor L. M. B. Aubert, the President of the Collegiate
Council, the students advanced, one by one, to the rostrum to receive
their academical diplomas. * * * There was at this moment a general bustle and a great deal of stretching of necks all over the hall to catch
a glimpse of the fair student, but no cheers or any other sign of sympathy
escaped her male colleagues. At an English university a most enthusiastic
reception would on a similar occasion undoubtedly have been awarded to
the fair one.   In the afternoon, however, a deputation from the students
waited upon Miss Thoresen to congratulate her, and to welcome her
amongst their ranks. She also received an invitation to the festival which
the students always give on the evening of the matriculation day, but this
is of such a wild and uproarious character that she very wisely excused
herself from being present. In the course of the evening her health was
proposed, and drank with the greatest enthusiasm." In a letter from Mr.
Berner, dated Christiania, December 5, 1882, he writes me : " It is my intention, next year perhaps, unless a similar move is made in other quarters,
to propose an amplification of the recent law, which will render it possible for
women to take the final university degree. It may be necessary to explain
that the law of June 15, 1882, permits them to aspire to only the first degrees. It was thought best to make haste slowly. Now these two degrees
do not confer any privileges, do not open any of the walks of life. It is

their brothers, were repealed some time ago, but the ghost of this half-heirship still survives in the habit of paying women less than men, whether it concerns the salary of an ordinary employment or the granting of a Parliamentary pension.* We have two women's reading-rooms, but I am acquainted with no other association. We have no organ in the periodic press ; we have no influence on legislation ; we take no part in political life.

---

only after passing this final examination that one may enter the civil service of the state, be a judge, clergyman, principal of a high school, lawyer, physician, etc. Such is the provision of the law of July 28, 1824. In order, therefore, to place women on an equality with men, this law must be changed, and the former admitted to this examination. I do not think this proposition will encounter much opposition now that a beginning has been made. We shall then see women competing with men for employment in the civil service, a calling for which they are admirably fitted. It is a reform of this description that I propose as the next step in the movement now begun."—T. S.

* Mr. Berner, in the letter already referred to, says : " But, while much still remains to be done by legislation to improve the social position of women, the education of public opinion concerning this woman question is of even greater importance. The law reformer is powerless against popular customs, which even destroy the force of existing laws. Thus we see how custom in the last few centuries has annulled the truly liberal provisions of our ancient jurisprudence regarding the rights of married women, and authorized the husband, by the mere act of marriage, to take possession of the wife's property, and to treat her as a minor. The tide is, however, now happily turning again. Marriage contracts or settlements are becoming more and more frequent, and although a bill concerning married women's property, similar to the one which has recently become law in England, was defeated in the Storthing this year (1882), yet the growing tendency towards marriage contracts shows that almost the same end will be attained by this means. It is scarcely necessary for me to add that I stand ever ready to do what I can to advance the interests of women. In my opinion, there hardly exists nowadays any other social problem which has a better claim on public attention. Until women are placed on an equal footing with men, we shall not have departed from the days of barbarism."—T. S.

9

Such is the sum and substance of woman's condition in Norway.*

A word may be offered, however, in extenuation of the humiliating figure which Norway makes in this great movement for the elevation of women.

It should always be borne in mind that Norway is a

---

* Miss Mathilde Gasmann, a talented Norwegian artist living at Paris, gives me these few notes which brighten a little Mrs. Collett's rather dark picture. "The number of Norwegian women who are school teachers," says Miss Gasmann, "is proportionally very great. It is relatively but a few years since women became teachers in the public and private schools for boys, and consequently the state has not yet founded normal schools for their training, although bills for this purpose have been laid before the Storthing by the government. For several years we have had state industrial schools for women, where the instruction is almost free. These schools are very much frequented. The number of our literary women augments every year. Public opinion has grown much more liberal as regards the part women may play outside of the domestic circle. A few years ago, the fear of being called a blue-stocking would have restrained many a woman from quitting the narrow sphere to which nature was thought to have limited her. To-day, however, women are frequently found discussing scientific subjects, lecturing on literary topics, participating in congresses, etc." Mr. Berner says on the subject of education : " Our system of girls' high school education, which has been so deplorably neglected, needs reforming. Such an improvement might be obtained by adopting the American plan of opening the high schools to both boys and girls. But the co-education of the sexes is admitted in this country only in exceptional cases, and then only up to the age of twelve or thirteen. This is a great mistake. It is as equally detrimental to woman as to man, and consequently to the family and society in general, to make education a means of isolation, a wall between the two sexes, holding up to the one ideals and aims in life widely different from those which are instilled into the minds of the other. *Non schola sed vita* ought to be the governing principle of every educational system, or, as Gambetta very truly put it : ' To join hearts, you must begin by uniting minds ' ('*pour unir les cœurs, il faut commencer par rapprocher les esprits* '). It is, however, rumored that the government has in course of preparation a bill for the establishment of girls' gymnasiums similar to those already in existence for boys."—T. S.

laggard among nations, because she is the most isolated of that triad of states called Scandinavia, both as
regards geographical position and political relations. Her
deliverance from Denmark, under whose yoke four long
centuries were passed in provincial stagnation, was not
accomplished until the second decade of the present
century. She had then much lost time to make good, ere
she could hope to cope with her sister countries, Sweden
and Denmark, and assume a distinctive place in general
European civilization. It does not fall within the scope
of this sketch to trace the successive steps by which the
nation, favored by an admirable constitution, and the
gentle rule of the Bernadotte* dynasty, which brought
as it were a spark from the south to material only awaiting ignition, has taken on a new life, and is to-day
thriving as never before. The effect is seen in every
department of our national activity. Art and literature
especially felt the change. Since 1814, the year of our
independence, the metropolis of Norway, from a small
starveling market-town of some eight thousand inhabitants, has swelled into a stately city of nearly a hundred
and thirty thousand souls. The land was as a desert.
Many of our lordliest alp-tracts then lay unexplored, and
few there were who dared the break-neck adventure to
gain nearer acquaintance with them. In some rural districts the dead were borne to the grave-yard bound on
horses. What has since been accomplished to facilitate
communication and to provide for the convenience and

---

* It is scarcely necessary to remind American readers that the founder of
the reigning house of Norway and Sweden was Napoleon's marshal, Bernadotte. It may be said in passing, that Mrs. Collett's opinion of the Bernadotte dynasty as regards its treatment of Norway is not shared with her by
all Norwegians.—T. S.

comfort of travelers throughout our wide-spread, strag-
gling territory, the annually increasing stream of native
and foreign tourists well know and fully appreciate.

The nation, therefore, has had, as I have already said,
much lost ground to recover in order to catch up with our
restlessly advancing age. But as yet she has not had the
might nor the time to test all the questions, and to solve
all the problems, which this same restlessly advancing age
has brought forward in its career. Hence it is that all
which concerns woman and woman's place in society has
lingered pretty much in its former state. Our over-
busy men have not yet found leisure to devote themselves to her.* Unfortunately our women lack, in a
certain measure, that Danish vivacity and mobility which
might prompt them to rebel against this spirit of masculine exclusiveness, which has become more and more predominant. Patiently, therefore, oh, how patiently! they
remain quiet, much like well-behaved children awaiting
their turn. The crushing character of our rocky mountains
and that isolation in which a great portion of our culti-

---

* There are a few exceptions to this statement, as has already been seen
in the indefatigable labors of Mr. Berner. Professor Lochmann, of the
Christiania Medical School, is also favorable to the enlargement of the
sphere of women's activity, and has recently pronounced, with the approbation of the faculty, for their admission to the pharmaceutic examination.
" Pharmacy is a field for which women seem peculiarly fitted," he says ;
" I have no doubt that they would conscientiously and carefully prepare and
dispense medicines, and experience has shown that there are many advantages in employing them in this department. They are indeed already
found there, and the general opinion is that they do their work satisfactorily. It would therefore be in the interest of society as well as that of
women themselves, to give an official stamp to their employment in this
profession, which could be very easily done by opening to them the pharmacy school connected with the university."—T. S.

vated people live and move, give a certain heaviness to our women which develops ultimately into a passivity too sluggish to will, too timorous to dare. There are parts of my country where girls become women, and women matrons, without ever having once heard the ominous words, "women's rights." And the religion of our land, which least of all may be termed "the joyous Christianity," does not hesitate to pronounce its yea and amen to this dumb stress of self-renunciation.

What I have just said of our rural population is equally true of the social life of our towns, where the absorption of business and especially the turmoil of political strife, which has begun to lift its Gorgon head in our heretofore so peaceful and happy land, scarcely leave a moment for the consideration of woman's interests.* It is still, as it was before 1814, regarded unfeminine for one-half of Norway to have any thing in common with the other half. The ideal of womanhood is to be as little remarked as possible, that is, not to leave the beaten path. If a woman should venture an opinion or put a question in a conversation among men on political topics, a polite

---

* Mr. Berner makes the following note on this sentence of the text: "'The turmoil of political strife' has already done much for women, and will surely do more. Our great national poets, Ibsen, and especially Björnstjerne Björnson, have exerted a great influence in liberalizing public opinion in regard to the woman question. In his well-known 'Lectures on the Republic,' he makes this very true remark : 'The first thought, or perhaps more correctly, the first deed in aid of women, will come from the republic. With gratitude and hope women ought to unfurl the banner of republicanism.'" Miss Frances Lord, of London, in the preface to the translation of Ibsen's "Nora" (*Ett Dukkehjem*), literally, "A Doll's House," gives an interesting biographical notice of the author, which brings out clearly the important part he has played in the European women's movement. This work, which appeared in 1879, procured for Ibsen the title of "Woman's Poet."—T. S.

response will of course be given, but it will be instinctively addressed to the man at her side.

Years may pass away before any one shall remind us that this cause exists. But that day must come, like the February sun, so ardently awaited in our northern clime. Coldly, weakly will fall those first rays into our shaded valleys. But welcome, February sun! Blessings on thy first, though feeble beam! It is the harbinger of many brighter ones to come.*

---

* The above sketch, although prepared for this volume, first appeared in the Christiania *Aftenposten*, of February 8, 1882, in the form of a letter addressed to me. Mrs. Collett has since done me the great honor of publishing, in the same journal, two other open letters on the woman question, similarly addressed.—T. S.

CHAPTER VI.

SWEDEN.

BY ROSALIE ULRICA OLIVECRONA.

[Mrs. Rosalie Ulrica Olivecrona (*née* Roos), born at Stockholm in 1823, was educated at the Wallin School for Girls (mentioned in the following essay), and was one of the first scholars of this pioneer institution for the instruction of women. Miss Roos went to the United States in 1851, and spent nearly four years as a teacher in South Carolina. During this period she devoted much time to a favorite study, botany, and collected a herbarium of American plants containing more than four hundred specimens. On her homeward voyage she visited Havana and New Orleans, went up the Mississippi, stopped at several western and eastern cities, and admired the Mammoth Cave, that natural wonder, Niagara Falls, and the Catskill Mountains. In 1857 Miss Roos married Dr. K. Olivecrona, one of the most distinguished jurisconsults of Scandinavia, then Professor of Law at the University of Upsala, and named in 1868 a member of the Supreme Court (*Högsta Domstolen*) of Sweden. Two years later Mrs. Olivecrona aided in the foundation of the *Home Review* (*Tidskrift för Hemmet*), the women's organ referred to at greater length in the following pages, to which she has contributed numerous essays on social and educational questions, on natural science, accounts of travel, biographies, stories and poetry. Mrs. Olivecrona has also published a volume of poems (1851) and the "Life and Work of Mary Carpenter" (1877), of which an abridged edition has been issued in French (Paris, 1880). Having taken the leading part in organizing the Swedish department of women's work at the Vienna International Exhibition (1873), she prepared, at the request of the Swedish commissioners, "Notes on Women's Work in Sweden" (*Weibliche Arbeiten, Schweden*), which were annexed to the statistical reports edited by them. These notes, revised and augmented for the subsequent great exhibitions, have been translated into English (Philadelphia, 1876) and into

French (Paris, 1878). By invitation of the Women's Centennial Committee of the Philadelphia Exhibition, Mrs. Olivecrona prepared, after much time and labor, a lengthy account of women's share in Swedish charitable work. The manuscript reached America in safety, but having been mislaid, a very unsatisfactory abridgment of the original was drawn up at the last moment and published as a supplement to the catalogue of charities conducted by women. Mrs. Olivecrona is the contributor for Sweden to the proposed "Encyclopedical and Biographical Dictionary of Celebrated Women" (*Dictionnaire encyclopédique et biographique des femmes célèbres*), edited by Miss Anne Marie Botteau, of Biarritz. She has taken part, as a member, in the Dublin Social Science Congress (1861), the International Prehistoric Archæological Congresses of Copenhagen (1869), Brussels (1872), Stockholm (1874), and Buda Pesth (1876), and the Stockholm International Penitentiary Congress (1878), at which Dr. E. C. Wines presided, and to which Mrs. Olivecrona contributed a paper on the reformatory work of Miss Carpenter. Mrs. Olivecrona's philanthropic labors have been in connection with the Upsala Ladies' Society for Poor Infants (1861–1868), the Stockholm Society for the Education of Idiots (since 1869), and the Stockholm Society for Promoting Female Industry (1872). She moreover founded the Ladies' Committee of the Red Cross (1871), the Bee-Hive (*Bikupan*), or shop for the sale of women's work (1870), and took part in the establishment of a Working Home for Idiots (1881). All of these institutions are at the capital.]

DURING the last twenty or thirty years an earnest movement, aiming to extend women's sphere of thought and action, has been manifest throughout all civilized countries. Sweden early felt its influence, quickly caught the spirit of the times, and made great progress in the amelioration of the condition of its women. The best evidences of this are found, on the one hand, in the many educational institutions which have been established for, or made accessible to, women; and, on the other, in a greater readiness, on the part of both private individuals and the State, to employ females.

The movement for improving the education of women may be said to have been inaugurated by the establishment of the Wallin School in 1831, through the efforts of Professor A. Fryxell, the eminent historian, under the patronage of the Archbishop of Sweden, J. O. Wallin. The next step was the opening, in 1859, at Stockholm, of Higher Classes for young ladies by some influential men, who were eager to raise the level of female instruction. The tuition, which was gratis, was given in the form of lectures and private recitations, and embraced religious exercises, the natural sciences, mathematics, history, Swedish grammar and literature, French, hygiene, and drawing; the scholars being at liberty, however, to choose their subjects. This course of study was continued for three years, and, having met with great success, it led to the foundation of the Royal Seminary for the Training of Female Teachers (*Kongl Seminariet för bildande af lärarinnor*), which was opened at Stockholm in 1861. Instruction at this institution is free; the curriculum covers a period of three years, and embraces, besides the branches already mentioned, geography, natural philosophy, pedagogics, German and English. The number of scholars admitted to the seminary since its beginning is 523, of whom 348 have received a teacher's diploma. Through the voluntary contributions of the pupils, a fund has been raised, the interest of which creates three scholarships. The Royal Normal School was established on the same premises in 1864, not only as a preparatory school for the Seminary, but also with the object of affording its students an opportunity of gaining some practical insight into the art of teaching. This school is much frequented, and, although the instruction is not gratuitous, it admits fifteen free pupils and five for a limited fee.

Including the Seminary and the Wallin School, there are altogether in the metropolis eight high schools for young women, with a total number of 1,800 pupils and 250 teachers.* Though they all aim to offer to women a good and thorough education, they are conducted on somewhat different principles — one admitting more liberty in the choice of studies and allowing the subjects to be independent of each other; another keeping more strictly to the regular courses. Two of them, the Wallin School and the girls' Lyceum, have added gymnasium classes to their curriculum, where the pupils are prepared for the matriculation examination,† which authorizes them to pursue their studies at the two universities (Upsala and Lund) of the kingdom. Besides these eight institutions, Stockholm has a great many schools on a smaller scale, which offer good educational advantages.

Even in the provinces, much has been done of late years to promote female education. Gottenburg has six girls' high schools, the most important of which was founded in 1867 by an association, the funds collected for that purpose amounting to 35,000 crowns.‡ Upsala has three very good schools, and there is, in fact, at the present time (1883) no provincial town of note which has not one or more high schools due to private munificence, or supported by the community. Most of them are in charge of graduates of the Royal Seminary at Stockholm, which is thus extending its beneficial influence all over the king-

---

* In 1881, Stockholm had a population of 176,745.—R. O.

† No student is allowed to matriculate at either of the Swedish universities without having previously passed a preliminary examination, called the students' examination, showing his competency to pursue university studies. —R. O. This is also the American and English system, but is not adopted in many continental countries. The word "gymnasium" in this sentence is employed in the sense of high school.—T. S.

‡ A Swedish crown equals about 27 cents.—T. S.

dom. Several good and well-organized boarding-schools are also to be found in the country. Notwithstanding the many efforts that have been made to procure for girls the same educational advantages which boys have long enjoyed—gratuitous instruction in schools established by the State—they have as yet met with only partial success. At the meeting of the Diet in 1873, the government asked for a grant with which to establish high schools for girls in four provincial towns, but the request was negatived. However, 30,000 crowns were voted to support private schools already in existence. This appropriation has gradually increased to 70,000 crowns, and makes it possible to furnish free tuition to many scholars in straitened circumstances.

Besides the institutions already mentioned, there are Courses of Lectures for young women who desire to pursue advanced special studies. The Classes for the higher education of women, established by Miss Jenny Rossander in 1865, have proved quite useful in this respect, enabling even young female teachers to supply defects in their education. More than a thousand women have profited by them. Owing to divers circumstances, these classes have lately been discontinued, but others are springing up in their place, and in some of the schools above mentioned, advanced classes have been established for those students who wish to continue one or more special branches.

In 1870 women were admitted to the universities, and in 1873 they were allowed to take the same academic degrees in arts and medicine as male students. Upwards of fifty young women—twelve in the single year of 1883 —have passed creditably the matriculation examination. Only a limited number have, however, pursued studies at

the universities, and still fewer taken academic degrees.*
One of the latter is a teacher in a boys' school at Stockholm.
At present (January, 1883) there are four female students
in Upsala, all belonging to the philosophical or arts faculty; † two in Lund studying medicine, and one in the
Stockholm Medical School (*Carolinska Institutet*). It is
with satisfaction I add that they are treated with perfect
deference by their fellow-students of the other sex. There
are three scholarships for female students, all founded by
private persons—viz., one at the University of Upsala,
another at the University of Lund, and the third at the
Medical School in Stockholm.

In 1867 a course of instruction for the training of nurses
for the sick was opened at the University Hospital in
Upsala, under the superintendence of a lady who had gone
through the Nightingale Institution for the training of
nurses at St. Thomas's Hospital in London. Several
women have followed this course in order to fit themselves for the position of matrons in hospitals and in-
firmaries. Similar courses were organized in 1877 in Got-

---

* This is doubtless due in part to the fact that it is a novelty and that the
practical advantages do not as yet correspond to the exertion. The number
of students and graduates is, however, steadily increasing.—R. O.

† One of them, Miss Ellen Fries, took, in the spring of 1883, the degree
of doctor of philosophy, and defended her thesis, which treated of the
diplomatic transactions between Sweden and the Low Countries during the
reign of Charles X., in an able and spirited manner before a large audience.
Some days after, the graduating ceremony (capping, as it is called in En-
land) took place with customary solemnity, and Miss Fries received her
diploma and the laural crown, the insignia of her new dignity. She was
accompanied home by her fellow-graduates, a delegation of students offered
her a magnificent banquet and the choir of the musical society gave her a
beautiful serenade. About the same time another of the female students
passed the examination of candidate of philosophy, which is preliminary to
the doctorate.—R. O.

tenburg, and in 1882 in Stockholm. In the hospital belonging to the Deaconesses' Institute, which was established at Stockholm in 1851, and accommodates upwards of fifty patients, all the attendance is performed by "deaconesses" with the assistance of one physician, and most of the medicine used is prepared by them. A school for poor children, a home for destitute children, a reformatory for women, a reformatory school for girls, and a school for the training of maid servants, owe also their existence to this institution.

Women have had access to the Royal Academy of Music, at Stockholm, since 1854; in fact there are instances of their having been admitted as early as 1795 and 1821, though this permission was afterwards withdrawn. The instruction is given by professors of both sexes. Many women profit by this privilege and pursue musical studies with success. For instance, the examination for organists, including harmony, singing, playing of the organ and piano, has been passed with credit by a large number of female students. The examination for musical director,* which covers a period of five years' study, and which includes, besides the subjects already mentioned, counterpoint, the history and æsthetics of music, instrumentation, the piano, violin and violoncello, was passed some years ago by Miss Amanda Maier, who also obtained the best certificate for the organ.

The Swedish capital contains many special schools which are frequented by women. The Royal Academy of Fine Arts was, in 1864, made accessible to female students, but the number being limited to twenty-five, many

---

* The passing of this examination is preliminary to the competitive examination for several posts, such as leaders of orchestras, of military bands, teachers at the university, etc.—R. O.

aspirants are annually turned away. The Industrial School was first opened to women in 1854. About 800, of whom a large proportion pursue technical studies, attend yearly this institution, and are allowed to compete for prizes. The telegraphic school, founded by the Government, has many female pupils. There are more than a dozen commercial and calligraphic institutes which admit them. Several are conducted by ladies. The Royal Central Gymnasium is open to women who desire to teach or study gymnastics. As early as 1820 female pupils were admitted to this institution, and about 1864 a regular course of training was established for women. More than one hundred have obtained diplomas and gain their livelihood as teachers of gymnastics.

Stockholm, Gottenburg and Lund have each a lying-in hospital for training in midwifery. The instruction is free, and includes obstetrics with and without instruments, the nursing of children, etc. The number of women who pursue the complete study of instrumental obstetrics increases yearly, as they are more entitled to public confidence, and are consequently in greater demand. Swedish midwives were allowed the use of instruments as early as 1829, and experience has shown the wisdom of this measure, for to this may be ascribed the slight mortality in childbirth. The number of practicing midwives in Sweden is upwards of 2,200.

I now turn from higher and special instruction to the subject of elementary and popular instruction. Sweden has five normal schools for primary school mistresses, which are much frequented. To these were added, in 1867, classes for teachers of infant and children's schools, where future school mistresses may have the opportunity of acquiring the art of teaching. There are also twenty-four normal schools devoted entirely to the training of teachers for infant schools. Primary schools for boys and girls are found everywhere in the country as well as in the cities. They are counted by thousands, and are of three kinds: stationary schools, of which there are about 3,600; ambulatory schools, about 862; and infant schools, about 4,300. Since 1870 have been established high schools for young peasants, which furnish more advanced instruction than that given in the primary schools. In nine among them there are also classes for girls, and the pupils—about two hundred in number—are especially educated with the view of becoming good housewives. Industrial and sewing schools for poor children, where instruction is given gratuitously in spinning, weaving, sewing, etc., are very common in the country as well as in towns. In Stockholm there are four institutions for the training of maid servants, the oldest being the Murbäck Institute, which was founded in 1747. Similar ones are also found at Gottenburg and other cities. All over the kingdom numerous children's homes are met with. Among the earliest establishments of this kind is the one founded by the Princess Eugénie in the Island of Gothland, near her summer residence. The children are received at an early age, pursue the same studies as in the primary schools, and are taught in addition needlework and domestic employments.

I shall complete this long list by a brief mention of three other classes of schools. Sweden possesses several dairy schools, especially at the agricultural institutes, where women are taught the management of farms and dairies, the care of cattle, etc. The State grants annually 3,000 crowns for this purpose. It is not an uncommon thing in Sweden for women to take charge of the dairy cattle on a farm as well as to do the indoor work of the dairy.   Sunday schools, where religious instruction is given to poor children, and mending schools, where poor girls are taught to repair their clothing properly, are thickly scattered throughout the kingdom, and are under the charge of young ladies.

Swedish women themselves have been unsparing in their efforts to procure for their sex the advantages of a good education, and it is in a large measure due to their perseverance that many of the above mentioned schools have been founded or made accessible to female pupils. The *Home Review* (*Tidskrift för Hemmet*) is also an important factor in this grand result. This periodical, which has always been a warm and energetic advocate of women's interests, was founded, in 1859, by Lady Sophie Leijonhufoud, at present the Baroness Adlersparre, and by the author of this sketch.   It was started anonymously, but having attracted public attention, the identity of the editors could no longer be concealed.   During the first years the editors were almost entirely thrown on their own resources, but gradually they enlisted the co-operation of many able writers, both male and female.   After an existence of a quarter of a century, it may be said that this review has done a good work, for to it is unquestionably due much of the progress which has been made in the educational and social position of Swedish women.*   The author of this sketch retired from the editorship of the *Review* after the lapse of nine years, but she has never ceased to contribute to its pages.   The Baroness Adlersparre then became sole editor, a posi-

* Mrs. Olivecrona might have gone farther and said that this periodical and the group of liberals who supported it exerted an influence throughout all Scandinavia.   See the chapter on Denmark which follows.—T. S.

tion which she still fills with great talent and untiring energy. Besides her literary work, the Baroness Adlersparre has been active in promoting reforms in the condition of her sex in other directions. Thus she established, in 1869, the copying office, which threw open a vast field of labor to women who there find remunerative work in copying and translating. In 1874 she founded the association of the friends of women's domestic industry, and through her exertions the first school for the training of nurses was organized, in 1867, at the university hospital in Upsala. To her efforts is also due the Ladies' Reading Room at Stockholm, which has been in existence since 1867, and whose object is not only to diffuse a taste for good reading, but also to put it within the reach of persons with limited means.

The *Home Review* does not offer the only instance in Sweden of the participation of women in periodical literature. Our magazines and newspapers count many able female writers among their contributors, and a number of women have successfully filled the post of editor. We have, also talented authoresses, among whom none are more worthy of remembrance and honor than Mrs. Lenngren (1754–1817), whose poetry is unsurpassed in humor and elegant versification; Freddrika Bremer (1801–1866), known and beloved throughout the civilized world; the Baroness von Knorring, Mrs. Emily Carlén, Mrs. M. S. Schwartz, and Mrs. J. Wettergrund.

The fine arts are much cultivated by Swedish women. Music is studied with predilection, as is evidenced by the many far-famed Swedish singers, as, for example, Jenny Lind, Louise Michaëli (1830–1875), and Christina Nilsson, and by the large part that this accomplishment holds in the general system of education. We have some female composers of vocal music, and for the violin, piano and orchestra. One of the harpists in the orchestra of the opera is a lady.

The first Swedish woman in this century who distinguished herself as a painter was Sophie Adlersparre (1808–1862), sister-in-law of the Baroness Adlersparre. Many of the difficulties against which she had to struggle have gradually been removed, and female artists occupy to-day a respected position. Several of them, such as Amalia Lindegren, Agnes Börjeson, Josefine Holmlund, Sophia Ribbing, and Adelaide Leuhusen, are known and admired even beyond the limits of their native land. Sculpture, the noblest and most difficult of the fine arts, is also cultivated by some female amateurs, among whom a member of our royal family, the Princess Eugénie, holds an eminent place. Mrs. Lea Ahlborn has been engaged, since 1853, as engraver of medals in the royal mint at Stockholm, and enjoys a high reputation in this vocation. At the Royal Academy of Sciences women are often employed to draw and paint Swedish plants for scientific purposes, and since 1860 female designers have been engaged in the archives of Swedish maps. Wood carving is executed by women with skill and taste. Sophia Isberg (1819–1875), one of the first among these artists, was the daughter of a poor tailor. She had great natural talent, although it was never duly cultivated. Her workmanship was, however, distinguished for great variety of ideas, often historical, and also for an elaborate execution. She received prizes at exhibitions in Stockholm, Gottenburg, Paris, London, and Vienna. Several of our best photographers are women, and xylography, lithography and engraving afford employment to many female artists.

The legislative power has co-operated with the advocates of woman's emancipation, not only in increasing the opportunities for obtaining instruction, but also in providing new means of self-support, all the more necessary since machinery has deprived women of many kinds of work formerly performed by them. Thus, to cite a few examples, the following laws have successively conferred on Swedish women new rights. In 1845 equality of inheritance for son and daughter was established and the wife was given the same rights as the husband to the common property.* In 1846 women were granted the right to practice industrial professions and to carry on business in their own name. In 1853 and in 1859 laws were passed enabling them to be teachers in the primary schools. In 1858 they were allowed to claim their majority at twenty-five, if they found it desirable—a proviso which was removed in 1863, when they were unconditionally declared of age at twenty-five. In 1861 they were permitted to compete for the situation of organist in the State church and to practice surgery and dentistry on producing proofs of competency. In 1863 minor positions in the postal and telegraphic service were, with certain restrictions, opened to them. In 1864 their rights in trade and industrial pursuits were enlarged. In 1870 they were admitted to the universities after having passed

---

* As soon as the marriage ceremony is performed the property of husband and wife is united, and each party has an equal share in it. The mere act of marriage renders the property of both parties common, with the exception of inherited landed property. At the death of one of them it is divided into two parts, the one devolving on the surviving spouse, the other on the heirs of the deceased. Country real estate is not included in this division. The landed property, inherited either by husband or wife, goes to the children, if there be any. If there are none, it descends to the next heir of the deceased.—R. O.

the students' or entrance examination, and to the medical profession, after having produced requisite proofs of ability. In 1872 women of twenty-five obtained full power to dispose of themselves in marriage (the father's, brother's, or relative's consent having heretofore been necessary).* And in 1874 married women became entitled to manage that part of their private property set aside for their personal use in the marriage contract, and to control their own earnings.

The civil law of Sweden is in many respects more liberal than that of other countries in its treatment of married women, not only allowing them equal rights with their husband to the common property but conferring on them at his death one-half of this property, with the exception of the country real estate inherited by him. This law has long been in use, but just and judicious though it be, it has, however, proved impotent to protect married women from the evil consequences resulting from the husband's mismanagement of the common property or from his spendthrift habits. To remedy this, a society for protecting married women's private property was formed in 1871 by Mrs. E. Anckarsvärd and Mrs. Anna Hierta-Retzius. This society aims at procuring for a married woman the lawful right of administering and disposing of her own private property, whether inherited or acquired, so that it may not be lost by the maladministration of the husband or seized to pay his debts. A sum of 3,000 crowns is awarded as prizes for the best essays on a projected law for this purpose.†

---

* The nobility held out longer. It was not until March 14, 1880, that a resolution was passed at a meeting of noblemen yielding the privilege of acting as sponsors for their own daughters.—R. O.

† This society would secure for Sweden a law similar to that which went

The efforts to enlarge the field of women's work have also secured the co-operation of the general public. Many females now find employment in professions formerly only open to males, as, for example, clerkships in private and savings banks, in joint-stock and insurance companies, in business and railroad offices. Almost all the larger shops have female cashiers. There are instances of women acting as superintendents of branch departments of private banks, and in one town the treasurer is a lady. The engagement of women in these callings is continually gaining ground. In 1880 there were 5,892 business women in Sweden, 3,101 of whom were in business on their own account. In this same year more than 1,900 were engaged in industrial pursuits, 650 of whom were owners of factories and workshops. During the past few years almost all trades and industries have been opened to women. Even in mechanics they are not wholly without representatives. Some very ingenious machines, an apparatus for tuning organs and harmoniums, an improvement on Grover & Baker's sewing machine, a contrivance for making nets, the patent of which Norway has bought for a considerable sum, bespeak female inventive genius.* Many women are watchmakers, one having even

---

into effect in England on January 1, 1883. The Swedish wife, however, is in a very different position from the English wife, for the former has equal rights with the husband as regards the common property, though not equal *control* over it.—R. O.

* "Women are accorded every talent except that of inventing. This is the opinion of Voltaire, one of the men who has been the most just to women and who knew them best. But, however, if men capable of inventing were alone to have a place in the world, there would be many a vacant one even in the academies."—Condorcet's Works, vol. ix., pp. 18, 19. In 1872 the French Academy of Sciences awarded Miss Caroline Garcin a prize for the invention of an automatic sewing machine.—Leroy-Beaulieu's "Women's Work in the Nineteenth Century," p. 461. Mrs. Matilda Joslyn Gage, in an

received a prize at a London exhibition. Two sisters are successful as goldsmiths in Stockholm. There are female shoemakers, lace-makers, glovers, bookbinders, japanners, mother-of-pearl workers, rope-makers, glaziers, hatters, comb-makers, painters, turners, upholsterers, confectioners and bakers, who carry on these various trades on their own account. Most of the weavers employed in factories are women. There are female type-setters, and some printing offices are owned and managed by women. At the china manufactories of Gustafsberg & Rörstrand a great deal of the work, particularly modeling and enamel painting, is performed by women. From Dalarne, one of the northern provinces, we get many clever female gardeners.

Among the many efforts of women to be of service to their own sex, I shall cite but two or three examples. The Governesses' Mutual Annuity Fund, founded in 1855 by Miss Deland, aims to provide a small annual income to aged lady teachers. At fifty-five the shareholders receive an annuity of nine per cent. on the paid investments, which have increased by the adding of the interest to the capital, and by the acquisition of the investments of contributors who have died before the prescribed age. On January 1, 1882, the capital of this society amounted to 190,713 crowns. The institution is entirely managed by women, the board of trustees consisting of nine ladies. For the disposal of such products of female workmanship as do not generally belong to the industrial market, a salesroom, called the "Bee Hive," was opened at Stockholm in 1870, under the patronage of several ladies. This

interesting little pamphlet entitled "Woman as Inventor," removes whatever misgivings the two greatest philosophers of the eighteenth century may have entertained concerning woman's inventive genius.—T. S.

effort to assist females in straitened circumstances, by affording them an opportunity to dispose of their work profitably, has proved highly successful. During the twelve years of its existence, the Bee Hive has sold goods to the amount of 218,000 crowns. Similar establishments have sprung up in several provincial cities. The third example is the women's societies which distribute among the poor, who cannot otherwise find employment, spinning, weaving, knitting and sewing work.

Among the many benevolent societies and charitable institutions for the aid of suffering womanhood may be mentioned the Society for the Relief of the Poor, at Stockholm, founded and patronized by the Queen; societies for the promotion of female industry, created by the late Queen-Mother;* the Lotten Wennberg's Fund for the destitute, founded by the late Queen Louisa † in memory of the philanthropist Miss Lotten Wennberg (1815–1864), whose life was devoted to the needy and unfortunate of the capital; the Friends of Poor Children, a society under the patronage of the Princess Eugénie ‡; the Patriotic Association, which originated with the late Queen Louisa, and aims to induce the working classes to provide against old age and times of need by making small investments in insurance companies; the Home for Released Female Prisoners, established in 1860 by the present Queen § with the view of assisting women punished for crime to reform and redeem their character; the Crown-Princess Louisa's Hospital,‖ for sick children; a Home for poor elderly

---

* Josephine, consort of King Oscar I., deceased 1876.—R. O.

† Consort of Charles XV., died 1871.—R. O.

‡ Daughter of King Oscar II.—R. O.

§ Sophie, princess of Nassau.—R. O.

‖ It was founded under the patronage of Queen Louisa, while still crown-princess.—R. O.

ladies, quite a magnificent establishment, founded and endowed in 1873 by the late Queen-Mother, Josephine, in commemoration of the fiftieth anniversary of her arrival in Sweden, and dedicated to the memory of King Oscar I., her late consort; another Home, with the same end, due to the exertions of Countess von Schwerin, and liberally endowed by Freddrika Bremer, has been in existence since 1862; a Deaf and Dumb Asylum, established in Stockholm in 1861, and an Asylum for Idiots (the first of its kind in Sweden) in the country, dating from 1866, owe their origin to women of small means and modest position; a temporary Home for maid-servants in want of employment, opened in 1877, and a Home for incurable children, established in 1881, both due to the untiring exertions of the Princess Eugénie, who entirely devotes her life and means to benefit suffering humanity.

There is in Sweden a society based on the same principles as the British and Continental Federation, and with the same end in view. It has both male and female members, the latter being particularly zealous to promote the cause they have embraced. To their efforts are thus due several institutions whose object is either the rescue of those of their own sex who have already been led astray, or the prevention of sin and misery, by providing work for unprotected and destitute females. In connection with the former I may mention the Home for Destitute Women, established at Stockholm in 1881 by Mrs. Andersson-Meijerhelm, where many women find shelter, food, work, and even clothing, and, upon leaving, are provided with good places or remunerative employment. The objects of this association are also embodied in the temporary Home for young girls who are out of work, which was opened at Stockholm, in 1881, by Miss Nordvall, a fund for giving assistance or loans to needy females, and several register-offices for working women, where addresses and references are left, and where employers may apply when in need of hands. In the spring of this year (1883) a bazar was held at the capital in behalf of a Home for aged maid-servants. There are many more associations and institutions in the varied fields of philanthropy, due to the benevolence and energy of women, but the above mentioned may be considered as fair specimens.

The domestic industry of the peasant women consists chiefly in spinning and weaving for family use. In the north of Sweden, however, where the soil is favorable to the cultivation of flax, there is an extensive linen industry; the linen there manufactured by hand forms an important article of internal commerce. In one of the central provinces, yarn and textile fabrics of undyed wool are produced in considerable quantities, and the women of that region travel about offering their wares for sale. In another of the central provinces, white and colored stuffs of cotton and wool are manufactured by hand in the peasant homes. This industry is very general. Contractors, as a rule wealthy peasants, furnish the raw material, pay small wages for the work, and the goods are carried all over the kingdom by peddlers. Knitting also forms a part of domestic industry. The peasant women knit not only stockings for the use of the family, but even warm and strong jackets for seafaring men. In some provinces curiously-worked and highly-ornamented worsted mittens are made by the women. Another branch of industry, lace-making, is limited to certain parts of the country. It flourishes mostly in Wadstena (Östergöt-land) and vicinity, and comes down from the olden time, when it constituted one of the chief occupations of the sisters of the far-famed nunnery of Wadstena, founded by St. Brigitta in the XIVth century. The late Queen Louisa, consort of Charles XV., encouraged and revived this industry, which had gradually degenerated, but now produces fine specimens of workmanship. Even in Dalarne, in the north, and in some of the southern provinces, lace-making exists, but is only carried on for the use of the inhabitants themselves, who employ it to ornament their national costumes. It is to be regretted that these costumes are gradually passing away, as they are the means of promoting greater variety in domestic handiwork. Where they are still worn the women generally display more taste and skill in their handiwork as shown by carefully-executed embroideries and richly-colored textures.

These specimens of elaborate work are not confined to the costumes, but are also to be seen in curtains, cushions, carpets, etc., serving to decorate the walls of the cottage on festive occasions, and frequently handed down from generation to generation. Many Dalecarlian women are skilled in making ornaments of hair, such as chains, bracelets, brooches, etc., which they peddle on foot, not only in Sweden, but also in the neighboring countries.

Even Lapland exhibits proofs of female industry. Women not only make all the garments worn, which consist partly of a coarse worsted material and partly of the skin of the reindeer, but they also manufacture shoes. They ornament their costumes with curiously-woven, gaudy-colored belts and a richly-embroidered bib, called *åtså-leppa*, on which they greatly pride themselves. A kind of zinc wire is used for embroidering, but their common sewing thread is made of the sinews of the reindeer, carefully twisted together.

As the directors of the Vienna International Exhibition of 1873 wished to see the female industry of the respective countries represented, a committee of our ladies undertook to arrange a section for women's work in the Swedish department of the Fair. The object of this committee was to collect specimens of all the different kinds of work suitable for display. In order to form a more correct judgment about the articles contributed for this purpose, a preliminary exhibition was held in Stockholm in the spring of that year. Many hitherto little-known or observed productions of female handiwork, especially that of the peasantry, attracted considerable notice. This gave rise to an association called the Friends of Women's Domestic Industry (*Handarbetets vänner*), which was organized in the spring of 1874, with a view to promote and develop female industry on the basis of native art. This association, which has met with much encouragement, is endeavoring to save from oblivion ancient patterns and modes of workmanship, and to introduce new ones based upon this early art. The society gives employment to a considerable number of women, and has received and executed orders not only for the home market, but even for Russia, England, Germany, and Austria. Among its patronesses are the present Queen and the Crown Princess.

Associations for promoting domestic industry (*Hushållningssällskap*) exist all over the kingdom, and have been very successful in carrying out this object among the country people. They employ many female teachers, who give instruction in different kinds of weaving, basket and straw work, not only to the children in the country primary schools, but also to peasant women. The encouraging results of these efforts may be noticed at the annual exhibitions of these associations.

I have left until the last the few words I have to say on the question of the political rights of women, for little progress has been made in this direction. However, in many affairs relative to the municipality, women vote on the same terms as men; as, for example, in the choice of the parish clergy and the municipal councillors, (*stads-fullmäktige*), and in the naming of the electors of the county council (*landsting*), which elects the members of the Upper Chamber. As regards women's admission to the complete elective franchise, which would confer upon them the right of voting for members of the Diet, no demands have been made in this direction nor any meetings held for this purpose.

The rapid sketch, which I have just given of the means of education and the spheres of activity now accessible to Swedish women, proves that the efforts made for the amelioration of their condition have not been in vain. Far from being limited to a minority, more or less numerous, these beneficial results have become the property of women of all classes of society, who at present enjoy advantages, which throw open to them new fields of work and knowledge, and which, in the not distant future, must render them intellectually, civilly and politically the equals of men.

CHAPTER VII.

DENMARK.

BY KIRSTINE FREDERIKSEN.

[Miss Kirstine Frederiksen was born February 6, 1845, on the Isle of Laaland, belonging to Denmark, in the Baltic Sea, and was educated at her father's country seat in the midst of a large family. She visited London in 1870, examined carefully the great charitable institutions of the English capital, and on her return home published an account of her impressions. Two years later Miss Frederiksen traveled in Italy and Switzerland, and the result of her sojourn in the former country was a sketch of Syracuse entitled " A Capital of the Remote Past." Soon after this Miss Frederiksen went to live in Copenhagen, where she has always taken an active part in all that concerns the improvement of women. For five years she was at the head of the Copenhagen Women's Reading Room, mentioned in the following sketch, and has been since 1875 a member of the Board of Managers of the Female Drawing School in that same city. In 1878 Miss Frederiksen passed the State examination for short-hand writing, the only Danish woman who has done so up to the present time, but was refused, on account of her sex, a position on the staff of stenographers of the Rigsdag, or Diet, by the president of the Landsthing, or Upper House. The following year she passed the State teachers' examination, and received an appointment in the public schools. Miss Frederiksen has contributed, to various home and foreign periodicals, translations from the writings of Frances Power Cobbe, the late Professor Jevons and Emile Laveleye; original essays on Mrs. Browning and William E. Channing, on the woman question, and on educational and pedagogic subjects.]

THE first thing to strike the student of the woman question in Denmark is the complete absence of any direct participation by women in the political affairs of the country. In the Danish Constitution of 1849, which established universal male suffrage, nothing is said of the political rights of the other sex.   In municipal and school-board elections the same thing is true.*   Women can exert only an indirect influence through their husbands and brothers.   But, it must be added, Danish women have not shown any very strong desire to exercise these privileges.†

The liberal movement which swept over Europe in 1848 was felt in Denmark, and had a beneficial effect on the legal condition of women in our country.   Thus, in 1857, a bill was passed making them of age at twenty-five, when men also reach their majority, and the laws concerning inheritance became the same for both sexes.

The principle of community of goods in marriage, or, as it is called in the Napoleonic Code, *communauté de biens*, ‡ has been in vogue for two centuries in Denmark.

---

* In Iceland, which is a dependency of Denmark, unmarried women and widows, if they are householders, vote at municipal and school-board elections.   This reform was brought about in 1882.—K. F.

† In 1660 a *Rigsdag*, or States-General, was convened at Copenhagen, and the four estates—nobles, clergy, commons, and peasants—voted together for the last time, the result being the conferring of absolute power on the king. On this occasion the nobles not only voted for themselves, but for their absent relatives, including their mothers and sisters, who probably held property in their own right.—K. F.

‡ The "community of goods" is a species of partnership between the husband and wife.   The property owned by each at the date of their marriage, except their lands, and all that may be subsequently acquired by either of them, except lands inherited or donated, are brought into and constitute the common fund.   This fund is chargeable with the debts of each existing at the commencement of the marriage, and with those subsequently contracted by the husband ; and he alone possesses the right to its control and management.   . . . .   This same partnership system has been adopted by the civil code of Louisiana, and to a partial extent by the statutes of California.—John Norton Pomeroy, Johnson's Cyclopædia, article "Marriage."—T. S.

But the term is a misnomer, for the husband alone has the control of the property and the income, so that the " community " consists in the wife giving up her all to the husband.   Every attempt to change this law has been, and is still, considered an attack on the sacredness of the marriage relation.   But the eyes of the public have been opened of late by numerous lawsuits—the publicity of our judicial proceedings is of recent date—to the abuses resulting from this unjust arrangement.   Discussions on this subject in several international Scandinavian law congresses have awakened Danish jurists to the importance of reforms, and, after the repeated efforts of Mr. Fredrik Bajer, a member of the Folketing, or Lower House, who was backed by a petition from several thousand women, a law was passed in the session of 1879–80 which gave to women the control of their own earnings.*   This step in advance was followed by another in 1881, when the Minister of Justice was authorized, by a clause in the budget, to legalize gratuitously marriage settlements, thus abolishing the heavy fees attending such acts and rendering them easier and more frequent.   We may say, however, that the general tendency of Danish law is to place married women, both as regards the control of their property and children, in the absolute power of the husband.

In close connection with this question is the important subject of the employment of women.   The belief, which is especially strong in every nation of Germanic-Gothic origin, that domestic duties are the proper and only sphere of women, has been handed down to us from our ancestors.   Two influences have modified this prejudice :

---

* Mr. Bajer writes me from Copenhagen, under date of February 6, 1883: " The complete text of this law may be found in the *Annuaire de législation étrangère, publié par la Société de Législation Comparée*, Paris, 1881."—T. S.

the necessity of procuring better paid work for single women and the example set by foreign nations, as Sweden, for instance. The State and the municipalities have employed women for the past twenty years, and we find them to-day in the postal, telegraphic and railroad service, in banks, in the government departments, and in the private offices of newspapers and merchants. But the higher posts are still exclusively reserved for men. Women have been refused employment as parliamentary stenographic reporters on account of the political associations which surround the position, as if more harm could come from taking down a speech in short-hand in parliament, than from reading the same speech in the newspapers or listening to it from the galleries. It is scarcely necessary to say that women are paid less than men. This is the case, for instance, in the public schools, where women have taught since 1860, where they perform the same labor as men with the full approbation of the authorities, and where they receive a similar pension after a service of a certain number of years.

University education is highly valued in Denmark, and the State has striven for centuries to improve it. In 1875 women were admitted to the University of Copenhagen—the only one which exists in Denmark—and are allowed to take degrees in every department except theology. The higher and lower forms of instruction—the primary school and the university—are thus open to women. But the whole intermediate stage, the vast field of secondary and professional instruction, depends entirely upon private initiative. It has, therefore, been a serious check to the higher education of women, that everything except the most elementary instruction has been until recently exclusively monopolized by men. The State supports thirteen gymnasia, or boys' colleges, but entirely neglects the other sex. In 1881, a young girl, who wished to prepare herself for the university, applied for instruction in the upper classes of one of these boys' colleges in the country, but after considerable delay the application was refused.

But Danish women have made noble efforts to fill up this gap in the system of female instruction, and the greater part of the talent and energy of the sex has been devoted to this end. Natalie Zahle (1826– ——), holds a prominent position in this field. In 1883 Miss Zahle exercised for the first time the right of conferring degrees—a great novelty in the history of education in Denmark. Her Institute, which was founded at Copenhagen in 1851, besides giving instruction in various branches of knowledge, embraces a normal school, and has established recently a preparatory course for those wishing to pursue university studies. This large establishment, which, in my opinion, is not inferior to similar institutions in other parts of Europe, is almost entirely managed by women, who give instruction in the highest, as well as in the lowest, branches. Our professional schools for girls are due to women and are directed by them. Such, for example, are Miss Caroline Testman's Girls' Commercial School, and the Drawing School and Institute for Arts and Industry, under the management of Mrs. Charlotte Klein. The latter was founded in 1874 when women were refused admission to the Royal Academy of Arts at Copenhagen. Both of these institutions are at the capital. Housekeeping schools for the instruction of servants and ladies in domestic economy are found at Copenhagen, and exist also in the country, for the benefit of peasant girls.

Besides these professional schools, women are also admitted to the *Folkehöjskole*, a peculiar outgrowth of the patriotic movement which swept over Denmark during the first half of this century, and which has spread to Sweden and Norway.* There are at least seventy of these schools in Denmark. Men and women of the highest culture, for the most part disciples of the poet and reformer, Grundtvig, have, especially since the unhappy Sleswick war in 1864, when the existence of our nationality was threatened, delivered semi-annual courses of lectures to the grown-up youth, in order to arouse in them an enthusiasm for the language, literature and history of their native land. Grundtvig planned the *Folkehójskole*, the first school being established in 1844. One of his followers, Cald, extended the benefit of the instruction to peasant girls. It was not until 1864 that the system was generally accepted in Denmark and received aid from the State. That deeply-rooted prejudice against educating the two sexes together has prevented even these liberal-minded teachers from lecturing to men and women at the same time. Co-education exists only in the country primary schools, and it is considered a sign of progress that the two sexes are separated in the cities.

Danish women have always taken an active part in charitable work. Ilia Fibiger (1817–1867), a noble-minded and highly gifted lady, although far from rich, opened her

---

* "The idea was to throw away all finery, all that had not vigor and breadth enough to become public property ; to make religion and patriotism the basis of civilization, and living influence and practical consequence the test of all its elements ; and then by an extensive scheme of education to lift the whole mass of the people up into this reconstructed civilization. And this idea was accepted with such an enthusiasm, and its realization inaugurated with such success, that the small tablet on which the Danish people records its life is, in this moment, one of the most interesting parts of the great picture of modern civilization."—Clemens Petersen, in Johnson's Cyclopædia, article " Danish Language and Literature."—T. S.

own house to seven orphans, and in 1867 founded a sort
of infant asylum which has since been widely imitated. In
1874, Jægerspris, the country seat of Frederick VII., was
bequeathed, along with a large fortune, by his widow, the
Viscountess Danner, for the foundation of an educational
institution for abandoned little girls, and it has since become the grandest charitable establishment in Denmark.
Miss Fibiger also took a prominent part in the movement
for the introduction of women into the sick-room, and set
a good example by offering her services as a nurse in one of
the hospitals of the capital, during the cholera epidemic of
1853. The innovation grew in favor with physicians, but
it was not until 1875 that a systematic organization of female nurses was introduced into our hospitals. There are
training schools for female nurses in the provinces, so that
the profession may now be considered open to women. But
it is a very humble position that these faithful nurses fill,
for the thought has never been entertained of confiding
to them the management of even the most insignificant
hospital. It is only at the Copenhagen training school,
founded in 1862, that the directress occupies an independent and responsible post. In 1876 a branch of the Red
Cross Society was established at Copenhagen.

Turning to woman in literature, we meet for the third
time the name of Ilia Fibiger, one of the most characteristic personages of modern times. Here, too, she appears
as a thorough woman. In poetry and prose she speaks
out plainly in favor of the free development of her sex
according to the laws of nature, and she teaches that the
true woman is not only to be found in the drawing-room
but also in the garret and cellar. Most of the women who
since 1848 have made a name in the literary world have
been animated, like Ilia Fibiger, partly by an interest in

the emancipation of their sex and partly by patriotic enthusiasm. Thus, the works of Pauline Worm (1825– —) display an almost masculine vigor, whether the author points
out with indignation in the novel how young women's
talents are trampled upon and smothered through prejudice, ignorance and stupidity, whether she sings in verse the
praises of her country, or attacks in sharp polemics those
religious doctrines which in her opinion undermine the
patriotism of the nation. The whole life of Mathilda
Fibiger (1830–1872), the sister of Ilia, was a martyrdom
to the independence and liberty of women. The cannon
of the war of 1848 between Denmark and Sleswick awakened her whole soul. Her model was Jeanne Darc, and all
her powerful literary talent was consecrated to the cause
of the admission of women into active life. She fell unquestionably before the resistance which her ideas met
with and which her sensitive nature could not support.
Athalia Schwartz (1821–1871), by her earnest writings on
the question of female education, did a great deal to prepare the advent of the new era in women's instruction
now dawning on Denmark.

If we look back to the past, Danish women of letters
present much the same characteristics as those of other
nations. Biographical and psychological subjects seem to
have been their favorite themes. In the early part of the
century we have the excellent descriptions of every-day life
among the upper classes by Mrs. Gyllembourg (1773–1856),
the mother of the poet Hejberg; Mrs. Hegerman Linden-
crone (1778–1853), and others. The correspondence of
Kamma Rahbek (1775–1829), the Danish Récamier, with
the leading men of her time, gives us a better insight, than
can be found elsewhere, into the inner life of the golden
age of our literature. In the eighteenth century, it is

likewise the correspondence of Charlotte Dorothea Biehl (1731–1788) which unravels for the historian the tangled diplomacy of the epoch. The memoirs of the unhappy Eleonora Christine (1621–1678), daughter of King Christian IV., who passed twenty-two years of her life in prison, depict in an admirable manner the peculiar mixture of grandeur and coarseness of the time, and form a unique memorial of the seventeenth century.* At a still earlier period many Danish gentlewomen collected large libraries in their castles, and rendered a real benefit to literature by preserving and copying the poetry of the Middle Ages.†

Danish women have not as yet accomplished much in the fine arts. It is worthy of note, however, that, in the theatre, where they earliest got fair play, women are by no means inferior to men, but have so distinguished themselves that there is every reason to presume, if it had not been for the impediment of language, names such as Anna Nielsen (— –1856) and Johanne Louise Heiberg (1812– —) would certainly have been known beyond the limits of our little country. Besides the late highly gifted Elizabeth Jerichau-Bauman, who, though born a Pole, was a Dane by adoption, the young Danish school of painting now in process of development contains female artists of great promise.

---

* Eleonora Christine fell into disgrace on account of her great and touching faithfulness to her husband, Carpito Ulfeldt, who was charged, not without cause, with treason to his country and his king. The reigning queen, Sofie Amalie, whose husband was the half brother of Eleonora, was jealous of her rare gifts, both mental and physical. This was, in fact, the real cause of her long imprisonment.—K. F.

† It may not be out of place to mention here the remarkable fact, that probably the most prominent personage who ever sat on the Danish throne was a woman, Margrethe, who died in the year 1412, the reigning queen of Denmark, Norway and Sweden.—K. F.

Among the professions where Danish women have yet to conquer a place is journalism.   They have already participated in discussions in the public prints, but have generally thought it necessary to conceal their personality under a pseudonym.   When, in 1845, for example, Marie Arnesen, a girl of twenty, wrote under the name of Valgerda a vigorous open letter to the aged Professor Arndt, of Bonn, to correct his statements concerning popular feeling in Sleswick, she was most earnestly entreated by her friends not to risk her reputation, by acknowledging her identity with the authorship of this polemic.*

Denmark has produced several journals devoted to the interests of women and edited by women.   The *Friday* (*Fredagen*), issued from July, 1875, to 1879, was conducted by Mrs. Vilhelmine Zahle, sister-in-law of Miss Natalie Zahle, whom I have already mentioned.   It was a bold, radical little sheet.   The name was probably taken from the *Woman's Journal and Friday Society* (*Eruentimmer Tidenden og Fredagsselskabet*), which appeared at Copenhagen, in 1767, under the anonymous editorship of a woman.   The aim of this paper was to improve the condition of women in the limited sphere in which they then moved.   The *Woman's Review* (*Tidsskrift for Kvinder*) began to appear in January, 1882, and is still (1883) in existence.   Its editor, Mrs. Elfride Fibiger, has recently associated with her Mr. Friis, a very earnest friend of the women's movement, who has given a more progressive turn to the paper.   It now advocates women's suffrage,—the first journal in Denmark to take this radical step.

---

* The same thing is true of continental Europe generally.   In France, for instance, several of the most popular contributors to the *Revue des deux mondes*, *Temps*, *Figaro*, and other leading Parisian periodicals, are women who sign their stories and articles with a masculine or fanciful name.—T. S.

It is still more uncommon for our women to appear on the public rostrum; but here too a beginning has been made. Among others, Pauline Worm, but more especially Benedicte Arnesen-Kall (1813– —), the authoress and the sister of Marie Arnesen, have recently, on the platform, brought several subjects successfully before the Danish public.

One of the most striking signs of progress among Danish women are the societies which they have formed during the last ten or twelve years. In 1871 a society auxiliary to the Geneva International Women's Rights Association (*Association internationale pour les droits des femmes*)* was organized, and was soon afterwards transformed into a national association. This organization still exists. As admittance to the Athenæum, the principal reading-room of the metropolis, was refused to women in 1872, a reading-room for their special use was established. This reading-room, as well as the drawing and commercial school for women, although their creation is due entirely to private munificence, have recently received some aid from the government. In 1876 a Society for the Protection of Animals was formed, chiefly through the vigorous exertions of Mrs. Julie Lembcke, and in 1877 an association for the improvement of morals, closely connected with the British Federation opposed to the legalization of prostitution. The Baroness Lili Stampe is the soul of this society.

The examples of individual women striving to do something to advance the interests of their sex are more and more frequent. They have come forward with propositions to modify the marriage ritual in a way more in

---

* For an account of this organization, see the chapter on Switzerland.— T. S.

keeping with the dignity of the sex, and have founded prizes for essays on subjects concerning the woman question. We also meet on every hand girls struggling through all manner of difficulties in order to secure the benefits of a higher education. It is plainly evident that Danish women are weary of the part allotted to them in the old society, a part well characterized by the saying attributed to Thucydides, that the best that can be said of a woman is, that there is nothing to say about her.

I began with the admission that the positive fruits of the women's movement in Denmark are not very conspicuous; I must close by expressing the belief that the future development of the reform will find in this country a well-prepared soil. A lady who once visited Denmark, and who had participated actively in the women's movement in her own land, remarked: "After living in Denmark, I understand why you Danish women are so passive,—you are too well off." This judgment is quite correct. A comparatively humane spirit reigns among all classes in Denmark. Abuses have never been so great that they have cried aloud for correction. Peasant women are not field-laborers, and scandalous lawsuits in the higher circles are infrequent. Hence it is that our women move so slowly, and at the same time act so earnestly when once their minds have been opened to the new doctrines.

It is beyond the scope of this short sketch to enter profoundly into a history of the origin of the women's movement in Denmark. I shall, therefore, treat the subject but briefly. The young Mathilde Fibiger, in her "Letters from Clara Raphael" (*Clara Raphael Breve*) which appeared in 1850, was the first to awaken an earnest discussion of the woman question. This great subject had been treated up to that time only with laughter and mockery by its opponents, and with timid sympathy by its friends. For twenty years thereafter the agitation seemed to sleep. But reports came to us of the activity of the English women; the writings of that original Norwegian author, conservative and radical at one and the same time, Camilla Collett, penetrated Denmark; we learned that in Sweden some of the best men pleaded our cause, and, when the struggle for our national existence ceased for a moment, after 1864, public opinion on the woman question was found to have changed. The sympathetic utterances of the greatest poets of the north —Björnson, Ibsen, Hostrup—have, perhaps, done more than all else to awaken an interest in the subject. The Swedish *Home Review* (*Tidskrift för Hemmet*) has also exercised considerable influence in Denmark.* But if some progress has been made during the last ten years, it is probably due in no small measure to John Stuart Mill's celebrated book, " The Subjection of Women," which was translated into Danish in 1869 by Georg Brandes, the well-known critic, and widely read throughout the country. It was from the educated women of the middle classes that issued the demand for better instruction and better paid employment for their sex, and it has been thought that the movement would keep within those limits. But women are human beings: give them an education and a competency, and they must have all the rest.

---

* For an account of this journal, see the chapter on Sweden.—T. S.

CHAPTER VIII.

FRANCE.

BY THE EDITOR.

CONDORCET, whom Mill, in his "Autobiography," pronounces "one of the wisest and noblest of men," spoke out repeatedly and plainly on the eve of the French Revolution in favor of the rights of women. His "Letters from a Bourgeois of New Haven to a Citizen of Virginia" (*Lettres d'un bourgeois de New Haven à un citoyen de Virginie*), which appeared in 1787, contain an able plea for women's suffrage, and his essay "On the Admission of Women to Citizenship" (*Sur l'admission des femmes au droit de cité**) sounds like an article in the Boston *Woman's Journal* or the London *Englishwoman's Review*. But the great philosopher did not stand alone. Michelet paints a vivid picture of the celebrated orator and member of the Convention, the Abbé Fauchet, speaking in 1790 for women's rights, with Condorcet among his listeners, in the circus, which once stood in the middle of the Palais Royal.† The Abbé Sieyès, Saint Just, and other leaders of the epoch, have left eloquent words in support of women's emancipation.

The press of the Revolution was not silent on the subject. Besides the numerous tracts, pamphlets and even

---

* This essay appeared in the *Journal de la société de 1789*, for July 3, 1790.

† *Les femmes de la révolution*, p. 74.

books which were written for and against the question, several newspapers came out warmly in favor of extended liberty for women. The *Orateur du peuple*, the *Chronique du mois*, which printed articles by Condorcet; the *Bouche de fer*, in which Thomas Paine sometimes wrote; the *Journal de l'état et du citoyen*, the *Cercle social*, and other journals, took up the discussion in a friendly spirit.

But this movement did not spend itself in words alone. The Assembly and the Convention determined to ameliorate the condition of women. The proposed code of the Convention, drawn up by Cambacérès, placed married women on an equality with their husbands, which leads a high legal authority to say, that "such a work of civil legislation was never elaborated in any age or among any people." * In the great question of primary instruction, to cite one more example, the Convention treated alike both boys and girls.

But far more interesting and remarkable is woman's own part in this effort for emancipation. She was no passive spectator.† The "Petition of the Women of the Third Estate to the King" in 1789, is very well written and deals chiefly with the lamentable position of

---

* Emile Acollas, *Le mariage*, p. 98. This is a very able and liberal little book, which presents the whole subject of marriage, both in its legal and moral bearings, in a very instructive and broad-minded manner.

† The historians of the French Revolution have never done full justice to the women of that epoch, sometimes through prejudice and often because of the obscurity which surrounds the subject. As an instance of this latter fact, Michelet (*Les femmes de la révolution*, p. 112) says: "We unfortunately know but little of the history of the women's societies; it is only in the accidental mention of the newspapers, in biographies, etc., that we find some slight traces of them." Lairtuillier (*Les femmes célèbres de la révolution*), has done something toward filling this gap in the literature on the Revolution.

women in the field of work.* Another petition of this same year prays for women's civil and political rights and their admission to the States-General, while still another begs that they be placed on an exact equality with men, and that even the pulpit be opened to them—not a slight request in a Catholic country. The petitioners did not hesitate to solve the most difficult social questions. "Remember that your happiness is absolutely dependent upon that of women," they said to the National Assembly; "the only way perhaps to render it mutually unalterable, is to promulgate a decree obliging men to marry women who have no dower." "The number of these documents makes them more significant and important," says M. Amédée Lefaure, and, I may add on the same authority, they are all the production of women themselves.†

But woman's activity was not confined to petitions. Mlle. d'Orbe, who, as president of one of the women's clubs, pronounced an admirable funeral oration on Mirabeau; the Marchioness of Fontenay (Mme. Tallien), "the woman who saved the city of Bordeaux from massacre,"

---

* Some idea of the industrial position of women prior to the Revolution may be gained from this paragraph by Condorcet (*Sur l'admission des femmes au droit de cité*): " Before the suppression of the *jurandes* [the governing bodies of the old trade corporations] in 1776, women could not acquire the *maîtrise* [the right to the complete exercise of a trade] of a milliner and of other callings, unless married, or unless a man lent or sold them the use of his name, in order that they might obtain the privilege. It is quite singular that a woman could be regent in France, but, until 1776, she might not be a milliner at Paris." Millinery is one of the few occupations which women have latterly gained from men.

† *Le socialisme pendant la révolution.* This book is most liberal in its treatment of the woman question, and contains very curious information concerning the part women played in the upheaval of 1789.

says Legouvé,* "and snatched Paris from the Reign of Terror;" Théroigne de Méricourt, who shouldered the musket in the revolutionary cause ;† Rose Lacombe, the leader of the women's clubs; Olympe de Gouges, the author of the "Declaration of the Rights of Women," and of a score of volumes on all sorts of social questions, are a few of the less known names of a long list of women, who in courage, generosity, breadth of mind, extravagance and acts of savagery, even, were unsurpassed by the men of the epoch.

Either singly or in mass, women were the authors of some of the most important episodes of the Revolution. The initiative act of the struggle, the famous petition of the Champ de Mars, which demanded that " neither Louis XVI., nor any other king," should be recognized, was drawn up by a woman, Mme. Robert, *née* Kéralio.‡ In the

---

* *Histoire morale de la femme*, p. 398.

† " The ballot and bullet argument," as it has been called, is often brought forward against women's suffrage. If you vote, you must fight, say the opponents of the enfranchisement of women. The defenders of women's political claims then cite the large number of women who, in all ages and in all countries, have borne arms. An obscure but very striking example of a would-be female warrior recently came to my notice. Mlle. Julie Jussot, of Vergigny, in the department of the Yonne, was placed on the official birth-register under the masculine name, by mistake, of Jules. On reaching twenty-one recently, she received a communication from the mayor of her *commune*, informing her that the moment for military service had arrived. She responded promptly, but on learning her sex, the authorities erased her name from the list of conscripts. In a letter to me, which, by its style and hand-writing, betokens a woman of considerable education, Mlle. Jussot says : " In regard to the conscripts' flag, I demanded permission to carry it, for one's heart ought always to be French, when the defence of one's country is concerned. If the day of revenge comes, although I am not a man, I assure you, sir, that France may count on me to defend her soil." This sentiment has the true ring of a Jeanne Darc.

‡ Michelet, *Les femmes de la révolution*, p. 188.

storming of the Bastille and at the *fête* of the Federation, Michelet pronounces women the prime movers. It was their energetic conduct which crowned with success the events of the 5th and 6th of October, 1789, and brought Louis from Versailles to Paris. A French historian has truly said: " Women were the advance-guard of the Revolution." *

Thus the advocacy of great men, and the activity and vigor of women themselves, seemed in the early days of the Revolution to portend the opening of a new era for the female sex. But the authors of the revolt wished only to use the women for the advancement of their own ends. No sooner was the insurrection gotten well under way, than they deserted their worthy coadjutors. In the beginning they encouraged them in the foundation of clubs, and applauded their ardor in the cause, only to abolish these clubs, check this ardor, and finally thrust them back into their old position when the end was gained.† Mirabeau, Danton, Robespierre, *et al.*, soon put a period to this women's movement. The Republic was gradually merged into the Empire, which was the *coup de grâce* of the aspirations of the women of 1789. The Empire not only dissipated their day-dreams, but it fastened the Napoleonic Code about their necks. This was a fatal moment for women's interests. The general public had not forgotten the many disorders in which they had participated, and was unfriendly. The codifiers were dry old followers of the Roman law, and Bonaparte, woman's evil genius, was all powerful. The spirit with which he entered upon the task may be judged by this remark to his

---

* *Les femmes de la révolution*, p. 24.

† Legouvé, *Histoire morale de la femme*, p. 405.

colleagues: " A husband ought to have absolute control over the actions of his wife; he has the right to say to her: madam, you shall not go out; madam, you shall not go to the theatre; madam, you shall not see such or such a person."*

Then came the Restoration and its philosopher, M. de Bonald, who pronounces the *ipse dixit*, " man and woman are not equals, and can never become so." Divorce is abolished, and an attempt is made by the government to re-establish primogeniture.† But this period contained at least one happy event—the birth of the socialistic schools, which, if they have sometimes brought the woman question into bad odor, have also done a great deal to ameliorate the condition of the female sex.‡

---

* Napoleon's misogyny was fully reciprocated. Mme. de Staël's hatred of the Emperor is well known. Ségur, (*Les femmes*), states that the women disliked Napoleon because of his wholesale slaughter of their sons on the field of battle. These mothers had perhaps more ground for their antipathy than the high-strung exile of Coppet. One of the bright spots in this dark period was the appearance in 1801 of Legouvé's " Women's Merit " (*Le mérite des femmes*), a rather heavy poem to-day, but which had a great success at a time when women were without friends at court, and few persons were disposed to sing their praises. Even this poetical defence of women was not allowed to go unanswered. Ménegault published, in this same year, " Men's Merit " (*Le mérite des hommes*), in imitation of Legouvé's poem, and as a set-off to it.

† This would have been a tremendous blow to women, for, as will be seen further on in this chapter, the French law of inheritance places daughters on an absolutely equal footing with sons, one of the very few provisions of the Napoleonic Code which treats women with the same justice as men.

‡ An old Saint Simonian, one of the dozen still alive, M. Charles Lemonnier, once told me that it was due to the efforts of his sect that women are employed by the railroad companies as guards at the highway crossings. The first railroad in France, that between Paris and St. Germain, which was inaugurated in the early days of Louis Philippe's reign, introduced this custom,

With the liberal re-awakening of 1830, the woman question again came to the front. The socialists, individual women, societies, and newspapers, began to take up the subject. Among the women's rights journals were *La femme nouvelle*, which appeared from 1832 to 1834, and the *Gazette des femmes*, which was published from 1836 to 1838, under the editorship of Mme. Poutret de Mauchamps. She based her agitation on the *Charte* or Constitution of 1830, and took the position that, in proclaiming the political emancipation of Frenchmen, the generic term was used, so that the new charter of liberties necessarily included Frenchwomen in its provisions.*

Mme. de Mauchamps appears to have understood the importance of attaching some well-known personages to her agitation. One of the articles is headed, "Men, Worthy of the Name, who Demand the Civil and Political Rights of Women." Then follows a list of some Parisian celebrities, and among others, Jules Janin, the distinguished critic of the *Journal des débats*, and Châteaubriand. The readers of the *Gazette* are informed that the latter "has called and said to us, 'Count me among your subscribers ; you defend a grand and noble cause.' " Jules Janin contributes at least one article to the paper, a fine estimate of George Sand ; and Charles Nodier, the

---

and I never see one of these sturdy women, as the train whizzes by, a baton at her shoulder, without thinking that the eccentric Saint Simon accomplished some practical good in the world.

* Mme. de Mauchamps held that *les français*, as employed in the *Charte*, embraced *les françaises*, and that *tous, chacun*, etc., wherever they occur in that document, refer to women as well as to men. She therefore addressed a petition to the King, with the following heading : " Petition of Frenchwomen to Louis Philippe I., praying that he declare, in virtue of the Charter of 1830, that he is King of Frenchwomen as he is King of Frenchmen " (*qu'il est roi des françaises comme il est roi des français*).

prolific author and member of the Academy, writes a short book review in one of the numbers.*

Every issue of the *Gazette des femmes* begins with a petition to the King and Parliament, praying for reforms in the Code, for political rights, for the admission of women to the Institute,† etc. In the number for January, 1838, a demand was made that women be admitted to the universities and given degrees. It was forty years before France would listen to this petition, and what was asked under the Orleans monarchy is only just beginning to be granted under the Third Republic. And yet these petitions, ably drawn up, and sensible in their claims, several times reported and briefly discussed, were heaped with ridicule in the Chamber and quickly forgotten.

That this movement had attracted a share of public attention is evidenced in many ways. The *Gazette* informs us that at one of the elections several voters, instead of casting their ballots for the candidate, gave them to his wife, as a protest against the exclusion of women from the franchise. Mme. Hortense Allart de Méritens, the novelist and historian, writes to the editor of the approaching foundation of an "Association for the Amelioration of Women's Condition," but I find no further mention of this

---

* Nodier could not have been under the influence of Mme. de Mauchamps when he penned for *Le dictionnaire de la conversation* his paper entitled *La femme libre.*

† Alexandre Dumas said in the French Academy a short time ago : "We frequently, and very justly, invoke the authority of Mme. de Sévigné and Mme. de Staël, and yet, if these two celebrated women were alive to-day, we would not give them a seat in our midst. We have, perhaps, been sometimes struck by this contradiction, by this injustice, and we must have said to ourselves : 'As woman can be man's equal in virtue and intelligence, why may she not also be his equal in society, in our institutions, and before the law?' "—Report on the Botta Prize, sitting of May 10, 1881.

16

organization. In September, 1834, appeared the *Amazone*. The National Library contains only the prospectus of this paper, which was to be a daily for " the political education of women," and which was to treat the question in a serio-comic vein.* The agitation attracted the attention of Mme. de Girardin, who refers to it several times in her brilliant " Parisian Letters " (*Lettres Parisiennes*).

Laboulaye's " Inquiries concerning the Civil and Political Condition of Women from the Times of the Romans to the Present " (*Recherches sur la condition civile et politique des femmes depuis les Romains jusqu'à nos jours*), and Legouvé's " Moral History of Woman " (*Histoire morale de la femme* †), both appeared during the reign of Louis Philippe, and did a great deal to direct the public mind to the lamentable condition of women before the law. M. Legouvé's book, conceived in a very liberal spirit, and written in a charming style, was soon read all over Europe. " Equality in difference " (" *l'égalité dans la différence* ") is its key-note. " The question is not to make woman a man, but to complete man by woman," says the author in another part of the volume.

While this Platonic consideration of the woman question was in progress, the Revolution of February suddenly burst upon France, and for a moment it seemed as if the

---

* Its epigraph was as follows :

> *Les hommes ne sont pas ce qu'un vain sexe pense,*
> *Ils sont trop étourdis pour gouverner la France.*

† Although this work was published after the advent of the Revolution of February, its contents had been delivered as a series of lectures at the College of France during the last year of the July monarchy. M. Legouvé is the son of the author of *Le mérite des femmes*, to which poem reference has already been made, and, for a Frenchman, holds very advanced ideas on the woman question.

era of the actual emancipation of women had come at last. But the magnificent dreams of the Second Republic were, in so far as concerned women, never realized. " In 1848 there was a grand agitation," Laboulaye once wrote me, " great demands, but I know of nothing durable or solid on this question." " The intrigues and fatal days of June, 1848, and June, 1849, absorbed public attention," Jeanne Deroin Desroches* writes me; " men of influence took little interest in social questions, and especially that of the emancipation of women. We were finally prohibited from having anything to do with the political clubs,† and the police aided in the getting up of meetings and societies of women, such as that of the *Vésuviennes*, composed of prostitutes, which burlesqued everything we said and did, in order to cast ridicule and contempt on our meetings and our acts." In a word, the movement of 1848—and there was a great movement at this epoch—was swallowed up in Socialism, and Socialism destroyed itself by its own extravagance.

But the women had some staunch friends at this time. Victor Considérant, the well-known disciple of Fourier, was "the only one of the nine hundred members of the Con-

---

* Mme. Desroches, one of the enthusiasts and martyrs of this period, is now living at an advanced age, at Shepherd's Bush, near London.

† It was a Protestant Minister, Athanase Coquerel, the most distinguished member of the celebrated family of clergymen, the Beecher family of France, who laid before the Chamber the bill for the exclusion of women from the clubs. He was very roughly handled for this act by several feminine pens. See *Almanach des femmes* for 1852. This curious little publication, in French and English, was due to the indefatigable Jeanne Deroin. The first number, which appeared at Paris in 1852, was seized by the police, and the subsequent numbers, those for 1853 and 1854, were issued at London. These modest little annuals throw a flood of light on a very confused period.

stituent," writes Jeanne Deroin, "who demanded women's political rights in the Committee on the Constitution." When, in the summer of 1851, it was proposed in the Chamber to deny women the right of petition in political affairs, M. Laurent, of the Department of the Ardèche, M. Schœlcher, the celebrated Abolitionist, the Garrison of France, and M. Crémieux, opposed the proposition, and it was defeated.* When the subject of the reorganization of the communes came up, in November, 1851, M. Pierre Leroux, the famous Socialistic Radical, offered an amendment to the first article of the bill, to the effect that "the body of electors be composed of French men and women of legal age." He supported his amendment in a speech which filled three columns of the official newspaper, and which was received by the Chamber with shouts of laughter.†

The Revolution of 1848 was as fecund in newspapers as it was in socialistic Utopias. Among the former were many women's journals. I have run over some of these and found them highly interesting, often amusing, but always sincere and earnest. *La politique des femmes*, "published in the interest of women by a society of working women," as we are informed, and which became, later, *L'opinion des femmes*, and *La voix des femmes*, edited by Mme. Eugénie Niboyet, a woman of considerable literary talent who died in 1882, are, perhaps, two of the best specimens of these women's rights' papers.

The French propensity to turn everything to ridicule— and there was, indeed, much material for its gratification at this time—found an outlet in *La république des femmes*, "the journal of the petticoats" (*cotillons*), as its

---

* See the *Moniteur*, June 24 and July 3, 1851.
† Id., November 22, 1851.

sub-title reads, which appeared in June, 1848, and poked fun at the women who participated in the public life of the day.

In April, 1851, M. Chapot proposed in the Legislative Assembly to restrain the right of petition in the case of men, and to suppress it entirely for women in all matters of a political nature. Jeanne Deroin, confined at St. Lazare as a political prisoner, issued a vigorous protest from her cell. M. Laurent presented this petition and attacked the Chapot resolution. A debate ensued, and the question was adjourned to July 2d. On that date M. Schœlcher, who is to-day a member of the Senate, offered an amendment protecting women's right of petition. M. Crémieux, who was later a member of the Government of National Defence, seconded the amendment, which was finally adopted. The Chapot resolution was then unanimously rejected.

But the Republic fell, and the Second Empire rose on its ruins. The women's movement was abruptly checked. In 1858 Proudhon published " Justice in the Church and in the Revolution " (*La justice dans l'église et dans la révolution*), in which occurs an extended sociologic study of woman. He favors the androgynous couple as the social unit, without, however, attributing an equivalent value to the two parties who constitute it. Man, he says, is to woman in the proportion of three to two. The inferiority of the latter is, consequently, according to Proudhon, irremediable. Newspaper articles, pamphlets and books, attacking this volume, appeared in large numbers, and among them, Mme. Jenny P. d'Héricourt's " The Enfranchised Woman," (*La femme affranchie*), and Mme. Juliette Lambery's (Mme. Adam) " Anti-Proudhonian Ideas on Love, Woman, and Marriage " (*Idées antiproud-*

honiennes sur l'amour, la femme et le mariage), which Professor Acollas pronounces "the most eloquent and the most peremptory refutation of the absurd opinions of P. J. Proudhon on woman." *

The writings of Michelet, Jules Simon, Emile de Girardin, Eugène Pelletan, Leroy-Beaulieu, Emile Deschanel, Mlle. Julie Daubié, and many others, touching upon different phases of the woman question, belong to this or a little later period. Michelet, in his "Woman" (*La femme*) and "Love" (*L'amour*), establishes his famous theory of the "sick woman" (*la femme malade*); Jules Simon, in his "Working Woman" (*L'ouvrière*); Leroy-Beaulieu, in his "Women's Work in the Nineteenth Century" (*Le travail des femmes au dixneuvième siècle*); and Mlle. Daubié, in "The Poor Woman of the Nineteenth Century" (*La femme pauvre au dixneuvième siècle*), show up the lamentable industrial position of women; Emile de Girardin calls attention to the condition of woman in the family; while Eugène Pelletan, in his volume entitled "The Mother" (*La mère*), demands the suffrage for women.† The opinions of these thoughtful and liberal-minded writers had a powerful influence on French public opinion, and prepared the way for those reforms in favor of women, some of which have already occurred, and others of which must follow in the near future, unless the reactionary party once more gets the upper hand.

---

* *Le mariage*, p. 35, note.

† "By keeping woman outside of politics, we diminish by one-half the soul of the country."—*La mère*, p. 233. The late M. Rodière, the distinguished Professor of the Toulouse Law School, in his "Great Jurisconsults" (*Les grands jurisconsultes*), published in 1874, is outspoken in favor of women's suffrage. See pp. 509–512. His language is the more remarkable from the fact that he was a strict Catholic, and, at the same time, a republican, a very rare combination in the France of to-day.

The women's movement took on a more organized form during the last years of the Empire, and M. Léon Richer grouped about himself and his paper, *L'avenir des femmes*, which still exists as *Le droit des femmes*, the more active friends of the question, and succeeded in securing the support of many distinguished writers and statesmen.

Under the Third Republic the woman question, like every other liberal measure, has gained new life and vigor. At the beginning of 1871, Mlle. Julie Daubié, "one of the worthiest women I have ever known," says Laboulaye, announced in the public prints the approaching organization of an Association for Women's Suffrage, but died before accomplishing her object.*

In 1874, at the time of the discussion of the new electoral law in the Versailles Assembly, M. Raudot, of the Right, proposed that every married elector or widower with a child should have two votes. Another deputy, M. de Belcastel, was in favor of the same proportion, but would give the widower two votes whether he had children or not. The Count de Douhet went still further: he would give every man, first a vote for himself, another for his wife, and finally one for each child. The committee to which these projects were referred accepted the principle, and article seventh of the bill which they reported read as follows: "Every married elector, or widower with children or grandchildren, shall have a double vote." Although this article was rejected, it shows that there are men in France who think that women and the family are not sufficiently represented under the present electoral system.

---

* "Mlle. Daubié," Mme. Griess-Traut writes me, "was the first female bachelor of arts in France. She encountered great difficulty in obtaining her diploma, but succeeded in 1862, I think."

In the summer of 1878 occurred at Paris the first International Women's Rights Congress, due in large part to
the exertions of M. Léon Richer. The Organizing Committee contained representatives from six different countries, viz.: France, Switzerland, Italy, Holland, Russia, and
America. Among the eighteen members from Paris were
two senators, five deputies, and three Paris municipal
councilors. Italy was represented by a deputy and the
late Countess of Travers. The American members were
Julia Ward Howe, Mary A. Livermore, and Theodore Stanton. Among the members of the Congress, besides those
just mentioned, were Colonel T. W. Higginson, and deputies, senators, publicists, journalists, and men and women
of letters from all parts of Europe. The work of the Congress was divided into five sections, as follows: the
historical, the educational, the economic, the moral, and
the legislative. The proceedings of these different sections have been published in a volume, which forms a
valuable collection of the most recent European and
American thought on the various phases of the woman
question. *

About this time was founded the Society for the Amelioration of the Condition of Women, of which Mlle. Maria
Deraismes and Mme. Griess-Traut are the moving spirits.
In 1876 Mlle. Hubertine Auclert, radical, earnest, indefatigable, established a Woman's Rights Society, whose
special aim is to secure the suffrage for women, and in
February, 1881, appeared the first number of its uncom-
promising organ, *La citoyenne*. Mme. Koppe, who though
poor in purse is rich in purpose, published at Paris, from
1880 to 1882, *La femme dans la famille et la société*, a

---

* *Actes du congrès international des droits des femmes*; Paris: Ghio, Palais-
Royal.

little journal which advocated bravely every good reform. In the autumn of 1882 two new women's rights associations were organized. M. Léon Richer created the French Women's Rights League, whose principal object is to improve the legal condition of French women, and Mlle. Hubertine Auclert converted her Women's Rights Society into a National Women's Suffrage Society, whose aims are sufficiently indicated by its name. During the past few years, mainly through Mlle. Auclert's efforts, meetings have been held and petitions signed in favor of women's suffrage both at Paris and in the provinces. But the reformers have encountered great opposition. Here is one remarkable example of this selected from a large number. M. de Goulard, Minister of the Interior in 1873, refused to allow Mme. Olympe Audouard, whose voice and pen have always been devoted to the interests of her sex, to speak at Paris on the woman question " for three reasons." Here are two of them : " 1. These lectures are only a pretext to bring together a body of women already too emancipated. 2. The theories of Mme. Olympe Audouard on the emancipation of women are subversive, dangerous, immoral." *

We have now glanced rapidly at the principal features

---

* Besides the books already mentioned in the course of the preceding pages, I give here, for the reader who may wish to examine more thoroughly this interesting subject, the titles of two short volumes written in a friendly spirit, and treating the question in a general manner. *La femme libre,* by M. Léon Richer; Paris : E. Dentu, Palais-Royal. *Essai sur la condition des femmes en Europe et en Amérique,* by M. Léon Giraud ; Paris : Auguste Ghio, Palais-Royal. M. Richer's *L'avenir des femmes* (Paris, 4 rue des Deux Gares), a monthly publication, and Mlle. Hubertine Auclert's *La citoyenne* (Paris, 12 rue Cail), also a monthly, give a good idea of current opinion in France on the woman question.

of the more radical phase of the women's movement in France since 1789 up to the present day. I shall next consider the actual situation, treating it under separate heads, as follows: 1. Laws; 2. Morals; 3. Religion; 4. Charity; 5. Instruction; 6. Literature; 7. Fine Arts; 8. Industry; 9. Socialism.

"The Revolution, as has already been seen, signally failed," writes M. Léon Giraud,* "in all that concerned woman. Especially in establishing her legal status did it deviate widely from its principles. This was due in no small degree to the writings of Rousseau. In his *Émile*, Rousseau discusses the theory of woman considered as a child, and adopts the principle of virile and non-virile functions which constituted the basis of ancient Roman law, but which the jurisconsults of the second and third centuries of our era had already begun to repudiate.† Curiously

---

* M. Léon Giraud, *docteur-en-droit*, is a graduate of the Paris Law School. His legal studies early convinced him of the necessity of a complete revision of the laws affecting the family. He gave himself wholly up to this subject, and sought, in travels in foreign countries, the justification of his own theories. His work on the "Condition of Woman in Europe and America" (*Essai sur la condition de la femme en Europe et en Amérique*) was sent to the French Academy in 1883, in competition for the Botta prize, and gave rise to a warm discussion in that learned body. In this synthesis of the woman question, the author comes out in favor of female suffrage. Hence the originality of the book and the cause of its ill-success at the Academy. An earlier volume, bearing the rather odd title, the "Romance of the Christian Woman" (*Le roman de la femme chrétienne*), was historical in its nature, and considered from an entirely new point of view the subject of the conversion of woman to Christianity. Various pamphlets and articles for periodicals preceded these publications. Among the former may be mentioned "Souvenirs of the Women's Rights Congress" (*Souvenirs du congrès pour le droit des femmes*), written apropos of the first International Women's Rights Congress, held at Paris in 1878.

† Gaius's "Institutes," Book I., § 190.—L. G.

enough Portalis's preliminary considerations on marriage
in the introduction to the Napoleonic code, are taken in
large part almost *verbatim* from *Émile.** Never, in a
word, was the idea of justice to women more foreign to
any code of laws than to that of 1804.

"Let us first consider married women. In the new
code, as in the old, they lose independence and become
incapable of ownership, with all its rights and privileges.
Of the different matrimonial systems placed by the code at
the disposition of the contracting parties, none guarantees
woman's liberty. Under none may the wife act, in regard
to her property, with the same freedom as the most ignorant man. In one case—the system of 'community of
goods' (*communauté de biens*)—she is treated as if weak-
minded and in need of a committee; in another—the system
by which each spouse is left the separate owner of his or
her property (*séparation de biens*)—she is looked upon as a
prodigal requiring a guardian. These variations of the old
idea, that the wife should be in subordination, are based
on principles borrowed from the common law (*coutumes*)
of the sixteenth century, and, in certain cases, are even
severer on women than the prescriptions of three hundred
years ago.

"It is true that the civil code says, with odd *naïveté* or
singular assurance, that the matrimonial systems which it
presents are only illustrations, limiting in no respect the
liberty of the contracting parties.† But do not believe it.
This pretended liberty is defined by the article which im-

---

* Compare Fenet's "Preliminary Reports" (*Travaux préparatoires*), Vol.
IX., pp. 177 *et seq.*, and all the first part of the fifth book of *Émile.*—L. G.

† The law does not regulate the conjugal union, as regards property, except in default of special conventions which the spouses may make as they
see fit. * * * —Civil Code, Art. 1387.

mediately follows, and which informs us that there is a marital authority, a husband who is the head of the family in this new code as in the old.*   And several other articles occur farther on in the code, thrice repeating the wife's subordination, stating what deprivations public order and morality require of her, and especially divesting her of that right *par excellence* of ownership, the alienation and free disposition of her property.†   It may be understood from this what is meant, when woman is concerned, by those 'imprescriptible' and 'inalienable' rights which were the motto of the Revolution; they are the rights which the husband has over the wife !   This statement must be read twice before it can be believed.   But the tenor of our law, which nobody questions, and the constant practice of eighty years, leave us no room for doubt.

" The right of alienation, which is an inherent attribute of ownership, and which, according to the economic principles of 1789, was so inseparable from the idea of property that the one could not be understood without the other—even mortmain having been abolished for the simple reason of its restrictive character—this right is a myth in so far as it relates to woman.   And yet this same woman

---

* The spouses may annul neither the rights resulting from the marital authority over the person of the wife and children, nor those pertaining to the husband as head of the family.   *   *   *   —Civil Code, Art. 1388.

†   *   *   *   she [the wife separated from her husband] may not alienate her real estate without the husband's consent.   *   *   *   —Civil Code, Art. 1449.   The husband retains the control of the real and personal property of the wife, and, consequently, the right to the revenues derived from her dower or from property coming to her during the marriage.   *   *   *   —*Id.*, Art. 1538.   *   *   *   she [the wife] may not alienate them [paraphernalia] or go to law concerning them, without the husband's consent.   *   *   *   —*Id.*, Art. 1576.

was solemnly declared, by the reform of the laws of succession, capable of absolute ownership and of a personal
and exclusive title to public riches. The daughter who,
as Pothier informs us, was formerly passed over in favor
of the sons as regards the greater part if not all of the
estate, inherits equally with the male children according
to the code of 1804, as was also the case in 1792. Neither
distinction of sex nor primogeniture is recognized in our
present laws of descent.* The daughter, who once
counted as a fraction or a zero, is now an integer. This
reform has become a permanent part of our legislation.
When in 1826, under the Restoration, a bill was laid before parliament for the re-establishment of primogeniture,
the effort broke down completely. But once married,
this same woman ceases to be an owner in the true signification of the word. Either our law of inheritance is
nonsense or our marriage system an error. We must accept one or the other conclusion. Our legislators cannot
consistently pronounce such contradictions in one and
the same breath, without displaying an absence of philosophy and logic, to be explained only on the ground of
complete indifference to the best interests of woman.

" If we now consider the more intimate relations existing between husband and wife and the authority of parents over children, we find that the dominant idea which
inspires this portion of our code has also been handed
down from the sixteenth century.

"Conjugal fidelity is declared reciprocal in a singularly
untruthful article,† and yet the husband and wife are in

---

* The children or their heirs inherit * * * without distinction of
sex or birth.—Civil Code, Art. 745.

† The spouses owe each other mutual fidelity, succor and assistance.—
Civil Code, Art. 212.

no respects treated alike. The latter is held strictly to account for any moral laxity, under penalty of separation,* and even of several years' imprisonment,† while the former has only to guard against one thing—the law declares it formally—persistent concubinage.‡ It is in fact polygamy which the law condemns. But the definition of marriage would have been sufficient to prohibit this. The wife, therefore, must submit to every license on the pa.. of her husband until this extreme is reached, and even then he is only slightly fined.§

" The father alone, as long as he lives, enjoys authority over the children.‖ He has custody over them, he may punish them, he superintends their education ; when they would marry, it is his consent which must be obtained.¶

---

* The husband may demand a divorce on account of his wife's adultery.—Civil Code, Art. 229.

† The wife convicted of adultery shall be punished with imprisonment for at least three months and not more than two years.—Penal Code, Art. 337.

‡ The wife may demand a divorce on account of her husband's adultery when he shall have kept his concubine under the common roof.—Civil Code, Art. 230. The first and last of the three foregoing articles are no longer in force on account of the abolition of divorce, but they are given as showing the spirit of the code.

§ The husband who shall have kept a concubine under the common roof, and who shall have been convicted thereof on the complaint of the wife, shall be punished by a fine from one hundred to two thousand francs.—Penal Code, Art. 339.

‖ The child, at whatever age, should honor and respect his father and mother.—Civil Code, Art. 371. He is subject to their authority until his majority or emancipation.—*Id.*, Art. 372. The father alone exercises this authority during marriage.—*Id.*, Art. 373. The last article destroys the force of the first two,—one of the many absurd contradictions of this much-vaunted French code.

¶ The son under twenty-five and the daughter under twenty-one may not marry without the consent of their father and mother ; in case of disagreement, the consent of the father suffices.—Civil Code, Art. 148. Could anything be more nonsensical than such an article as this ?

The mother is regarded legally as if she did not exist. When she becomes a widow, her inferiority is further emphasized, for she is still kept under a sort of marital power which discredits her in the eyes of her children. This situation is not justified on the specious pretext of the necessity of there being a head as between two rivals, and its character is the more humiliating for this very reason. The widow is indeed made the legal guardian of her children, but her husband on dying may impose upon her an adviser, without whose consent she cannot exercise the duties of guardianship,—which amounts to taking away with one hand what is given with the other.* It is scarcely necessary to say, that the dying mother possesses no such prerogatives in respect to the widower. Again, the widow who marries may see the guardianship of her children pass completely from her control to that of a custodian, named by a family council.† Furthermore, the power of sending children to prison undergoes a singular modification when transferred from the father to the mother, becoming less energetic in her hands.‡

"Such are the principal features of woman's position in the family. But she has other disabilities than those already mentioned. For example, she may not be a guardian nor a member of a family council, except in the ascending line, as mothers and grandmothers; she may not be a witness to any legal document, nor the publisher of a political newspaper; she may not call a public meeting.§ Nor is this all, but from these facts we readily per-

---

* Civil Code, Art. 391.
† Civil Code, Art. 395.
‡ Compare Civil Code, Arts. 376 and 381.
§ This list might be made much larger. But, more important than the number of these disabilities, is the unwillingness shown by French legis

ceive what is the legal status of woman in France, and are able to judge whether the wife and mother, in the narrow sphere to which she has been relegated, enjoys the influence and rank which she merits.

"We now take up the grave question of the young girl. And this brings us face to face with the important subject of affiliation (*la recherche de la paternité*). According to our code every child born outside of wedlock is considered to be fatherless,* unless, of his own free will, the father formally acknowledges his offspring. Statistics show what a poor resource this is for the bastard: it occurs but once in fifty times.† In no case, except rape, which is almost unknown in France, can the father of an illegitimate child be prosecuted. He is under no obligations to the child any more than to the mother. A promise of marriage, even when made in writing, counts for nothing. A cohabitation extending over many years, even a whole life-time, creates, in the eyes of the law, no presumption against the man. The same thing is true of any private papers containing reiterated avowal of

lators to remove any of them. One instance of this is worth citing : In the month of March, 1881, M. de Gasté introduced into the Chamber of Deputies a bill making women electors for the tribunals of commerce, which decide many of the differences arising between tradesmen. The bill did not pass, and Gambetta, who was then Speaker, seized the occasion to perpetrate a witticism at the expense of the women. It should be remembered that in no country of the world are there so many women occupying important and independent positions in trade, as in France.

* Affiliation is forbidden.   * * *   —Civil Code, Art. 340.

† For valuable details on this subject of affiliation, see the remarkable report of Senators Schœlcher, de Belcastel, Foucher de Careil and Bérenger, which was printed in the *Journal Officiel* of May 15, 1878. See also the bill of M. de Lacretelle on the re-establishment of turning-boxes (*tours*) introduced the same year. It may be added that the Senate took no action on either of these propositions.—L. G.

paternity and of measures taken, either at birth or later, for the maintenance and support of the child.* A man may employ every means in his power, short of brute force, to seduce a girl, but no reparation can be obtained. Such is the harsh doctrine of our law. The truth of this statement cannot be questioned. The text of the code, the preparatory reports and the practice of our courts, all agree in this interpretation. Since the promulgation of the Napoleonic code, four score years ago, you cannot find in the whole history of French jurisprudence one single case of a man forced to acknowledge his child. Our ancient jurisprudence contained this maxim: 'The author of the child must support it' (*'qui a fait l'enfant doit le nourrir'*).† What a change from one epoch to another! It could not be more complete.‡

---

* The proposition of M. Demolombe, one of our first jurisconsults, to make affiliation depend on the treatment of the child as one's own (*possession d'état*), met with no favor. See Demolombe's Commentaries on Arts. 319 *et seq.*—L. G.

† Loysel's " Institutes of Common Law " (*Institutes coutumières*).—L. G.

‡ One example selected from thousands may be given to prove, that not only are the statements of the text not exaggerated, but that they are even too mild. M. Alexandre Dumas has just published a powerful arraignment of the French code in its treatment of affiliation. The pamphlet was called forth by a recent decision of the French Court of Appeals. Mlle. G—— became a domestic in the house of M. G——, a farmer and married relative much older than herself. They became intimate and two children were born. Mlle. G—— found a place at Paris, when M. G—— ceased to aid her. Thereupon her guardian sued for damages, basing his claim on seduction, the youth of Mlle. G——, and the fact that her seducer was her relative and should have been her protector. The provincial court, where the case was tried, condemned M. G—— to pay 6,000 francs. He appealed, and the Paris Court of Appeals decided on June 28, 1883, that the seduction had not been accomplished by actionable means, and that M. G—— was responsible only before " the tribunal of his own conscience." It reversed

"And does the State, since it does not hold the father responsible for his illegitimate children, do anything to supply his place? At the beginning of the century, and almost up to the second half, the country undertook on a large scale the care of foundlings, by the establishment of turning-boxes (*tours*), which allowed the unfortunate mother to deposit secretly, and without being subjected to any formalities, her child in the hands of those who would care for it. But, strange to say, at the moment when the turning-boxes were the most necessary on account of the increasing number of abandoned infants, they were gradually suppressed (from 1840 to 1860). In a word, the State in its turn forsook the children and broke the solemn promise, given the mothers of France in 1811, to repair in part the great injustice done them, when it relieved the fathers of all the duties of paternity. Abortion and infanticide consequently increased, until they have reached such a point that the juries, weary of punishing without producing any effect, now often simply acquit the culprit. Such is the present situation: the seducer responsible neither to the child nor its mother; the latter, if poor, reduced to infanticide or prostitution.

"And what does the code do to protect the girl? Almost nothing. While it affords man every facility for the gratification of his passions, it shows an indifference for woman to be found probably in no other system of laws. We guard the girl up to the age of thirteen, but

---

the decision of the lower court, and ordered the poor girl not only to return the 6,000 francs, but to pay costs. Such inhumanity seems almost impossible at Paris, "the capital of civilization," and in the last quarter of the nineteenth century. And yet the creation of this abominable code is considered one of the greatest of Napoleon's honors.

beyond that year she must look out for herself.* The code does not shield her, but rather shields the man. From 1832 to 1863, in which year the law was put on the statute book, the young girl was protected only until the age of eleven, and previous to 1832, girls of the tenderest years might be defiled, provided violence was not used † Is not the source to be found here of many of the cancerous evils which are fast eating out the life of our social system?

"Is woman sufficiently protected when, according to our penal code and the firmly-established practice of our courts, the inciting of minors to debauch, even when systematic and long-continued, is not punishable, provided the debaucher is seeking to gratify his own passions and is not acting the part of a pander? ‡ Is she sufficiently protected when the father, who has made a traffic of his daughter's virtue, does not thereby lose paternal authority over the other children, who still remain subject to his exclusive and dishonorable control? § Is she sufficiently protected when the husband's adultery is permitted up to a point where it becomes almost complete impunity? Is she sufficiently protected when our system of legalized prostitution owes its very existence to the con-

---

* Any outrage on decency consummated or attempted without violence on the person of a child of either sex under thirteen years of age, shall be punished with imprisonment * * * —Penal Code, Art. 331.

† See commentary on Arts. 331 and 332 of the Penal Code.

‡ Whoever outrages public morals by habitually inciting, aiding or abetting the debauchery or corruption of the youth of either sex under twenty-one years of age, shall be punished * * * —Penal Code, Art. 334. The commentary on this article reads : "Art. 334 is inapplicable to him who, in inciting minors to debauch, is acting for himself and not for others." Three decisions of the Supreme Court, supporting this view, are given.

§ Compare Penal Code, Art. 335, second paragraph, and Civil Code, Book I., Title IX.

stant, unpunished practice of inciting minors to debauch? *
No; it is too evident that so long as the Napoleonic
code thus forgets almost every one of the material and
moral interests of woman, so long will it hang as a mill-
stone about the neck of our France, so bravely struggling for her political regeneration.

" The divorce question now occupies a great deal of the
public attention of this country, and is very closely connected with the existing system of partial divorce or the
separation of a married woman from the bed and board
of her husband (*séparation de corps*). One of the chief
reasons given for the re-establishment of divorce, which,
introduced by the Revolution, existed until 1815, is the
effect it will have on this class of women. We have
already seen that the wife's separation from the husband
does not free her from marital power, even when she is
the applicant, which is the case nine times out of ten.
She continues to bear his name, and sees her fortune still
subject in a measure to his control, so that the husband,
if he would take revenge for an adverse judgment, finds
here an excellent opportunity to hector his former wife.
Although our publicists, both those for and against
divorce, have spoken out in opposition to this state of
things, no change has been made.

" Another anomaly of this partial divorce was suppressed, but in favor of the husband, it must be said. I
refer to the presumption that the husband was the father
of any children born after the separation, even when all
cohabitation had ceased.† Since 1850, however, the husband has only to confront the date of the child's birth

---

* See Yves Guyot's " Prostitution " (*La prostitution*).—L. G.

† The old maxim put it: *Pater is est quem nuptiæ demonstrant.*—L. G.

with the date of the separation, to prove that he is not its father. This reform is perfectly just, but it is a curious fact that our law-makers introduce innovations only when their own sex is to be benefited thereby.

" What would be the situation of the divorced wife if, without any other changes in the code, M. Naquet's bill, which is the project the most likely to succeed, were to pass in the Senate as it has already done in the Chamber ? In the first place, the wife would of course be emancipated from the marital power, which is not the case under the present system as we have just seen. M. Naquet also places husband and wife on the same footing as regards adultery, which is not now the case. But with these two exceptions, M. Naquet's bill justifies the apprehensions of its adversaries, even when the wife's interests are alone considered. Many provisions of the code would sadly clash with her new liberty. Divorce should be the coping of any reform of our marriage laws, not the foundation stone.

" Let us, in the first place, consider the children. It is evident that the divorced wife does not obtain complete control over her children, especially if she remarries. In this case she falls into the same category as the widow, whose disabilities we have already noticed. She will still be subject to the decision of the family council as regards preserving the guardianship of her children, and will have less authority over them than the other divorced parent. Such inequality would cause her to look with disfavor upon divorce not backed by other reforms, and she would probably have less and less recourse to it.

" Furthermore, would not the possibility of divorce be a temptation to the husband to abuse the powers which the law gives him over the fortune of his wife? At present he is required to at least provide for her wants. What limit would there be to his depredations if M. Naquet's bill passes? Many an honest lawyer will admit that the husband has a thousand ways of ruining his wife under whatever system they are married. By the dissolution of the marriage tie, the husband, after spending his wife's fortune, could disembarrass himself of her, while she would not be able to hold him to the slightest obligation.

" If now we consider the advantages of divorce, we find an aspect of the question quite peculiar to France. I refer to divorce in its relations to nullity of marriage, which modifies in this particular the narrowness of our civil code. It will be remembered that in France the civil law and canon law are absolutely distinct. The causes which make possible the nullity of a marriage are not the same in the two systems. The first, which is very severe, admits of but one case,—error concerning the person.* Our courts have decided that this means the marriage of a man or woman to another than the individual he or she had in view,—a mistake which, it may be said, never occurs. Once married, two beings are bound together for life, whatever their past has been, or whatever their future may be.

" Such was not the doctrine of the old canon law. The church of course held to the principle of the indissolubility of marriage, but of marriage normally contracted and uniting certain conditions. The theory of nullity of marriage was very liberal, there being not less than sixteen cases in which the contract could be broken. It was declared null *ab initio*, and thus the doctrine of indissolubility was left intact, while the present intoler-

---

* See Civil Code, Art. 180, and the commentaries on this article.

able situation, from which there is no escape, was avoided. By the re-establishment of divorce, so as to recognize exactly the causes accepted by the canon law, religious scruples would be gotten over, and those who combat the Naquet bill from church prejudices would be able to unite with its advocates. Thus, with the tolerance of Rome and the consent of the State, divorce might become a living fact again." *

I next take up the moral condition of French women. A Paris journalist has written: " It is not necessary to go to Constantinople to find the harem : one need not leave Paris, with this single difference, that instead of being confined to the narrow walls of a palace, it overflows the limits of the fortifications." † This is no exaggeration. The vital statistics published each week in the daily papers—to cite but one of many proofs—establish only too firmly the truth of this statement. I select at hazard one of these official reports. During the sixth week of 1882 there were 1,268 births at Paris, of which 937 were legitimate and 341 illegitimate.‡ That is to say, nearly one-third of all the children who come into the world each week at the French capital are born outside of wedlock,—some 17,000 bastards launched on to life annually in one city of France. In such a state of things the

---

* The general subject of the legal position of women in France, is briefly and clearly treated by M. Léon Richer in his volume entitled, the "Women's Code" (*Le code des femmes;* Paris: Dentu, 1883). I would recommend, as a convenient edition of the civil and penal codes, the two little volumes of M. Rivière (*Les codes français;* Paris: Marescq, 20 rue Soufflot). The different matrimonial systems are clearly explained in Professor Emile Acollas's interesting little book, " Marriage " (*Le mariage;* Paris : Marescq, 1881).

† M. Albert Rabou, *La France,* February 9, 1881.

‡ *Le Temps,* February 12, 1882.

France of to-day would do well to imitate the Convention, which issued the celebrated decree that " every girl who supports her illegitimate child during ten years, by the fruit of her own labor, may claim a public recompense."*

Mme. Emilie de Morsier,† than whom no woman in France is more competent to speak for the moral condition of her sex, writes me as follows : " It may be thought surprising that French women have not demanded the abolition of State regulated vice (*police des mœurs*) before advancing their claims for civil and political equality. Ought not the first protest of woman to be against a law which makes property of her very person ? Her body is not her own ; under certain circumstances it may become the property of the police, and an object of speculation for dealers in human flesh, whose business is protected by this same police. This law condemns women to the life of a public prostitute under the surveillance of the authorities.

" Now and then a voice has been raised against the infamies without name concealed under the hypocritical expression of the *police des mœurs*. Eugène Sue, in his 'Mysteries of Paris,' stigmatized this official sentine

---

* Legouvé, *Histoire morale de la femme*. Legouvé also cites the following ordinance of the Convention, one of the many examples of the fair treatment of women by that body : " Every mother whose work cannot support her family, may claim aid from the nation." Professor Acollas's work, " The Child Born Outside of Wedlock " (*L'enfant né hors mariage*), may be read in connection with this subject.

† Mme. de Morsier, besides taking an active part in all philanthropic and reformatory movements in France, is the translator into French of Miss Phelps's " The Gates Ajar " and " Hedged In," Mrs. Ashurst Venturi's " Joseph Mazzini, a Memoir," and of Mazzini's two essays, " The Duties of Man " and " Thoughts on Democracy."

called the 'bureau of morals' (*bureau des mœurs**), and the heart-rending life of the poor Fleur de Marie is no exaggerated invention of the novelist, but a daily actuality. Mlle. Julie Daubié, in a little tract entitled 'The Toleration of Vice' (*La tolérance du vice*), indignantly condemns this infamous system; but this noble woman died in the midst of her campaign against immorality.

"In 1873 Mrs. Josephine E. Butler arrived in Paris. She had been for several years at the head of an English movement, whose aim was to combat this same system introduced into some parts of Great Britain by act of Parliament. She held, with good reason, that as this curse came from the Continent, it should be denounced and attacked at its source. Mrs. Butler was the first woman who spoke in France before large meetings on this delicate question, and those who heard her remember the profound impression she produced.

"At the same time, a Frenchman, M. Yves Guyot, spoke out against the iniquity, and began in the press a campaign, which he continued later in the deliberations of the Paris municipal council. Having laid the responsibility for these infamies at the door of the prefect of police, he was condemned to six months' imprisonment, so that a man was the first to suffer for having championed the cause of these slaves of vice.

"Members of the British and Continental Federation for the Abolition of Prostitution, which owes its origin to Mrs. Butler, have several times visited Paris to advocate their cause, and the organization of a French committee was the result, with Mrs. Dr. John Chapman and

---

* This is the bureau of the police department, where the girls receive their cards (*cartes*), and here is the dispensary (*dispensaire*) where the doctors practice their inspection (*visite forcée*).

Yves Guyot as presidents. One might have thought that the movement, once gotten under way, would have grown in public favor. But such was not the case. Many persons were, indeed, convinced of the justice of the cause, but as soon as the novelty of the first impressions wore off, they fell back into their former state of indifference, and few passed from conviction to action. France does not yet know what self-government means. When people express the desire for a reform, they sit down, fold their arms, and wait for the government to act. It cannot, therefore, be said that there has been in this country a genuine movement of public opinion in favor of the abolition of State-regulated vice. If M. Yves Guyot had not kept up the agitation, the question would probably long ago have dropped out of sight and out of mind.

" The Paris Society for the Improvement of Public Morals (*Comité parisien pour le relèvement de la moralité publique*) follows much the same lines as the Federation, and is doing a good work.

" The various associations in France for the promotion of this cause have always been composed of men and women, but it must be admitted that it is not the feminine element which has predominated. This question, so essentially a woman's question, does not awaken their interest. It has been said that ' women make the morals,' but it would be more correct to say that they *accept* them. Through a deplorable frivolity, by a wish to please at any price, they tacitly accept men's opinions and yield to their wishes. This culpable complaisance is sometimes carried to such a length, that wives strive to imitate the dress and manners of a class in whose society their husbands occasionally find a moment's pleasure, hoping, by debasing themselves, to retain an affection which they fear may escape them. On the other hand, conscientious women, religious ones above all, scarcely dare to glance into these abysses of vice, and, brought up to believe that they have nothing to do with the outside world, say : ' These things do not concern us : men make the laws.' Selfishness, ignorance and prejudice must be great indeed, when wives and mothers do not see the depth and breadth of this question. The cause lies in the tacit acquiescence of women in the current opinions held by men on this subject of morals. They have accepted their theory of the necessity of vice, and firmly believe that the house of ill-fame is a hygienic requisite."*

There is a small body of Catholics in France, including such men as M. de Falloux, the Bishop of Amiens (M. Guilbert), and the Abbé Bougaud, who cling to the forlorn hope of conciliating Rome with the new society born of the French Revolution. But their efforts have met with no success, and every day the breach widens, the republi-

---

* The literature on this subject of public morality, especially that which treats of the grave question of State-regulated vice, has grown to immense proportions within the past few years. The *Actes du congrès de Genève* (September, 1877) and the *Compte-rendu du congrès de Gênes* (September, 1880) are rich in information on this subject. The continental organ of the Federation is *Le bulletin continental*, a monthly under the editorship of M. Aimé Humbert. These three publications may be obtained by addressing M. Humbert, 19, rue du Château, Neuchâtel, Switzerland. *La prostitution*, by Yves Guyot (Paris : Charpentier, 13, rue de Grenelle St. Germain), is perhaps the best French book on the subject. The *Westminster Review* for April, 1883, contains a paper written by Dr. John Chapman, and entitled " Prostitution at Paris," which explains very clearly and fully the system of *police des mœurs* as practiced at the French capital. M. Fallot, 17, rue des Petits-Hôtels, Paris, Secretary of the *Comité Parisien*, mentioned in the text, can furnish documents and information concerning the general condition of morals in France.

cans and freethinkers on one side, the monarchists and priesthood on the other.

This freethinking party is strong and active. On the evening of Good Friday, 1882, for example, occurred twenty-two banquets of "freethinkers and atheists" at Paris alone, and fourteen more in the environs. M. Léo Taxil's Anti-Clerical League (*Ligue anti-cléricale*) and his bold little paper entitled the *Anti-clérical*, keep up the rubadub of agitation. This rebellion against the church takes on various forms. On June 28, 1881, was founded the Civil Marriage Society (*Société du mariage civil*), with one of the mayors of Paris as its president. The great question of the separation of church and state is constantly before Parliament, and has called into existence a society and newspaper devoted specially to the advocacy of this reform. Another society is exclusively occupied with the propagandism of freethinking doctrines.

"The question of the enfranchisement of woman and the recognition of her rights," says Maria Deraismes,* "is closely connected with the anti-clerical question or free-thinking movement. Woman, since the commencement of the world, has been the victim of religious tradition. It is often said that Christianity lifted woman out of her

---

* Mlle. Deraismes is one of the ablest lady speakers in France and an active leader in the anti-clerical movement. She has always been a zealous worker for women's rights, was temporary president of the Paris congress of 1878, and is to-day editor and proprietor of a strong free-thinking organ, the *Républicain de Seine-et-Oise*. Mlle. Deraismes is probably the only woman in France who is a Freemason. Her reception a year or two ago by the Lodge of Le Pecq, a small town near Paris, created no little sensation, for it was a double blow at the church, which, prohibiting even its male members from becoming Masons, could only look with holy horror on a woman's entrance into this organization. Mlle. Deraismes was president of the Paris anti-clerical congress of 1881, in which some of the most important public men of France participated.

degradation; that before the coming of Christ she was a mere thing, an object of amusement, an instrument of reproduction. But this is only a legend and has no historical foundation. The servitude of woman in antiquity has been considerably exaggerated. The fact is that she was subjected far less than many people are willing to admit.*

"The advent of Christianity scarcely modified this situation. The new doctrine condemned one sex to submit to the other; it taught that woman was made for man, and not man for woman. According to St. Paul and all the fathers of the church who came after him, women should cover their heads in the churches as a sign of submission; they are ordered to keep silence, they may not preach, they are commanded to respect their husbands, because man

---

* The divine element, according to the ideas of the ancient world, was composed of the two sexes. There were *dei feminei*, and hence temples sacred to goddesses, holy sanctuaries where were celebrated mysteries in which men were not permitted to participate. The worship of goddesses necessitated priestesses, so that women exercised the sacerdotal functions in the ancient world. The wives of the Roman consuls even offered public sacrifices to the divinities at certain festivals. This important part played by woman in the religious sphere could not but have an influence on her general position. In the Orient she put on the sovereign purple in the absence of male heirs. The modern world has not done better. Roman law permitted married women to control and enjoy their paraphernal property. The wife as well as the husband could make application for a divorce. The dramatic authors of the epoch show us that matrons exercised, when it was necessary, considerable authority in the home. The more property the wife had, the more rights she had.—M. D. "It must be admitted, although it shocks our present customs, that among the most polished peoples, wives have always had authority over their husbands. The Egyptians established it by law in honor of Isis, and the Babylonians did the same in honor of Semiramis. It has been said of the Romans that they ruled all nations but obeyed their wives. I do not mention the Sauromates, who were, in fact, the slaves of this sex, because they were too barbarous to be cited as an example."—Montesquieu, "Persian Letters," letter xxxviii.

is the head of the family as Jesus is the head of the church. Who can discover in such ordinances the elements of emancipation and equality? They are, on the contrary, a solemn and definitive proclamation of the social inferiority of woman. Christians were so uncertain as to the real value of woman, and the teachings of Jesus were so obscure on the subject, that the Council of Mâcon asked if she had a soul! Although the Virgin Mary occupies the largest place in the Catholic Church, to the exclusion of the persons of the trinity, still this preponderance of the female element in the doctrine and in the service has not improved the social condition of women.

" The French republicans of to-day are striving to establish a democracy, and they encounter on every hand a tremendous obstacle,—the church. Now of all the allies of this church, women are the most zealous, the most influential, the most numerous. They it is who have prolonged the existence of a doctrine condemned fatally to disappear. Remove women from the church, and the Catholic edifice receives a mortal blow. Our men, who have so long neglected women, now begin to perceive the whole extent of the folly of which they have been guilty in refusing them knowledge. They are now trying to repair this fault. They are rapidly organizing a system of instruction for girls which shall be secular, and the same for both sexes. They see that knowledge is the source of all liberty.*

---

* The growing belief among French republicans that the realization or failure of their efforts to found a lasting republic in this country depends in no small measure on the women of France, is one of the most interesting features of the present political crisis. It has often been said, notably by Michelet, that women gave the death-blow to the first republic and powerfully aided the victory of the church and old beliefs. The radical publicist, M. Léon Giraud, one of the most active and intelligent friends of the women's

" Every woman who desires to obtain her rights, or who wishes at least to escape from tutelage, should second the freethinking movement. In breaking with the Catholic legend woman revokes the primordial decree which smote her, and which has rendered her an object of universal reprobation. Hence it is that freethinking makes numerous recruits among the sex which seemed doomed to be forever the prey of superstition. A large number of women are members of the anti-clerical societies, which are multiplying every day and spreading into the provinces. Turning their back on churches, they attend our gatherings, take part in the discussions and become officers of our meetings and societies. Among the many friends of this cause are women distinguished for their learning, literary talent and eloquence. I have room to name but a few, such as Mesdames Clémence Royer, Gagneur, André Léo, Angélique Arnaud, Jules de La Madélène, Edgar Quinet, Edmond Adam, Griess-Traut, Louise David, Rouzade, Feresse-Deraismes, and de Barrau."

Women participate very largely in charitable and philanthropic work. "I am happy as a French woman,"

movement in France, writes me on this subject as follows: "It is a statement which I think true and which I have tried to explain in my book 'The Romance of the Christian Woman' (*Le roman de la femme chrétienne*)." In a speech against the decrees which drove the unauthorized religious orders from France, Laboulaye said in the senate, on November 16, 1880: "If you were present at the expulsion of the congregations, you saw women praying, supplicating. Do you think they will have any affection for the republic? Hatred of the republic is becoming a feminine hatred, and a government cannot resist that." Referring to this speech a few days before his death, Laboulaye said to me in a laughing mood: "Somebody has remarked that a government is lost which has the cooks against it, because they each have a cousin in the army!"

Mme. Isabelle Bogelot* writes me, " to be able to say that our beautiful France contains many large-hearted women, and private charity is extensive. There is still much misery, for it is impossible to remove it entirely. To obtain the results we desire, and guard women from dishonor and starvation, is a problem whose solution must be sought elsewhere than in charity. I shall cite a few of these private charitable organizations at Paris, which will give an idea of the work throughout France.

" The Philanthropic Society (*Société philanthropique*), which was founded in 1780, has been a blessing to poor women for a hundred years. Among its many benefactors may be mentioned Mme. Camille Favre, whose recent liberality has made it possible for the Society to establish dispensaries for children, which will soon be opened in all the outlying quarters of Paris.† The Society for the Amelioration of the Condition of Women, already mentioned several times in this chapter, has charitable aims. The Society for Released Female Prisoners of St. Lazare (*Œuvre des libérées de St. Lazare*), founded by Mlle. Michel de Grandpré, comes to the assistance of those liberated from this well-known women's prison. Mme. de Witt has created a folding-room in connection with the extensive publishing house of Hachette & Company, which gives employment to two hundred poor women. They are fed, and the money which they deposit draws ten per cent. interest. Mme. Dalencourt has organized a society which provides needy women with

---

* Mme. Bogelot (4, rue Perrault, Paris), who is one of the most liberal-minded and active friends of the poor and unfortunate, is a member of the board of managers of the Society for Released Female Prisoners of St. Lazare (*Œuvre des libérées de St. Lazare*), of which Mme. de Barrau is director.

† The office of this society is 17, rue d'Orléans, Paris.

work and food at a very reduced price, and assures them ten per cent. on their savings. Such are a few—perhaps the most characteristic—of the Paris charitable institutions due to women and for women."

Among other benevolent works in which women participate, may be mentioned the Paris Society for the Protection of Animals, which counts many ladies among its officers and members. Female charity is sometimes of a patriotic nature, as in the case of the Association of French Ladies, which was founded in April, 1879, and whose principal object is to care for the wounded in time of war. The Association has several branch societies in the provinces and supports schools for the training of nurses at Paris and in other cities of France.

The sister of charity must not be overlooked, for in France as elsewhere she is an important factor in benevolent work. It may be said that we have in her the germ of the female physician, for in the dispensary she is a pharmacist, and at the sick-bed a doctor. The sister of charity is, therefore, acting a grand part in accustoming the public to this progressive step in the medical profession.*

---

* Concerning printed information on French charities, Mme. Bogelot writes : " *Le manuel des œuvres* (Paris : Poussielque, 15, rue Cassette), published every two years, gives an account of all public institutions and those of a private nature which have been officially recognized. *Manuel des bureaux de bienfaisance*, by Molineau (Paris : Marchal et Billard, 27, place Dauphine), is valuable. *Les gens de bien*, by Mme. Demoulin, of St. Quentin, will soon be published and will give the names of all those who devote their attention to charity in France." M. Maxime du Camp, of the French Academy, has well described the public and private charities of Paris. For the first, see the *Revue des deux mondes*, June 15th, August 1st, September 1st and 15th, 1870, and October 15th and November 1st, 1872 ; for the second, see the same periodical, April 1st and May 15th, 1883.

In order to fully appreciate what has been accomplished in the matter of girls' instruction, we must know what was its condition when the work began. The situation previous to the Revolution may be judged by this extract from one of Mme. de Maintenon's essays on education: " Bring up your girls of the middle classes as such," she says; " do not trouble yourself about the cultivation of their minds; they should be taught domestic duties, obedience to husband, and care of children. Reading does young girls more harm than good; books make wits and excite insatiable curiosity." As regards history, Mme. de Maintenon allows that girls should have a slight knowledge of it, in order to know the names of their own princes, so as not to mistake a king of Spain or England for a ruler of Persia or Siam. But ancient history is proscribed. " I should fear," she says, " lest those grand traits of heroism and generosity exalt their mind and make them vain and affected."

But the Revolution modified French ideas concerning women's education. A descendant of La Fontaine, Mme. Mouret, who edited a women's educational journal in 1790, read at the bar of the National Assembly a plan for the instruction of girls, which was received in most complimentary terms by the president.* It was the Convention which first spoke out clearly in France for girls' instruction. But the Convention was too short-lived to accomplish its work, and war and bad government adjourned for many long years the realization of its liberal plans.†

---

* *Dictionnaire de la presse*, p. 161.

† M. Auguste Desmoulins, the radical member of the Paris Municipal Council, in a speech at Foix, on the occasion of the unveiling of a statue to Lakanal, September 24, 1882, pointed out how this great Minister of Public

The Empire did nothing for the instruction of women, and the Restoration was worse than the Empire, for it was clerical. But the culpability of Napoleon and the Bourbons is of a negative nature. It is not the same with Louis Philippe, however. When the July monarchy, in 1833, at the instance of Guizot, created primary instruction for boys, the girls of France were entirely neglected. This was positive culpability. It must have been at this period that Balzac exclaimed: "The education of girls is such a grave problem—for the future of a nation is in the mothers—that for a long time past the University of France has not thought about it!" Efforts have since been made to remedy this fault, but there are still 3,281 *communes* which have no primary schools for girls, and 31.34 per cent. fewer girls' than boys' schools in all France.

The history of girls' intermediate instruction is still less creditable to the country. Although private initiative has nobly endeavored to supply a crying want, the State began to act but yesterday. M. Duruy, Minister of Public Instruction under the second Empire, created, in 1867, courses of lectures for the intermediate instruction of girls, but it was not until December 21, 1880, after a long and bitter struggle of three years' duration, that M. Camille Sée saw his bill become law, and France offered its girls something more than an elementary training.

Instruction under the Convention, who considered "the education of girls as indispensable as that of boys," saw his hopes, blasted in France, realized in the United States. "It is not sufficiently known," said M. Desmoulins, "that the vast system of national instruction so brilliantly consummated at this hour across the Atlantic, is the direct and natural result of all that was thought out by our encyclopedists, longed for by our grand revolution, and prepared by the National Convention."—*Bulletin de la ville de Paris*, September 30, 1882.

" Our law is at one and the same time a moral law, a so-cial law, and a political law," said M. Sée, in the Chamber; " it concerns the future and the safety of France, for on woman depends the grandeur as well as the decadence of nations."

The manner in which this reform has been received by French women shows that they were only waiting for an opportunity to improve their minds. I cannot resist citing a few examples of their enthusiasm in what has become, in so far as France is concerned, a second Revival of Learning. The day before the Rouen College (*lycée**) opened, in October, 1882, the names of 202 girls were already on the register. The Amiens College had, during its first term, 60 day and 40 boarding scholars. At Lyons, a very clerical city, although the college opened very late in the autumn of 1882, some 40 scholars were in attendance. When the Montpellier College—the first girls' college in France—was organized, it had 76 scholars, at the end of the year more than 100, and during the autumn of 1882 the lectures were attended by 215 girls. The college at Grenoble began on April 17, 1882, with 47 girls, and in January, 1883, this number had risen to 112. This same tendency is seen in the lecture courses founded by M. Duruy, to which reference has already been made. Whereas, in 1875, these Sorbonne studies were pursued by 165 girls, in the collegiate year 1881–2 there were 244.

But the Government and the municipalities enter as heartily into the work as the women themselves. The Chamber voted, in 1882, ten millions of francs for the

---

* In the French system of secondary instruction the establishments are of two classes, those which have a State subvention and those supported entirely by the *commune.* The first are called *lycées*, the second *collèges.* I use our English word, college, for both classes.

creation of girls' colleges. Rouen, one of the first cities to demand a college, found that it would cost a million francs; the municipality forthwith contributed half that sum and the Government the other half. At the end of the first year after the promulgation of the Sée law, the following results had been obtained: The foundation of a superior normal school for women at Sèvres,* the opening of four colleges, all the preliminary steps taken to the same end in twenty-six other cities, while similar negotiations had been begun by thirty-eight other municipalities. To-day (October, 1883)—less than three years after the Sée bill became law—still greater progress can be reported, and almost every month a new girls' college is added to the vast system of public instruction in France.

University education for women was secured long before intermediate education, due mainly to the fact that no new schools had to be created. From 1866 to 1882, 109 degrees were conferred upon women in France. There have been 49 bachelors of arts, 32 bachelors of science, and 21 doctors of medicine; 98 degrees have been conferred in Paris alone. Many foreigners, especially in medicine, are found among these 109 graduates, but within the last year or two—particularly since the Sée law has created a demand for educated teachers—the number of French women studying for university degrees has greatly increased.

---

* This is a national institution corresponding to the celebrated superior normal school for men in the Rue d'Ulm at Paris. Its aim is to fit women to become directors and professors of girls' colleges. It was created July 28, 1881, at the instigation of M. Sée, by a vote of Parliament, and opened December 12 following, with about 40 scholars, ranging from 18 to 24 years. In October, 1882, 40 new scholars entered. The course of studies now covers two years, but efforts are being made to extend it to three years. The director of the school is Mme. Favre, widow of the celebrated Jules Favre.

The history of women's medical instruction in France is very significant, and shows most strikingly the growth of public opinion in regard to the higher education of women generally. In 1864 Legouvé wrote: "The reader must not think that I desire to see women mingling with male students on the seats of the law or medical school; this would indeed be a poor way to provide for their improvement." In 1875, Dr. G. Richelot, President of the Paris Medical Society, styled the study of medicine by women "that deplorable tendency," "a malady of our epoch." But Legouvé has lived to see women sitting on the same benches with male students without detracting from the improvement of either sex, and Dr. Richelot's malady has become an epidemic. There was a time when the female students at the Paris Medical School were almost without exception from abroad. But this is not the case to-day. The first Frenchwoman to take a medical degree in France was Mlle. Verneuil, who is still practicing at Paris. She graduated from the Paris Medical School in 1870. Up to 1881 six more Frenchwomen had followed her example, five taking their degree at the capital, and one at Montpellier. Since that time several new names have been added to the list, the last being Mlle. Victorine Benoît, who was graduated at Paris in August, 1883, with the highest approval of the board of examiners, composed of such doctors as Potain, Strauss, Rendu, and Monod.

That the Paris Medical School has not shut its doors against women, in marked contrast with the action of so many other medical schools, is due in no small measure to Laboulaye. He once told me that some years ago the question of refusing women admission to the Paris Medical School was brought up in the Department of Public

Instruction. The matter was referred to him. His report to the Minister was to this effect: The rules of the school say nothing on the subject ; it would therefore seem the best and the simplest course to require of women who desire to pursue medicine the same preparatory studies and the same tests for graduation which are demanded of the male students, and thus allow both sexes to enjoy the advantages offered by the school. This sensible and just advice was followed, and the question has never been mooted since.

The co-education of the sexes is not unknown in France, although the average Frenchman, who has a very strong repugnance to the system, would be astonished at its prevalence. There are 17,728 primary schools for both sexes (*écoles-mixtes*), nearly one-third of the primary schools of France, with 633,697 scholars. They are found in every department, and there are seven in the department of the Seine. For the past thirty-two years there has been an agricultural orphan asylum for the two sexes (*asile agricole mixte*) at Cernay, in the Haut-Rhin. "These schools," says Mme. Griess-Traut, "have produced here, as in other countries, excellent results."* In the universities, co-education is accepted with scarcely an objection, and every year it becomes more and more a matter of course among professors and students alike. In fact, this rapid and hearty admission of women to the

---

* I take the figures in this paragraph from an admirable article by Mme. Griess-Traut, in the *Phare de la Loire* for November 21, 1882. The objections raised to this primary co-education, even by the most distinguished educationists of France, are always amusing and often absolutely puerile. M. Francisque Sarcey even goes to the United States to find arguments against it. In the *Dix-neuvième Siècle* for October 19, 1880, he says : " The Yankees commence to lose faith in this system, which will soon disappear " (!).

French faculties is one of the most significant and re-markable social revolutions of recent years.*

"A comparison of the condition of French literary women of to-day," says Mme. Henry Gréville,† "with

---

* Primary and intermediate co-education have become an integrant part of our American school system, but university co-education is still strongly opposed by a large class. In France, on the contrary, the first are condemned, while the second is now generally accepted. Lumping together the opinions on this subject held in the two countries, we find the system approved in the three degrees of instruction, which shows that the objections on both sides of the Atlantic are only prejudices.

A concise, learned, and very interesting account of women's education in France, past and present, and more especially of intermediate instruction, is found in *L'enseignement secondaire des filles* (Paris: Delalain, 1, rue de la Sorbonne, 1883), by M. Gréard, one of the leading educationists of France. This is the latest and most authoritative essay on the subject. Jules Simon's *L'école* (Paris: Hachette, 79, Boulevard St. Germain), while ably treating the whole subject of public instruction, devotes a large portion of his volume to a rather liberal consideration of women's education. *Histoire de l'éducation des femmes en France* (Paris: Didier, 1883), by Paul Rousselot, was awarded the Botta prize in 1883 by the French Academy. *L'enseignement secondaire des jeunes filles* (Paris: Leopold Cerf, 13, rue de Médicis), a monthly, edited by M. Camille Sée, with the co-operation of Henri Martin, Legouvé, and others, gives, besides short essays on the subject of women's education, all the current news on the question.

† Mme. Gréville (whose maiden name was Alice Marie Fleury) is the daughter of M. Jean Fleury, who was born at Vasteville, in Normandy, and is now professor at the University of St. Petersburg. She was born at Paris, Rue de Grenelle St. Germain, October 12, 1842, and is the wife of M. E. Durand, who was born at Montpellier in 1838. It will be seen, therefore, that Mme. Gréville is thoroughly French by birth as well as marriage. I give these details because she has been claimed by other countries, by Switzerland and Belgium to my personal knowledge. In 1857 Mme. Gréville went to Russia and did not return to her native land until after the Franco-German war in 1872. A few years later her literary career began in the form of remarkable novels depicting Russian society, and the *Revue des deux mondes*, the *Journal des débats*, and the *Temps* delighted their readers at one

that which they occupied during the first half of this cent-
ury, presents at the very first glance a remarkable difference. What then seemed abnormal, odd, almost reprehensible, is now universally accepted without exciting any comment.   In fact, from 1800 to 1850, women who had a taste for writing sought to excuse themselves before the public for indulging in this extraordinary caprice, and some, like Mme. Tastu, Mme. Ancelot, Elisa Mercœur, and Mme. Desbordes-Valmore, succeeded in being pardoned their mania by dint of good grace, amiability, I may almost say, humility.   Others resembled George Sand, who came to an open quarrel with all prejudices, and lived for her art alone. Through the force of genius, she succeeded in compelling even the most recalcitrant to accept her, but only after a long and perilous struggle. Conscious of greatness and indifferent to public opinion, she was able to alleviate her vexations, but not to remove them.

" To-day a woman may write on any subject,—on science, art, and pedagogics ; she may take up fiction,—every path is open to her. The public judges her as it would a man, retaining, however, that fine, almost involuntary deference, the result of habit and good breeding, which every Frenchman—whether he shows it or not by his outward acts—feels for the woman who respects herself. This notable change, which, relatively speaking, has come about rapidly, is due principally to the fact that female writers of the present time do not entertain the same

---

and the same time with charming creations from this rapid and prolific pen. But Mme. Gréville is not only a talented and clever novelist, she is also a broad-minded, liberal thinker on all the great reform and progressive questions of the hour, and her artistic little house on the heights of Montmartre is an influential centre for the propagation of modern ideas.

ideas on literature as formerly. When a woman fifty years ago boldly took up the pen, she declared herself by this very act at variance with prejudice. Her avowed object was glory ; she desired that her name should make a noise in the world. This name, therefore, was rarely a pseudonym unless circumstances rendered a disguise necessary. From 1850 to 1880 a change, which has become the rule, took place. In order to enjoy greater liberty, almost all women who felt themselves pushed toward literature sheltered themselves behind a pseudonym, often a masculine one, whose secret was sometimes kept for many years. Their glory thus became less personal, was associated more with the talent than the individuality of the writer, was freer from alloy, and womanly dignity gained thereby. There is evidently an advantage in being discussed under a borrowed, rather than under one's real name. The family is not touched in the combats of the press, and may, up to a certain point, remain ignorant of the quarrels of literature, while, at the same time, the domestic hearth is benefited by the material rewards of literary labor. No wonder, then, that many young girls turn toward this new field of work.

" At the same moment that the prejudice against female authors began to diminish in force, a more substantial education—still far from what it should be, however—provided these literary neophytes more ample means for the attainment of their aspirations, which first assumed the form of verse, so true is it that the impulse to sing, less definite, more subtle, precedes that of speaking. Many volumes of poetry with the names of women on the title-page were born, ran their short course, and died. Then the movement became more strongly marked, took on a more precise form, and, after some groping, the feminine

novel, properly so-called, was produced.* Thereby were
women not only presented in a new light, but were
afforded new means of existence. At the same time,
numerous collections for young people were published,
and a large number of distinguished women made their
first literary efforts in this department. Many continue
to devote themselves to juvenile literature, while others
have gained a reputation in the higher walks of fiction.

"Public opinion changed so rapidly that the expressions, 'feminine studies,' 'feminine style,' were soon considered to carry with them praise rather than blame, and men
even began to choose feminine pseudonyms at a time when
women were borrowing their *noms de plume* from the masculine part of the calendar. But so complete a revolution
was not produced without profound causes. Female authors—to cite the most important of these influences—
were formerly considered, justly or unjustly, to neglect
their homes so as to devote themselves more entirely
to literature. The stockings in holes, the house in disorder, the children uncared for, the husband treated as an
unwelcome intruder sapping the inspiration of his spouse,
—all these repugnant details of domestic imperfection had
passed into a proverb and brought literary women, often
unmeritedly, into discredit. When the profession became
the appanage not alone of a few eccentrics, but of a large
recognized class of industrious, poorly paid women, it
was perceived that they were, generally speaking, none
the less good mothers and excellent housekeepers anxious
for the reputation of the home. Their aim in taking up
the pen was commonly to add some dainties to the dry
bread of the daily existence of an aged mother or sick

---

* George Sand being an exceptional genius should be considered a pre-
cursor, not the creator of modern feminine French fiction.—H. G.

child, to come to the aid of sons who must be educated, and daughters who must be endowed. How many cases might be cited of women who, abandoned by a prodigal, unquestionably culpable husband, and reduced to the alternative of choosing between poverty and something worse, found their salvation in a return to the studies of their youth. Exhausted strength, the lack of a teacher's diploma, false pride which cannot brook an employment after having enjoyed independence, the incapacity to suffer humiliations never before experienced,—all these circumstances, singly or united, have often forced from the soul of a cruelly tried woman, cries of anguish and passion which have found an echo in the public heart. ' Where have they discovered that ?' is asked. In the tortures of a blighted existence. Hence it is that women have been able to say things which men would never have thought of or divined. The public has done them justice, believing that they do not the less merit its respect for having discreetly expressed these sufferings. This indulgence has brought into prominence a galaxy of feminine names and surrounded them with consideration and sympathy. But talent may be germinated otherwise than by misfortune. Happy souls speak in equally touching accents. The joys of the family, the frenzy of passion, and the drama of existence are subjects of study and reflection as inexhaustible for happy as for sad hearts.

"Thérèse Bentzon, Albane, the delicate author of ' Madeleine's Sin' (*Péché de Madeleine*); Juliette Lamber (Mme. Edmond Adam), Etienne Marcel, André Gérard, Georges de Peyrebrune, Jeanne Mairet,* Jacques Vincent,

---

* It is a high compliment to Jeanne Mairet that she should be classed by Henry Gréville among French authors, a compliment which may be shared by American women, for the wife of the well-known Paris journalist, Charles

and many others whose names I omit with regret, have produced works full of true sentiment and actual experience, which enable us to study the soul of the women of to-day as we never could those of the past. Other female pens have taken up philosophy and morals. The delicately penetrating reflections of Mme. Julia Daudet, her poems full of natural sentiment; the gloomy, merciful morality of Mme. Blanchecotte, who takes from humanity its afflictions, which she shares, and, whether in prose or verse, gives comfort in return; the philosophy (which rejects an invisible, unknown enemy) of Mme. Ackermann, who, standing almost alone in this order of ideas, has spoken out concerning the nature of our existence in such clear, energetic language,—such are a few of the female philosophers and moralists of the France of to-day. In another department, I may cite those clever women, *femmes d'esprit*, Daniel Darc, Ange Bénigne, and Gyp, worthy successors of Mme. de Girardin.

"The problems of education, many of which are still unsolved, could not fail to attract the attention of women, in whom the maternal sentiment is oftenest the most predominant. Mme. Pape-Carpantier's ideas on this subject gave evidence of womanly patience and good sense, and she showed the devotion of an apostle in putting them into practice. In creating object-teaching in the infant schools (*salles d'asile*) she opened her arms, like St. Vincent de Paul, to all the little ones, the hope of the future and the care of the present. But these arms were not only her own, they were those of all France. What the infant asylum (*crèche*) had done for the first months of

---

Bigot, is the daughter of Healy, the American artist. Her new novel, "Marca," was highly praised by the *Temps*, and won a prize from the French Academy in 1883.

the baby, Mme. Pape-Carpantier did for the age when the turbulent child is a danger to himself in the house, at a time when he is capable of learning a great deal in the infant-school. Object-teaching produced a large number of educational works, and gave a start to juvenile literature, which was quite backward in France, although very able women had not disdained to consecrate their time and labor to this important branch of letters. Nothing is more difficult than to address one's self to the young in language which instructs and improves, at the same time that it amuses. Mme. de Witt, *née* Guizot, followed by Mlle. L. Fleuriot, Mme. Colomb, and many others, gave themselves up to this work, often so ungrateful, and yet all the more meritorious, as it is harder, less remunerative, and does not command so much applause as the higher kinds of fiction. Pedagogics, properly so-called, have found an able expounder in the person of Mme. Coignet. And in proportion as intermediate instruction for girls is developed in our country, writers now little known will come forward to elucidate questions as yet but poorly understood. The number of young women who take degrees in science and letters increases every year, and scientific literature will undoubtedly in the near future find among them adepts of a scientific and philosophic turn of mind, such as Mme. Clémence Royer, whose works embrace a vast portion of the human thought of the present time.

" During a certain period, toward the middle of the century, a mystical tendency gave birth to writings of a lofty inspiration, which by their form almost attained to poetry. Mme. de Gasparin and Mlle. Eugénie de Guérin were the high priests of this school. But the current has changed, and these two meritorious women have left no disciples. Quite different is the elegant superficial literature of the society journals, in which the toilets and pleasures of the fashionable world are described. Mme. de Peyronny, whose brilliant pseudonym is Etincelle, understands wonderfully well the volatile art of giving form to that which is as delicate as the wings of the butterfly. To treat lightly light things is not an easy task, and nothing is more difficult than to be always clever. A knowledge of foreign languages plays an important part in our literature, especially since the war of 1870-'71, and every book of value published abroad has been translated into French, generally by women. Although this kind of work does not admit of great latitude for the development of any individuality, Mme. Arvède Barine, by a thorough study of Russian, German and English literatures, has made a deserved reputation as a specialist in this department of literary labor.

" Women have not played a prominent part in French theatrical literature. I do not mean to say, however, that they have not the ability and desire to write plays. The material difficulties, such as the getting up of the piece, the rehearsals, etc., would be enough to discourage them even if the directors were not to turn their back upon them. At a time when the newspapers throw wide their columns to feminine pens, *impresarios* cling to the old prejudice and shut their doors—except in a few extraordinary instances — against every piece written by a woman. The case of a lady is cited—and she is probably not the only one—who, in order to have her play produced, had to hire a theatre, engage actors, and take upon herself the responsibility of the whole representation. She was probably more persevering and had more money for the realization of her dream than other feminine play-writers, since her example has not been followed. As no physiological reason has been advanced to prove that women, who are capable of contriving good novels, are incapable of making good plays, we may hope that this last prejudice will soon go to join the others in the oblivion of the past.*

"In such a short and rapid sketch I can only give the principal features of the epoch, and many names worthy of mention must be passed over for lack of space. This paper would miss its aim if I were to turn bibliographer. More important than persons is the movement, which, starting from a fixed point at the beginning of the century, is pushing on toward the hidden future of its close. In looking back at the first half of this period, it is impossible not to be struck by the marked improvement, during the past thirty years, in the literary status of French women. The future has still greater ameliorations in store for us if we continue to preserve that sense of dignity which, with very rare exceptions, characterizes to-day the female authors of France. If, at some gathering of artists or *literati*, the eye is arrested by a woman attired in tasteful simplicity, if she converses with graceful ease, if she

---

* The visitor to the Théâtre Français will notice among the large and interesting collection of busts of famous French playwrights which adorn the halls and stairways of this theatrical pantheon, the marble figures of two women, not the least of the galaxy, George Sand and Mme. de Girardin, who have added many admirable dramas to the repertory of the House of Molière. Since 1680, when the Français was founded, about sixty plays by women have been acted. Mlle. Arnaud, whose *Mademoiselle du Vigean* was given at the Français for the first time on June 28, 1883, is the latest female dramatic writer at this theatre. Dramas by women have been produced at other Paris theatres. The most recent instance is the *Autour du mariage*, a comedy in five acts, played at the Gymnase in the autumn of 1883, and due to the joint authorship of the Countess de Martel (Gyp) and M. Hector Crémieux.

knows how to listen to the recitations and the music, it is very probable that this is one of those women of whom French literature is proud. It was not safe formerly to entertain such an opinion, but blue stockings have disappeared since authoresses daily ply the needle."

"Somebody," Mme. Léon Bertaux* writes me, "has said 'Thought, daughter of the soul, has no sex.' A president of Oberlin College declared in 1867: 'While admitting that the two sexes are equally capable, I do not mean to affirm thereby that there exists no normal difference between the intelligence of women and that of men.' This incontestable diversity, this variety in the essence of expression, renders feminine art the corollary of masculine art. It is precisely in taking our stand on this precious result, that we demand for the woman, who devotes herself to art, those opportunities for elementary culture afforded by the School of Fine Arts, in order that she may possess a solid foundation on which to build her artistic conceptions. If a goodly number of

---

* Mme. Léon Bertaux is one of the most distinguished of modern French sculptors. Besides the statues which she has exposed during a long series of years at various exhibitions, she is the author of a number of monumental works, two frontals of the Tuileries, decorative statues for several public monuments, and a large fountain composed of eight bronze figures at Amiens. Mme. Bertaux is the only Frenchwoman who, having taken three medals in sculpture, is *hors concours*, that is to say, she may be a candidate only for the medal of honor, which is conferred each year at the annual exhibition (*salon*) on one sculptor. Mme. Bertaux is the founder and presiding genius of the Society of Female Painters and Sculptors (*Union des femmes peintres et sculpteurs*), the earliest organization of the kind in France. "The object of this international association," says Mme. Bertaux, "is to offer its members annually an opportunity to exhibit their principal works, to defend their interests, and to afford young talent a chance of making itself known."

19

Swedish women take an honorable position in our exhibitions and treat successfully historical subjects, it is because they have the means of developing at an early hour their artistic taste, for Stockholm has a National School of Fine Arts where women may study from the living model.*

"The interesting personality of Mme. Vigée-Lebrun (1755-1842) opens the series of the French female artists of the century. Marie Anne Elisabeth Vigée, daughter and pupil of the painter of this same name, whom she overshadowed, gave evidence in early youth of a great talent for art. At seven she is said to have drawn a man's head, full of promise for the future, and at twenty she had become celebrated for portraits commanded by the State. D'Alembert, in the name of his colleagues, gave her access to all the sittings of the French Academy, and in 1783, under the absolute monarchy, she was made a member of the Academy of Painting and Sculpture, notwithstanding the opposition of some of her future associates.

"To-day, when the female painter or sculptor is no longer looked down upon by a prejudiced society, but, on the contrary, is rather courted for her artistic talent, is it not strange that the only obstacles which she encounters are those thrown in her way by the very institutions which ought to befriend her? Does not common sense revolt against the check which they place on her

---

* That Frenchwomen are only waiting for the opportunity to participate in the valuable instruction of the School of Fine Arts is evidenced on every hand. M. Emile Guiard, for example, the secretary of the institution which he mentions, wrote me in January, 1883 : "Women are admitted to the School of the Louvre (*École du Louvre*), and every one of our lectures, however dry they may be, has at least five or six female listeners."

emulation? It is true that no fixed law limits women's artistic ambition, but a hidden influence, all the more mischievous because of its disguise, militates against our success and public recognition. I shall cite but one example among a thousand. Is there a male artist of the ability of our great portrait-painter, Mme. Nélie Jacquemart, who has not been awarded a first-class medal and membership in the Legion of Honor?* The directors of the Department of Fine Arts, who have succeeded each other from time to time, have been influenced by prejudice and arbitrary routine rather than by equity, so that, since the foundation of the Third Republic, they have systematically refused female artists this important honor. The wrong is increased by the advantages enjoyed by men, for whom the country has smoothed the way, permitting them, without expense, to reap the benefits of the School of Fine Arts until their thirtieth year, if necessary, while, at the same time, the female painters and sculptors pay their portion of the taxes for the support of an institution which is an obstacle to them throughout their whole career.† It is easily understood, therefore, that the female

---

* Mme. Bertaux herself presents a striking instance of this same injustice. Sculptors of far less merit were long ago made members of the Legion of Honor. To fully appreciate the importance of this exclusion, it should be remembered that these distinctions are very highly valued in France. But fifteen women, by the way, are members of the Legion of Honor.

† The justice of Mme. Bertaux's complaint can be fully appreciated only by those who have carefully examined the question. A French male artist who is not a graduate of the State School of Fine Arts, who is not a member of the State Academy of Fine Arts, who stands outside of the authorized official circle, labors under the greatest difficulties. The annual art exhibition, which up to 1882 had been controlled by the State, passed, in that year, into the hands of an independent body of artists (*Association des artistes français*). The prime cause of this change was the desire to escape as much as possible the evil influence of an official art *coterie*. If the male artists of

artist, who is unequally armed for the combat, and whose honors are not adjudged after the same rules of merit, occupies only a secondary place in France. These difficulties explained, the talent of the individuals mentioned in these notes stands out all the more prominently.

" The number of women still living who have received official medals since 1824 is not less than fifty-five, of whom three are sculptors and four engravers. The three sculptors are Mme. de Fauvau, Mlle. Thomas, and the author of these notes. Mme. Felicie de Fauvau, who received a medal of the second class in 1827, was one of that galaxy of romantic artists who substituted for the bad classic school of the Restoration a rather characterless style, which may be called—if we may be pardoned the pleonasm—neo-renaissance. Mlle. Mathilde Thomas, an animal sculptor of great merit, received a third class medal in 1881.* Among the forty-eight painters who have taken medals, the name of Rosa Bonheur is most

France found the yoke unbearable, it is easy to imagine what the female artists suffer, who have against them not only the State but also the extra-State organization. It must not be inferred, however, from what has just been said, that female artists are entirely ignored. The following women took honors at the *Salon* of 1883 : Second class medal, Mme. Demont-Breton, who also received a gold medal at the Amsterdam Exhibition of 1883 ; third class medal, Mlle. Lucie Contour and Mlle. Léonie Valmon ; honorable mentions : Mme. Fanny Prunaire, *née* Colonny, Mlle. Blau, of Vienna ; Mme. Van Marcke-Diéterle, Mme. Hélène Luminais, Mme. Lavieille, Mme. Marie Bashkirseff, of Russia ; Mme. Signoret, Mme. Bénard, Mlle. Delattre, a pupil of Mme. Bertaux ; Mlle. Lancelot, and Mme. Desca. This list includes painters, sculptors, engravers, etc. The last five names are those of sculptors. The State purchased the work of two of these artists. In the summer of 1883, Mlle. Martin finished the bust of Le Verrier, which had been ordered by the French Academy of Sciences.

* At least one female sculptor has the honor of being represented in the collection of art at the Théâtre Français—Fanny Dubois Davesnes, the author of the bust of the once famous dramatist, Marivaux.

widely known, although the talent of a young artist, Mme. Demont-Breton, whose fine canvas, " The Beach," (*La plage*) secured a second-class medal at the *Salon* of 1883 and was purchased by the State, places her in the front rank. Mlle. Bonheur studied under her father, and her first work seemed to give promise of a sculptor. It was a fine study in plaster of a bull that thus early revealed the solid qualities of the future artist. In 1848 she produced her masterpiece, ' Nivernese Ploughing ' (*Labourage Nivernais*), which is found in the Luxembourg, and in 1865 the Empress bestowed upon her the Cross of the Legion of Honor.*

" But there is ground to hope that in a very near future women will experience in the career of arts a juster treatment; opportunities for study similar to those enjoyed by men, a school of fine arts, the prize of Rome as a stimulant, and the same artistic and official distinctions. I should also demand, although this will not be so generally accepted, that women form part of the juries at our art exhibitions.† The success of the public exhibitions of the Society of Female Painters and Sculptors proves that the victory is socially won. The second exhibition, that of 1883, occurred in the Palais de l' Industrie, the same edifice in which the great annual *Salon* displays its vast international art collection. This is an important and significant concession. It means that the day is indeed approaching when Frenchwomen will be on an exact

---

* I must pass over in silence many female artists of talent, such as Mlle. Élodie La Villette, the marine painter ; Mlle. Berthe Wegmann, the historical and portrait painter ; and Mme. Euphémie Muraton, the painter of still life.—L. B.

† Mlle. Thérèse Schwartze was a member of the jury on Fine Arts at Amsterdam in 1883. This is the first time in the history of international exhibitions that a woman has held such a position.

equality with Frenchmen in everything pertaining to that grandest of studies, the Fine Arts."

" One of the principal careers open to women," writes Mlle. Laure Collin,* " is the honorable and modest calling of teacher, and especially teacher of music, in which department large numbers have distinguished themselves. Most of these successful teachers are graduates of the well-known Paris Conservatory, which is open, when vacancies occur, to every woman under twenty, who possesses the necessary means, and who can pass the competitive examinations.†

---

* Mlle. Laure Collin, the author of several admirable manuals on musical subjects, may be considered to be the presiding genius of musical instruction in the French public school system. She is professor in the Girls' Superior Normal School at Fontenay-aux-Roses, the Normal School for Mistresses of the Seine at Paris, and the Normal Courses for Maternal Schools, at Sceaux and Paris, where she teaches a remarkable and very successful method approved by the Minister of Public Instruction. Mlle. Collin is also the author of a history of music.

† As several American girls have already studied with success at the Conservatory, and as others doubtless contemplate following their example, I subjoin some remarks on this institution which Mlle. Collin has been kind enough to furnish me. "The Conservatory," says Mlle. Collin, " is a school of high virtuosity. To keep one's place is almost as difficult as to get admitted to the school, for it is absolutely necessary, under penalty of expulsion, to pass the periodic examinations. This requirement forces talents to multiply and develop, I hardly know how, for there is no uniform method pursued, each professor being free to apply his own, if he has one. But I explain the success of the institution in this wise. There are families of artists, forming a sort of privileged class, in which virtuosos succeed each other generation after generation, and the children, while at their play, so to speak, imbibe good musical traditions. The girls who fill the classes of the Conservatory come generally from these families. Let us take a student of ordinary ability and follow her step by step from the moment she enters the school. If a member of one of the three or four elementary classes, she will have to undergo the trimestrial examinations, when her progress will be

"France possesses many talented female pianists. Léonie Tonel—a very exceptional case—was unanimously awarded a certificate by the Conservatory jury of admission, her remarkably skilful execution exempting her from the competitive examination. One of our most celebrated pianists was Mme. Pleyel, *née* Moke, a pupil of Jacques Herz, Moscheles and Kalkbrenner. After playing with great success in all the capitals of Europe, she became, in 1847, professor at the Brussels Conservatory, and died in Belgium in 1875. Mme. Farrenc, whose death occurred a few years ago, was also a pupil of Moscheles, Hummel and Reicha, and was distinguished as a composer, writer and virtuoso. In 1869 the Institute awarded her the Chartier prize for the best compositions of music. Mme. Farrenc's class at the Conservatory has turned out

---

ascertained and promotion into the upper classes will follow. Her aim must now be to secure prizes awarded at the public competitions which occur in the month of July. These examinations consist in the execution of a piece of music designated beforehand by the jury, and the reading at sight of an unpublished piece. The first is the same for all the competitors, but its interpretation varies according to the style of the different professors, for it is evident that the pupils of M. Delaborde will give another rendering than those of M. Lecouppey or Mme. Massart. The fate of the pupil depends upon the result of these public competitions. She may try three times, a year apart. If she secures, the third year, an honorable mention, for example, she has two more trials, but is pitilessly dropped from the Conservatory after two new successive failures. The professors, of course, look with most favor on pupils endowed with a talent for execution and capable of shining at these musical tourneys. But it often happens that the unsuccessful students succeed better as teachers than their more fortunate companions. It has been the custom during the past ten years for Mme. Erard to present the winner of the first prize one of her pianos, while the Pleyels do the same for the second prizeman. The present director of the Conservatory, M. Ambroise Thomas, has introduced many changes in the curriculum of studies, and to-day the pupils receive a most complete musical and dramatic education."

a legion of good female pianists. Among our most highly appreciated contemporaries, I may mention Mesdames Massart, Josephine Martin, Montigny-Rrémaury, whose talent for execution is very remarkable, and among the number of those who have secured a first prize at the Conservatory, and who follow the modest calling of teacher, I may name Hortense Parent, who has struck out a new path and founded a normal school for the piano, which has rendered great service to extra-State instruction.

"Among celebrated singers, who, though dead, are not forgotten, I may cite Mesdames Cinti Damoreau, Dorus-Gras, Nau, and Stolz, all of whom became famous at the opera; Mlle. Falcon, whose magnificent voice, lost, alas! so soon, has not yet had its equal; Mme. Vandenheuvel-Duprez, cut down in her prime and at the zenith of her success; Mme. Cabel, who, although Belgian by birth, won naturalization on the stage of the Opéra Comique; Mesdames Marie Sasse, Gaymard, Darcier, Wertheimber, and Delagrange; Mme. Gallimarié, who gave such an original creation to so many rôles; that eminent artist, whom we are still permitted to enjoy, and whose style is marked with such rare distinction, — Mme. Miolan-Carvalho; Mme. Bilbaut-Vancheld, whose first-rate talent immediately placed her in the front rank; and lastly, that brilliant singer, eclipsed after shining an instant like a meteor, —Mme. Adler Devriès.*

"I must not forget two celebrated female musicians of quite different styles, Mesdames Viardot and Ugalde.

---

* The name of Mme. Adler Devriès, a native of Holland, reminds me of several other foreigners who have made a reputation in France, as Sophie Cruvelli (the Baroness Vigier), who gave new life to Spontini's *Vestale;* Krauss, who is to-day our leading operatic singer; the Countess de Sparre and the Countess Merlin, whose sweet voices charmed drawing-rooms at the time when Malibran electrified the public at the Italian Theatre.—L. C.

Auber said of the latter, 'She would have invented music,' and Charles de Bernard pretended that she must have been born in a piano. This was indeed almost true, for Delphine Beaucé (who became at sixteen Mme. Ugalde), a pupil of her mother and her grandfather, the composer Porro, won a medal, when six years old, in a competition, where she performed a part in a composition for two pianos. She taught music at nine, and three years later sang the mezzo-soprano solos in concerts given by the Prince of Moscow. Her voice soon developed into a soprano of great compass. Her *début* in 1848 at the Opéra Comique in the *Domino noir* created a sensation. Engaged several times by this theatre and by the Lyrique, Bouffes, Porte St. Martin, Châtelet, she created twenty-one important rôles. Mme. Ugalde (married in 1866 to M. Varcollier) has for several years devoted herself to teaching, and no one has had greater success in forming artists for the lyric stage. Marie Sasse, for example, is one of her pupils.

" Mme. Viardot (Pauline Garcia), daughter of the Italian singer Manuel Garcia, goddaughter of Paër, and sister of Malibran, is, beyond question, one of the greatest artists of our epoch. Her sweet mezzo-soprano voice, supported by a masterly style, has breathed new life into the *Orphée* and *Alceste* of Gluck, which had too long lacked that powerful interpretation without which they fail. Mme. Viardot has been heard in all the great cities of Europe and has sung in the language of each country she visited. Among her most remarkable creations are Gounod's Sappho and Fidès in *Le Prophète.* She has had for some time a class at the Conservatory, and is the author of several unpublished partitions.

" Several Frenchwomen have taken up operatic composition and some of them have succeeded in it. At their head stands Louise Bertin, who, shortly after the appearance of Victor Hugo's ' Notre Dame of Paris, ' composed an opera, *Esméralda*, the subject of which was drawn from this book. Mme. Tarbé des Sablons is the author of two operas, *Les Bataves* and *Les Brigands*, founded on Schiller. Mme. Pauline Thys has written an opera in four acts entitled *Judith*, and several operettas which were well received. Mme. Olagnier composed, a short time ago, a very original comic opera, *Le Saïs*, which had a great success, Capoul creating the principal rôle.*

" In the symphonic style of composition I must again mention Mme. Farrenc (aunt of M. Reyer of the Institute), the author of a symphony which was performed at the Conservatory and much admired. I may further name the Baroness de Maistre, the Countess de Grandval,† who has composed some fine religious and instrumental music; Augusta Holmès, who has written a symphony, *Les Argonautes ;* and lastly, Mlle. Chaminade, whose very remarkable compositions were executed in 1882 at the Pasdeloup concerts in Paris.

" In ballad music I must recall the names, forgotten today, of Pauline Duchambge, a master in this department of music, and of that other well-known artist, Loïsa Puget (Mme. Gustave Lemoine) who followed her. Mlle. Puget was the author of her own ballads, which she sang with great charm and spirit. Mme. de Rothschild is the author

---

* " If an opera by a woman succeeds, I am delighted, for it is a confirmation of my little system that women are capable of doing everything we do, with this single difference between them and us, that they are more amiable than we are."—Voltaire, October 18, 1736, to Mr. Berger, director of an opera-house.

† Mme. de Grandval was awarded in 1883 the prize offered by the Minister of Fine Arts at the competition of the Society of Composers.

of a sweet melody which all Paris sang, and Pauline Thys, whom I have already mentioned, has shown talent for ballad music. The refined drawing-room of Mme. Marjolin, daughter of Ary Scheffer, was recently charmed with the melodies of an artist of great merit, Mlle. Wild, a pupil of Barbereau. Her style is large and pure. She has written several masses, among others a pastoral mass, some remarkable hymns, and pieces for the organ. She composed almost, at her *début*, a quatuor for string instruments which won the approbation of masters like Onslow.

" I have spoken of some of the leading female teachers of the piano, and I have now to mention what we have done in vocal instruction. Eugénie Chauvot, a pupil of Duprez, has secured a high place as professor of singing, and has grouped about her the most distinguished artists. Mme. Féret, a pupil of Révial, whose poor health greatly limits her work, has carefully collected the excellent principles of the master and transmitted them to her disciples. French women play also an important part in the musical instruction given in the public and normal schools. The author of these notes has labored in this field.* The popularizing of musical instruction has made great progress in the last few years, and its development bids fair to soon place France on a level with the nations the most favored in this respect. I am proud to say Frenchwomen have contributed to this progress in the most remarkable and efficacious manner."

" I may say, without exposing myself to the imputa-

---

* I have witnessed with astonishment the wonderful results of Mlle. Collin's method, and I do not hesitate to recommend its careful examination to the teachers in our American schools, where the science of music is too often sacrificed to the learning by ear of a few patriotic songs.

tion of indulging in national vanity," writes M. Paul Foucart,* "that in no other country of Europe does woman, in proportion as her situation requires it, work as much as in France; that nowhere does she, in every grade of society, associate herself so closely and effectively with the husband in his efforts to assure the moral and material prosperity of the family. Those foreigners who have learned, by a long residence in France, to understand the country, are powerfully struck by this fact. ' No housewives are more perfect than the French,' says Karl Hillebrand,† ' who, without boasting of being housekeepers after the German fashion, know how to superintend domestic affairs with a judicious and firm hand. Many of them even take the husband's place in business. . . Ambitious to the highest degree, passionate under a cloak of coldness, clever in what they undertake, elegant in appearance, endowed by nature with a grace carefully cultivated by a skilful education, possessing above all a firm character and a strong will, they direct husband as well as brother or son, urge him on, smooth his way, and take all the necessary and difficult steps to secure his success. In a word, they conquer him a place in the world and help him to defend it.' ‡

"The most natural and legitimate method of securing

---

* M. Paul Foucart, of Valenciennes, is a close student of industrial questions in France, and is the author of a pamphlet entitled the "Industrial Function of Women" (*Fonction industrielle des femmes*), the substance of which was given as a lecture at Havre in 1880.

† "France and the French during the Second Half of the Nineteenth century" (*La France et les français pendant la seconde moitié du XIXe siècle*), Chapter I.—P. F.

‡ I do not pretend that there are not exceptions to Karl Hillebrand's complimentary estimate of Frenchwomen, but these exceptions are much rarer than people generally imagine.—P. F.

that grand *desideratum* of society, the division of labor, would be for the women of all classes, supported by the men, to devote themselves entirely to household duties. But almost always among the lower classes, women are forced to seek occupations directly remunerative, which, on account of the brusque development of the great industries and the exactions of a fierce competition, compel them to confide their children to mercenary or charitable institutions, thus inflicting on the family, in exchange for insignificant pecuniary gains, incalculable moral losses.

"Without believing that the world is degenerating and that the ideal of humanity must be sought in the past, I hold that before the advent of the industrial revolution born of the general use of steam machinery, the condition of the women of the lower classes was, in certain respects, more normal than it is to-day. Manufactories employing hundreds of hands were then very rare, while many occupations—spinning, lace making, tulle work, the weaving of muslin, the reeling and weaving of silk, the sorting, picking and winding of wool bobbins, etc.,—were followed at home. In this way women gained at the domestic hearth a sum which considerably augmented the resources of the family, without depriving it of maternal care and influence. If young girls left the paternal roof, it was only to labor in the fields, to become servants, or to work as apprentices in small shops,—callings in which agility, address, or taste were the all-important requisites.

"Toward the second third of the nineteenth century were felt for the first time with all their force, the consequences of a production which developed more rapidly than the demand, and which occasioned stoppage and famine where its promoters predicted abundance. Weeks without work for the husband and misery at home! How is the family to be kept from starvation? Many wives imagined that the shop, the cause of the evil, might also prove its remedy. If the husband and wife were both at work would not the home realize twice as much, at least in ordinary seasons? And when the hard times came, it was not probable that all industries would be affected; when the shops stopped, it would be rare if both husband and wife were thrown out of work. Will not life therefore be made easier? The answer to this question is found in the following table,* published in 1882, by the minister of commerce, which gives the actual wages of those employed in textile industries in France.

		Ordinary Wages.	Maximum Wages.	Minimum Wages.
Spinning.	Cotton,	1.78	2.29	1.40
	Wool,	1.71	2.15	1.37
	Silk,	1.61	2.04	1.34
	Hemp and Flax,	1.68	2.19	1.38
	Averages,	1.69	2.17	1.36
Weaving.	Cotton,	2.03	2.66	1.64
	Wool,	1.82	2.31	1.56
	Silk,	1.75	2.41	1.33
	Hemp and Flax,	1.69	2.19	1.36
	Averages,	1.82	2.39	1.47

" It appears, therefore, that it is for the miserable pittance of one franc and eighty-two centimes† that so many

---

* This table is taken from the " Statistical Annual of France " (*Annuaire statistique de la France*) for 1882.—P. F. The money figures in this and the tables which follow are in francs and centimes. A franc equals about nineteen cents, and a centime about a fifth of a cent.

† About thirty-five cents in American money. It may be considered, however, that thirty-five cents has the purchasing power in France of at least fifty cents in the United States.

women abandon home and children, thus doing a great injury to themselves as well as to those women who cling to the old customs. The competition of the factory has reduced the price of manual labor in many industries still practiced at home. Embroidery and hand-made lace, for example, although they have much declined, continue to give employment, the first to 150,000, and the second to about 220,000, women. The pay of an ordinary embroiderer in the Vosges has fallen to one franc and ten centimes, while the apprentice of fourteen, who copies only simple easy models, earns one-half that amount.* Still worse is the condition of lace-makers. At Valenciennes, of which they were formerly one of the glories, they have entirely disappeared. At Alençon, in Auvergne, at Chantilly, at Bayeux, they earn only from one to one and a half francs, and it is probable that all of these poor souls will have to soon lay aside their bobbins unless they wish to die of hunger.

"In the workshops of the small manufacturers the situation is scarcely any better, as is shown by the careful investigations made by the Paris Chamber of Commerce in 1860. At that time 106,310 women were employed in the various industries of the capital. The Chamber of Commerce divided them into three classes according to their occupations and wages :

First Division.	1,176 women earning	0.50
	2,429 " "	0.75
	6,505 " "	1.00
	7,013 " "	1.25
	17,203	

---

* Augustin Cochin, " Monograph on the Workingwoman of the Vosges " (*Monographie sur l'ouvrière des Vosges*).—P. F.

	16,722	women earning	1.50
	7,644	" "	1.75
	24,810	" "	2.00
	7,723	" "	2.25
	17,273	" "	2.50
Second Division.	2,055	" "	2.75
	7,588	" "	3.00
	411	" "	3.25
	2,250	" "	3.50
	1,264	" "	4.00
	88,340		

	278	" "	4.50
	270	" "	5.00
Third Divison.	146	" "	6.00
	73	" "	7 to 10
	767		

" If we leave out of the account the first of these three divisions, composed principally of girls under sixteen and of women whose aim is simply to add to their own comfort or supplement their husband's salary by needle-work, and who are often lodged and boarded ; and if, for quite different reasons, we do not take into consideration the third division, made up of women who enjoy exceptionally high wages,—the second division will alone furnish the data with which to arrive at the average pay of Parisian working-women, engaged chiefly in the important departments of tailoring and the manufacture of textile fabrics. It appears that this average is two francs and fourteen centimes a day,—a small sum ; greater, however, than the reality, as M. Leroy-Beaulieu has proved by pointing out certain elements which had been neglected in the calculation.*

---

* "Women's Work in the Nineteenth Century " (*Le travail des femmes au XIXe siècle*), first part, Chapter IV.—P. F. Mme. Caroline de Barrau also has shown, in her able "Essay on the Wages of Women at Paris" (*Étude sur le salaire du travail féminin à Paris*) that the average pay of working-

"Since 1860, on account of the increased depreciation of money and the corresponding rise in the price of food, these figures have gone up a little. But the following table, taken from the statistical publication for 1882 already referred to, which places Paris side by side with the capitals of the departments, shows how small this increase has been:

DAILY WAGES, WITHOUT BOARD, OF A WORKING-WOMAN IN THE SMALL INDUSTRIES.

	1. AT PARIS.			2. IN THE CAPITALS OF THE DEPARTMENTS.		
	Usual.	Maximum.	Minimum.	Usual.	Maximum.	Minimum.
Washer-women ...3.00	3.50	2.50	1.70	2.09	1.47	
Embroiderers 3.00	4.00	2.50	1.69	2.19	1.36	
Corset-makers 2.00	3.50	1.50	1.60	2.08	1.28	
Dress-makers.....2.00	4.00	1.50	1.62	2.06	1.35	
Pantaloon-makers.4.00	6.00	3.00	1.62	2.08	1.30	
Lace-makers......3.00	4.50	2.00	2.03	2.57	1.56	
Artificial flower-makers 3.00	3.50	1.50	1.87	2.45	1.51	
Vest-makers 3.00	4.00	2.00	1.65	2.08	1.32	
Makers of linen garments 2.00	3.50	1.50	1.45	1.83	1.20	
Milliners 2.00	3.50	1.50	1.49	2.03	1.20	
Sewers on shoes..3.00	4.50	2.00	1.66	2.10	1.30	
Averages 2.80	4.10	2.00	1.67	2.14	1.35	

"Less than three francs at Paris and less than two francs in the chief towns of the provinces,—such are the daily wages of working-women in the small industries of France. And it must be further borne in mind that this

women is far below the figures given in the statistics. She considers it even under two francs. M. Othenin d'Haussonville (*Revue des deux mondes,* April 15, 1883, p. 859) says: "Having noted the large number of women who earn but two francs or less than two francs, I am led to believe that Mme. de Barrau is right."

20

pittance becomes still more beggarly, or is reduced to nothing, in moments of sickness, during a dead season or complete stoppage. To the wife whose husband also earns something, it is a very appreciable help; for the virtuous girl or widow it is scarcely enough to keep body and soul together; for the woman who has family cares —aged parents to support, young children to bring up— it is the source of terrible misery, mendicity or prostitution.

"Such is the present condition of things in France, similar to that found in many other countries in Europe. The picture of the fearful consequences of this situation has been often drawn, especially by Jules Simon [*] and Leroy-Beaulieu,[†] and I myself have endeavored to suggest the moral and material remedies for the disorder."[‡]

French socialism, at all epochs and under every form, has always been more or less friendly to women. The working-men's congresses of late years have passed resolutions in favor of giving women the same pay as men for the same work, and, in some instances, demanding their political equality. But the dreams of theorists and

---

[*] " The Working-woman " (*L'ouvrière*).—P.F.   Jules Simon's book tends to this conclusion : Woman should be the guardian of the domestic hearth, and man alone should go forth into the world to win the daily bread.

[†] " Women's Work in the Nineteenth Century " (*Le travail des femmes au XIXe siècle*).—P. F.

[‡] " Women's Industrial Function " (*Fonction industrielle des femmes*).—P. F.   The State employs women in but one department, if I am not mistaken. A chief clerk of the Minister of Posts and Telegraphs informs me that 5,500 females are engaged in France in the postal and telegraphic service. They are paid from 800 to 1,800 and 2,000 francs a year, and at the end of a certain period are retired on a pension.   The sale of tobacco, which is a government monopoly, is entirely in the hands of women.   No man is ever given a tobacco shop in France.

the resolutions of public assemblies have found their realization, probably, in but one instance,—the remarkable Social Palace at Guise.

M. Godin* writes me : "The foundation of the *Familistère* reposes on principles which are a synthesis of the practical ideas forced upon the attention of the world by the St. Simonian, phalansterian and communistic schools of the early part of this century. But it is above all for women and children that our creation at Guise has proved a happy event. The Association of the *Familistère* is, I think, the only institution which has, up to the present time, put into practice respect for the rights of women, who are treated as the equal of men in all the affairs of life. This idea of the equality of the sexes was borrowed from Fourier. The *Familistère* could not change the laws of French society, but, as members of the Association, women enjoy all the rights of men. They may aspire to all the honors at the disposal of the Asso-

---

* In order not to endanger the success of the *Familistère*, M. Godin felt constrained for many years to hold aloof from public affairs. But in 1870 he broke a long silence by publishing a manifesto, in which he vigorously attacked the Imperial *plébiscite* of that year and predicted the misfortunes it was to entail on France. A month later M. Godin was chosen a member of the Council General (*conseil général*) of the Department of the Aisne. When the Franco-German war burst upon the country, he, as mayor of Guise, firmly protected the interests of the city against the exorbitant demands of the enemy. Elected in February, 1871, a member of the National Assembly, M. Godin sat five years on the liberal republican (*Union républicaine*) side of the Chamber. He retired from national politics in 1876, but has always retained his seat in the Council General of the Aisne. In the midst of political and industrial occupations, M. Godin has found time for literary work. The ideas so briefly treated in the text are fully developed in a number of valuable volumes on social questions, but more especially in "Government, What it has Been, What it Ought to Be, and True Socialism in Action" (*Le gouvernement, ce qu'il a été, ce qu'il doit être, et le vrai socialisme en action*).

ciation; they are electors and eligible; they may form a part of all committees and councils. They perform these duties with faithfulness, and have shown themselves inaccessible to cabal, which has not always been the case with the men.

" In order that women may profit by the social liberty to which the present current of ideas is leading them, a change must be made in the system of family life: domestic economy must be modified and perfected. The emancipation of women will remain in the domain of speculation, as long as our institutions and customs impose on the father and mother the entire responsibility of the care of the family. The *Familistère* has solved this problem by assuming the bringing up of the children from the moment of their birth, so that the mother has to bestow on them only her milk and caresses, and the family, its tenderness and affection. But even in the absence of mother and family the children are not neglected. They always receive the closest attention. At every stage of their growth the children are under the eye of the Association. Separated into nine divisions in nine different rooms, each division has its nurses and teachers, who give instruction in keeping with the age of their pupils. In this way the mother and father can confer on their offspring the delights of family life, without inflicting on them, at the same time, any of its discomforts. The care and education of the children—which are the same for both sexes—being thus assumed by the Association, the duties of maternity are reduced to nursing during the early months of the child, and the mother is not hindered from attending to her other occupations. Women, therefore, find themselves emancipated, in so far as they desire it, from one of the most monopolizing obligations; they recover their liberty and may devote themselves to work and culture.

" In order to introduce this innovation, it is indispensable that the isolated habitation give place to the common dwelling, the phalanstery or social palace, so that the bringing up of children may be made a distinct organized part of the family system. The *commune*, therefore, must be architecturally reformed, and all the common household duties be placed in proximity to the home. It is necessary, furthermore, to bring about the division of domestic labor; to establish for the children a nursery, infant schools, primary schools, etc.; to organize kitchens, laundries, public halls, etc. Only in this way is it possible to reconcile household duties and family cares with the exercise, on the part of women, of civil and political rights and lucrative employments."

CHAPTER IX.

ITALY.

I.—A GENERAL REVIEW.

BY AURELIA CIMINO FOLLIERO DE LUNA.

[Mrs. Aurelia Cimino Folliero de Luna was born at Naples, and is descended from a noble family of Spanish origin, her grandfather being a grandee. At the age of fifteen it was discovered that the young girl had a fine and powerful voice, and after hearing Ungher she was seized with a passion for the operatic stage. But her parents objected, and these aspirations after artistic fame were abruptly cut short. Later in life, however, when a political exile in England, Mrs. Cimino found that her musical talent stood her in great stead, and singing lessons mitigated the hardships of a forced residence in a foreign land. In 1846 she married a young Neapolitan poet, Cimino, and when he was banished two years later for participation in the revolutionary movement of 1848, she accompanied him into exile. She now passed several years in England, France, and northern Italy, and in due season became the mother of ten children. Mrs. Cimino's literary career began at Milan, in 1857, where she published, in the periodical *Gabinetto di Lettura*, some articles translated from the English. She next wrote for the *Italie*, a journal founded at Turin, with the co-operation of the Princess Cristine Belgioioso, and began later her advocacy of woman's rights by a series of letters to *La Nazione* and the *Rivista Europea*, of Florence. In 1872 Mrs. Cimino founded in that city, under the patronage of Queen Margaret, then Princess of Savoy, *La Cornelia*, a bi-monthly, especially devoted to the moral and material interests of women, which counted many distinguished Italian liberals among its contributors. Numerous family and literary occupations forced Mrs. Cimino to resign the editorship of the periodical in 1879, when it ceased to exist. Mrs. Cimino is the author of a novel (*Gabriello*), "Miramar, or Maximilian of Austria" (*Miramar, o Massimiliano d'Austria*), of a volume of travels, "Marshes, Mountains and Caverns" (*Lagune, Monti e Caverne*), of an essay entitled "Idleness in

taly" (*L'indolenza in Italia*), etc. Mrs. Cimino's last work is "Social Questions" (*Questioni Sociali*), a collection of scattered essays now forming a
part of the "Library of Social Science" (*Bilioteca di Scienze Sociali*), which
is being issued at Cesena. Mrs. Cimino has been sent by the Italian government on two important missions: the first, in 1878, by the Minister of Public Instruction, Coppino, to study the agricultural establishments for women
in France, and the second, in 1882, during the Berti ministry, to visit the
Trieste Exhibition and to make a report thereon to the Minister of Agriculture. This report appeared in 1883 in the *Italia Agricola,* a periodical published at Milan.]

THE emancipation of women is not a modern idea in
Italy,—not a result of the example set by the United States
and England. Italian women, even before they had an
exact notion of their rights, intuitively resisted the laws
and customs which taught that they were ignorant non-
entities, and subject to men's authority. Antiquity shows
us that Roman women had made many steps toward
freedom, under the empire of Augustus, who, perceiving
that high-minded women hesitated to marry because of
the legalized profligacy of the husband, promulgated the
Papian law, which corrected many abuses and encouraged
marriage. Claudius and Septimus Severus continued
the good work, and Justinian, with the assistance of the
Empress Theodora, published to the world his famous
Code, which mitigated the perpetual tutelage to which
women were subjected.* We may add to these facts the
opposition of Roman ladies to a proposition of the
senate to levy on them a severe war tax, which was defeated after a speech by Hortensia, daughter of the celebrated orator Hortensius, and, like him, noted for her

---

* "The Emperor Julian accorded to wives the right to apply for divorce, a
privilege which husbands alone had enjoyed since the earliest days of Rome,
so that the least gallant, perhaps, of the Cæsars was the most just toward
women."—Condorcet, "Letters of a *Bourgeois* of New Haven to a citizen of
Virginia."—T. S.

eloquence; the frequent attendance of women upon the lectures of the most renowned rhetoricians, and their presence at the lyceums for the youth. Hence I am permitted to affirm that, even in ancient Rome, there is evidence of a movement in favor of the equality of the sexes.

At a later period, during the *Renaissance*, women distinguished themselves not only in prose and poetry, thereby proving their equality and sometimes even their moral superiority to men, but they filled with distinction several of the most important chairs in the universities of Italy. Although they had no opportunities to study the sciences and the classics, many, nevertheless, took high rank in these departments of knowledge. At the epoch when the famous medical school of Salerno flourished, in the fourteenth century, Abella, a female physician, acquired a great reputation in medicine and wrote books in Latin, and in the following centuries women professed the sciences and the classics in the universities of Bologna, Brescia, Padua, and Pavia. It is during this period that we encounter the names of Bettina Gazzadini, of Mazzolini, whose bust is found among those of the most distinguished savants in the anatomical museum of Bologna; Laura Bassi, who lectured on physics in Latin; Marie delle Donne, Elena Cornaro, Clotilde Tambroni, and the celebrated Gaetana Agnesi, whom no women and few men have ever equaled in the extent and profoundness of her learning and in the goodness of her heart. I shall not speak of the beautiful Novella di Andrea, of Laura Cereta-Lerina, at twenty professor of metaphysics and mathematics at the University of Brescia; of the celebrated Neapolitan, Martha Marchina, professor in a German university, an honor enjoyed at that epoch by Italian women alone; of Pellegrina Amoretti, of Isotta da Rimini, and of so many other heroic souls who, toiling in isolation and surmounting unheard-of difficulties, ever protested with word and pen against the inferiority attributed to their sex, and finally won the admiration of men.

The liberal ideas of to-day, which have made Italy a new, powerful and free people, find an echo in our women, who, in this national regeneration, feel more keenly their own subordination and inferiority to men. Along with this desire for general equality is a growing demand for the practical education of women, which will open to them lucrative careers and make it possible for girls, standing alone in the world, to support themselves. Here it was that the example of America and England was useful to us; while we were still under foreign domination and ignorant of the solidarity of sex, Anglo-Saxon women were freer and more united. Almost immediately after the formation of the kingdom of Italy, courageous women arose, able orators and writers, such as Anna Maria Mozzoni, Malvina Frank, Gualberta Alaide Beccari, and many others. The last-named lady founded at Venice *La Donna*, a journal now published at Bologna, which, although a little exaggerated in tone, has done much to awaken women to a consciousness of their rights and to bring their demands to the attention of the public. A few years later I established at Florence *La Cornelia*, which counted among its contributors, besides talented female writers like the Princess Dora d'Istria, distinguished jurists like Gabba, Forlani, Mauro Macchi, Urtoller, and others, who treated with marked ability the legal side of the question. The periodical was honored by the patronage of the Princess Margherita, now Queen of Italy, which shows that our young sovereign was early favorable to the new ideas.

Pressed on by the liberal spirit of the time, the government began to make some concessions. In 1866 the widow, or the wife in the absence of the husband, was given the control over her own children, and the married woman in certain cases was secured in the management of her personal property. Thus the barbarous principles of the Roman law concerning the family, so opposed to the dignity of the mother, were in some measure modified. In 1876 a committee of the Chamber, of which the deputy Peruzzi was chairman, reported a bill in favor of conferring on women the right to vote on municipal and provincial questions (*voto amministrativo*), a privilege which they had formerly enjoyed in Lombardy and Venice under Austrian rule. This bill was reintroduced in 1883 by the Depretis ministry, and will soon come forward for discussion.* On the eve of its fall, the Bonghi ministry laid before the State board of education (*consiglio superiore*) a plan for the establishment of government normal schools, which gave Domenico Berti, who presided, the opportunity to enlarge the scope of the bill, by including high schools and professional schools for women. An anterior decree of the same minister had opened the uni-

---

* The Paris *Temps*, of April 7, 1883, gives the substance of the new law concerning the *voto amministrativo*—which must not be confounded with political suffrage, or the right of electing members of the Chamber of Deputies—about to be submitted to the Italian Parliament. The first clause declares that "all citizens of both sexes, who know how to read and write, are electors." The justice of this measure is recognized by many Italians who are far from considering themselves friends of the women's movement. A resident of Turin told me recently, that he knew a lady who owned almost the whole of the land in a certain township, but who had to submit to see her interests cared for or abused—the latter generally being the case—by her own tenants, members of the municipal council. They could cut roads through her estate, they could levy taxes on her—in a word, they had her completely in their power, while she, their proprietress, could not lift a finger in her own defence.—T. S.

versities to female students. Thenceforth Italian women could obtain a professional education and pursue the higher branches of knowledge.

The professional instruction of women was first advocated by Laura Mantegazza, who founded the earliest professional school in Milan, and who was ably seconded by the Marchioness Tanari and Alessandrina Ravizza. These distinguished ladies understood that scientific or industrial instruction, that is to say, a training which made self-support possible, was the real key to the woman question; that material independence, united with a higher moral and intellectual education, was the surest way of putting an end to the social inferiority of women. These ideas found influential friends among those in power. The director of the telegraphic service, Commendator d'Amico, began to employ females, in spite of the violent opposition of some narrow-minded men. The Minister of Public Instruction, G. Coppino, wished to open a new field to female activity by establishing courses in agriculture for women. In 1878 I had the honor of being sent to France by the government to study the agricultural schools of that country, and to prepare an official report thereon. Although this useful reform has not yet been realized, the conduct of the minister offers a striking example of the interest taken in the woman question by our leading statesmen. Not less remarkable was the mission confided to Miss Anna Maria Mozzoni by M. de Sanctis, a member of the ministry at that time, to represent the government at the International Women's Rights Congress, held at Paris in 1878.* Among the best known ministers

---

* Miss Mozzoni is one of the ablest and most active leaders of the women's movement in Italy. She is the author of several thoughtful publications on the various phases of the woman question, and is an eloquent

and ex-ministers of Italy who, although not all members of the same political party, are more or less friendly to the women's movement, may be mentioned the names of Domenico Berti, Cesare Correnti, Pasquale Mancini, the distinguished Italian professor; De Sanctis, G. Coppino, Ubaldino Peruzzi, Marco Minghetti, and Dr. Ber-

---

orator, as I can vouch, having listened to her opening address at the Paris congress mentioned in the text. But her grandest oratorical effort was the speech delivered in February, 1881, at the Universal Suffrage Congress of Rome, when she offered and supported a resolution in favor of women's suffrage, which was carried by a large majority. (See the *Free Religious Index*, of Boston, May 19, 1881, where I gave a complete translation of this speech.) Miss Mozzoni wrote me from Milan in August, 1882: "Since 1878, when I published my little pamphlet on the 'Civil and Political Condition of Italian Women' (*Delle condizioni civili e politiche delle Italiane*) nothing has changed, except that the progress of socialism is slowly liberalizing public opinion on the woman question, and that the number of female students in the universities increases every year. The development of the higher education of women is checked by the difficulties attending their admission to the gymnasiums, which depends entirely upon the good-will of the professors. I had to make a vigorous personal effort in order to secure a place for girls in the Milan gymnasium. When it was perceived that my friends in the Chamber intended to interpellate the ministry on the subject, the authorities yielded, and to-day girls may pursue their studies at our State schools. During the year 1881-2 there were twenty-five female students at the Milanese School of Fine Arts, several of whom have shown remarkable talent. Public opinion in northern Italy is more advanced on the woman question than the actual situation would seem to warrant. Our women are very intelligent, and there is a tendency among them—especially at Milan—toward liberal ideas. The extraordinary density of the population in this portion of Italy will be for a long time to come a great impediment to their admission to industrial pursuits and public employments. The most insignificant post is sought after by scores of capable men who are very jealous of aspiring women. Public opinion does not rebuff women who seek employment, but it does not aid and encourage them. In a word, we advance slowly. People know that we are in the right, they recognize the justice of our claims, and hold us, who preach the new doctrine, in esteem. But the generation which gov-

tani. To this list of our advocates may be added many members of Parliament and writers of talent and reputation.

These liberal-minded men of Italy have been well seconded in their efforts in favor of our sex by some distinguished women, who have not looked on with folded arms. I shall not attempt to enumerate the periodicals, the books, the societies and the labors due to these champions of their own cause. The roll is too long. But I may remark, that many generous ladies have opened at their own expense primary and industrial schools, as for instance the Antona Traversi Infant School (*Asilo Antona Traversi*) near Pavia, the Comparetti Raffalowich School in Venice, both named after their foundresses, and the school at Burano, near Venice, established by the Countess Marcello and the deputy Fambri, where instruction is given in the making of Venetian point lace (*punto di Venezia*)—an art which was almost lost. This institution now employs several hundred women, and has restored life to a little spot on the verge of decay.

---

erns to-day fought for liberty ; it was not brought up in liberty. Since the unification of Italy, we have gained a point or two in the code. Divorce and affiliation stand high on the calendar of Parliament, though I am aware that they will not be passed without a long struggle. The Senate, the nobility, the clergy, the queen—who is very devout, very aristocratic and not very intelligent—hesitate at every reform measure. There will be another hard-fought battle over the proposed administrative suffrage, but I think we shall here come off victors. The League for the Promotion of Women's Interests (*Lega promotrice degli interessi femminili*), of which I have the honor to be president, was founded at Milan in 1881. It is a very active organization, and counts among its members senators, deputies, priests, professors of the university, distinguished writers of both sexes, and a large number of working-men and women."—T. S.

Before closing this brief sketch, I desire to mention with deep gratitude the name of the man who first lifted up his voice in the Italian Parliament to defend and protect women. Salvatore Morelli deserves the veneration of every Italian woman. His first book, "Woman and Science" (*La donna e la scienza*), dedicated to Antona Traversi, was animated by a just and noble spirit, too radical, however, to meet with universal approbation. When he entered Parliament, Morelli, with the same courage, constancy, and radicalism, demanded the complete emancipation of women. Conservatives laughed, and many friends of our movement trembled for the cause. Ably seconded by Mancini, he succeeded in securing for women the right to testify in civil actions, a dignity which they had not previously enjoyed, although, by an absurd contradiction, they could be witnesses in criminal cases, convict of murder by a single word, and send the criminal to the scaffold. One of Morelli's last public acts was a divorce bill, which was examined by the Chamber. Guardasigilli Tomman Villa, the then Minister of Justice, was inclined to accept it, but death, which occurred in 1880, saved poor Morelli the pain of seeing his proposition rejected. An appeal to women has been made to raise a modest monument to Salvatore Morelli in memory of his good deeds.*

The reforms called for by Morelli and the other leaders of the Italian women's movement have not all been granted ; some have not even received serious attention. But I make no doubt, that in a few years the woman

---

* The editor of this volume has been requested to receive subscriptions to this fund in America and Europe outside of Italy. Such subscriptions will be acknowledged and forwarded to the committee in Italy. They should be addressed to Theodore Stanton, 59, rue de Chaillot, Paris, France.

question will be better understood in this country, will be regarded from a more elevated standpoint, and will obtain more general and more hearty support ; for, if we turn to the past, we are astonished at what has already been accomplished in this direction.

II. THE EDUCATIONAL MOVEMENT.

BY DORA D'ISTRIA.

[The Princess Hélène Koltzoff-Massalsky (Dora d'Istria), born Princess Ghika, first saw light at Bucharest. In 1849 she married Prince Alexander Koltzoff-Massalsky, of the elder branch of the Rurikowitchs, descendants of the founders of the Russian Empire, and lived for some time in intimacy with the court. Dora d'Istria is also the niece of Prince Gregory IV., the first to introduce into Wallachia the liberal institutions of modern civiliza- tion, while the members of her own family, the Ghikas, were among the most distinguished princes, or *hospodars*, of that country. An Italian journalist and author, Giovanni Boglietti, has well described the cosmopolitan char- acter of Dora d'Istria when he says that she is "Albanian by family origin, Romanian by birth, Greek by alliance, and still more by sympathy, and, lastly, Russian by marriage." Boglietti might have added that Dora d'Istria is French by language, for, although versed in a large number of modern tongues, she prefers to write in French, and is Italian by adoption, since, while Austria bore down on Italy with an iron hand, she boldly pro- claimed, as early as 1856, the idea of Italian unity, which then seemed an idle dream to statesmen, and took up her residence at Florence, where she still lives.* Dora d'Istria has traveled widely in Europe, the Orient, and the United States, which she visited in 1880 ; has published numerous ac- counts of her journeys, and is an honorary member of the French Geograph- ical Society. Her first publication, "Monastic Life in the Greek Church" (*La vie monastique dans l'église orientale*), was produced in 1855, and has since been followed by a large number of historical, political, social and literary works. She has written largely on the woman question. Her "Women in the Orient" (*Les femmes en Orient*) is a very valuable contri-

---

* Bartolomeo Cecchetti, director of the archives of Venice, wrote in 1868 : "The cause of nationalities finds in Dora d'Istria one of its most valiant and indefatigable supporters. The Greeks, the Albanians, the Romanians, and the southern Slaves, must admit that, if their history has been made intel- ligible and accurate, and questions most essential to their political and social future have been set forth so strongly that they have only to await an occasion and the means in order to attain their development in a happy and durable manner, it is due to this illustrious writer."

bution to this obscure subject, and her "Women by a Woman" (*Les femmes par une femme*), is a very able, complete, and remarkable book. Her voice and pen have also been employed in opposing war. The well-known author, Carlo Yriarte, has said of Dora d'Istria: "She is Parisian like Gavarni, Italian like Belginoso, Spanish like Larra, German like Goethe, Russian like Pouschkine, Wallachian like a Ghika, and Greek like Bozzaris or Lord Byron, with whom she divides the honor of having received from the Athenian Parliament the rights of 'Grand Citizen.'"]

DURING the age of the Italian republics, the women of Italy were famous for their learning. The brilliant and learned author of the "Literary History of Italy" (*Histoire littéraire d'Italie*), the Frenchman Ginguené, says that his compatriots can scarcely endure seeing women in the robes of the Muses, much less resign themselves to their putting on the doctor's cap. Italians were not so narrow. A tradition of the fourteenth century relates, that Dota Accorso taught at the celebrated university of that proud Bologna, whose device was *Docet*. In the fifteenth century Laura Cereta-Lerina was a professor of the University of Brescia. Padua, which occupies an exceptional place in the annals of learning, saw Helen Comaro Piscopia teaching philosophy in its university, and Novella di Andrea, as beautiful as learned, filling *ad interim* her brother's chair of the canon law. The large number of female poets shows how general was the cultivation of letters among women. In the sixteenth century, "so rich in illustrious women," as Rosalia Amari has truly said, there was scarcely an important city in Italy which did not possess its poetess. Ariosto does not hesitate to promise them immortality in the twentieth canto of the "Orlando Furioso," and Ginguené is surprised at this "extraordinary number of female poets." The Italian language itself, which speaks more emphatically on this point than any theorizing, created a long list of words, still lacking in the French, like *poetessa*, *autrice*, *dottoressa*, while in the fine arts occur *pittrice* and *scultrice.**

With the fall of the Italian republics and the domination of the foreigner, the season of intellectual women came to an end, and, if it had not been for the church, one-half of the Italian people would have been condemned to total ignorance. The history of the Roman church shows that every monastic order strove to create a female branch, Catholicism understanding much better than many of its rivals, that all propagandism which does not include women can never produce very great results. From this epoch dates the creation of those various religious orders for the education of girls, which still exist, and which, if not so much needed in the nineteenth century, did a good work in their day.

Two facts, which have occurred in recent years, are des-

---

*Sismondi is not mistaken when he goes still further and says, that " at Rome, women, while trying to please, were eager for authority." They did indeed often strive to rule the State and the papacy, which at this period had already become a power. Two patrician women, Theodora, and her daughter Marozia, disposed of the tiara during sixty years.—D. I.   Professor C. F. Gabba, of the University of Pisa, gives in the appendix to his remarkable work on the " Legal Condition of Women " (*Della condizione giuridica delle donne*), a most valuable list of the distinguished women of Itlay and other countries. The roll is very long and very brilliant.   This work cost Professor Gabba two years of incessant labor, and is, in many respects the most complete treatise on the legal position of women that has ever been produced.   He is now busy on the second volume, which will discuss the philosophical, political and social aspects of the woman question.   The first edition, issued in 1861, a small octavo pamphlet of less than two hundred pages, was the earliest publication on this subject which appeared in Italy.   Oscar Greco's " Bibliobiography of the Italian Authoresses of the Nineteenth Century " (*Bibliobiografia femminile italiana del XIX secolo*), an octavo of over 500 pages, published in 1875, gives a list of not less than 418 Italian female writers.—T. S.

tined to exercise a growing influence on the Latin nations of Aryan and Iberian origin. Anglo-Saxon civilization carried into North America tends more and more to diminish the intellectual inequality (the greatest of inequalities) of the two sexes. In the United States I have myself seen that women are capable not only of grasping intermediate instruction, but of participating in the advantages of a higher education. It is, therefore, possible to predict that the day must come when science will no longer be any more the monopoly of a sex than of a caste. At the same time, in the greatest of the Slavonic states, in Russia, woman has secured a body of rights which she does not yet enjoy in any other Christian nation. She may reign, vote, and control her own fortune. It is difficult to refuse to those who exercise such privileges, the necessary education which will teach the best use to be made of them. Hence Russia is gradually organizing for women a broad system of higher education.

Intellectual equality being admitted by the most powerful of the states of young America, and political and civil equality not being denied by the largest empire of old Europe, it was only natural that the Latin nations, to whom Rome had given the same civilization and the same religion, should at length become convinced that they had much to do for the instruction and education of women. Italy especially feels this influence, receiving into her midst, as she does each year, foreign women seeking a milder sky among celebrated cities embellished by masterpieces of art. It is impossible that the women of this beautiful land should not experience a certain sentiment of emulation, when they perceive that, in the capitals which have supplanted Athens and Rome, their sisters are becoming day by day more deeply initiated into the knowl-

edge of which the century is so proud. Italian statesmen begin to feel that the dignity of the country demands
a reform in this matter. It is said that Cavour was seriously thinking of ameliorating the condition of women,
and he was too intelligent not to perceive that instruction
was the first step in this direction. If this devoted patriot
was unable to realize all his plans, his successors have not
thought it possible to accept the situation left by the absolute governments. Since the creation of the kingdom
of Italy, each successive ministry has not only given much
attention to primary instruction, but has endeavored to
organize a system of intermediate instruction, which
should confer on girls the privileges hitherto enjoyed
only by boys.

Before the revolution which made a kingdom of Metter-
nich's " geographical expression," the state of public instruction was not the same in all the provinces. The
violent reaction, corresponding with the epoch of the
famous concordat made by Pius IX. and Francis-Joseph I.,
dates only from 1856, when girls' schools were attacked
with special fury. Napoleon I. had created at Milan, the
capital of his kingdom of Italy, a girls' college. The
Austrian government, which succeeded that of France,
went further. From 1822 to 1830 it organized fourteen
intermediate and one thousand and forty-four primary
girls' schools. These figures will, with good reason, seem
very insignificant in the United States, but in Italy they
were so exceptional, that Austria may boast of having
been the first to take an interest in the instruction of her
female subjects,—an interest which contrasted sadly with
the shameful disregard of the Italian princes.

Little disposed to follow the example of Austria, the
Sardinian government could not shut its eyes to the con-

duct of France, which did not inspire the same repugnance as the Germanic nation. Beginning under Louis Philippe with the reform of primary instruction for boys, and coming down into the Second Empire with the same thing for girls, France exercised an immense influence on the educational problem in Italy; for during that period, it must be borne in mind, France was the oracle of the Latin nations. When the king of Sardinia, throwing down the gauntlet to Austria, adopted the line of policy which was destined to transform him into king of Italy, the school question came to the front. The Casati law (November 13, 1859,) attempted to introduce into the provinces, which then obeyed Victor Emmanuel II., the same principles which Guizot had made triumph in France under Louis Philippe. Girls, however, were not forgotten in Italy in 1859, as they had been in France in 1833. The girls' primary schools were exclusively confided to female teachers, and normal schools for the preparation of such teachers were to be established.* The illiteracy among women—and men were not much better off in this respect—showed the crying need of the reform. In spite of the efforts made in Piedmont and Lombardy, one-half of the population in the north and centre of

---

* The Casati law renders primary instruction compulsory. Every father or guardian who neglects to send his boy or girl to school, subjects himself to a penalty. This law, however, must be considered a pure ideal which liberated Italy opposed to the Italy of absolutism. The lack of money not only renders difficult the foundation of schools, but it is a great obstacle to securing teachers. A salary which scarcely supports life, and no pension for old age, do not present very seductive prospects. If these drawbacks are taken into account, there need be no surprise at the poor progress made in the department of instruction since the foundation of the kingdom of Italy. Although the Italians have not yet been able to introduce the Casati law into every part of the country, it must never be lost sight of, if they wish to regain their former rank among nations.—D. I.

Italy, and almost the totality in the south, were steeped in absolute ignorance. In Piedmont and Lombardy, the most cultivated provinces, there were 450 persons out of every 1,000 who could not read ; 493 in Modena, Parma, Tuscany, the Marches and Perugia ; and 938 in the kingdom of the Two Sicilies.

Intermediate instruction, such as it is, is not an innovation in the Italian peninsula.* However, the country is beginning to understand better the necessity of it, and there is a growing tendency, scarcely noticed prior to the unification of Italy, to spread its benefits wider and wider. The convents were not content to give the daughters of the rich a simple primary education, and the Italian rulers of foreign origin felt the importance of creating establishments for girls' intermediate instruction. Thus, the Bourbons founded at Palermo in 1779 an institution for girls (*Educatorio femminile Maria-Delaide*), Napoleon, at Milan, a royal girls' college (*Collegio reale di fanciulle*), as I have

---

* Professor Gabba sends me the following notes : "A large number of private schools, which furnish a very good education, are found in several of the Italian provinces, and especially in Lombardy. Some of these institutions—particularly those of Milan—enjoy an ancient and well-merited reputation. The State supports six schools of a high intermediate order called *educandati*, where girls from seven to eighteen years of age receive a careful training. Verona, Milan, Florence, and Palermo have each one of these institutions, while Naples has two. A girls' gymnasium was opened a few years ago at Florence by a private society. The cause of education is greatly aided by the normal schools for the training of primary and intermediate teachers, one of which is found in almost every provincial capital. They are generally supported by the State. Among the State normal schools, that at Florence is the most important, as it has a ' superior course for perfectionment.' It is a significant fact that, of the 2,000 young women who graduate annually from these schools, at least two-fifths do not intend to become teachers. They are the daughters of well-to-do parents, sometimes of the aristocracy, studying simply for the improvement of their own minds."
—T. S.

already said, and the Grand Duke of Tuscany, in 1823, another girls' institute (*Instituto della S. S. Annunziata*).

But the bad administration of the absolute governments, which bore sway in Italy through force of arms, had in time checked the realization of the ideas of the founders of these institutions, as was proved by the inspection made in 1865, by command of the Minister of Public Instruction, Natoli. The 200,000 francs at the disposal of the most celebrated of these establishments, to cite but one example, educated only 30 girls. It was, therefore, found necessary to reform these schools and to create new ones more in harmony with modern ideas.

I shall terminate this sketch with a few words concerning the higher education of women. No law of the kingdom now hinders women from entering the Italian universities and taking degrees. A short time ago, to cite but one example, a Russian lady, Miss Paper, passed the examination for doctor in medicine at the University of Pisa, took her diploma, and is to-day practicing with success at Florence.*

The efforts made in the Latin countries to emancipate women from the heaviest of servitudes, that of ignorance, —have they been as discouraging as we should be led to believe by the theories of Prudhon and Michelet? The answer may be best given by a man who had a long expe-

---

* " Higher scientific instruction for woman is not neglected in Italy," writes Professor Gabba. " It may even be said that more has been done in this direction in Italy than in several other European countries. Our universities are open to women as listeners and students. Several, during the past few years, have taken the doctorate of medicine and the doctorate of literature. Besides the universities, a superior girls' college was established at Milan in 1861 and at Turin in 1866. A law of June 25, 1882, established at Rome and Florence a Superior Normal School for Women with twelve State scholarships. The curriculum covers four years." —T. S

rience in matters of education, and who had studied the subject in both the old and new world. "It has been asked in Italy, as often among us," says the late M. Hippeau, "why young men, who have finished their classical studies, generally write much worse than girls who have received an instruction which is less complete and erudite. Among the questions put forth by the last (Italian) Commission of Inquiry was this: 'Whence does it arise that in what concerns composition and style, girls' schools present an incontestable superiority?'"* The inspectors in their reports to the Minister of Public Instruction unanimously affirm, that the female pupils are much superior to the males in the normal schools, as regards discipline, application and progress in their studies.†

---

* *L'instruction publique en Italie. Enseignement secondaire, VI.*—D. I.

† This fact contradicts all that has been said about women's intellectual inferiority, which forms the base of M. Renan's theories. The celebrated physiologist, Karl Vogt, in his "Studies of Man" (*Leçons sur l'homme*), has shown that the skull of the French of the Middle Ages was much smaller than that of the contemporaries of La Fayette. It is evident that exercise of the encephalon has developed that organ, as the arm is fortified by action and the leg by locomotion. Before pronouncing woman an inferior species, a simple transition between "man and nature," as Michelet has said, it would perhaps be better to wait and see if intellectual culture may not have on her the same effect as on the men of "the good old time." The late Dr. Kurz, the eminent historian of German literature, who had also great experience as an educationist, states in an article on women, published by the *Illustrirte Zeitung,* June 23, 1860, that in Germany, where all the children of both sexes attend the primary schools, he had never been able to signal any difference intellectually between the boys and girls of the working classes and peasantry. But, on the other hand, he found that as one rose in the social scale, there was an increasing change in favor of the male sex. He thought this was due to the limited number of women taking part in intermediate instruction, and their complete exclusion from the lectures of the University. I have observed the same thing in Italy, where the boys and girls of the cities, who have pursued the same studies in the primary schools, do not differ in intelligence, while among the upper classes and aristocracy, the women often seem

When the aristocracy of Italy cease to send their daughters to the convent, when the primary and intermediate schools are more largely attended, then we shall certainly see re-born in this country the era of great female scholars.

---

to belong to another nation and epoch, so lacking are they in the intellectual culture of the age.—D. I.

CHAPTER X.

S P A I N .

BY CONCEPCION ARENAL.

[Mrs. Concepcion Arenal de Garcia Carrasco was born in 1820, at Ferrol, Galicia, Spain. Her father was a distinguished patriot, who threw aside his books for the sword when the war for independence broke out in 1808. On the return of peace, he suffered persecution under the despotic government of Ferdinand VII., because of his liberal ideas, and died in exile at an early age. After the death of her father, Concepcion went with her mother to Madrid, and began in private her own education, which has ever since been her chief care. In 1847 she married Fernando Garcia Carrasco, an able lawyer and author, and one of the earliest writers on the *Iberia*, the most important political newspaper of that period (1853-'5), to whose columns she often contributed leading editorials. In 1860 the Madrid Academy of Moral and Political Sciences awarded the first prize to Mrs. Arenal's remarkable work, "Benevolence, Philanthropy and Charity" (*La Beneficencia, la Filantropia, y la Caridad*).* Her next publication was entitled " Poor Visitor's Manual" (*El Manual del Visitador del Pobre*), an excellent little book, which has been translated into five foreign languages. " The Woman of

---

* Mrs. Rosario Zapater de Otal, of Madrid, gives me the following account of the awarding of this prize. " Public opinion in Spain," says this talented lady, " forces women to associate their real name as little as possible with their writings. If they participate in a literary or scientific competition, this prejudice has to be taken into the account, or they may not be allowed to enter the lists. Mrs. Concepcion Arenal, a very remarkable author, had recourse to a subterfuge when she took the prize of the Madrid Academy. Several able essays were presented, but it was found, when the envelope was opened, that the successful one came from the pen of Mr. Fernando Angel Carrasco y Arenal, Mrs. Arenal's son, a boy of ten! A month later the mother acknowledged to the Academy that she was the real author of this admirable production."—T. S.

the Future" (*La Mujer del Porvenir*) takes the ground that the assumed inferiority of women is only a result of old prejudices and injustice, and has no foundation in fact. Mrs. Arenal has written a great deal on penitentiary science, and on this subject is pronounced by Dr. Wines " an authority in her own country and in Europe." Her "Essay on International Law" (*Ensayo sobre el Derecho de Gentes*) is the first and only work by a woman in the *Biblioteca 'Juridica,* a collection emanating from the most distinguished Spanish jurisconsults. Among Mrs. Arenal's other productions, may be mentioned two volumes entitled "The Social Question" (*La Cuestion Social*), and "Popular Instruction" (*La Instruccion del Pueblo*), which was "crowned" in 1878 by the Academy of Moral and Political Sciences. She is the founder and principal contributor to the fortnightly review, *The Voice of Charity* (*La Voz de la Caridad*), which is now in the twelfth year of its publication at Madrid. As a poet, one of her anti-slavery poems gained the first prize from the Spanish Abolition Society. During the recent civil war in Spain, Mrs. Arenal was the secretary of the Red Cross Society. "The Woman at Home" (*La Mujer de Su Casa*) is the last production of this able pen. This little volume, conceived in a most liberal spirit, appeared in 1883.]

IN this sketch of the present condition of Spanish women, I shall treat the subject under seven heads, in the following order: I. Work; II. Religion; III. Instruction; IV. Legislation—civil, administrative and criminal; V. Public Opinion; VI. Morals; VII. Progress.

I. The Spanish woman is a very imperfect manual laborer, so that for this and other reasons her work is not highly valued and is poorly paid. Without any opportunities for an industrial education, she is forced to take up with kinds of handicraft which do not require it,—unskilled, brute labor, where it is perfectly well known she is very inferior to man. In the trades which are considered to belong especially to her sex, such as sewing, embroidery, dress-making, millinery, and the like, she is neither clever nor tasteful, and is excelled by the women of other countries, whence are introduced on a large scale into Spain ornamental needle-work, ready-made clothing, cravats, etc.   It is impossible to estimate even approximately the value of these articles imported into the country, but it is certain that the sum foots up many millions.   Nor is this all.   Foreign milliners and dress-makers, who supply the wants of the elegant classes of society, are found in all our large cities.

At the same time our own women lack employment, and enter into a deadly competition in the very limited number of occupations left to them by foreign superiority and masculine exclusion.   Indeed the army of needle-women is so large that their pay often falls to a figure scarcely credible, and is always too low to supply the physical wants of the laborer.   Unfortunately I do not, therefore, exaggerate the situation, when I qualify this competition as *deadly*, for incessant toil which does not procure sufficient food and a decent lodging, ruins health and hastens death.   The condition of needle-women who do not own sewing-machines—still a very numerous class—is worse than that of their more fortunate sisters as regards earnings, though probably their health is better.   Statistics do not give the number of obscure victims who sink slowly away, but, from personal observation, it seems to me that women cannot be the motor of the sewing-machine without great harm to their health.   Factory-women are about as badly off as needle-women; they earn scarcely enough to keep body and soul together, for they are paid like apprentices, and the supply is so great that they are without work a large part of the year.   As regards brute labor, in the fields, mines, etc., a woman is compared to a young boy, and, although in some cases she performs as much and even more work than a man, she is paid far less.

If Spanish women have no trades, or at least if those which they exercise are very poorly compensated, they have no profession either, for how can we apply this term to the lowest branch of teaching, at a salary which does not support life? And, with the exception of a few large cities, such is the situation of school-mistresses throughout Spain, unless they have other resources than those gained in the class-room.

As artists, Spanish women fare little better than as sewing-women and school teachers. Custom and lack of knowledge shut against them architecture and sculpture. As painters, they make some copies and decorate fans, boxes and *faience*, but works of real merit are exceptionally rare. About the same thing is true of music. It is only in the great cities that a few women support themselves by giving piano lessons. At this moment I am aware of no actress or singer of distinguished talents in our theatres, while I know that their pay is very low. Our women are ignorant of the sciences, and if, as is very rarely the case, they acquire some scientific knowledge, as medicine for instance, they may make no use of it as a means of subsistence, for public opinion and the law of the land present insurmountable obstacles.

This unfortunate state of things is due to many and different causes which may be reduced to the four following: 1. Want of education; 2. Force of custom; 3. Unlimited competition; and 4. Disdain of public opinion.

1. If the elementary education of boys is neglected, the condition of that of girls may be imagined. It may be said that girls do not go to school in Spain, or if they do, it is only to learn to read badly, and to acquire a superficial acquaintance with rudimentary studies, which the mistress, almost as ignorant as her pupils, can scarcely

teach. This is true even in towns of some importance, where alone girls' schools exist. Such an education, if it indeed deserves the name, renders women unfit for any but the most material kind of work. They are seldom taught trades, they have no industrial skill, so that their labor is of an inferior quality.

2. Custom, without reason but with great obstinacy, shuts out women from the most lucrative occupations and trades, and even from those for which they are peculiarly fitted by nature. Delicate mechanical arts which do not require strength, and other crafts which demand exactitude, patience, and assiduity, are practiced exclusively by men, without there being any justification for this on the ground of women's intellectual inferiority, since those who hold that they are wanting in intelligence, are obliged to admit that they have enough for many occupations which custom refuses to let them undertake.

3. This limitation of the field of work for women produces a plethora in those paths which lie open to them, and, as I have already said, a deadly competition is the consequence. As the working-woman finds nobody to protect her, as labor associations are unknown, and as she cannot sell directly to the consumer, she becomes the prey of the speculative middle-man, and when the latter is a shop-keeper, she may be considered a real victim of competition.

4. The contempt of public opinion is another reason why women's industry is so poorly remunerative and why they are paid less than men for the same work. It is not true that competition *always* renders products cheap, and that the degree of cheapness depends upon how much the supply surpasses the demand. Spain offers several examples to the contrary. But for the sake of brevity I shall

not cite them, and shall simply say that, the effects of competition not being neutralized by the good-will of public opinion, Spanish working-women toil for a beggarly return. Thus the economic condition of our women is most deplorable, and though I am perfectly well aware that these same evils are shared in common with the working-women of Europe generally, I also know that in the more advanced countries the field of female industry is not so contracted and participation in manual labor not so discredited as in Spain. If the misfortune is not limited to this land, it has here attained greater gravity than elsewhere.

II. I now pass to the second division of my subject: Is the Spanish woman religious? This question may be answered by a Yes or by a No, depending on what is understood by religion. According to my own definition of the word, I do not hesitate to respond in the negative. Spanish women, as a rule, are not religious, though there are of course exceptions. They are devout, pious, superstitious; the worship, the rites, the form, the superficial, are everything; the depths and heights of true religion, its soul, its genuine constituents, are little or nothing. Religion of this sort does not exercise much moral influence on its devotees, contributes but little toward their improvement, and in some instances even becomes an obstacle in the way of all amelioration. It is noticeable that, among the women who consecrate themselves to God, as they say, appearances and formalism are regarded as more important than moral considerations. This fact is more applicable to the nuns who come from the middle and upper classes than to those sprung from the people. The sisters of charity, who do some good in the world, are, with few exceptions, recruited from the masses, while young ladies enter the cloisters and spend their existence, not so much in efforts to benefit suffering humanity, as in the performance of rituals and in contemplation, a plan of life which, we may say in passing, is not very effective for the regeneration of the sinners whom they gather together.

III. Education in Spain is at a very low level, much lower indeed than foreigners suppose, who, after an examination of the statistics, found their conclusions on the attendance at the elementary and intermediate schools and at the universities, instead of on the quality of the instruction given in these institutions. If men are poorly trained, if a university degree stands for a privilege and not for the intellectual calibre of him who holds it, what must be the education of Spanish women can be easily imagined.

In girls' schools—where they exist—the major part of the time is employed in manual branches, and it is an exception if the school-mistress knows how to read intelligently, to write without violating the rules of orthography, and to explain the most elementary parts of arithmetic. In the institutions frequented by the children of the upper classes, the course of studies embraces a little geography, history, piano and French, which are taught in a very superficial manner. Nothing resembling solid instruction is given, and even this poor beginning is soon forgotten, for on leaving school our women generally read only novels and religious books. It is now becoming possible to find some young girls who write passably well and who understand the simpler rules of arithmetic, but it is still often difficult to obtain a secretary or treasurer who can keep clearly and correctly the minutes and accounts of a charitable society. At a recent competitive examination for the position of principal of a normal school, which, because of a relatively large salary attached to it, ought to have been and was much sought after, the majority of the candidates gave proof of the greatest ignorance, and when it is stated that they held teachers' diplomas and that many of them are at the head of schools, the little value of academic degrees and the shameful deficiency of our educational system become painfully evident. There are exceptions, but, speaking generally, the Spanish mistress ought to attend school herself.

IV. I shall next touch upon the laws, beginning with those of a penal nature, which in Spain, as is more or less true of all countries, are in contradiction to the civil, political and administrative usages in all that concerns women. While the latter close against them the civil service, the professions, public life and in some cases pronounce them minors, the former always consider them perfectly responsible beings and never admit their sex to be an extenuating circumstance for softening the severity of a penalty. In Spain, the only distinction made in their favor is that female prisoners have beds and are never chained, alleviations not enjoyed by men.

The administrative and school regulations exclude women from the civil service and from all callings except those of teacher in the lowest schools, vendor of postage stamps, stamped paper and tobacco—a government monopoly—and telegraphist, when a husband, father, or brother is engaged in the same occupation.

The civil position of women is not the same in all parts of Spain; in some provinces they are more favored than in others, especially when they become widows. But

22

everywhere the law falls into a strange contradiction when it touches the rights of married and single women. The latter, on reaching their majority, enjoy the same privileges as men in regard to property, and, like them, may inherit, will, let, sell and buy. But the moment they marry, they return to the condition of minors. The husband controls everything, without having to render any account of his stewardship. He may lavish on concubines the patrimony of his wife, while she cannot dispose of a farthing without his consent. If the husband, who is a father and a soldier or employed in the civil service, abandon his wife and children, she may obtain, after fulfilling a certain number of requirements, the end of which is often never reached, a small portion of his pay. The law is again inconsistent when the wife, who, while the husband lives, stands on such an unequal economic footing with him, once a widow, comes in for half of the acquest—that is, the increment, during the marriage, of the common fortune—which on her death goes to her heirs. Within the past few years a step has been taken in the direction of the civil equality of the two sexes, and the widow now enjoys paternal authority over the children.*

The girl who is a minor and would marry, must have the consent of her parents and guardians. But if they refuse, she may, after complying with certain legal forms, dispense with it. A Spanish woman lays but little stress on the religion of her husband, provided he consents to go through the form of receiving the sacrament. If, which is very rare, the *fiancé* holds to a religious belief other

---

* The Spanish woman confers upon her husband the titles of nobility and the other privileges attached to them which she possesses at the moment of her marriage. The wife always retains the family name received from her father and places it before that of her husband.—MRS. ZAPATER DE OTAL.

than the Catholic, and if he is honest enough to admit it, this circumstance does not form an obstacle to the marriage, except in the eyes of Rome. Neither the *fiancée* nor the family abandon the projected union on this account, and it is only old women who never saw such scandalous proceedings in their day, and young women, who perhaps would be but too glad to secure the heretic for themselves, who are shocked, and deplore the impious act.

Divorce does not exist in Spain, and the same thing may almost be said of partial divorce, *a mensâ et toro*, because of the difficulties which lie in the way of its consummation and the disfavor with which it is regarded by society. Abandonment, on the other hand, is very easy and very common, for the husband may desert his wife and children without running the risk of any punishment.

It is scarcely necessary to say that Spain confers no political rights on women, although—the Salic law never having obtained in the Pyrenean peninsula—a queen may rule the nation.

V. In its treatment of women, Spanish public opinion may be likened unto a flood whirling along in its current a helpless body, driving it hither and thither and finally swallowing it up. How much ability and intelligence, what a vast part of the moral and intellectual life of our women, is sterilized and annihilated by erring public opinion! In this division of my subject I do not wish to consider the opinion of men alone, but, as it has an influence incomparably greater than that of women, I shall take it up first and dwell on it more at length.

Spanish men generally entertain sentiments of consideration and respect for mother, wife and sister, and paternal love also has a favorable effect on their ideas of women. But when untouched by feelings of tenderness, the sex falls very low in their esteem. They consider women their inferiors in everything and look down upon them with the disdain of veritable oppressors. Although, as I have just said, affection and chivalry sometimes outbalance contempt and neutralize or soften it, man does not form an exception to the rule, but despises what he considers beneath him and oppresses what he despises.

In a country where brute force is still greatly preponderant, muscular feebleness is necessarily looked upon as a serious defect, and, if we examine the subject carefully among the people, the largest and coarsest part of the nation, we find that this is the origin of man's arrogating to himself superiority in everything. Among the upper classes, man cultivates his mental faculties and strengthens his whole character. Religion, which has but little influence on him, and which might neutralize the frivolities to which the existence of woman is condemned, not only does not effectively combat these evils, but sometimes even increases them. Thus man finds himself clothed with advantages whose importance he exaggerates, and which, though not natural, are positive. Armed with these odds, he drives woman from all skilled and lucrative occupations, while she, degraded in the economic, and belittled in the intellectual, sphere, may forsooth inspire tenderness, interest, compassion, but cannot command respect. As neither love, generosity, nor anything can take the place of justice when masses of individuals are concerned, he who persistently refuses it, oppresses, however much he may varnish and gild the yoke. And this is the very way public opinion treats Spanish women.

Prompted by the Epistle of St. Paul,* man, under the most favorable circumstances, surrenders his rights only for harmony; he does not recognize those of woman. We know how often he prefers his privileges to concord and yields nothing, so that dissension instead of peace reigns, with the advantage, whether in marriage or outside of it, on his side.

The natural affections and refined sentiments which distinguish some men, who are not satisfied with the condescensions of a slave, establish equality in the spiritual domain and strongly affect the other spheres of life. But it may be truly said that man oppresses woman when he does not love and protect her. As workman, he drives her from the most remunerative trades; as thinker, he will not suffer her to cultivate her mind; as lover, he may trifle with her affections; and as husband, he may desert her with impunity. Public opinion is the real cause of all these wrongs, because it makes the laws or because it violates them.

But my readers may ask, Have not the liberal-minded men of Spain a higher ideal of woman? Several circumstances must be taken into account in answering this question. Our enlightened men, in the first place, are too few in number to exert an influence on the public. Again, though their minds are open on certain subjects, they are very ignorant on this woman question. They recognize in woman only the female, and nourish the illu-

---

* I would not have anybody surpass me in tenderness, respect and enthusiasm for the Apostle of Men, whose precepts and advice relative to women were an immense progress for his time, although they are to-day behind the age. Love, charity and kindliness constitute a powerful and indispensable social factor. They are auxiliaries of justice, but they cannot supplant it. Permanent peace does not spring from the yielding of one's rights, but from recognition of, and respect for, the rights of others.—C. A.

sion, which is akin to folly, of pretending that she is a reasonable being without exercising the reason. However strange this statement may appear, it is true of a large number of men, even of those who have received some education.

There is still a third class among our liberals who differ from the preceding more in theory than in reality. They make a speech or write an article on the necessity of educating women, but they do nothing in order to lift their wives and daughters out of ignorance. What are the elements of this contradiction? Perhaps there enter into it in equal proportions indolence, carelessness, the love of superiority, a lingering doubt as to the capability of women to receive a solid education, and an uncertainty as to whether it might not harm them, for there is ordinarily a long lapse of time between the theoretical acceptance of a new idea and its penetration into the mind and soul with a resulting effect on the conduct. Many men who favor women's education and are working industriously for this end, belong to this category. They are ever asking themselves the question, Have women the intellectual capacity for a sound education, and if so, may it not be dangerous to give it to them? There are men, on the other hand, who are thoroughly convinced of the necessity and possibility of imparting to the female, the same development as to the male, mind, and who are doing their utmost to popularize this idea. But, as I have already said, their number is too small to make a permanent impression on public opinion, which continues to deny woman's aptitude, to consider the cultivation of her mind an evil, and to refuse her the means for her intellectual improvement. It is evident that a society which judges thus, or to speak more exactly, which decides thus, must oppose even the consideration of women's rights, and especially their participation in public affairs.

All these currents, tainted with error and injustice, are found united in the spirit which governs the relations between the two sexes, where the law is often silent or a dead letter, and where public opinion misleads and plays the despot. It is considered but natural that the husband, who makes the money and who knows something, should be at the head of the family, and no objection is made if he pass from this rôle to that of a tyrant, provided his tyranny be not too brutal. Nobody, as a rule, blames him for a partial and moral abandonment of his family; and absolute desertion, which is very common, is not anathematized. The frequency of this last sin cannot be explained except on the ground of the complicity of public opinion, which pronounces the law wrong and renders it null.

If public opinion does not condemn him who sets at naught his duties as a husband and father, the base acts of the lover awaken, of course, no honest indignation, but rather feelings of contempt for the victim. If the woman who has been betrayed and abandoned is a mother, if she finds it impossible to nourish her children, and they perish in misery, if they become idlers and criminals, or if she yields to despair in any of its forms, even in suicide, he who has been the cause of these crimes and misfortunes does not see his future blasted,—is not censured by society. The woman, crippled by the shutting against her of the highways to self-support, disarmed for the battle of life, must be strong in herself, must master her affections, her instincts, the natural propensity to believe in him who loves her, who is able to protect her, and who promises to do so. The sin of the strong is called *triumph,* that of the feeble, *fall;* and public opinion, which leads the latter to destruction, spits on her and tramples her under foot once she is down.

It should be remarked, that this same public opinion which abandons and scoffs at weak women, whose faults have many extenuating circumstances, looks with favor on some whom it ought to denounce. Elegant adulteresses, whose loose morals seem to add to, rather than detract from, their social success, are well received and even applauded if they are rich, stylish and pretty, or if they are set off with a title. It sometimes happens in aristocratic circles that the most unrestrained immorality defies public opinion, laughs at it, so that adultery becomes not a tragedy but a very comedy.

Though women are refused the vote, they have a certain opinion and influence on public affairs. The dictum, that those who are born in slavery are born for slavery, may be applied in part to Spanish women, who, bred in ignorance, are more disposed to censure than praise those of their sex who strive after knowledge. They are early taught to accept the intellectual superiority of men, and they tolerate it. But their conduct is not the same when they have to do with educated women. They turn their backs on them, ridicule them and think to see only danger to the domestic hearth in this feminine book-learning. This belief is generally sincere, although of course there is no foundation for the alarm, and, being fortified by that of the great majority of men, it augments the difficulties which lie in the way of the instruction of women.

In the moral domain women's opinion has a still more deplorable effect, for in all that concerns the relations between the two sexes, it becomes an accomplice in the iniquities of men. No matter how scandalous a man's life may be, it does not militate against his success, but, on the contrary, it rather favors him in his love affairs and secures him a more advantageous marriage. A rake, whose intrigues are town talk, is more acceptable and makes a more brilliant match than a young man of good habits, who spends in work the time devoted by the other to dissipation and vice. The profound moral perversion of our women which this situation reveals, is the result, the *résumé*, the quintessence, as it were, of all the influences which conspire to their detriment. The women who thus encourage the vicious by marks of preference are not themselves immoral. Their conduct in all other respects may be irreproachable,—which only brings out in still bolder relief the deterioration of their taste and reason. And to this complacent tolerance of the vices of men, is often found united a Puritanical severity for those of their own sex, thus completing the acts by which they contribute to their own injury.

Besides these influences, which may be called special and direct, there are others of a general nature which conduce not less to the errors and misfortunes of women. The atmosphere in which they live, pervaded with material pleasures, and the delights of vain luxury, where poverty, however honorable, is looked down upon, and where riches are adored, often regardless of how they were obtained, is a powerful cause of this unfortunate situation.*

VI. The reader, who has reflected a little on what has been written in the preceding pages, will not find it diffi-

---

* I may say here once for all, that there are honorable exceptions to the various strictures on Spanish society which I am forced to make throughout the course of this sketch.—C. A.

cult to guess what will be said under the head of morals;
for if women stand on such a low plane in education, art
and industry, and are so despised by public opinion, they
cannot occupy a very high moral position.

The birth rate shows 5.55 illegitimate to one hundred
legitimate children. One woman is sent to prison for
every twenty men, while there is one female convict for
every 21,000 inhabitants. But, as the terms of imprisonment extend over several years, the actual criminality is
much less than this statement would seem to indicate.
Prostitution is very prevalent, and there are few countries where this cancerous disease is more widespread
than in Spain.

The love of luxury occasions a veritable ravage among
Spanish women, and becomes alternately the cause and
effect of immorality. It absorbs the resources which ought
to be devoted to necessary wants or to charitable purposes; it troubles domestic peace, sacrifices honor and
smooths the way to prostitution ; it enters the most humble homes and is often found allied with misery.   In view
of all the circumstances which surround our women, this
weakness is easily explained, and, though not an enigma,
it is none the less a misfortune for themselves and for
their country.

The terrible woman, that type dreamt of or invented by
travelers, and who might be described as "the female of
the Spanish brigand," does not exist.   There are women
among our criminals, but they are just like those of other
countries, neither braver, more wicked, nor more romantic.
It is true, I am ashamed to say, that a great many of our
women frequent bull-fights, but they are from the lower
classes and the aristocracy,—the ladies of the royal family
among the number.   They belong to the badly dressed

vulgar, and to elegant society. There are exceptions, but this is the rule.

When we wish to determine the moral condition of a people or a class, we generally proceed in a manner which produces inexact results. By the aid of statistics and other means, we discover the infractions of law and morality, we count the crimes and vices, and then we conclude that virtue is in an inverse ratio to this sum. But our reckoning is not correct. This is a double-entry account: its debits are bad acts, its credits, good acts. If we neglect the latter, our sheet does not balance.

Spanish women, through no fault of their own, are not given all the credit which they deserve, and are not permitted to gain all that of which they are capable, because their sphere of action is very much restrained and consequently the sum of their social merits is diminished. Men generally prefer in their wives and daughters only the domestic virtues, so that a lady often declines participation in a charitable work because the husband objects to her membership in a society or association. It is not surprising, therefore, that women who unite for benevolent purposes are subjected to criticism and ridicule, although the development of female usefulness is thus unwittingly stunted. Men are chiefly to blame for this, yet the other sex often unite with them to laugh down those of their number who may band together for charity.

When we consider how many noble movements and lofty aims, which owe their origin to women, are opposed and wrecked by hostile public opinion ; when we observe the fearful moral depravity of the nation, we are sometimes led to ask how it is that Spain continues to exist and even progresses, slowly though it be. The cause, which seems almost inexplicable, is found in the solid virtue, proof against every attack, of a strong nucleus of women of the lower and middle classes, who, with merit known of God alone, and of which they themselves are generally unconscious, give to a social fabric, almost ready to fall, the cohesion necessary to its preservation, and powerfully contribute to render the moral atmosphere, if not entirely salubrious, at least breathable.*

VII. I shall now take up the last division of my subject, viz., the signs of progress in Spain, which, more meagre than I could wish, will be treated in the same order as the foregoing part of this sketch.

The gradual growth of our national industries has opened to women new fields of labor in the factories, and female operators, under certain restrictions already mentioned, are often employed in telegraphic offices, where however, they are paid less than men for the same work. The number of female teachers is rapidly increasing, and a recent law places infant schools under their exclusive charge. Some years ago, musical instruction was entirely in the hands of foreigners; but to-day, many of our women follow this profession at Madrid, and earn far

---

* Generosity is the cardinal virtue of the Spanish lower classes. The wife of the laborer shares her mite with the poorer neighbor. It often happens that, when a friend or an inmate of the same house dies and leaves young orphans, women, as needy as they, divide among themselves, amid tears and sobs, the homeless children " that they may not have to go to the asylum," and from that moment they become as their own. When, on the occasion of some terrible inundation or other calamity, appeals are made to public bounty, it is a touching spectacle to see these poor people deprive themselves of the very necessities of life in order to contribute something. This conduct is all the more praiseworthy as their names will not appear in the newspapers and be lauded in the drawing-rooms. Woman is the soul of this noble generosity. The workman's wife does not lay away; what is left over each day is given to those who want, so that it is rare under these humble roofs to find any provision made for the morrow.—MRS. ZAPATER DE OTAL.

more than they could in occupations considered "proper for the sex."

Progress is noticeable in the religious sphere. As it is an indisputable fact that the funds of the church have diminished, that the revenue from the sale of quadrigesimal indulgences is decreasing, while, on the other hand, the population and riches of the country are increasing, it is evident that the priesthood is losing its hold on the nation. This is especially true of our women, for, if they still believed that the purchase of these bits of paper was a question of eternal salvation, they would buy them in spite of the ridicule of husbands, fathers, and brothers. But it is plain that they no longer think so ; indulgences are becoming a drug in the market, and consequently faith in their efficacy is dying out. I am told that many priests no longer ask women at confessional if they have bought these bulls, and I believe that this prudent course is getting to be quite common. The full significance of this fact comes out when we remember, that the precept thus set at naught is enunciated by an absolute power, by an authority infallible in Catholic eyes, whose wisdom and justice is of God himself, and disobedience to whom is punished by eternal damnation. I have never heard of a marriage not being celebrated because the groom held to a belief different from that of the bride, or because the former professed no religion at all, which is very frequently the case. If the husband is kind, the wife is satisfied with her choice, and does not think him lost if he declines to attend mass, to confess, and if he eats meat when she eats fish. It is true that the monks and Jesuits have returned to Spain, and that they still have a very strong hold on the women of the wealthier classes, but we who are advanced in life can testify that their influence, especially that of the monks, is not what it used to be. To-day, they do not mingle with the people; they do not find every house open to them; they do not interfere in all family affairs, as we well remember was their wont. I might cite examples, which have come under my personal notice, to prove that the religious fanaticism of Spanish women is no longer what it was, nor what some still imagine it to be.

Although the ignorance of our women is deplorable, when we compare the instruction they have with what they ought to have, we must admit, however, that progress in this direction has been made in all classes of society, whether we consider the increased number of female criminals who can read and write, or those ladies who have learned French, geography and grammar. This improvement is observed in country and city alike, and especially at Madrid, where, in the schools founded by the Association for the Education of Women,* nearly five hundred girls pursue courses in pedagogics, commercial studies, modern languages, painting, etc. This instruction, for the most part gratis, is given by professors who devote their time and strength to this noble object without receiving any remuneration,—worthy continuators of the grand work of the founder of the Madrid High School for Women,† Fernando de Castro, of blessed memory, one of the most philanthropic men I ever met, who so loved mankind that his name should be known in every land.

Nine hundred and eighteen girls attended the session of 1880–1, of the School of Music and Declamation at Madrid,

---

* The various publications of this admirable and active association furnish very full and complete information concerning the whole subject of the educational situation of Spanish women. The secretary, César de Eguilaz, may be addressed as follows: Asociacion para la Enseñanza de la Mujer, Bolsa, 14, Piso segundo, Madrid.—T. S.

† This institution was established in 1869.—C. A.

and the number has since increased. A few years ago, a School of Arts and Trades was founded at the capital, and women were admitted to the classes in drawing. In 1881 one hundred and thirty availed themselves of this privilege. In 1882 one hundred and fifty-four female students were present at the institutions (*institutos*) throughout Spain for intermediate education. The co-education of the sexes, therefore, is not unknown to us. Valencia, Barcelona, Gerona and Seville each counted sixteen, while the single girl at Mahon discontinued her studies on the ground that she preferred not to mingle with boys. At Malaga, the only female aspirant for the bachelor's degree took seven prizes, and was "excellent" in all her studies. During the academic year 1881–2 twelve women attended lectures in the Spanish universities. The three at Madrid were all working for the doctorate, and one has passed the necessary examinations; the two at Valladolid were occupied with medicine, while at Barcelona five were studying medicine, one law, and one pharmacy. Three of the medical students have passed their examinations, but, instead of the degrees, which are refused them, they are granted certificates, which do not allow them to practice.

The recent creation of two periodicals devoted to the question of female education, and the exclusion of male teachers from the infant schools, as has already been noted, are small but significant signs of progress. I may also mention in connection with this subject that Spain possesses some scholarly women and several female writers, especially poets, who hold a high place in current literature.*

---

* Francisca Lebrixa, daughter of the celebrated grammarian and historian Lebrixa (1444–1532), often filled her father's place in the University of

Public opinion is progressing, as is evidenced by the laws, and especially by the educational reforms, which are the exclusive work of men. The Council of Public Instruction, a consulting body holding by no means advanced ideas, was called upon a short time ago to decide whether the university certificates conferred upon women could be converted into regular degrees, which would entitle the recipients to the privileges attached to these titles. The learned council discussed, hesitated, tried to decide the question, but finally left it in a situation which was neither clear nor conclusive. This hesitancy and vagueness are very significant: a few years ago a negative decision would have been given promptly and in the plainest terms.

Public opinion seems to be changing for the better in its ideas of what ought to be the relations between the two sexes; and, although this transformation is very slow and almost imperceptible, there are indications, which I omit for the sake of brevity, which prove that here, too, I may report progress.

In the moral sphere, it may be said that female criminality appears to have diminished and the number of natural children to be less, when the increment of the population is taken into account. My own opinion is that

---

Alcala, and Beatriz Galindo, of Salamanca, was called "the Latin" ("*la Latina*"), because of her thorough knowledge of that tongue. Both of these women, as well as Isabel de Losa, of Cordova, who was a great theologian, were versed in the ancient languages and were real savants. Among the intellectual women of our own day I may cite the celebrated Fernand Caballero, whose admirable descriptions of Spanish life, translated into several tongues, are known and admired throughout Europe, and the Infanta Maria Isabel, the eldest sister of King Alphonso, who, by her private virtues and her vast acquaintance with art, history and the languages, is one of the most cultivated princesses of Europe.—MRS. ZAPATER DE OTAL.

Spanish women are better than they were, if we compare those of to-day with those painted in the history and literature of the past. A nation's moral condition cannot be determined by its vices alone; we must also consider its virtues. If a great number of our women are still on the same low plane as their progenitors, more of them have risen to a higher level; that is to say, although the bad may be as bad as of yore, the good are better. This conclusion is based on observations extending over a period of forty years, and I believe it unquestionably true.

There may be those who will accuse me of painting my country in too dark colors, or of allowing my sincerity to run away with my patriotism. What harm would there be in softening the picture a little, they will say, just as he who is blind of one eye offers the faultless side of his face to the artist? My answer is, that never have I tried or wished to separate patriotism from truth and justice; and, furthermore, if this volume, international in its nature, is to be useful, it must be true. It must be history, not romance, so that from a comparison of certain facts, exact and valuable conclusions can be drawn. If this object is not attained, it will not be because the notes on Spain are wanting in accuracy. The Spanish collaborator, with the proverbial nobility, *hidalguia*, of her race, has told the truth, disagreeable though it be, with a frankness which reveals strength and gives hope for the future.

23

CHAPTER XI.

PORTUGAL.

BY RODRIGUES DE FREITAS.

[Mr. Rodrigues de Freitas was born at Porto, January 24, 1840. From 1855 to 1862 he was a student at the Polytechnic Academy of his native city, where he took several prizes and was graduated as a civil engineer. He became a professor at this institution in 1864. Mr. de Freitas was elected a member of Parliament in 1870, 1871, 1878 and 1880, being the first representative of the republican party to enter the Portuguese chamber of deputies. He has written for several newspapers, and especially for the *Porto Commercial* (*O Commercio do Porto*). His principal works are: "Notice on Portugal" (*Notice sur le Portugal*, Paris, 1867) ; the "Social Revolution" (*A revoluçaõ social*, Porto, 1873) , an analysis of the doctrines of the International ; "Elements of Book-keeping" (*Elementos d'escripturaçaõ mercantil*, Porto, 1882), and a treatise on political economy which is now (1883) in press.]

AN English traveler, who visited Portugal in 1789, thus described Portuguese women: "They are generally endowed with excellent qualities. They are chaste, modest, and extremely attached to their husbands. None of them would think of leaving the house without first obtaining his permission or that of his family. In order that not even the shadow of a suspicion may rest upon them, men, even when relatives, are not permitted to enter their apartments, or to sit near them in the public parks. Their lovers, therefore, rarely enjoy the pleasure of seeing them, except at church, the only spot where sighs and signs of affection may be manifested. In spite of the greatest vigilance on the part of the duennas, lovers sometimes succeed in exchanging notes, but so adroitly that one must be a lover himself to perceive it. The altar boys are often the bearers of these tender messages. . . . On leaving the church, it often happens that the lovers' hands meet, as if by chance, in the same holy-water basin, are pressed together with a secret joy, and exchange notes. Ladies rarely go out for a promenade, unless it be to the neighboring church, which they visit regularly at least once a day. Weddings are very expensive, and are often the ruin of the poorer classes. Women are economical and sober, generally drinking only water. This dieting on the part of Portuguese women has a singular effect on their complexion ; they are pale and wanting in vivacity. Their style of dress scarcely changes throughout a whole century. The lower classes of both sexes are passionately fond of ornaments, fish-women often adorning themselves with gold necklaces and bracelets." *

If this picture is correct, what great changes have been wrought in a century among Portuguese women, and especially among those of the cities ! As regards dress, Paris styles prevail in Portugal, although somewhat modified and stamped with a strong Portuguese character. Imported fashions have succeeded in driving out the national costume, except from the interior of a few provinces which are in imperfect communication with the cities. And even here it is doomed to soon disappear.

The Portuguese are not an economical people. There are very few savings banks, and aid societies are rarer still. And yet many women will pinch themselves in necessary

---

* This citation is translated from a French edition of James Murphy's "Travels in Portugal," which will account for any discrepancies between it and the original text.—T. S.

expenditures so as to be able to spend more on dress. Wives and mothers, who have no time to see to the bringing up of their children, to look after the kitchen, and to aid their husbands, often destroy their lungs and eyes in toiling for long hours that they may array themselves after the newest modes. The peasant women continue to buy jewelry, which happily often proves a valuable resource when misfortune comes. The middle classes of the cities do not care so much for the precious metals, and waste very little money on them. Their chief aim is to dress fashionably, and to pass themselves off as rich. The paleness and inactivity of which the English traveler speaks, are still found in the large cities, and especially at Lisbon, among those women, who, though poor, wish to appear wealthy. This unhealthy and vulgar rage for show produces at the capital the greatest physical and moral ravages. Some people hold that this wanness and wasting away are due to the bad sewerage of Lisbon. It is quite true that the waters of the Tagus are not always *eau de Cologne*, and that the subterranean pipes do not perform their work thoroughly ; but the chief source of the evil is not under the ground, but in the head. The conduits of the mind are not pure ; in some instances they have never been cleansed ; and if this head be a woman's, if this woman is without education, or has received a completely false one, if she or her husband does not possess wealth, to what lengths may not this monomania for luxury carry them ? For a few strips of goods the stomach is left empty. Greater sacrifices than even health are made ; life itself is shortened and rendered useless.

Lisbon suffers much more than any other Portuguese city from this diseased condition of women's ideas and habits. It possesses an excessive number of public functionaries on small salaries, who feel obliged to spend as much as they can in order to keep up a social position. Although the old nobility has almost disappeared, the rich commoner takes its place, and is only too eager to display his wealth. Above this class is the court, which is passionately fond of luxury. The Queen Maria Pia, daughter of Victor Emmanuel, prides herself on being the most elegant lady of Portugal. She has the true bearing of a sovereign, and dresses in exquisite taste, but she sets a bad example. In 1882 the king and queen of Spain came to Portugal. Although the Spanish court is far richer than our own, the Portuguese queen surpassed the queen of the neighboring country by the magnificence of her robes and diamonds. On this occasion the pawnbrokers of Lisbon loaned a very large sum of money, which was spent, it is said, by the families who participated in the extraordinary *fêtes* of this occasion.

These facts pour a flood of light on the domestic life of Portuguese women, who, having recently acquired a little liberty, are laboring under the difficulties always experienced in a society not yet emancipated from the evils of long centuries of prejudice. It is not astonishing, therefore, if the frivolities of Paris are more conspicuous in our society than the grand qualities of the French capital,— if its faults are more generally imitated than its virtues. And yet Portuguese women have good natural instincts, and parents give much more attention to-day than formerly to the instruction of their daughters. It was once considered dangerous to teach girls to read and write. But such opinions are entertained no longer. This change, however, has not been entirely in the right direction. Our young girls are taught to play the piano, to sing, and to speak two or three foreign languages, of which French has the preference. But the course pursued is mechanical and uniform. It does not vary with the capacities of the scholar; it does not aim, above all things, to develop the faculties; and it has no regard for woman's mission as housekeeper, wife and mother. The result is, that after marriage, wives generally lay aside their books and soon forget all they have learned.

However, the progress which has been made, in spite of everything, is really remarkable. Public opinion being no longer what it was thirty or forty years ago, it seems to me that the weary tentative period is now approaching its end, and a better understanding of what ought to constitute female education and instruction is taking its place. Primary instruction is compulsory for boys and girls between the ages of six and seven. The course of studies is the same as that generally pursued in primary schools. Good female teachers are quite rare, and the school-houses, except those in some of the large cities, are very bad. Portugal possesses but two normal schools for the training of female teachers—one at Lisbon, and another, established in 1882, at Porto. On October 31, 1880, there were 320 public primary girls' schools, including those of the adjacent islands of Madeira and the Azores. Of the 820 female teachers, but 43 were graduates of the normal school at Lisbon—the only one which then existed. The census of 1878 reveals the lamentable ignorance of Portuguese women. The female population of Portugal is 2,374,870, of whom only 254,369 can read and write, while 2,120,501 can do neither. Perhaps these last figures are too high, but it is an unquestionable fact that female instruction, especially in the country districts, is greatly neglected.

There is not a single intermediate school for girls in all Portugal. In 1883 the Portuguese Parliament took up the subject of intermediate instruction, and discussed the question in relation to women and the progress in this direction realized in France during the last few years. A deputy, opposing the reform, recalled the words of Jules Simon, pronounced in a recent sitting of the Council of Public Instruction at Paris : " We are here a few old men," remarked this philosopher, "very fortunate, gentlemen, in being excused from having to marry the girls you propose to bring up." Our Minister of the Interior, who has charge of public instruction, followed, and declared that he was in favor of the establishment of girls' colleges. "It is true," he continued, "that M. Jules Simon considers himself fortunate in not having to marry a girl educated in a French college, but I think I have discovered the reason for this aversion. He is getting in his dotage, otherwise he would experience no repugnance in proposing to such a girl, provided, of course, that, along with an education, she was at the same time pretty and virtuous." The Chamber laughed. And such is the situation to-day: the minister favorable to the better instruction of women, while neither ministers nor deputies make a serious effort to bring it about.

This dark picture is relieved, however, by one or two bright touches. There are many private boarding schools where families in easy circumstances send their daughters, who learn to speak several languages, are taught a little elementary mathematics and geography, and acquire a few accomplishments. Some of the pupils of these institutions pass with credit the examinations of the boys' lyceums or colleges. Article 72 of the law of June 14, 1880, on intermediate instruction, reads as follows : " Students of the female sex, who wish to enter the State schools, or pass the examinations of said schools, come within the provisions of this law, except as regards the regulations concerning boarding scholars." That is to say, girls enjoy in the State intermediate schools the same privileges as male day scholars. Many girls have availed themselves of this opportunity to pass the lyceum examinations.

Women are admitted to the Royal Conservatory of Music at Lisbon, and also to the courses on midwifery in the medical schools of the capital and Porto. These courses cover two years and furnish a theoretical and practical knowledge of the elements of this science. Mid-wives, however, may not employ instruments, except in the presence of a male surgeon.

I shall next consider briefly the legal position of women in Portugal. Women, like men, reach their majority at twenty-one. Emancipation is a consequence of marriage contracted after the sixteenth year, and when all the legal formalities have been observed. The minor may also be emancipated by the father, or, in default of the father, by the mother, and in default of both, by the family council. In the last case the minor must be eighteen years old. The control of the wife's personal property belongs to the husband, but she may make a reservation, which gives her the right of receiving and freely disposing of one-third of the income of that property. Under the marriage system known as the " community of goods," the wife may contract debts without the authorization of the husband, if he is absent or incapacitated, provided the object for which the debt is incurred will not admit of a delay for the return of the husband or for his rehabilitation. In these two cases—the absence or incapacity of the husband—the wife controls the common property, but she cannot lawfully alienate the real estate without the authorization of a family council. The husband has the right of disposing freely of the common chattels. But if he gives them away without the consent of the wife, the sum thus lost will be charged to the husband in the common fund. The consent and accord of both parties is necessary to alienate or mortgage real estate, even when it belongs to one of the two parties. In case they cannot agree, the courts may decide the question. The husband cannot go to law concerning questions of property or the possession of real estate without the consent of the wife.

Debts contracted during the marriage without the consent of the wife, must be paid out of the husband's own funds. His portion of the common property is alone affected by such debts after dissolution of the marriage, or after partial separation (*séparation de biens* in French jurisprudence). An exception is made in the case when the debts were incurred for the benefit of the " community," or in the absence or incapacity of the wife, and when the circumstances will not admit of a delay for her return or rehabilitation.

Under the " dotal system," the husband may dispose freely of the dower, unless the marriage contract contains a stipulation to the contrary. But when the union is dissolved for any cause, he must restore the whole fund to the wife. The dotal real estate is inalienable, except in the following cases: 1. To endow and establish the common children ; 2. For the repairs of other dotal property; 3. To pay the debts of the wife, or of him who endowed her, anterior to the marriage ; 4. To procure family necessities, which could not otherwise be had; 5. To exchange it for something of equal or greater value ; 6. For public expropriation; 7. Where the property is indivisible with third parties. Outside of these cases, the wife may revoke the alienation of dotal real estate. There are cases when she may even do the same as regards chattels.

The civil code requires of husband and wife mutual fidelity and assistance. The wife especially owes obedience to the husband. She is obliged to live with him, to follow him, except to a foreign land, and not to publish any writings without his consent. She may, however, obtain from the courts, in case of unjust refusal on the part of the husband, the right to publish her productions.* She may not go to law without the consent of the husband, except to preserve and insure the rights which belong to her, to take measures against the husband, and to exercise her rights concerning the legitimate children, or the natural children belonging to her and a man other than her husband. It is scarcely necessary to add, that the husband's consent is not required if the wife is prosecuted criminally.

Our code does not recognize divorce, properly so called, *a vinculo matrimonii.* Marriage is a perpetual contract. The wife, however, may demand the separation from the bed and board of her husband, *a mensa et toro,* or, as it is known in French law, *séparation de corps et de biens,* for the following causes: 1. For adultery on the part of the husband which becomes a source of public scandal, or when he introduces his mistress into the common home ; 2. When the husband is condemned to prison for life ; 3. For grave cruelty and bodily injury. But, notwithstanding

---

* The married authoress may not publish her writings without the consent of her husband. But an order from the courts, in case of unjust refusal, will suffice.—Art. 1187, Portuguese Civil Code of July 1, 1867.—R. F.

this partial divorce, conjugal relations are always permitted between the separated parties. Adultery on the
part of the wife, whether it become a subject of public
scandal or not, is sufficient ground for the husband to demand a separation.

CHAPTER XII.

BELGIUM.

BY ISALA VAN DIEST, M.D.

[Miss Isala Van Diest began her medical studies at Bern, Switzerland, in April, 1874. In order to prepare herself for the new work, she had already spent some time in Germany, mastering the language, mathematics and Latin. " I had a strong taste for the sciences," Miss Van Diest writes me, " and especially for chemistry, which opens such a vast field for theorizing, and I determined to take the degree of doctor of sciences." This she did in 1876 at Bern, and next turned her whole attention to medicine, securing the degree of M.D., in May, 1879, from the same university. Her thesis for the doctorate of sciences was an " Essay on the Gonolobus Condurango " (*Etude sur le gonolobus condurango*), a substance much praised in America for its curative effects on the cancer; that for the doctorate of medicine was entitled, " Hygiene in Prisons" (*Hygiène des prisons*). " I chose this subject simply as a pretext," Miss Van Diest says, " in order that I might expose my views concerning man's responsibility for crime, and that I might have an opportunity of criticising the repressive system in vogue in the Swiss penitentiaries." Besides these two theses, Miss Van Diest has published anonymously some essays on social questions. " Conscious of the great moral influence which the physician who relieves physical suffering exercises over women," Miss Van Diest remarks, " I decided to study medicine as a means of opening their hearts to me, and of exhorting them to throw off their apathy, to help each other, and to demand the rights which belong to them. My efforts are very limited, the struggle has only begun, and I shall probably not live to see the end. But if it be permitted me only to see the question taken up in every country, and above all in my native land, where such powerful causes are at work to hold women in subjection, I shall die happy, certain of the triumph of our cause in a not too distant future." Miss Van Diest is the first and only female physician in Belgium. But she cannot secure the authorization which will allow her to practice. " I fear that I shall soon be obliged to give up the fight," she wrote me recently, " and go to France, England or Holland, unless I wish to lose the fruit of all my studies."]

THE situation of woman in Belgium is about the same as in France. The manners and customs of the two countries resemble each other, and the same code, which regulates the conduct and rights of civil life, governs both nations. In Belgium, even more so than in France, the condition of the women of the lower classes is very unfortunate. In our great industrial centres, woman at the tenderest age becomes the slave of the most brutalizing labor. Who has not witnessed with sorrow in our manufacturing cities the stream of workers—poorly dressed women and children, with their pale, wan, thin faces—moving slowly on and disappearing behind the gates of our factories? Shut up in these prisons from early morning until night, with scarcely an hour's repose during a long day, they breathe a foul, mephitic atmosphere, surcharged with miasma, steam and dust. Placed in the midst of the deafening noise of the machinery, the whirlwind of belts, flies and wheels, the slightest imprudence or thoughtlessness, a misstep, may cost the loss of a limb if not of life itself. Our large cities contain many such cripples of labor.

Family life does not exist for these miserable creatures. Constantly separated from her children, how can the mother give them the necessary care? Poverty and fatigue plunge her into such a state of moral and physical helplessness, that she can do nothing to improve the lot of her offspring. As soon as the child is old enough, he follows his mother to the factory. These poor children receive no instruction. Their mental, like their physical development, is entirely sacrificed because of the miserable pay which their week's toil produces. Death reaps a rich harvest here, and those who chance to escape its ravages are etiolated from their earliest youth.

From a moral point of view, the workshop is a loathsome centre for women. Ignorant, with no idea of the difference between right and wrong, without a check or guide, how can these poor souls resist vice? Is it necessary to describe all the terrible consequences and endless sufferings and misery which such a condition entails on girls of the lower classes?

Many well-known voices have been repeatedly raised in Belgium to protest against this state of things. Several other countries long ago regulated by legislation the employment of women and children in factories. In Germany the minimum age for the constant employment of children is ten years, while in France it is twelve years. No such law exists in Belgium. Nearly ten years ago, at the instigation of the Royal Academy of Medicine, a bill was laid before our Chamber of Deputies concerning the employment of women and children in factories. But up to the present time (1883) it has never been acted upon. The National Hygienic Congress, held at Brussels in 1852, the press and a large number of savants and publicists have demanded, and are still demanding, a reform in this direction. But all in vain. As far back as 1843 the government ordered an inquiry concerning the labor of women and children in the mines. Competent authorities were consulted,—chambers of commerce, engineers and medical commissions, and all recommended their exclusion from this terrible field of work. The report revealed all the sad evils of the situation. It established beyond question what everybody had already said and repeated a thousand times, viz., that women are not made for the hard labor of miners, that their employment in the mines is the cause of unspeakable depravity and disorder, and that it has as a result the degeneration of the population. The report of the medical commission of the Province of the Hainaut declares, that those who employ women and girls in mines are guilty of an abuse which disgraces humanity and which no pretext can justify. Years have passed since then, but the demands and protests of our own countrymen and women, as well as the examples set by foreigners, have accomplished nothing,—a striking instance of the difficulty which a question of humanity and justice encounters in the effort to prevail over an evil.

The poor girl of the country is also sacrificed. There, too, her toil is a source of speculation and her interests are quite forgotten. Many townships of Flanders have their convents which, while pretending to be schools for instruction in reading, writing and the catechism, are in reality only workshops where little girls are taught to make lace. Children as young as five or six years of age are kept, during long weary days, seated with a large lace-pillow on their knees, leaning over their work, the chest doubled, and toiling without a rest. Many of these young laborers here contract the germ of a fatal malady. Happily the progress of industry and modern invention has dealt this trade a heavy blow and it is slowly disappearing from the number of female occupations. Some years ago it was not uncommon to see, in the streets of our country villages, poor women, who had been brought up in the convents, busy at lace-making before daybreak in order to gain their bread. At present the pay is so small that it does not suffice to support them, and the industry is now limited almost wholly to religious establishments.

Such a situation, like that of the employment of women

and children in factories and mines, demands energetic protective measures. But that this reform may be radical and produce all the fruits legitimately expected, it should be combined with a law rendering instruction obligatory.

If we mount a round higher in the social ladder, we meet with the woman of the lower middle class, *la petite bourgeoisie.* Although she is not the slave of the factory, she is an industrious worker, has a calling, keeps store, exercises a trade. Often by her activity, her labor, her strong will, her real genius for order and economy, she becomes, more than man, the bread-winner and support of the family. She nourishes love of home and transmits to the children the ideas of duty and virtue. Possessing some instruction herself, she endeavors to develop their minds. The father is busy with his occupations far from home, and in the hours of repose seeks for amusement outside of the family circle. The mother is more with the children; she brings them up and is their guide. And yet this woman, often the real head of the family, is kept by the law in a condition of perpetual tutelage. But I need not dwell upon the general question of how the married woman is treated by the Napoleonic code; the subject is too well known.* One point, however, which has struck me most painfully, I would briefly touch upon here. The code takes great care to save the fortune of the wife when it is endangered by the prodigality of the husband : when her dower is in peril, she may demand a " separation of goods " (*séparation de biens*). But in order to ask for this separation, the wife must have a dower (*dot*); in other words, she must belong

---

* See the chapter on France, where this topic is ably handled by M. Léon Giraud.—T. S.

at the moment of the marriage, to a well-to-do family, which can bestow on her a dower. The code has entirely overlooked the poor wife, who, by her own industry, has slowly acquired a little sum. What protection does the law afford her against the prodigality and dissipation of the husband? None whatever. The separation of goods —whether there be a dower or not—would frequently be a blessing to many families. Under the present law, a husband may dissipate in a single day the hard earnings of a long life-time, without the wife being able to lift a finger in her own defence. Is this not a sovereign injustice?

And what will-power, energy and tenacity of purpose women must have in Belgium, as elsewhere, in order to secure a little footing in the world! Women's work is very poorly paid. The larger number, if not all, of employments, trades, and professions are monopolized by men. Women are generally considered incapable of doing anything. The example of other countries, however, has modified this situation, and the liberal spirit of our government has removed barriers which shut women out from certain employments. A good beginning has been made. In certain cities of Belgium, women are admitted to the postal and telegraphic service. But the circle of their activity should be enlarged, so that a greater number might have the means of procuring an honorable and independent position. Let us hope that the advantages already obtained will encourage further progress in the same direction.

To give women work is to save them not only from starvation but from vice. Recent lawsuits, the discussions of the press, and various publications, notably those of the Brussels Society of Public Morality (*Société de moral-*

24

ité publique*), have revealed misery and shame which would never have been suspected. A woman who has once fallen finds herself, under the *régime* of legalized prostitution which exists in Belgium, in such a position that it is almost impossible for her to break from her chains. That noble woman, Mrs. Josephine E. Butler, well said at Neufchatel: "This modern slavery, with its train of atrocities, is an outrage, not only on women, but on all humanity;" and M. Emile de Laveleye, the eminent Belgian publicist, has also remarked: "Persons object to the State charging itself with the instruction of the people, and deny still more strongly its right to protect women against excessive labor which destroys their health, and yet these same persons tolerate the State enrolling women by force in the ranks of the army of legalized debauchery." The legalization of vice appears to me to be such an odious thing, and the powers put in the hands of the police are so excessive, that I cannot understand how the abuse, once pointed out, is suffered to continue.

Mounting one more round of the social ladder, we reach the opulent commoner, or *bourgeoise*, and the aristocratic lady. Although these women form two very distinct classes in society, meeting but never mingling, the instruction and education which they receive and the influence which they exercise in their respective centres, are very much the same. I think I may say that, with few exceptions, this influence is null, and may be taken as the measure of the moral and intellectual development of

---

* This society is the representative in Belgium of Mrs. Butler's association for the abolition of legalized prostitution. Its secretary is the liberal-minded publicist, M. Jules Pagny, of Saventhem, and its president, the distinguished professor of Liege, M. Emile de Laveleye.—I. van D.

these women. We find here no brutalizing toil, no precarious existence, no worry about the daily bread, which fetters body and mind and checks the proper development of both. But, while difficulties which embarrass the upper classes are not the same as those with which the poor are forced to contend, they are none the less disastrous, and greatly modify the advantages of position and fortune, which might make it possible for the girl and wife to become strong, original individualities, capable of understanding their mission and of fulfilling it intelligently. The daughters of the fashionable world are early seized upon by the convents. The religious sisters, whose duty it is to instruct and prepare these young girls for the existence awaiting them outside of the cloister walls, have no idea, or at least a very wrong one, of real life, which they know only through the medium of exaggerated or false narratives, or the dim recollections of their youth. The sentimental and imaginative faculties are abnormally developed, to the utter neglect of sound reason and the practical things of this earth; and in this condition they are taken from their seclusion and launched into society. Provided with a very poor stock of knowledge, some precepts of conduct which they never find means of applying, and with a few accomplishments, they give themselves up to a round of *fêtes* and pleasures, until the object to be accomplished—finding a husband—is attained. If the girl is not very attractive, if wanting in energy, or if her education has destroyed what little she ever had, she will accept the first man who presents himself fulfilling the conditions required by her family, and from parental tutelage will pass to that of her husband, doomed to live and die a perpetual minor. But if perchance she wakes up one day to a full consciousness of her position, and perceives the extent of her misfortune, how this existence which she has thoughtlessly accepted weighs upon her! She will revolt perhaps, seek amusement and endeavor to find some compensation for her painful lot, unless the grand duties of maternity come to sustain her, to console her and to fill the void in her heart.

Thus, following different routes, we find at both ends of the social ladder the same result : woman's intelligence neglected and left in a state of infancy. I fear it will be a long time, if we may judge by the present condition of things, before our Belgian girls, in imitation of their aristocratic sisters of England, will themselves rise up and assume as high a rank in the intellectual sphere as that which they hold in the social world.

A word remains to be said concerning the admission of women to the walks of higher education, and notably to the study of medicine. There existed in Belgium some years ago a law which required students who would enter the university, to pass the examination of graduate in letters (*gradué en lettres.*) Candidates for this degree were expected to know how to translate Greek and write Latin. But as there were no schools where girls could study the dead languages with the thoroughness of boys, who were trained six years in the classics, the former were almost entirely shut out from enjoying the advantages of an university course. This *graduat*, however, no longer exists, and the entrance of women into our universities is now possible. Female students are found to-day at Brussels, Liege and Ghent, but their number is still very small. It was in 1880 that the first woman entered the university of Brussels, but it was not until 1883 that their admission became general. They pursue, for the most part. scientific studies, thereby securing more lucrative positions as teachers, and pass their examinations for graduation with success. The higher education of women is still an open question in Belgium, and there are those who oppose it. But the experience of Switzerland, England and France, not to mention other countries on both sides of the Atlantic, answers victoriously all objections. And does not the long list of the world's distinguished women prove that the female sex is capable of the highest intellectual culture? Not to go outside of belles-lettres, and the limits of Belgium, we have Miss Nizet, Marguerite Van de Wiele, the Countess de Kerchove de Denterghem, the Loveling sisters, Mrs. Courtmans, Mrs. Van Ackere, and many others.*

The progress of modern ideas tends to destroy day by day the prejudices which still exist in Belgium against the emancipation of women. We are far from the time when woman was a slave and grave bishops in council doubted whether she had a soul. Let us hope that the age is past when woman can be left in ignorance, and that soon the means will be no longer lacking by which she can elevate herself to the intellectual level of the other sex. Then will Belgium enjoy all the other reforms, and woman will become the equal of man in every department of life.

---

* Mr. Emile de Laveleye, writing me from the university of Liege in January, 1883, said: "Our female students have not yet taken their degrees. But as they are working very hard, I have no doubt they will be successful. But co-education will not be so exempt from danger here as in America. Our morals are very inferior to yours." Mr. de Laveleye, in an interesting little pamphlet entitled, "University Education for Women" (*L'instruction supérieure pour les femmes*, Bruxelles, Librairie Européenne, 1882), gives an account of the movement in favor of female instruction in Belgium. These pages show that many of our American Universities could learn lessons in liberality from their sister institutions of Belgium.—T. S.

CHAPTER XIII.

SWITZERLAND.

BY MARIE GŒGG.

[Mrs. Marie Gœgg, whose maiden name was Pouchoulin, was born at Geneva in 1826. Her family, which is of French origin, was driven from Dauphiné by the revocation of the Edict of Nantes, and took refuge in Switzerland, where, for several generations, its members have belonged to the Genevese *bourgeoisie*. She early showed intellectual tastes, and, while still very young, devoured a mass of good books, especially histories. At a later period, she mastered the English and German languages. The troubled period of 1848–1854 drove many political refugees from different countries to Geneva, and among the number Mr. Amand Gœgg, who was condemned to death for contumacy by the courts of his native land, the Grand Duchy of Baden. The subject of this sketch married the proscribed German, and then began the life, often so hard and so full of vicissitudes, of a political exile. They lived successively at London and Geneva; in 1862, after the amnesty, they returned to Baden; the year 1866 found them at Bienne, and in 1868 Mrs. Gœgg settled definitely at Geneva. By her travels, study and own experience, she perceived the unfortunate situation of her sex; and, although greatly occupied with the education of her three sons, determined to devote her life to the amelioration of women's condition. What she has done not only for the women's movement, but for humanity in general, is modestly told in the course of the following pages.]

To give an account of the progress made in the ideas of a people is always difficult, and especially so in regard to the development of the Woman Question in Switzerland, for our little country has, up to the present moment, remained almost a stranger to this important subject; or, if its attention has been turned in this direction, it has been much more as an indifferent or mocking spectator than as an interested actor. I, therefore, hesitate to undertake the task. The difficulty is still further increased by the division of the nation into twenty-five cantons, each one of which has had, until very recently,* its own legislation, its purely cantonal code ; so that an innovation introduced into one canton was confined to its narrow boundaries, and was often regarded with astonishment by the sister cantons. The primitive cantons,† and especially the Catholic ones, have lagged behind the Protestant cantons, which, in their turn, outstrip one another in the race for progress. Geneva, for example, whose population, composed of varied elements, is directed by the descendants of those superior emigrants who fled the political and religious persecutions of the last centuries, has always stood at the head of the Protestant cantons. Although subject to the Napoleonic code, Geneva has never known that debasing principle of the French law, the tutelage of women, which existed in the other cantons, even in intelligent Vaud, where it was not done away with until 1873,‡ and which was in force in several other cantons as late as 1881, when a federal law abolished it throughout all Switzerland.

It is scarcely necessary to explain that the law of the tutelage of women, assuming without question their intellectual and moral inferiority, kept them all their life, no matter what their intelligence, education and social position might be, under a masculine protectorate of some

---

* The new federal constitution of 1874 consolidated a large part of these separate laws.—M. G.

† The primitive cantons are the three which began the formation of the confederacy : Uri, Unterwald and Schwytz, and those which joined them soon afterward, as Lucern, etc. They are all Catholic.—M. G.

‡ This reform was due to the activity of the Solidarity (*Solidarité*), the Women's Rights Society, which will be spoken of further on.—M. G.

sort. Thus the father or the husband, and in case both were dead a son, if of age, or a friend, or even a stranger, might, according to his own will or pleasure, grant or refuse a woman the enjoyment of her own revenues. In a word, it was a mark of degradation put upon women from the cradle to the grave, not to speak of the danger with which this law threatened their material interests, the guardian of their fortune being thus legally tempted to use what was not his own—a temptation to which more than one succumbed—so that the numerous examples of women ruined by the very persons appointed to protect them, long ago proved the injustice of this state of things.

Since the laws of a people are generally the reflection of its customs, its beliefs, its aspirations, we may say that Geneva, whose statute-book is pervaded by a spirit of very great liberality, has shown, in its treatment of women, remarkable generosity and breadth of mind, when compared with the conduct of states living under an almost similar code, but which have been held back by despotism and ultramontanism. For example, Geneva preserved divorce when France re-established the indissolubility of marriage;* Geneva accorded to married women the control of their own fortune; granted them the right to deposit and draw their savings from the bank without the authorization of the husband; created more than 30 years ago excellent intermediate schools for girls; and opened the university to women in every department.

---

* The possibility of divorce has somewhat ameliorated the condition of women in Switzerland, when compared with their condition in other countries. The divorced woman regains, which is not the case everywhere, the control of her own property, and the right to her own earnings, and often, depending upon the causes of the divorce, the entire education of her children.— M. G.

However, notwithstanding these liberal measures, which denote a breadth of mind among our law-makers in keeping with the age, Switzerland, taken as a whole, has been one of the least disposed of European countries to accept the idea of the civil emancipation of women, and much less the conferring upon them of political rights. From 1848 to 1868 the claims of American women were looked upon here as the height of extravagance. Yet Switzerland has given to the world so large a number of distinguished women that it is unnecessary to defend before public opinion the proposition of female intelligence.* But belief is one thing, and practice is another. Between the admission of women's intellectual capacity and the logical application of rights which naturally result therefrom, yawns a vast abyss of prejudice and injustice. The echo of the demands of which we have just spoken rarely crossed the ocean to trouble the minds of our thinkers, and the general public was completely ignorant of them. From time to time some newspaper, for lack of other material or for the amusement of its readers, would tell how the women had assembled in the United States, at New York or elsewhere, to demand " emancipation." This word emancipation, thrown out on the public without any limitation of its meaning, gave a wrong impression as to the aims of these women, and created an unfortunate prejudice against them and their claims. But ideas are like flowers whose seeds are scattered far and wide. The germ deposited in America in 1848, although its growth was difficult, finally took root in Europe. English women,

---

* Further on in this chapter I give the names of some of my countrywomen who have distinguished themselves in letters and the fine arts.— M. G.

supported by the celebrated economist Mill, who had just
given to the world his grand book, the " Subjection of
Women," began to see and understand all the evils produced by the legal subjugation of their sex, and established a National Society for Women's Suffrage. Germany also had its awakening in 1865, at almost the same
time as England ; but German women, in also forming a
National Society, overlooked their civil and political
rights, and began by the improvement of the educational
and industrial condition of their sex.

In March, 1868, Switzerland, in its turn, began to move.
At that date I published a letter in the *United States of
Europe* (*Etats-Unis d'Europe*), inviting the women of all
nations to form a society, which might serve as a bond of
union between them and promote their common interests.
In 1867 I was present at the Peace Congress held in that
year at Geneva, and was struck with the advantages resulting from the meeting of all those superior men, come
together from the four quarters of the globe to protest
against war, and who, for the most part unknown to each
other, now became acquainted, discussed the questions
which interested them and finally separated, but not until
they had created the International League of Peace and
Liberty. Why should not women imitate this good example, and also assemble to consider their rights and to
found an international society ? This simple and natural
idea was the origin of the invitation sent forth in the
spring of 1868. In July of this same year the Women's
International Association was created, and I was elected its
first president. The constitution of the new organization
limited the membership of the central or executive committee to women, and this committee forthwith set to
work. One of its first acts was to address a letter to the

central committee of the International League of Peace and Liberty, which had announced its next meeting in September at Bern, asking that women be admitted to the congress. After a long discussion, the president of the committee, Gustave Vogt, of Bern, now a distinguished lawyer and journalist of Zurich, replied, that not only would women be admitted to the congress, but that the last day—Saturday, September 26th—would be given up to those women who wished to speak, adding that " it was not by gallantry, but by a sentiment of real justice, that the League afforded women an opportunity to make known their claims." This society, therefore, has the honor of being the first in Switzerland to admit women into its midst as equals.

Although, during the whole week, the Bernese public had followed the proceedings of the congress with deep interest, the session of September 26th may be said to have awakened the greatest curiosity. The platform and the body of the house were filled to overflowing. " The women are going to speak to-day ; it will be funny," was whispered in the crowd. But the crowd was mistaken. It was not funny, but eloquent. The audience was carried away by the very simplicity of the statement, and by the truth of the reasoning. Mrs. Virginie Barbet, of Lyons, and the author of this sketch, in the name of the association of which she was president, exposed from different standpoints the reasons which militated in favor of women's rights. They were listened to with deference and sympathy ; they were even applauded ; and—a detail worthy of note, for it is really extraordinary, when we remember the state of public opinion in 1868—not one voice in that vast assemblage was raised to combat the conclusions of these two women. Several members of the

League, of different nationalities, came to their support, and proposed that henceforth women be admitted to membership in the organization on the same terms as men. The vote in favor of the resolution was unanimous.*

The brilliant manifestation at Bern drew attention to the association, and adherents came from all sides. It may be said that from 1868 to 1870, there was in all countries great enthusiasm for the question of women's rights. It was like an awakening of the public conscience. Everywhere distinguished men and women were discussing the subject, and whether they spoke for us or against us, they all helped to let in new light on this important topic. During these two years, the association, responding to a real demand of the hour, had the honor of rallying around it many noble minds, and of affording a common center for their efforts and longings. When, therefore, the association held its first general meeting, on March 27, 1870, it counted fifteen strong local societies, each representing the needs of the country and canton where it existed. At this meeting, which was very largely attended, I, as president,

---

* It may be added that the International League of Peace and Liberty has ever since continued to be an ardent friend of the women's movement, not only in Switzerland, but throughout the world ; and Mr. Charles Lemonnier, of Paris, editor of its organ, *Les Etats - Unis d'Europe*, and elected its president two years later, both of which posts he still (1883) holds, has never let an occasion pass to say a good word for us.—M. G. The central committee, at the close of the Bern congress, not only chose Mrs. Gœgg one of its members, to which position she has been re-elected each year, but she was afterward made treasurer of the League, member of the board of administrators of the journal, and publisher. These facts prove both the liberal spirit of the association and the capacity—so often denied—of women for business. "They [women] are perhaps better fitted for administrative work than men," says Michelet (*Les femmes de la révolution*, p. 314). "The Revolution, which renewed everything, in opening active careers to men, should certainly have employed women in sedentary callings. I find one woman among the clerks of the Committee of Public Safety."—T. S.

read a report on what the association had accomplished. (1.) The organization of the fifteen societies just referred to. (2.) A petition to the Swiss National Council, which was never granted, asking for the recognition by the constitution of Switzerland of the equal civil rights of women. (3.) A petition, which was supported by Emilio Castelar in a fine speech, to the Spanish Cortes, at the moment when its members were called upon to draw up a new constitution, demanding that women be represented in the State. (4.) A petition—read amidst the applause of the whole left—to the Italian Chamber of Deputies, asking the Minister of Public Instruction to provide laic instruction for girls. (5.) A petition to the Grand Council of Geneva, praying for the creation by the State of a girls' orphan asylum similar to that for boys,— which was done a few years later. (6.) A petition to the English Parliament, in concert with Mrs. Josephine E. Butler and her English society, requesting the repeal of a recent law tending to legalize prostitution in England. With the object of advancing the young movement, I established, at my own risk, a bi-monthly, the *Women's Journal* (*Journal des femmes*). But this was a violation of that good old Latin motto, *festina lentè*, and, at the end of a few months, the paper suspended publication. Swiss public opinion was not yet ready to support such a venture.

It may be pointed out here, that, except in England, all the women's societies created in Europe had, up to the time of the organization of the International Association, refrained from touching the question of the political rights of women. The Swiss association, on the contrary, always included this subject in its programme. But, unfortunately, at the moment when our efforts were meeting with success, and the future was full of promise for the cause which we advocated, the terrible Franco-German war broke out, and, for various reasons unnecessary to go into here, I felt constrained to resign the presidency, and the association came to an end.

Two years later, when peace and calm began to reign again, a group of women, faithful to the ideas which had united them in the International Association, resolved to begin anew. A call was therefore issued, convoking, for June 9, 1872, the friends of the movement at the house of Mrs. de May de Rued, at Bern.*

The Bern reunion gave birth to a new society, the Solidarity (*Solidarité*), whose name signified the spirit which ought to unite all women. Mrs. de May de Rued was made president, and Bern was fixed upon as the seat of the Central Committee. Mrs. de May de Rued, who was Bernese, was known for her articles in the newspapers on the different codes of the Swiss cantons, and enjoyed a well-merited reputation in her native city. The Solidarity began immediately to organize auxiliary societies, and to agitate. In the spring of 1873 the society, through Miss Mathilde Boisot, president of the Lausanne branch, petitioned the Grand Council of the Canton of Vaud for the abolition of the tutelage of women, and were rewarded by having their prayer granted, the petition receiving the support of several Vaud deputies. Unfortunately the

---

* This circular letter was signed by the following women : Josephine E. Butler, Liverpool ; Caroline de Barrau, Paris ; Marie Gœgg, Geneva ; Fanny Keller-Dorian, Mulhouse ; Julia Kühne, Stettin ; Christine Lazzati-Rossi, Milan ; Mrs. de May de Rued, Bern ; Marianne Mentzer, Dresden ; Louise Roeder-Wiederhold, Jerusalem ; Rosalie Schönwasser, Düsseldorf ; Caroline Varesi, Milan ; Mathilde Boisot, Lausanne ; Maria Bosak-Hauke, Geneva ; Louise Estève, Serignan ; and Mathilde Hunziker, Aarau (Switzerland.)— M. G.

health of Mrs. de May de Rued permitted her to hold the presidency but a year ; at the general meeting of 1873 she resigned, and died two years later.

On the resignation of Mrs. de May de Rued, I was pressed to take the vacant position, but again declined, as I had done the previous year, and urged the committee to accept Miss Mathilde Boisot, who had long devoted her time and talent to the cause, and who had succeeded in creating a strong society at Lausanne. But Miss Boisot had in the meanwhile become Mrs. Dumas-Boisot, and the claims of married life rendered it impossible for her to perform the duties of president of the Solidarity. At a meeting at Geneva, September 15, 1875, I succeeded Mrs. Dumas-Boisot, and my election was renewed annually until 1880. During these five years, aided by a few faithful friends, I published a quarterly, the *Solidarity Bulletin* (*Le bulletin de la Solidarité*), which was very well received, and which, besides containing articles whose aim was to popularize the subject of women's rights, gave a general account of what was being done in this direction in other countries. But for financial reasons it was again found necessary to give up the periodical, and on September 20, 1880, the society and the journal ceased to exist. " The dissolution of the Solidarity," said the president in her farewell speech on this occasion, " ought not to discourage us, but ought rather to cause us to rejoice, for all the national women's societies which have been created recently in different countries prove that the Solidarity has succeeded in its work, and we have only to retire before the present movement, which has everywhere taken on a national character, an evident sign of its development and its force."

Such is the history of the women's rights organizations

in Switzerland.   Since the fall of the Solidarity no attempt has been made to establish another national association. What is the cause of the indifference or inertia of Swiss women in a matter which concerns society and themselves in so high a degree? There are many.   The principal one, perhaps, is the reluctance which a woman feels to take a new step in a little center where everybody knows his neighbor.   In France, England and America the women's movements have begun generally in large cities, where one is not a slave to what people say and also where friendly co-operation is more easily secured.   But Switzerland is composed only of big villages and small cities. Again, more so in Switzerland than elsewhere, the term "emancipation" was confounded with immorality.   This fact was so well known, that our women's societies have always substituted for this terrible word, the term "equality of rights."   But the stigma has nevertheless remained attached to the agitation, and great moral courage and a profound conviction of duty have always been necessary to decide a woman to take up this question in Switzerland.   In the great countries just mentioned, eminent men associate themselves with the movement, and the women's societies enjoy the support of lawyers, deputies, and senators.   This has never been the case in Switzerland.   Not a man holding an official position, cantonal or federal, has come to our aid and publicly approved our efforts to secure equal civil rights.   Our isolation is consequently complete.   Another impediment to our success has been the impossibility of working toward a common end. The differences of nationality, of religion, and of legislation in the various cantons have produced a variety of customs, habits and characteristics, which are extremely dissimilar, and which render Switzerland a composite having but one solid bond of union, but a very solid one,—a mutual veneration for the federal flag. How can anything be accomplished under such circumstances, where, instead of one obstacle, twenty-five must be gotten over one after the other?

Two or three other societies, though not devoted especially to women's rights, have, nevertheless, done much to better the condition and open the minds of women. The Swiss Society for the Public Good (*Société suisse d'utilité publique*), which has branches in almost all the cantons, has often touched upon the woman question and the measures that ought to be adopted to enable women to gain an honorable livelihood. It is regretable, however, that the noble and devoted members of this society, so earnest in their desire to see women gain material independence by remunerative employments, are strongly opposed to the idea of women's equality before the law. The British Federation (*Fédération britannique*) has its central committee at Neufchatel under the direction of Mr. Aimé Humbert, a very able and liberal-minded man, who would broaden the scope of the society if the matter rested with him alone. But, such as it is, the British Federation is an excellent organization, due to the initiative of that philanthropic woman, Mrs. Josephine E. Butler, who attacks that basest form of prostitution, the connivance of government, the legalization of vice, the establishment of infamous regulations, which, while they weigh on women, do not punish men. Besides these two admirable societies, Switzerland contains a large and varied number of charitable associations, many of which were created and are directed by women.*

---

* Among Swiss ladies the most widely known for their active charitable work, I may mention the following : At Geneva, Mesdames Butini, Eynard,

33

Our women have distinguished themselves in literature and the fine arts. Among the large number of female writers whom Switzerland may point to with just pride, I shall mention only a few of the more celebrated, for I might fill whole pages with the names of contemporaries who are pursuing with success the vocation of letters. It is scarcely necessary for me to say that their productions are healthy, moral, and instructive; that their aim is not only to interest and amuse, but to improve and elevate. Mme. de Staël, whose mother was Vaudoise and father Genevese, belongs unquestionably to Switzerland; Mme. Necker, the mother of Mme. de Staël; the Baroness de Montolieu, author of more than a hundred volumes, and Miss Frossard, may represent Vaud; Mesdames Necker de Saussure, Tourte-Cherbulier, de Gasparin, Geisendorf, Pictet de Seigneux, and Berthe Vadier, Geneva; Mesdames Alice de Chambrier, and Franel, Neufchatel; Mesdames Anna Rothpletz, Sophie Haller, and Maria Dössekel, Aargau; Mesdames Pestalozzi (*née* Anna Schultess, wife of the celebrated educationist), Spirry, and Zehnder, Zurich; Maria von Berg, St. Gall; and Marie Walden, Bern. Such is a brief list of the literary women of Switzerland, past and present. I am aware that I have overlooked many, perhaps some of the best.

In the fine arts, I may cite among sculptors the Princess Colonna, *née* d'Affry, celebrated under the name of Marcello, and a native of the canton of Freiburg; and Miss Thérèse Rey, of Geneva. Among painters, I select the names of Mesdames Rath, Couronne, Mérienne, Vouga,

Annevelle, Lenoir-Poulin, Genecand, Tronchin-Calendrini, Munier-Romilly, Gaussen, Ritter, and Vernet ; at Neufchatel, Mrs. Aimé Humbert ; at Zurich, Mrs. Trudel ; in Vaud, Mrs. Germond.—M. G.

Landesmann, Lagier, Munier-Romilly, Hébert, Stry-jenska, L'Hardy, Annen and Lamunière, who have been, or are still, known at Geneva for their talents in various styles; Mrs. Elizabeth Kelly, St. Gall; Mrs. Maria Custer, Winterthur; Mesdames Stockar-Escher and Fries, Zurich; Mesdames Lennziger, and Tschiffeli-Christern, Bern; and Mrs. Favre-Guillermod, Neufchatel.

In October, 1872, I sent a petition to the Grand Council of Geneva, asking that women be admitted to the University of Geneva on the same footing as men. The state of public opinion on this subject in Switzerland, and especially in Geneva, may be judged from the fact that, fearing to compromise the demand if I acted in my own name, or in that of the Solidarity, the petition was presented as coming from the "mothers of Geneva." Our prayer was granted. The following table gives the number of female students who have pursued their studies at the Geneva University:

Year.	Sciences.	Medicine.	Letters.	Total.
1876–'77	1	.	..	1
1877–'78	..	4	..	4
1878–'79	3	2	..	5
1879–'80	5	4	..	9
1880–'81	6	7	..	13
1881–'82	8	6	..	14
1882–'83	12	8	1	21

This table shows that the number of students is steadily increasing.* The list of female graduates up to

---

* But still more interesting is the fact that, with one single exception, all of the female students have pursued scientific or medical studies rather than those of a literary nature. The experience of the University of Geneva, therefore, seems to contradict the position taken by Professor John LeConte, M. D., late President of the University of California, when, referring to co-education in that institution, he says: " I think the young women show a

December 31, 1882, gives nine bachelors of science, physical and natural, and one doctor of medicine.* In Germanic Switzerland, at Zurich for example, the number
of female students is much larger than in the universities
of Romanic Switzerland, and they are for the most part

---

preference for and attain a greater proficiency in the classical and literary
branches of study. With a few exceptions, they seem to have an aversion
to mathematical studies, and to those branches of exact science which involve
the application of mathematics. This is true not only in relation to the
higher branches of mathematics, but likewise in relation to the elementary
mathematics (algebra, geometry, trigonometry,) required in the classical and
literary courses. Our experience here seems to me to fortify the *a priori*
deduction that the physical organization of the female has a reflex influence
on the intellectual manifestations of the sex." ("The Admission of Women
to the Universities," p. 9.) It is to be noted that the half-dozen other college
presidents who give their testimony on co-education in this little pamphlet,
issued in 1883 by the New York Association for Promoting the Higher
Education of Women, do not share the opinion of President LeConte,
which is, however, that of many friends of this movement. My own study
of the question, both in Europe and America, does not lead me to accept
President LeConte's conclusions, and the reader of this volume will notice,
in the course of its pages, several instances as strong as this of the University of Geneva, which go to prove that men and women are intellectually the
same. While correcting the proofs of this chapter I have met with a remarkable declaration to this same effect. Ernest Legouvé, of the French
Academy, referring to a recent competition for fellowships in the University of France, says : "A very singular fact, which is worthy of attention, was produced at this examination. The papers of the scientific candidates were greatly superior to those of letters. This result contradicts a
very general opinion, which I myself have strongly supported, viz., that
scientific studies, the abstract sciences and mathematics, must hold a subordinate place in women's education, because they are incompatible with the
nature of the female intellect. We have been mistaken."—(*Temps*, October
21, 1883.) —T. S.

* The rector of the University of Geneva, Mr. G. Julliar, writes me, under
date of February 8, 1883 : "Our female students are principally Russians.
. . . Besides the diploma of doctor of medicine given by the University,
the Confederation confers a medical degree on examination. This degree
has been taken by three women, who passed their examinations very well.

Russians.* The admission of women to the University of Nuefchatel dates from 1878, but few have profited by the concession. Fifteen ladies, non-matriculates, have listened to a course of lectures on general history and the history of modern literature, and one female student has matriculated, but up to the present time (May, 1883) no degree has been conferred on a woman.

. . . Some of the courses of lectures of the Faculty of Letters are attended by unmatriculated female students who are freely admitted on payment of a fee. A great number of ladies profit by this opportunity, but they pass no examinations and take no degrees. Up to the present time, the presence of women in our University has occasioned us no inconvenience, except in some lectures of the medical school, where the subjects are not always of a nature to admit of their treatment before mixed classes." Professor Pflüger, of the University of Bern, writing me under date of April 27, 1883, says : " Since February 2, 1876, up to the present time, thirty-five women have taken degrees at our medical school. The courses are, on an average, attended each semester by from twenty-five to thirty women, while from three to six female students follow the lectures on philosophy and letters. The presence of women at our university has occasioned no serious inconvenience, and many of my colleagues favor it. As for myself, I have no objection to the education of women, but they would probably appear to better advantage in other departments of study than medicine. I have occasion sometimes to lament the insufficiency of their preparatory instruction and their not participating in the examinations, so that I never know just what they are capable of."—T. S.

* Unfortunately the statistics of the University of Zurich from 1873 to 1883 have not yet appeared. They are being collected, however, and will be published in the autumn of 1883, on the occasion of the semi-centennial celebration of the foundation of the University.—M. G.

33*

CHAPTER XIV.

RUSSIA

BY MARIE ZEBRIKOFF.

[Miss Marie Zebrikoff was born in 1835, at Cronstadt, her father being an officer in the navy. She received a home education, which was broadened by extensive reading, and she published in 1868 her first critical essay, a review of the female characters of Leo Tolstoi's "Our Grandmothers." Similar articles followed, and the works not only of Russian authors but of Spielhagen, Auerbach, Shelley, George Sand, George Eliot and the other English female novelists, were criticised by Miss Zebrikoff's keen intellect in the pages of such periodicals as the *Contemporary Annals* (*Otechestvennya Zapiski*), *Herald of Europe* (*Viestnik Evropy*), *The Word* (*Slovo*), *The Act* (*Dielo*), and *The Week* (*Nediclia*). From 1875 to 1880 Miss Zebrikoff was at the head of an educational review, and at the same time edited, translated and compiled many English, French, and German books, as, for example, Mrs. Ellet's "Women of the American Revolution" (compiled with an historical essay as a preface) ; "The Three First Years of a Child's Life" (*Les Trois Premières Années de l'Enfant*), by Bernard Pérez, (translated) ; John Morley's "On Compromise" (translated with an essay) ; "The Emile of the Nineteenth Century," (*L'Emile du XIXᵉ Siècle*), by Alphonse Esquiros (translated), and "The New Life" (*Neues Leben*), by the late Berthold Auerbach. One of Michelet's histories, translated by some ladies, was edited and introduced to the public by Miss Zebrikoff in aid of the courses for the higher education of women—mentioned in the following pages—of whose exective committee she is a member. Miss Zebrikoff is a contributor to many educational periodicals, and is the author of some children's books.]

AN American woman—Miss Blackwell—was the first to open to her sex the untrodden path of medical science; a Russian woman, Miss Nadiejda Souslova, was the second.* Nearly twenty years have elapsed since that day, and Russian women have given many shining proofs of their ability, their perseverance and their courage, and have won academic distinctions in numerous universities of Europe. This remarkable innovation, in a field considered too rough for women's weak feet and forbidden them by popular prejudices, which, alas! are still too strong, has been a source of great astonishment alike to every friend and enemy of the woman question. I have often been asked, in my travels in Germany and Switzerland, the following question: "How is it that Russia, which by no means occupies the foremost rank in European civilization, is first in this matter of women's emancipation?—for no country in the Old World can vie with Russia in this respect." The answer to this question cannot be given in a line, but requires an explanation of some length.

Every new movement, however slight it may be, has its roots deep down in the national life. The great and successful impulse of Russian women toward scientific education is due to causes which spring from the political and social state of the country. Russia, although she came later than the other nations of Europe to work in the vineyard of modern civilization, has reaped certain benefits from this very tardiness. Hers is the lot of the youngest brother, who strives to emulate the best qualities of his seniors, but whose eyes are open to their defects,

* Miss Souslova, daughter of a peasant who had acquired some fortune, was the first Russian woman graduated in medicine at a foreign university, Zurich. Graduates of foreign medical schools, in order to practice in Russia, must submit to an examination in that country. Miss Souslova passed her Russian examinations so brilliantly that she astonished our medical celebrities, and has since won the reputation of being a very able physician. She has a very large practice in St. Petersburgh.—M. Z.

errors, and faults, and who grows wiser by their experience, seeking a lofty ideal which they have yet to attain. This lateness, therefore, has assigned to Russia a peculiarly important part in the work which the other nations are called upon to perform.

Although the historical antecedents of the United States and Russia are as widely separated as the poles, the former being freedom-seeking Europe removed from its old dwelling-place to a new one, still there are some striking points of likeness between the Russian Autocracy and the American Republic. The most remarkable of these resemblances is that both countries are thoroughly democratic. We may in some respects apply to Russia the following sentiments addressed by Goethe to the United States:

> Amerika Du hast es besser
> Als unser Continent das alte,
> Hast keine verfallenen Schlösser
> Und keine Basalte,
> Dich stört nicht im Innern
> Zu lebendiger Zeit
> Unnützes Erinnern
> Und vergeblicher Streit.*

We have had no feudal aristocracy which made women slaves and victims to the dynastic interests of the family, and which, though modified by the vivifying breath of the eighteenth century, is still a formidable stumbling-block to the advance of liberty and equality in Europe. In spite of the old barriers dividing the nobles from the merchant and peasant classes, Peter the Great himself could not

---

* America, thou art much happier than our old continent; thou hast no castles in ruins, no fortresses; no useless remembrances, no vain enmity will interrupt the inward working of thy life. (*Den Vereinigten Staaten in Sprüche in Reimen*).—T. S.

engraft primogeniture upon our institutions. The nobility clung to the democratic custom of dividing the property equally among all the sons, so that no hereditary aristocracy was called into life. Women were thereby benefited. When there are no male heirs—that is, no sons—the property is divided equally among the daughters, and the mother receives one-seventh of the real estate and one quarter of the personal property. The widow or orphan daughters do not run the risk of being driven from their father's house, as is the case in England when an estate goes to a male heir of a collateral branch.*

The question of woman's emancipation was first openly discussed by our newspapers and became a factor in Russian progress when the chains of the serfs were broken on February 19th, 1861. The spirit of liberty and equality is like rising water: it cannot mount in one portion of society without reaching the same level in every part. In England, to take another example, the women's movement sprang into life when the emancipation of the workman became a burning theme in the press, in public meetings and in parliament. But the woman question in Russia has not yet emerged from the ideal phase, and can boast of but very few practical victories,—scarcely more

---

* There are many other examples of the democratic spirit in Russia. Before the time of Peter the Great all government offices were held by men of noble blood. The aristocracy (*boyars*) and the gentry (*dvorianstvo*) divided among themselves the few positions which then existed in the crown service. Since Peter the Great, not birth but education has been the necessary qualification. The son of a peasant, merchant or mechanic, if he has been educated at an intermediate school (*gymnasium*), is a candidate for a place under government. Since the abolition of slavery, in the last reign, all Russians have been placed on the same level of equality. There is but one exception,—peasants, workmen, and small shopkeepers may be punished with the rod.—M. Z.

than three. Our women are mistresses of their own fortune; they participate in the choice of members of the municipal council and county assembly, through the agency of a male friend or relative who represents them at the polls, and they enjoy the means of securing a higher education, wrung by their own brave efforts from the reluctant hands of society and the bureaucracy. The first two privileges have come down to Russian women from the centuries, while in liberal England they have only recently been secured, and in republican France they are utterly unknown.*

Notwithstanding these advantages, the condition of the Russian woman as regards the relations between parents and children, and husband and wife, is that of a dependent being. As a daughter, she is in the absolute power of her parents until their death. On reaching her majority, she does not become free to act and think for herself. Her lot is complete obedience, except in the two cases where the parents incite their daughter to crime, or order her to do an illegal act. And even here, everything is against the daughter. She must prove the truth of her allegations before the courts—a very difficult proceeding where it is the vogue to surround all criminal actions with mystery, and witnesses are in bad odor.† The text of the Russian law is explicit. The authority of parents over their children ceases only with death, except in the case of a son entering the crown service or when a daughter

---

* Miss Zebrikoff might have added that the same thing is true of the United States as a whole, democratic and republican though they be.— T. S.

† Russian law considers women's testimony of less weight than that of men. A clause in the code reads : '' When two witnesses do not agree, the testimony of an adult outweighs that of a child, and the testimony of a man, that of a woman.''—M. Z.

marries, for, as the law reads, " one person cannot reasonably be expected to fully satisfy two such unlimited
powers as that of the husband and that of the parents."*
Obedience to parents, therefore, cannot be required of a
married daughter to the same extent as of her unmarried
sister.

Parents have the right to punish the rebellious child,
and both the secular and ecclesiastical authorities are
armed by the law with power to aid them.   On a simple
request made by the parents, without any judicial examination, the child may be sent to the house of correction,
sentenced to hard labor, or confined in a monastery, there
to undergo religious discipline in the form of vigils, fasts,
and prayers, and to be subjected to hardships scarcely
less severe than those of the house of correction. Happily
Russian society has outgrown these barbarous laws, and
instances of their application are extremely rare, and
always occasion a great hue and cry. They are, however,
sometimes enforced.   Ten years ago the newspapers told
of three men, one thirty-five, the other two seventeen and
twenty years respectively, who were sent to the house of
correction for four months, not as a punishment for the
very grave crimes of which they were guilty—one of them
had nearly committed murder in a fit of intoxication—but
simply, on the demand of their parents, to restrain them
from going to greater excesses.   The youth of seventeen
and the man of thirty-five were imprisoned at the instance
of a widowed mother, a poor music teacher, struggling for
her own and her daughter's sustenance, while the third
owed his confinement to a widow of seventy, who trembled for the future of her youngest son.

---

* Volume X. of the Russian Civil Laws.—M. Z.

It will have been noticed that the Russian mother is on a footing of equality with the father in exacting filial obedience. The slave of yesterday may be a tyrant to-day, if a mother whose husband allows her some freedom of action, or if a widow. It will also have been observed that the same submission is required of the son as of the daughter, except when the former enters the service of the State. Neither may marry without the parents' consent. In but two provinces of Russia—Pultava and Chernigoff—a daughter, on attaining the age of twenty-one, may take legal measures to force her parents to consent, and then only when the father or mother is guardian of the property belonging to her.* Women, however, derive but little benefit from this law, as it is applicable only to those who possess property, and who have lost one of their parents, so that the surviving parent is the guardian of this property; or to those who, both parents living, have inherited property.

If the girl is not free in her choice of a husband, the parents cannot force her to take a husband against her will. If she may not marry the man of her choice, she can at least remain single. Peter the Great established this law prohibiting marriage where one of the contracting parties objected. The priest may not begin the ceremony if the bride declares that her parents have forced her to accept the groom. But it must be borne in mind that the assertion of this right requires no small amount of moral courage on the part of the young girl, who, after the

---

* Pultava and Chernigoff were a part of Little Russia, formerly an independent state of Zaporogue Cossacks, who, to escape from the thraldom of Poland, submitted to Russia on the condition that their laws and customs should be respected. This is the origin of the exception referred to in the text.—M. Z.

public scandal occasioned by such a declaration, must return to parents irritated at her disobedience, and, as their conduct proves, wanting in all true affection for her. But to-day such marriages never occur among the educated classes,—a proof of progress in civilization, and at the same time of independence among our young women.

The Russian marriage laws are a little less severe than those of Catholic origin. Civil marriage is unknown. Marriage is a religious rite—a sacrament—and is indissoluble except on three or four grounds. A great and salutary victory will be gained when the marriage laws of Russia are radically reformed. Ill-usage and immorality are not considered sufficient causes for divorce. By marriage, a woman becomes the subject of an autocratic lord. With the exception of her dowry—for she is the absolute mistress of her own fortune—the wife is in the full power of the husband. If her choice proves unhappy, she must bear her lot. Her husband may be a dissolute drunkard, immoral, dishonest; but she remains his wife. If he ill-treats her, she may have him cast into prison by complaining to the justice of the peace, but she is still his wife when the term of punishment has expired. The law does not here recognize any ground for divorce.

There are but four cases in which divorce is granted in Russia. The first is physical incapacity for marriage either on the part of the wife or the husband, and in the latter case the wife must prove her virginity after three years of married life. The second is adultery by the husband, which must be established by two witnesses present at the moment the crime was committed, a requirement which renders proof of infidelity almost impossible. The third is the disappearance of the husband for a period of five years. In this case the wife may apply to an ecclesi-

34

astical council for the annulment of the marriage. But this court is as dilatory as it is venal. The divorce is granted only when the husband fails to answer the summons of the court, and the slightest rumor that he has been seen or heard of in some quarter, often protracts the proceedings to such an interminable length, that the poor wife loses both the bloom and strength of youth. The fourth and last ground for divorce occurs when the husband is deprived of his civil rights and is exiled to Siberia. The wife may follow her husband, but all children born after the father's disgrace are considered to belong to the lowest class in society, though the wife and the children born before his condemnation preserve their social position.* When the wife, taking advantage of her husband's degradation, applies for a divorce, the religious authorities grant the request, and the secular power gives her a pass,†

---

* Russian society is sharply divided into four classes, rising one above the other. The last and lowest is made up of peasants and the petty shopkeepers of the towns. They are looked down upon by all the other classes, and are subjected to corporal punishment for delicts. The wife who accompanies her husband to Siberia may see him and her children subjected before her own eyes to the degrading penalty of the rod.—M. Z.

† A *pass* is an official paper giving the name, rank, profession, etc., of the holder of it. Every Russian subject must have a pass. On arriving in any town, in changing lodgings and the like, the pass must be sent to the police to be viséed. When a woman marries, she is inscribed on her husband's pass, and if she wishes to visit another town, she must obtain a pass from him. Otherwise she may not leave him. This document is generally worded as follows: " I give this pass to my wife that she may inhabit any city or village she chooses." It depends entirely upon the husband to name the term for which the pass is good, and when it expires, the wife must return or get it renewed. The daughter stands in the same relation to her parents as the wife to the husband. They give her a pass, which is registered by the police and stamped. Among the working classes, the wife and daughter often obtain their pass only after paying a stipulated sum to the husband or parents.—M. Z.

stating her new condition. She may then re-marry. To the honor of Russian wives be it said, that few seek for a divorce under this fourth head, but rather, on the contrary, many share the lot of their exiled husbands, or remain behind only in order that their children may receive an education which could not be found in some remote Siberian village. The *via dolorosa*—the highway to Siberia—has often witnessed men staggering on under the weight of heavy chains, while their wives, with infants at the breast, follow on foot or in rough open carts.*

The Russian civil law recognizes a separation between husband and wife, but this must not be confounded with divorce. It occurs only when both parties consent to it, and neither has the right to marry again. The law gives the daughter to the father and the son to the mother, on the ground that the stronger should support the weaker. When the wife is without fortune, the husband is obliged to furnish the means for her maintenance and for the maintenance and education of the children, if there be any. If the wife willfully leaves her husband, he may force her to return to him, and if necessary call upon the police for aid. If a man of cruel nature, he may compel her to submit to an escort of armed policemen along with the vagabonds and criminals who are being conveyed from one prison to another. The late Third Section, or department of secret police, which has left behind it throughout all Russia such a loathsome and dreaded name,

---

* It is worthy of note that in this fourth case the church departs from its principle of the indissolubility of marriage, binding the wife to her husband for weal and for woe, and accepts the considerations of the civil law. It may be added that a marriage is null when unlawfully contracted, when the bride's protest was disregarded, when the man was married under a false name, etc.—M. Z.

had at least one redeeming feature, in that it frequently shielded women from brutal husbands. Often has its occult power snatched from the tyrant his victim whom the ecclesiastic and secular laws did not protect, and forced him to give her a pass which allowed her to live unmolested. If, on the other hand, the husband deserts his wife, she may claim from him enough money to support herself and children.

The pecuniary independence of the Russian woman— for she is mistress of her own fortune, as I have already stated—has led to her obtaining the few other privileges which she enjoys. As she owns property, she pays taxes, and therefore participates in the choice of the members of the municipal council *(gorodskaya ouprava)* which expends her money.* Women do not go to the polls themselves, as I have said before, but are represented by some male relative or friend who votes for them.† They choose in the same way the members of the county assembly, *(zemstvo)*, who appoint the board or committee which supervises the public affairs of the county.

These rights possessed by Russian women must not be measured by a European or American political standard. The powers of the municipal and county assemblies may

---

* The advocates of women's rights in the United States have been proclaiming for forty years that "taxation without representation is tyranny," while Russia, the land of autocracy, has been practicing this fundamental principle of justice since the days when we were colonies. Here, as in many other places in this book, Americans will notice that in our treatment of women we are often far behind what we are pleased to call "effete monarchies." —T. S.

† Mrs. Worden, Seward's sister-in-law, adopted a somewhat similar plan. She required all the men who worked on her farm near Auburn to vote as she wished, for, being a taxpayer and yet a widow without father or son, she felt that she ought to be represented at the polls.—" History of Woman Suffrage," I., 462.—T. S.

be likened to those of a housekeeper or an intendant of a great estate; they gather the taxes and expend them on schools, hospitals, roads and canals. But they may make no laws, vote no supplies, in a word, do nothing to change the ordained order of things. Yet the *gorodskaya ouprava* and the *zemstvo*, although they have no voice in legislating for the nation, nor even for their own province, county, or town, exercise a great influence in their narrow circle, and are a step toward self-government. Before their creation, the work which they now perform was in the hands of a crowd of government agents *(tchinovniks)*, who were an absolute plague to the country.

American women ask for participation in the enactment of the laws which they are bound to obey. But Russian women cannot make such a lofty demand, for men even do not enjoy this right. We can feel, however, that politically we are almost the equal of men, although we may not, like them, deposit our own votes and are not eligible to either of the public bodies of which we are electors.*

The Russian peasant women are in a much worse state than the women of the upper classes. They must obey not only the laws of the empire, but those of custom— a sort of common law—which vary in different provinces. Their lot is hard and miserable in the extreme, and our renowned poet, Nekrassoff, has given a vivid and pathetic picture of it in his poems. In Great Russia, that is, in all the provinces of north, east, and middle Russia, where the system of the village " commune " exists, these laws of custom protect women in some respects.

---

*Universal suffrage does not exist in Russia. The ownership of property or the payment of a certain tax is the necessary qualification of an elector. Every woman who meets this requirement, votes.—M. Z.

34*

In these village communes, the land is considered to belong to all the inhabitants in common. The village council (*mir*), after the lapse of a certain period of years, divides the fields and meadows into lots, according to the number of families and the size of each family. A numerous household receives a larger lot than a small one. The father may not sell or mortgage his lot, but it is his for tillage until the new period of division comes round. If he concludes to abandon his peasant state and become a merchant or denizen of a town, his land reverts to the commune, though his cottage, cattle, furniture, harvest, carts, implements, etc., are considered to be his. The principle in the communes of Great Russia is this: the land belongs to the tiller of the soil, but only so long as he tills it.

This idea, firmly planted in the mind of the people, sometimes redounds to the advantage of the peasant women. When an industrious wife is tied to a worthless husband who is undermining the prosperity of the family, she complains to the *mir*, which often transfers the lot of land to the wife, who thus becomes, *de facto*, the head of the family. When a widow can, by her own and her children's exertions or by the aid of a hired man, cultivate her late husband's lot, she becomes its owner and has a voice in the *mir*. There are numerous examples of women continuing to represent the family, even after the eldest son has reached his majority. When a member of the commune enters the army, his wife is provided with a lot of land, if she is ready to cultivate it. An orphan girl, if she declares her intention not to wed, demands a similar favor. Girls generally marry in another than their own commune and rarely bring a husband into it, for otherwise, in either case, the new family would have to be given a lot, which would lessen the extent of the existing holdings.

This *mir* is a powerful and important little body. It often acts as a judge in quarrels between husband and wife; sees that the land is well cultivated; that the taxes are paid; and it names the school boards and the school patrons and patronesses.* I recall a curious instance of one of these patronesses, who, the daughter of a rich peasant, could neither read nor write, and who, with tears in her eyes, related how her father had forbade her acquiring these elementary branches of knowledge. But once appointed patroness by the *mir*, the father could no longer check her, and she finally learned to read and write by daily intercourse with the scholars in the school-room. The Russian *mir*, however, must not be thought, from these few instances of liberality, a friend of women's emancipation. It is only too ready to lend a helping hand to parents or husbands when they desire to crush the spirit of independence in daughter or wife.

Some communes unite, form what is called a *voloste*, and choose judges, who are appealed to in the case of small delinquencies, family differences, petty thefts, etc. I know of instances where this peasant justice has been favorable to women; as, for example, where a wife, declaring that she would drown herself rather than return to her husband, this *volostnoy* tribunal obliged the latter to give her a pass, so that she might earn her own livelihood as a domestic. Such decisions, although perfectly binding in the eyes of the peasants, are in reality illegal,

* There are three sorts of elementary schools as regards their origin: those founded by the government, by the *zemstvo*, and by private individuals. When the peasants create one of the third class, they choose a patron or patroness who has leisure and money to devote to the school.—M. Z.

as they are in opposition to the written code of the empire.   No regularly-constituted court of justice could compel a husband to give his wife a pass, unless he chose to do so of his own free will.

Among the peasants, the bride's preferences are seldom heeded by the parents when they arrange her marriage, and it is but poor consolation that the bridegroom is treated in the same way.   She must accept her fate, and bear it patiently unto death.   In the words of Pope, slightly changed,

> She is but born to try
> The lot of man,—to suffer and to die.

She cannot take advantage of the divorce law in the few cases already mentioned, for the legal, medical, and other expenses are too large for a peasant woman's purse. Divorce is available to her only when her husband loses his civil rights.

The subject condition of Russian women is one of the principal causes of the rapid growth among the people of certain radical Christian sects, some of which resemble in many particulars the American revivalists and Anabaptists.   The despotism of the family drives the peasant woman to these sects, which teach that there can be no domestic ties *de jure* where none exist *de facto*, and that it is degrading to observe the letter when the spirit is dead.   She flies from her home, and lives under an assumed name, lest she be dragged back to her former servitude.   She feels raised to a condition of equality and independence by her faith in a religious doctrine, and ardently embraces the new belief.   The maiden, or woman married against her will by the State church, having once thrown in her lot with these enthusiasts, may marry among them. Until within the last two years Russian law did not recognize these marriages, and *de jure* the wife was always free to leave her sectarian husband, without his being able to restrain her. In some of these sects, the husband and wife stand on an equal footing, and the marriage lasts as long as both parties are satisfied. On entering the conjugal state, they declare their intention before the elders of the church, and on sundering the union, they do the same. Until very recently these sects were persecuted, and many a peasant woman, by her devotion and heroism, has shown herself worthy of the martyr's halo. Women often preach, and the greater number of these religious bodies are distinguished for a high moral level, purity and tenderness of domestic life, which is all the more remarkable, when it is remembered that an entire dissolution of all family ties is permitted by some of their peculiar doctrines.

Besides the sects just mentioned, there are others of an ascetic nature, in which the women take vows of chastity and consecrate their lives to nursing the sick and studying the Bible. A new sect has very recently sprung up, whose distinguishing feature is the exaltation of woman. She is placed above man because she can give birth to another immortal being. Her pain and travail are so great, that exempting her from all other physical suffering and annoyance would be but a poor reward ; she is entitled to the deepest gratitude and reverence of mankind.*

---

* It is not the Russian sectaries alone who award women a higher place than that generally given them. In 1506, C. Agrippa wrote a treatise entitled, "On the excellence of woman above that of man." (Legouvé, *père, Mérite des femmes*, p. xlii.) Toussenel, says M. Pelletan, "has appealed to physiology to prove the superiority of woman to man." (*La mère*, p. 362.) M. Valentin de Gorloff, the young French African traveller, has said : "The

Certain writers who have studied these religious phenomena, speak with great admiration of some young girls gifted with remarkable oratorical talents and wonderful depths of mystical thought. The sects to which they belong seek sanctity in the acts of every-day life. A member of one of them—a psalm-reading old maid—said to a proud bishop riding in a carriage: " Christ went barefooted."

The spirit of the Russian sectaries in favor of the emancipation of women shows what a vital hold the woman question has on even the lowest orders of our national life. What the upper and educated classes of women seek in the sciences, higher education, and the liberal professions, the poor, ignorant peasant women find in mystical religion.

The subject of women's emancipation was first called into life among the enlightened classes of Russia, about the year 1840, by the writings of George Sand. The new ideas were confined to a narrow circle of thinkers and authors, and continued in a latent form until the freedom of the serfs caused them to burst forth with renewed force. No agitation can be pure gold : there must be some alloy in it. Errors were mingled with the young movement, and enmity and calumny magnified the demand for freedom into a cry for the destruction of the family. We have grown wiser by the faults committed at the inception of the struggle, and to-day our claims can be considered subversive only by those who wish

men of the Touareg tribe are not allowed to have more than one wife, and she possesses the greatest influence, not only in domestic but in political affairs. The Touareg women are far more highly educated than the men. They can read and write well, they possess some musical talent, and their poems are celebrated in the desert." (London *Times*, weekly edition, April 28, 1882.)—T. S.

women to be ignorant and spiritless slaves. The Russian woman seeks knowledge and the professions, not for the purpose of destroying the family, but that she may serve it the better. She does not ask emancipation from duty, but emancipation from chains. The freedom she yearns for is not the freedom of giving loose rein to all the whims of unprincipled fancy. She wishes to have the liberty of marrying whom she will, of breaking the bond which binds her to an immoral husband, of enjoying every facility for earning her own livelihood, and of removing all obstacles thrown in the way of acquiring knowledge which may·open to her the highest positions in life. She desires to be no longer a zero in public affairs, but an active working force.

The reforms of the last reign gave a great impetus to the movement for women's independence, though this was not one of the results intended. The bureaucratic reform caused the discharge from the public service of hundreds and thousands of office-holders and governmental agents; and their daughters, who up to this time had lived in a state of more or less ease, were now thrown suddenly out upon the world to support themselves. The liberation of the serfs had the same effect. Before this reform was accomplished, a vast number of small land-owners found they could make more money by teaching their slaves trades than by cultivating their fields. So they increased their slaves, instructed them in all kinds of mechanical work, hired them out in the towns, and required of them an annual payment of from twenty to thirty rubles,* and in the case of a skillful hand even a larger sum. When emancipation came, the masters re-

---

* A ruble is worth from seventy-five to eighty-six cents, depending on the coinage.—T. S.

ceived an indemnity for the lots of land given by them to the slaves employed in agriculture, but no compensation was made them for the artisan slaves who gained their liberty at the same time. The landlords were entirely unprepared for this revolution, and were forced to hire laborers and buy machines to do the work which formerly cost them nothing. Many of them were ruined, and their daughters had to shift for their own livelihood. Thus, hard necessity made welcome the notion of women's independence, which without these two influences would have long remained in the realms of theory, for no idea ever triumphs in actual life without the way being prepared for it by economic causes.

But it is in the field of education that the greatest progress has been made. The difficulties that this movement has encountered and at last overcome would require too much space for enumeration, and could be understood in their full significance only by Russians, or by those foreigners who are well acquainted with the country. They show the importance of the victory, and are a happy omen for the future.

The vastness of the Russian Empire and the paucity of its population are in one respect favorable to this movement. Russia is sadly lacking in intellectual workers. The numerous villages disseminated throughout her wide plains want teachers and physicians. The professional emancipation of women is not therefore threatened by that inveterate opposition observed in densely peopled countries which annually disgorge into America their surplus of population. Our *zemstvo* needs and pays for the education of physicians in the woman's medical school at St. Petersburg, and for teachers in the various normal schools of the country, on the condition that the

women who enjoy these scholarships serve five years the
county which grants them. This scarcity of brain force
constrains even the government to further the cause of
women. We had a striking example of this in the recent struggle with Turkey, when the war department was
only too glad to avail itself of the assistance of female
physicians for the army.

The moral and intellectual power of women is recognized not only by the progressive, but also by the retrogressive, element of Russian society, and the latter class
does not hesitate to use it. When, in 1867, three ladies,
delegated by some of their own sex, requested the late
Minister of Public Instruction, Count Tolstoi, to establish
university lectures for women, they were met by a decided
refusal. Thereupon the professors of the St. Petersburg
faculty, taking advantage of their right to lecture in
public, opened, under the auspices of a committee of
ladies who managed the enterprise, a course of lectures,
which, while not so considered officially, were in fact
instituted for women. Although these lectures were
attended by both sexes, women alone were allowed to
use the library and cabinets in connection with them, to
be examined if they wished, and to receive certificates
from the professors. Ten years had not elapsed when the
same minister who, in 1867, forced the scheme for the
higher education of women to begin life under the guise
of public evening lectures, acquiesced in the plan of insti-
tuting at St. Petersburg superior courses for women.
Count Tolstoi wished to introduce into Russia his classical system—a profound study of the Greek and Latin,
in imitation of the German gymnasiums—but not having
the necessary number of teachers, on account of the aversion of the youth to pursue the classics to the extent he

35

desired, the minister hoped to render the idea popular by having these languages taught in the girls' schools. So women were invited to acquire Latin and Greek, in order to fill the new positions; and thus was Count Tolstoi glad to avail himself of women's learning, and thus was he brought over from an enemy to a very reluctant friend of women's higher education.

The honor of the initiative step in this movement belongs to Mrs. Konradi. In 1866 she addressed a letter to the members of the association of natural and physical sciences, which met that year in St. Petersburg, requesting them to do something for women's university education. Her letter met with warm sympathy, and from that moment our men of science * have taken an active part in the work, so that to-day Russian women may pursue their studies not only at the capital, but also at Moscow, Kief, Kasan, and, in a word, in almost all the provincial cities where universities exist.

The curriculum of studies at St. Petersburg is very extensive, and is divided into two grand divisions,—the historical and literary, and that of the natural sciences and mathematics. The latter embraces anatomy, physiology, botany, zoölogy, chemistry, physics, geology, mineralogy,

---

* The chemist Louguinin subscribes annually five hundred rubles to the St. Petersburg courses for women, and Professor Bestoujeff is always ready to assist needy girls who cannot pay the tuition fee of fifty rubles a year. The celebrated professor of physiology, Siechenoff, has lectured in aid of a fund for a physiological cabinet for women, while Professor Miller, Professor Ovsiannikoff, and others have contributed money. Mr. Mendeleieff, professor of chemistry, and Mr. Vagner, professor of zoölogy, have lectured in our courses without pay. All the other professors offer their services at the modest charge of two hundred and fifty rubles a year for one hour, five hundred rubles for two hours, and so on. The same spirit is shown in the other university centres. In Moscow the literary and historical courses are superintended by Professor Guerié, who founded them.—M. Z.

astronomy, cosmology, and mathematics even in the highest branches. Lectures on agricultural chemistry are delivered to those women who are preparing themselves for agricultural pursuits, and a series of lectures on the civil law is given annually. The same studies with modifications are pursued in the other towns.

The courses for women in St. Petersburg were opened in 1878. The students are divided into four classes, each class representing a year's work. An examination occurs annually for all the classes. The first examination for graduation took place in the summer of 1882, when ninety-nine young women secured degrees in the literary and historical department, and sixty-four in the scientific department. About nine hundred students attend these lectures every year, and up to September, 1882, two hundred and one new matriculations had been registered for the session of 1882-3.* These numbers are all the more remarkable when it is remembered that as yet women derive no practical advantage from these long years of study, for, while the aim of the courses is to fit graduates for positions in the higher classes of girls' schools, men alone may fill them. Every man who desires a place in the intermediate schools must pass a teacher's examina-

---

* These figures prove that women desire a university education as much as men. This fact is almost universally accepted in the United States, though, as a general rule, it is only just beginning to dawn on the continental mind. Few American universities can boast of as many students and annual graduates as this St. Petersburg institution. The curriculum of studies destroys another objection to women's higher education almost as prevalent in the new world as the old, viz., that women are not capable of pursuing the same studies as men. If now the St. Petersburg reformers could only bring about co-education—a very easy step it would seem under the circumstances—they would be on the high road to the ideal educational system of the future.—T. S.

tion before the university authorities. Now our courses prepare women for these very examinations, from which, however, they are excluded. The professors of the University of St. Petersburg, and the members of the committee superintending the women's courses, have petitioned the government to admit women to the teachers' examinations. No answer has yet been given, but when it comes, it will doubtless be a favorable one, for a refusal would leave unsatisfied one of the most crying wants of Russian education.

The intermediate girls' schools (gymnasiums, as they are called), though they are far from perfect, are evidently considered a *pia desideria* in France, for a short time ago the French government sent a commission to Russia to study them. They owe their origin to the late Empress Maria Alexandrovna, who modeled them after the German *Töchter Schulen.* The course of studies covers seven years, and embraces the Russian, French, and German languages; arithmetic, and the rudiments of the sciences; but falls far short of what is needed for entrance into the university. This gap has to be filled by private study, and herein lies the grave defect of these schools.

The Minister of Public Instruction has established girls gymnasiums which lengthen the course of studies to eight years. These schools, although a thorough reform of the scope of their instruction is needed, have done a great and good work in spreading knowledge through the middle classes of Russian society, without, however, bridging the break just mentioned.

Government institutes, founded by the Empress Catherine II., and patterned after Madame de Maintenon's Maison de Saint-Cyr, of the time of Louis XIV., were the only girls' intermediate schools which existed in

Russia previous to the gymnasiums. Unlike the latter, class distinctions are observed in these institutes. Some of them receive the daughters only of the hereditary nobility, or of military and civil officers of high rank, while in others are educated girls from the families of the lesser nobility, of rich merchants, and of clergymen. The pupils are shut up in these schools from the age of seven or eight, until they reach their sixteenth, seventeenth, or even eighteenth year, and during this long period they seldom leave them, except on great holidays, and at the summer vacation. The instruction is superficial, and the scholars go forth entirely unprepared for real life. The gymnasiums are much preferable, as they do not separate the girl from her family, and from the active, practical world without.

Considered from a pedagogic standpoint, the gymnasium can fit its pupils only for the primary schools or for the lower classes of the gymnasiums. The government, in order to complete this deficiency, established, some time ago, a series of courses on pedagogics, which cover three years, and prepare teachers for the middle classes of the gymnasiums. This action was taken after the presentation of the petition asking for the admission of women to the teachers' examinations, which thus seems to have had some effect on the authorities.

The highest professional instruction for women is given in the medical courses, which began in a way that may appear strange to those not acquainted with Russian life. A young woman gave fifty thousand rubles for this object, but the sum was not large enough to cover all the expenses of the proposed school, and the undertaking would have fallen through if the War Department had not come to its aid. The Minister of War patronizing the medical

35*

education of women seems odd at the first blush. But his conduct was in fact very natural and very practical. The Academy of Medicine was already under the superintendence of the Minister of War, its chief aim being the education of surgeons for the army and navy, and, as it occupied a very large building, a part was handed over to the women for lecture rooms and clinics.*

The tentative of the government was very timid, not to say amusing. The female graduates were to be called "learned midwives;" † they were to study only the diseases of women and children ; and when they went forth to practice the healing art, women and children were alone to be their patients. But the Minister of War builded better than he knew. The professors were real men of science, and found it impossible to keep within the narrow limits prescribed by the government. They gave a full course in medicine, added a fourth year, and then a fifth year, threw open the wards of the hospitals to their new pupils, and, in a word, treated the women just as they treated the men. And Russia was soon a thousand-fold

---

* Since these lines were written the medical instruction of women at the capital has entered upon a severe crisis. Recent reforms in the War Department call for economy, and the Minister has been forced to refuse the usual subsidy and to close the hospital and clinics. The St. Petersburg municipality offers to take the women under its protection, and furnish them a building and a hospital. Nothing is yet decided in the matter. The women who are now (October, 1883) studying will be allowed to finish their course, but no new students will be received. A public subscription, in aid of the Women's Medical Courses, has been opened at the capital. A women's medical college is about to be founded at Moscow, but it will, unfortunately, be far less complete than the St. Petersburg courses. —M. Z.

† This was the term used in the government plan, and was meant to distinguish the women who had received a scientific medical education from ordinary midwives.—M. Z.

repaid for what it had done. Twenty women followed the army in the last war, and gave admirable proofs of courage, skill, and tenderness on many battle-fields and in the hospitals, amid the ravage of the typhoid fever. The late emperor, who witnessed their conduct, always entertained a high opinion of them.

There are now in St. Petersburg fifty-two female physicians, and about two hundred and fifty in all Russia, although it is not yet ten years since medicine was opened to women. Many Russian women have also pursued their medical studies abroad in the Universities of Zurich, Bern, and Paris. I may also mention as among the professional institutions frequented by women, a school for the training of nurses, and two schools of midwifery in St. Petersburg, and one in Moscow. Women also study obstetrics in many of the hospitals.

I shall say nothing of the School of Painting at St. Petersburg, which owes its foundation to an association of artists and friends of art, and which receives students of both sexes; nothing of the Industrial Gymnasium, where girls are taught various trades, and which is a creation of the government; nothing of the good work done by the Froebel Society of St. Petersburg; nothing of the association formed two years ago at the capital for the establishment of girls' industrial schools, and to which one lady contributed 20,000 rubles,—but shall hasten on to the more important subject of the employment of women.

The elementary public schools offer our women the largest field of work. But the pay is so poor that men generally seek other callings, though there are many persons of both sexes who devote their lives to this humble occupation. The rôle is a difficult one and requires great fortitude and self-sacrifice, and yet many young girls take it up with genuine ardor. In some remote parts of Russia the schoolmistress is cut off during the long winter months from all intercourse with the world. She toils many hours each day for a beggarly reward; sees no books, reviews nor newspapers; lives in a log cabin deprived of all comforts; eats coarse food, and very seldom enjoys the society of persons of equal culture. And yet, notwithstanding all this devotion and acknowledged ability, the teacher's profession is, in the case of women, stunted in a most lamentable manner. They may instruct in elementary schools and in the lower classes of girls' gymnasiums and institutes, they may be governesses in private families, but they may aspire to nothing higher.

In medicine, we find similar restrictions. Although they pursue all the studies and pass all the examinations, women are not physicians in the eyes of the law. They may treat the diseases of women and children, but that is all. In the country, where there is often no male physician within the distance of fifty miles, our women might have employment and confer immense blessings upon the poor peasants of both sexes. Some years ago a woman passed a brilliant examination and defended with success a thesis on the diseases of the eye. But she could not become an oculist. And yet women, by the delicacy and flexibility of their fingers, are far better fitted physically than men for this calling. There have been instances of some of the medical inspectors in the provinces interfering with the practice of medicine by women, although invited by the *zemstvo* to come into their midst, by prohibiting the apothecaries to put up a prescription emanating from a female physician.

Some time ago an attempt was made to open the

law to women. After the reforms in our judiciary and the establishment of the order of advocates, some law offices employed women. Professors were invited to lecture on law before the women's courses at St. Petersburg, and some women went abroad to study the science in foreign universities. But the government forbade lawyers to accept their services as clerks, and the movement was nipped in the bud.

The government employs women only in the Fourth Section, the Department of the Empress, which directs the girls' gymnasiums and institutes. Women also find something to do in the railroad and telegraphic service. In the latter department they perform the hardest work, receiving and sending telegrams, while the much easier and better paid positions, as chief clerks and the like, are closed against them. Female telegraphists are paid only from twenty-five to forty rubles a month.

Women have yet to fight their way into the republic of the sciences. No woman has ever received a degree in our universities, while those who have been more successful abroad—and the list is long and brilliant—have asked in vain to be permitted to pass the examinations and defend the thesis for the degree of master of sciences. No positive law exists which bars women from securing university honors, for such a case was never foreseen. This fact is considered to be favorable to the claims of female aspirants. Mrs. Kovalevsky* and Mrs. Litvinova, doctors of mathematics of foreign universities, are now preparing themselves for the degree of master of sciences. If this stronghold is once gained, women will have the right to become professors in the superior courses for women.

---

* Mrs Kovalevsky has just (October, 1883) been appointed *privat-docent* at a college in Stockholm, and will lecture on mathematics.—M. Z.

There are many fitted for this career by their talents and learning who cannot enter upon it for lack of these degrees.

The scientific societies are more liberal than the universities. They do not shut their doors in our faces. The law society of St. Petersburg counts among its members Miss Evreinova, who took her degree of doctor of laws at Paris. The medical society is not afraid to affiliate with female physicians. Miss Nadiejda Skvortzova, whose ability has been recognized by the Paris medical celebrity, Dr. Charcot, is one of the women more recently received by this society.

It is in literature alone that women stand on the same footing with men.* This success depends entirely upon their talents. No certificate or degree here obstructs their path. But if a woman would enter journalism, if she would be the editor of a political or scientific newspaper, the case is different. When Mrs. Konradi, whom I have already mentioned in connection with women's higher education, and who is well known by her writings, wished to edit *The Week* (*Nediclia*), a political journal, permission was refused her by the censor of the press, and she had to put her husband forward as the nominal editor, though he was in no respect qualified for the position. Women may be editors of educational reviews, children's papers, eclectic magazines, and the like, and they may

---

* They are paid the same as men. The best known female writers receive as high as two hundred rubles for sixteen printed magazine pages, containing from 30,000 to 40,000 letters. The average remuneration is fifty, sixty, or seventy rubles, depending upon the reputation of the author and the popularity of the magazine. Many women support themselves by translating, but, as Russians are generally proficient in foreign languages, the market is overstocked and the pay is fifteen rubles or less for sixteen printed pages. The price for scientific translations is twenty-five rubles.—M. Z.

act as publishers of newspapers, reviews and books without having to make application to the censor. There are at St. Petersburg four or five children's papers and educational reviews which are edited by women, and one or two literary and political periodicals which are published by them.

The novel is the branch of literature in which Russian women have gained the highest reputation. After the two renowned names of Tourguéneff and Leo Tolstoi, the greatest novelist of which our literature can boast is a woman, Krestovsky,* the pseudonym of Mrs. Nadiejda Zayontchkovsky. During a long literary career, which extends over a period of about thirty years, she has given to the world a large number of tales and novels of first-rate merit, and presents the rare example of a genius which, instead of weakening by the advance of age, grows in strength and depth. I know of no woman in European literature who is her equal, an opinion which is generally accepted. She may be compared to George Eliot. Inferior to the Englishwoman in the profundity of philosophical thought, she surpasses her in the warmth and vividness of her pictures. Her short stories are much better than the long ones, and all aim to depict some phase of Russian society. They are pervaded by the spirit of one seeking a lofty ideal, of a great-hearted patriot bleeding for the woes of her country, a lover of all that is pure and humane, a hater of all that is base and tyrannical. Many of Krestovsky's best pages have not been made public for political reasons. The freedom

---

* Krestovsky (pseudonym) is, as I have said in the text, an authoress. There is also a man, whose real name is Krestovsky, who writes sensational novels in which he paints in very dark colors the young generation striving for liberty and women seeking their emancipation. There is not much danger, however, of the two writers being confounded.—M. Z.

with which she lays bare the faults of our society may appear to be poor patriotism to those who take a narrow view of this feeling, and who too often magnify their own personal vanity into a national sentiment.   There is a Russian proverb which reads : Who loves well, chastens well.   But the dire necessity of chastening is a source of deep moral suffering.

This feature of Russian character, as reflected in our literature, is generally misunderstood, and yet it is one of the surest signs of our progress.   It is a proof that the conscience of the nation is not lulled to sleep by self-adoration, but wide awake to the duty of striving to attain the loftiest ideal of human perfection.   Russian society does not present the same comparative uniformity of level which, in spite of all the differences of parties, opinions and classes, exists in Europe and America.   With us, one may see side by side representatives of the ideas of a hundred years ago, of the present century and of the ages to come, when the opinions which now count but few adherents will receive the right of citizenship in the world.   Russian progress may be compared to an army's painful march through deserts and swamps, where the vanguard is so far in advance of the main body that it is supported with difficulty, but pushes bravely on without noticing those who fall by the way.   It often happens that even in the narrow circle of the family, members are found as widely separated one from the other as this vanguard from the main army.   All Russian authoresses of any reputation march in this vanguard. The retrogressive party can boast of no woman's name distinguished for thought or talent.   Severin, the pseudonym of Mrs. Nadiejda Merder, Mrs. Olga Shapir, Mrs. Smirnova, and many others, have all published their works in the pages of progressive magazines. Vesseniev, the pseudonym of the late sister of Mrs. Zayontchkovsky, who was as sympathetic a writer and who wielded even a bolder pen, never contributed a line to the organs of the *statu quo.*

In other departments of literature I may cite the names of Mrs. Manasseina, author of many scientific articles on medicine and physiology, and of an excellent book on the physical training of children ; Mrs. Alexandra Efimenko, who has written many interesting essays on the Russian *mir* and the laws of custom among the peasants ; Miss Catharine Nekrasoff, who has published essays on Russian folklore ; Mrs. Vodovasoff, the author of a very important work for the young, "The Life of European Peoples " (*Jyzn evropeishih narodow*), and of many other children's books; Mrs. Olga Novikoff, friend of Mme. Adam of the *Nouvelle Revue,* who has, besides magazine articles, printed a work on Russia ; and the late Mrs. Vernadsky, who published some twenty years ago a book on political economy, which is now forgotten, but was very honorably mentioned in its time. The tales of Ukrayna (Little Russia) by Marco Vovchok, the pseudonym of Mrs. Marie Markevitch, are a plea in favor of the political rights of the peasant classes, and are full of pathetic beauty. Some of them have been translated into French. I must not close this partial list of our female authors without mentioning one of great promise, but whose brilliant career, just opening, was suddenly cut short by death. Mrs. Sophy Bruloff was the daughter of Professor Kavelin, and in early childhood showed remarkable talents. Later she developed a strong taste for history, was sent abroad where she studied historical subjects with the greatest assiduity. She has written some very able

essays on historical questions, and was making the preparatory notes for a great work on the epoch of Catharine II. when she died, at the early age of twenty-four.*

The Russian women's movement has one characteristic feature in which it differs from the similar movements elsewhere,—it is ever true to the ideas of progress.
Whilst in other countries we sometimes see women striving for their own rights alone, for their own well-being,
and in their eagerness to secure them, only too prone to
make themselves the instrument of the church and con-.
servatism, Russian women do not separate their cause
from the great cause of human progress. The Jesuits
in Europe have well understood, in their struggle for
the preservation of old prejudices, what a powerful arm
they should find in women equal and independent members of society and at the same time subservient to the
will of the order. In England many Tories and high
churchmen voted with Mr. John Stuart Mill in favor of
women's suffrage. No retrogressive element in our
society can count upon the aid of one woman battling
for equality. The women who muster under that banner
are quite satisfied with their dependent, inferior position,
and pronounce as heresy every utterance for the emanci-

---

* Mommsen, in a note to me, referring to this female historian so full of
promise, says : " The question is not, if women are capable or not, of high
proficiency in every branch of learning, but if the average standing of man's
and woman's capacity for these researches is equal or not, and this question
cannot deal with exceptions." Montesquieu appears to answer the German
historian when he says: " The powers [of the sexes] would be equal, if their
education were too. Test them [women] in the talents which have not been
enfeebled by the way they have been educated, and we will then see if we
are so strong" (Lettres Persanes, lettre xxxviii.) L. Aimé Martin wrote, a
half century ago : " It is in spite of our stupid systems of education that
women have an idea, a mind and a soul."—T. S.

pation of their sex. Russian women who have risen to the consciousness of their right to knowledge and independence, consider these blessings as means with which to serve the people and improve the condition of their native land.

CHAPTER XV.

POLAND.

BY ELISE ORESKO.*

[Mrs. Elise Oresko, *née* Pavlovska, was born toward the end of the first half of this century at Grodno, where she now resides. The young girl was placed by her parents under the care of nuns, who gave her an education which they did not intend should produce a woman of letters. Married when a mere child, she was rather checked than encouraged in her bent, which revealed itself at an early hour. Shortly after 1863 the periodicals of Warsaw began to publish stories and poems signed by her name, and in a few years the Polish people perceived that its national literature was enriched by a new writer of exceptional talent, whose pen was untrammeled, vigorous and original. She wrote and studied at the same time. Study sustained and increased her powers, and to-day Mrs. Elise Oresko occupies the place of honor in contemporary Polish literature. Her field is the novel which depicts customs ; but she does not neglect science for romance, nor fear to speak out plainly concerning the questions of the day. In the domain of science she prefers philosophy, as is shown by her *Patriotism and Cosmopolitanism (Patryotyzm i Kosmopolityzm)*, which appeared in 1880. This work gives evidence of vast stores of information drawn from a close study of solid authors like Buckle, Draper, Spencer and Darwin, whom she grasps and utilizes. Her reasoning is logical and compact, and her style is clear.

---

* Mrs. Oresko in a recent letter, concerning the publication of this sketch, says : " On account of the peculiar spelling of my name, which foreigners can neither decipher nor pronounce, please be kind enough to print it *Oresko* and not Orzeszko. The former is more easily pronounced, and does not affect the Polish of the name." I give this explanation lest it may be thought by some that I have changed the orthography inadvertently. —T. S.

She defends patriotism, which she considers not as hostile to cosmopolitanism but as the foundation of it, for cosmopolitanism is itself an expression of that condition of the future in which peoples will no longer nourish mutual enmities. In the mean while it is patriotism, as much an historical as social product, which constitutes the moral safeguard of nations. Such is the dominant idea of Mrs. Oresko's able book. Philosophy is also the foundation of her imaginative productions. Just as the chemist treats the elements of which he composes a new body, so she, in all her novels—and the number is large— blends together into a harmonious whole the various parts of the question she wishes to bring out. The new creation of Mrs. Oresko is a philosophic idea, bearing ordinarily on a social topic, which she advances and demonstrates. She is not contented with dramatizing a situation, with tangling and untangling a plot of more or less interest for the amusement of idlers. Her stories are advocates in action ; she pleads the cause of the unfortunate, the disinherited, the injured, of those who suffer and know not their duties nor their rights. Now it is a woman who struggles against the social current and is overpowered in the uneven contest (*Martha*) ; again, it is a family unable to comprehend the new lot which has befallen unhappy Poland, and is lost in the labyrinth (*Eli Makover* and *Rodzina Brochwiczow*); or it is young women, admirably endowed by nature, who, meeting with so many obstacles, one misstep following another, finally stumble into the wrong path. It must be admitted that what she narrates, describes and vivifies is not gay ; she likes dark colors ; but the colors speak, implore, and at the last page of each of Mrs. Oresko's works the reader is forced to ask himself : Whose fault is it ? The question is answered. Among the disinherited, she has chosen the disinherited *par excellence*—the Jewish population, which forms almost ten per cent. of the inhabitants of the former Republic of Poland. The Jews, who established themselves in the country centuries ago, at the time of the merciless persecutions to which they were exposed in Europe, multiplied and remained in the same state as at the moment of their coming. Steeped in ignorance and superstition, strangers, defiant, hostile, they formed a separate social order which was but superficially understood by the Christian population. Mrs. Oresko sets herself the task of studying this caste, of examining into their mysteries and their misery, with the hope of discovering the remedy. There are, perhaps, few persons in Europe who understand the Jewish problem in its very essence so thoroughly as the author of *Meïr Ezofowicz*, a remarkable novel, in which the condition of this interesting people is described with photographic fidelity. Her theme is the awakening of aspirations toward civilization—an awakening which will come, and is, in fact, coming in the midst of an ignorance as profound as it is superb and proud. The hero, a very young man, turns his face, toward the light and struggles against the influence of those about him who are ruled by the rabbi.   The latter character, a great cabalist, disdaining everything which is not connected with cabalism, and not knowing even the language of the country in which he lives ; the *melamed** slovenly and quick-tempered ; the grandfather and the great-grandmother of the hero, as well as the hero himself, all show admirable correctness of observation and appreciation on the part of the artist who has created them.   The author introduces us into the midst of an unknown world, deeply interesting in many ways to those who love to study the life of by-gone ages.   Europe little imagines what ethnological, sociological and archæological riches lie hidden in her bosom.   *Meïr Ezofowicz* reveals some of them in the attractive dress of a story of great artistic merit, which the French public will soon have the opportunity to read and enjoy·in a translation.   Mrs. Oresko has still a long literary career before her.   She is young, active, courageous and enterprising.   Her presence in the liberal and progressive party is a powerful acquisition to that body.   Her pen is as useful as agreeable, and her work is intelligent, influential and durable.   In any literature Elise Oresko would occupy a high place and be a source of deep delight.†]

IN the first quarter of the present century there lived in Poland a great writer named Clementine Hoffmann *née* Tanska.   She was not a genius like Mme. de Staël or George Sand, although her literary ability, which was almost mediocre, attained nearly to genius through a profound knowledge of, and a noble devotion to, public interests.   In her numerous works she speaks out plainly against the worship of foreign lands, which was spreading in an exaggerated form among the wealthy classes ; against the low moral and mental plane on which our women moved, given up to coquetry and idleness ; and she strove to correct these faults by appeals to patriotism and civic

---

* Jewish *argot* for the master of a Hebrew school.—E. O.

† This admirable little biographical notice of his distinguished literary compatriot is written for its place at the head of this chapter by my friend, Mr. Z. Milkowski ("T. T. Jez"), one of the best known of Slavonic novelists, whose numerous works are now being translated into French, and whose fame will some day, I am sure, cross the Atlantic.—T. S.

virtues. She declared that the nation needed all its forces to rise again, or at least to escape total obliteration. One of these forces was woman. Woman's mind, therefore, ought to be more fully developed and her ideas of domestic life more elevated. This last demand touched a chord ever sensitive in Polish women, and Clementine Hoffmann was but faithful to the past in recalling to her sex their numerous and important duties, and especially those of the family circle. Thus her writings, telling only what the best of Poland already knew, were everywhere heartily welcomed, and, by their appeals to a glorious by-gone age, enjoyed an enormous popularity. As late as 1850 the works of Clementine Hoffmann were the Bible of our women, and, though to-day they no longer meet the demands of the hour, and are quite neglected, the influence which they exerted throughout a long period of years has been rich in good results. They snatched Polish women from complete degeneracy and prepared them for the grand possibilities of the future.*

Clementine Hoffmann had quite a large number of female literary contemporaries, some of whom were distinguished for their talents, and all for the intelligent interest which they took in public affairs. It has in fact become such a fixed characteristic of Polish literary

---

* It may be interesting to mention that when Clementine Hoffmann was dying, she expressed the wish that her bones might be laid in the cathedral of Vavel, at Cracow, where are buried the great men of Poland. Modest and undervaluing the merit of her life-work, she asked for an humble spot. The request was granted; her heart was placed in this Polish Westminster Abbey, and a little tablet on the wall near the door bears this inscription: "To the talented author and brave citizen." This brief epitaph is as significant as it is touching. It stands as the symbol of the part—no ordinary one, as the student of our history knows—performed by Polish womanhood in this Pantheon of national toil and glory.—E. O.

women, that when even ladies of noble birth take pen in hand, instead of selecting as their theme a chronicle of their own charming but frivolous existence, they prefer to treat questions of a political and social nature.*

Besides the invocation by leading female authors of the old spirit of woman's participation in the public interests of the Commonwealth, Romanticism formed another powerful factor in this awakening of Polish woman. The poetry of this school, addressing itself to the people, the richest source of its inspiration, drew general attention to an element of the nation neglected until then, and democratized a society to which the nobles had given an aristocratic turn. Furthermore, even by its exaggeration of fancy and passion, Romanticism combated materialistic tendencies and urged upon mankind a healthier ambition, more elevated pleasures and nobler aims than the tranquil enjoyment of riches and the gratification of vanity.

Along with the writings of Clementine Hoffmann, the poetical works of Adam Mickiewicz, and that galaxy of Romantic bards who revolved about this sun, have been the mental food of several generations of Polish

---

* There are many examples of the truth of this statement. ·For instance, Anna Iablonowska, *née* Princess Sapieha, wrote many large volumes on the condition of the Polish peasantry, and nobly practiced what she preached by freeing all the serfs on her vast estates and establishing for their use hospitals, schools, printing-offices, libraries, etc. Anna Mostowska, *née* Princess Radziwill, and the Princess Isabella Czartoryska are two more illustrations of this fact. The latter has published a great deal on agriculture, is the author of the best popular history of Poland, and has founded at Pulavy (an estate and château which formerly belonged to the family), a museum of archæology and art, with this inscription at the entrance: "The Past for the Future." The Princess de Wirtemberg, *née* Princess Czartoryski, who was in her day the first of Polish novelists, may also be cited in connection with this subject.—E. O.

women. It is true that this nourishment, like everything else in this world, has produced good and evil results. The latter, which have survived even unto this day, form at this moment one of the greatest obstacles in the way of the struggle for the emancipation of women. But in frowning on the petty vanities of women, which hold too prominent a place in contemporary life, and by directing the attention of our sex toward the people, Romanticism brought them over to the study of serious questions, to Democracy, so that to-day they are prepared for the solid, broad, democratic existence of the near future.

The third and last influence came from occidental Europe. Poland had a traditional affection for France, and was in direct communication with Germany, so that our society readily received the new truths sent to us from the West. The idea of the emancipation of women, although confused and defective, reached us through the widely read novels of George Sand, while German philosophy, with its many followers in Poland, also had an effect on our women. Here, as elsewhere, along with much that was good and sensible in the young movement, was mingled much that was bad and ridiculous. For one woman ennobled by the consciousness of her rights and true dignity, there were a dozen erring Lélias talking nonsense, or female adventurers who quoted *Léone Léoni* or *Jacques* to justify their thoughtlessness and their vices. But the few well-balanced minds, who proclaimed the new faith with good sense and energy, snatched their countrywomen from that state of nothingness with which they were threatened by society and education. They stand forth as shining examples to their contemporaries, for it is they who have modified public opinion and opened untrodden paths to the women of the future.

About 1840 the movement entered a new phase 'in Poland: a singular and remarkable group of women, the Enthusiasts (*Entuzyastki*), who represented the good and some of the bad elements of the three influences just mentioned, came upon the scene Although the Enthusiasts did not form a regularly constituted association, they acknowledged as leader a female writer of great talent, but still more distinguished for her force of character, Kazimira Zmichowska, whose pseudonym was Gabrielle, and who grouped them about her and inspired them with her own ardor. Freedom of thought and conscience, the independence of women, their rights in education and industry, love of the people, patriotism, and contempt of public opinion as long as it opposed these ideas by word or act,—such was the doctrine which they taught by pen, speech and the example of their own lives. Courageous even to insolence—as is often the case with novices, and especially with feminine novices—they sometimes went too far; in philosophizing at random, they often fell into error; and by imitating men in gesture and dress, they brought ridicule upon themselves and their cause. They were women of the purest lives; and while they believed in human perfectness through knowledge, labor and love of mankind, they were far from being Mystics. They professed for the most part a very liberal Christianity, which bordered on freethinking, and demanded equality before the law for both sexes and for all classes of society. They spoke out boldly for popular liberty when the people were sunk in slavery, and for women's right to knowledge and professional labor at a time when the question of the emancipation of their sex was scarcely ever mentioned. From this noble group sprang a large number of enlightened teachers, writers and philanthropists who have done a good work for humanity.

Toward 1863 the Enthusiasts had become very numerous. They were well acquainted with each other, as they often assembled at chosen places and kept up an extensive and frequent interchange of letters. But they disappeared with the storm—the insurrection of 1863—which broke upon our country. Some did not survive it, others died soon afterward, while the few who remained led a life of retirement. There are, however, now and then instances of Enthusiasts who still take an active part in the progressive movements of their country. Mrs. Baranowska, for example, the wife of the distinguished physician of Warsaw, is still the centre of a body of young people of both sexes, who come to her for encouragement, advice, books, and even pecuniary aid. By her breadth of mind, her philanthropy, and her elevated patriotism, Mrs. Baranowska stands to-day one of the best representatives of that noble band under whose influence the modern advocates of women's rights in Poland passed their childhood or early youth. In fact, it may be truly said that we are the descendants of the Enthusiasts who prepared public opinion to receive the ideas which we now proclaim.

The vividest imagination could scarcely picture to itself the rapidity with which the most radical changes occurred in Poland in the short period of about two years (1863 and 1864). Never, perhaps, in the history of any people, has so much been destroyed and set up in so brief a time. It may be said that the flames of the revolutionary conflagration, and the means employed to extinguish them, gave birth to a new world. During a decade, however, we thought only of the ruins of the past. Nobody had the heart, the leisure, or the force to look the situation in the face and to begin work anew. There was no society,—only the débris of a society. All was chaos.

After the lapse of several years, about 1870, the Russian rule grew less implacable, and the Polish nation, by mere force of habit, became more accustomed to their situation. Fear diminished, and another generation sprang up. A fresh life began, and a new treatment of social questions. In the foreground stands out that grand reform, the emancipation of the peasantry, with all its material and moral consequences. It was a blow at the nobility; from simple consumers they became producers. It opened new careers to the lower orders, dignified toil, and rendered society democratic. The Russian Government had shut the court and civil service against Poles, so that the nobles, driven from their lands, were forced into commerce,—until then entirely in the hands of Jews. Here was another democratic result. Again, although the idea of nationality had not perished, we now determined to keep it alive, not by revolutions, but by industry, by activity in the callings which despotism still left open to us. The new society recognized as its foundation the people, the family, education, agriculture, and industry. Liberal ideas commenced to take possession of the public mind.

These great changes affected women as well as men, and gave a new turn to their aims and existence. But, of all these mutations, there was one which especially touched women. Marriage is much more difficult in Poland than elsewhere. In the period immediately following the revolution of 1863 the country lost one-half of its male population, for besides those who died on the field of battle, or were sent into exile, many emigrated to foreign lands. For ten years a marriageable man was a rarity in Poland. Since that time, however, the numerical relation between the two sexes has become more normal, although the contraction of the old fields of activity, and a lack of thorough acquaintance with the new, still throw great obstacles in the way of marriage. Certainly in no country are there so many men who remain celibates in spite of themselves, and so many women who, through the impossibility of matrimony, are compelled to earn their own livelihood.

There are, therefore, many good reasons why Polish women should have free access to every calling, and the public recognizes the fact. Since 1870 a marked movement in this direction has been noticed in the press, which is the only medium in Poland for the expression of opinion, and the principal instrument of propagandism. This great subject of women's education—and I use the word in its broadest sense—is one of the chief topics of discussion in our periodicals, and, although there are differences of opinion on the question, all parties unite in demanding better instruction and more lucrative employment for the female sex. Some hold that their education need not extend beyond domestic requirements, the science of teaching, and a knowledge of a few trades, while others would fix no limit to their culture and activity. There are extreme conservatives and journalists who oppose these reforms, but their number is so small, and their influence so insignificant, that they are far outweighed by our moderate liberals and radicals, who favor the movement. The writings on this subject, very numerous and widely circulated, are from the pens of Polish authors of both sexes, or translations from foreign languages. Mill, Legouvé, Laboulaye, Daubié, Paul Leroy-Beau·

28

lieu,* etc., are read by most Polish women either in the original or in translations. Hence arises new enthusiasm, fresh energy, which the native leaders strive to direct.

Since 1809 the civil law of the Kingdom of Poland † has been the Napoleonic code, while the other Polish provinces of the Czar are subject to Russian law. The position of women under the Napoleonic code is well known : it departs from the custom of the middle ages by giving them an equal share of the patrimony, while it keeps to this same past by making married women perpetual minors. Russian law is, in one particular at least, not as fair toward women as French law, since it gives the daughter but a fourteenth part of the paternal inheritance, thus sacrificing her rights to the profit of her brothers, and since, in case of her death without issue, her brothers and their male descendants alone inherit her property, to the complete exclusion of her sisters and their descendants, male or female. But, on the other hand, Russian law is more just than the French code in its dealings with the property rights of married women, who, on reaching their majority, at twenty-one, have complete control of their fortune.‡

Women's subordination is brought out still more clearly than in the laws by their lamentable educational and industrial position.

In Poland, as elsewhere, the system of education is di-

---

* The productions of these French writers which treat of the woman question are mentioned in the chapter on France.—T. S.

† At the division of Napoleon's Grand Duchy of Warsaw at the Congress of Vienna in 1815, the eastern and largest portion was formed into what Alexander was pleased to call the "Kingdom of Poland," and annexed to Russia.—T. S.

‡ This subject of the Russian law in its relation to women is discussed more fully in the chapter on Russia.—T. S.

vided into three stages, viz., elementary, intermediate and university. Of the three, it is only the first which is the same for boys and girls ; the second is neither so wide-spread nor so complete for the latter as for the former ; and the third, although exisiting for women in Russia, is quite unknown in Poland. If a Polish woman would pur-sue university studies, she must go to St. Petersburg, or to the universities of western Europe.

The belief in the natural inferiority of women is most deep-rooted in the lower classes. Although girls as well as boys in the Kingdom of Poland are commonly given the rudiments of an education, this is almost never the case in the Polish provinces. The peasant will send his boy to school, but only the influence of enlightened and progressive public opinion can save his girl from growing up in complete ignorance, and in localities where no such pressure exists, the instruction of the female peasantry is entirely neglected. The Polish peasant woman is well described by Legouvé in his "Moral History of Women," when he calls her "a primitive soul in a vigorous body attenuated by toil." In the Polish provinces of Austria, where the system of popular education has improved, departure from this prevailing type is not uncommon ; in the Kingdom of Poland a slow modification is in progress; but in the other provinces it persists in its immobility. The situation is better in the cities. A larger proportion of girls attend school, and the opinion that they should know how to read and write is more generally held. In fact, a girl ignorant of these rudiments would be a rare exception in our cities.

I now take up intermediate education. The number of girls' gymnasiums responds better to the public demands

than is the case with those for boys. In the latter instance there are more pupils than seats in the class-room.*
But it must not be imagined from this fact that girls do
not seek an education as eagerly as boys. They are often
taught at home or in private boarding-schools, which are
under the supervision of the government, and which have
the same course of studies as the boys' gymnasiums. Administrative centres, like Warsaw and Wilna, possess several girls' gymnasiums, and each provincial town has at
least one, while the number of pupils in these establishments varies from one hundred and fifty to five hundred.
The curriculum embraces the modern languages, the
sciences, history, etc., and these institutions might be regarded as fulfilling their office sufficiently well, if only the
methods of teaching were better and if the spirit which
pervades them were more practical, more elevated and
more liberal. But, perhaps, their greatest fault is the
utter neglect of the Greek and Latin languages, so that
their graduates are not prepared for the universities of
Russia and western Europe.

A better education is afforded by the girls' boarding-
schools, which, although under the supervision of the
government, as has just been said, are managed by private individuals. Warsaw possesses a dozen such institutions, and every town of the kingdom, however small, has

---

* There is a singular Russian custom in Poland of limiting the number of
scholars which a gymnasium may receive. For example, the gymnasium of
such or such a city is allowed to have 300, 400, or 500 pupils, and each
class 30, 40, or 50, as the case may be, but when this quota is filled all applicants are driven to seek admission elsewhere, or—which is generally the
case—to return home. This practice is not regulated by law, but is a temporary measure applied to those parts of the empire which are in disgrace, and
depends entirely for its enforcement upon the good or ill will of the ministry
and their representatives in the provinces.—E. O.

at least one. They are completely wanting in the provinces, for the reason that it is there unlawful for Poles to
teach, so that those unfortunate portions of Poland must
send their daughters to us for education.

There are two reasons why these private schools are
superior to those of the State. In the first place, although
everything must be taught in the Russian language, the
professors are Poles, and consequently take a deeper interest in the instruction of their countrywomen than could
be the case with the foreign teachers—the Russians—
of the State schools; and, in the second place, these institutions are founded and directed, almost without exception, by women of a high intellectual and moral order,
and are animated by a lofty spirit of patriotism and duty.
Some of them have a wide reputation and count among
their professors many of the most distinguished savants
and authors of the country, but their expensiveness and
the long distances which separate Warsaw—where the
best of them are found—from the other parts of Poland,
render these excellent seminaries accessible only to the
well-to-do classes.

The higher education of women. In pronouncing these
words I am prompted to put on sackcloth and ashes; for
throughout all Poland there is not one single institution
for university instruction. It is true that the subject has
been discussed at great length in the periodical press of
Warsaw; it is true that in 1879, on the occasion of the
celebration of the fiftieth anniversary of the literary début
of the famous writer Kraszewski, it was proposed to
open, in connection with the university for men at
the capital, a similar establishment for women; and
it is also true that the government might be prevailed
upon to give its consent and that the opponents of

the measure are so few and feeble that they could do but little to check it. But, for three important reasons, nothing substantial has as yet resulted from all these projects and all this agitation. In the first place, the large amount of money necessary for the foundation of such an institution is an insurmountable obstacle ; and even if this were partially gotten over by annexing the creation to the men's university, the expenses would still be too great for a society scarcely risen from its ruins. If there were a representative body of any kind, a congress, a parliament, a diet, to take the initiative in raising subscriptions, the matter would be more easy of accomplishment; but, unfortunately, no such thing exists in Russia. The second circumstance which militates against the measure is a hesitation on the part of even the most progressive minds, as to whether it is best for society and women themselves to increase a class, which, owing to the exclusion of men from the judicature, the civil service and the profession of teacher, has created an intellectual proletariat scarcely able to keep body and soul together and forced to seek in Russia and occidental Europe the livelihood which cannot be found at home. The third objection—a serious one to every true Pole— is that, in the proposed university, instruction would have to be given in the Russian language. These are the principal reasons, backed by several minor ones, why the higher education of women is entirely wanting in Poland.

But the current in favor of women's intellectual development sweeps on in spite of these barriers. Every year hundreds if not thousands of our girls leave Poland to pursue their university studies in Russia or the West. Zurich has its Polish female students, the Sorbonne at

Paris counts many in its lecture-rooms,* and from all
parts of Europe come reports of the taking of university
degrees by Polish women. But it is the Russian capital,
only thirty-two hours from Warsaw and twenty hours
from Wilna by rail, which is the Mecca of these thirsters
for knowledge. Far from home, in a strange, large,
expensive city, with small means and a poor preparation, these brave girls surmount difficulties which are
often almost overwhelming. Public opinion in Poland
does not favor this practice, the press discourages it, and
families regard it as a misfortune. But this does not
mean that society is opposed to the higher education of
women *per se*. No, far from it. We recoil at the dangers
and sufferings to which our girls must be subjected ; we
know too well the evil influences of foreign capitals, and
we fear lest their patriotism diminish. The facts prove
that these objections are well founded. The only female
physician in Poland was educated at Zurich. The
graduates of the St. Petersburg Normal School and the
Bestugew institute have been forced to seek in Russia the
employment refused them in Poland, where the law does
not permit them to teach, while those who prefer home
to a perpetual expatriation have had to accept other

* My own acquaintance with the Latin Quarter confirms this statement.
M. Zévort, of the Department of Public Instruction, on the occasion of the
recent establishment of the Superior Normal School for Women at Sèvres, took
a young Polish girl from her studies at the Sorbonne and made her a teacher of mathematics in that institution. Another Pole, Mrs. Abdank, *née*
Wscieklica, invented an admirable electric lamp in the winter of 1881-2, while
attending lectures on mathematics and physics. Miss Antoinette Milkowska,
daughter of the novelist Milkowski, was busily at work for her baccalaureate
when she was named professor at the new girls' lyceum at Lyons, while
Miss Tomaszewicz, sister of Mrs. Dr. Tomaszewicz-Dobrska, mentioned
farther on in this sketch, is still attending lectures on mathematics and
physics.—T. S.

work than that originally chosen. But these last have not toiled at their books in vain. The presence in society of a group of superior women, with minds broadened by serious studies, and with characters strengthened by trials, elevates the intellectual level not only of their sex but of the nation in general, and acts as a spur to public opinion. They are the pioneers who smooth the way for further progress. Aye, more than pioneers, they are martyrs, for they cannot use their talents, nor gratify the noble longings of mind and heart. The number of these women, who are grander, braver and more industrious than happy, is quite large in Poland. It is difficult to be exact, but those who have received a higher education in the establishments of St. Petersburg during the past ten years may be counted by thousands.

I shall now consider the opportunities afforded educated women to use what they have learned. No law closes the civil service to them, but so strong is custom in the Russian bureaucracy that a woman could not obtain even the most humble position. An exception to this statement must be made in favor of the telegraphic service. In 1878 thirty females were employed in this department at Warsaw alone, who received from five hundred to fifteen hundred rubles,--very high salaries when we consider the general pay of women. But I must add that these thirty fortunate individuals were Russians. The railroads belonging to private companies sometimes employ females in clerical capacities, but the instances are very rare, and are encountered only in the Kingdom of Poland. In these directions, therefore, there is but little encouragement.

The teacher's profession offers in the Kingdom of Poland a better field for the employment of women. The primary and private boarding-schools contain many female teachers, and, although the pay is beggarly, and the work hard and disagreeable, the positions are eagerly sought and admirably filled. The salary of the female teachers in these private boarding-schools is much lower than that of the male teachers. The latter command from one to three rubles an hour, while the former can earn but between fifty copecks and a ruble.* The most famous literary women cannot obtain more than a ruble. Thus the highest price paid women is the lowest in the case of men.

But what is said here is true only of the Kingdom of Poland. In the rest of the vast Polish territory under the sway of the Czar, Russians of both sexes may alone fill these positions. Thus, driven from the State schools and the boarding-schools, which, it will be remembered, are under the partial control of the government, female teachers with official diplomas, and those without these diplomas—the latter as ignorant as they are poor—crowd into the field of private instruction, where the supply being much greater than the demand, the pay is very low. A woman may earn in the city, perhaps, six hundred rubles a year,—a sum which can scarcely keep the wolf from the door. The highest price paid is fifty copecks an hour, and the lowest is often but ten copecks. If we subtract one hundred and fifty days (Sundays, holidays, and vacations) from three hundred and sixty-five, we find that a teacher works two hundred and fifteen days; and if she is in the school-room eight hours each day, and receives ten copecks an hour, she will have earned at the end of the year just one hundred and sev-

* A copeck is worth about three-quarters of a cent, and a ruble, about seventy-five cents.—T. S.

enty-two rubles! This is a pitiable return for hard work and weary toil often performed by those who, if it were not for political causes, might secure an honorable and lucrative place in society.

Medicine, literature, and the fine arts are accessible to women if they are not discouraged by the obstacles which lie in the way of a preparation for these callings.

In medicine, besides a foreign diploma, the candidate must be a graduate of the St. Petersburg Medical School. It is true that the same rule holds good for men, but I have already shown how much more difficult it is for women to fulfill these conditions. What has become of the Polish female medical students at the Russian capital? One practices at Riga and another at Polock. Where are the rest? It is a difficult question to answer. Three or four years ago Mrs. Tomaszewicz-Dobrska returned from Zurich to Warsaw, and is still the only female practitioner in the Kingdom of Poland. Her success is evidenced by the increasing number of her patients, which equals that of the most celebrated physicians of the Polish capital, and which shows that society, far from opposing the innovation, heartily approves it. I must add, however, that this friendly disposition of the public is due in no small measure to the admirable conduct of Mrs. Tomaszewicz-Dobrska, who knows how to unite simplicity with learning, and modesty with independence. The diseases of women and children, and the great demand for female physicians in the country, where men do not willingly go, open a grand field of lucrative work for our sex, which will doubtless be quickly filled when the difficulties blocking the way to a medical education are removed.

Polish women take an active part in letters, especially

in the departments of poetry, romance, criticism, pedagogics, and children's literature. Here, again, the lack of
facilities for education is a serious obstacle, but, nevertheless, some of our female novelists have gained the first
rank, in the opinion of both the public and competent
critics, and enjoy a popularity and exert an influence
which, in both cases, is very considerable.* There are
newspapers at Warsaw which women have edited for the
past sixteen years, and which have much weight with the
public. The lyceum platform is very popular in Poland,
and female lecturers—for the most part authors—are generally as successful as men. The remuneration for literary labor is, as a rule, the same for both sexes. As translators, women perform more work than men; but in
scientific literature, with the exception of pedagogics,
they play a very insignificant part.

Here, as in the rest of Europe, the dramatic art offers
a lucrative employment to women. Many of the actresses
and *prime-donne* who have made distinguished reputa-
tions in Europe and America are Poles. Painting is followed by several well-known female artists. Some of our
great painters admit women to their studios, but the
School of Fine Arts at Cracow is not open to female students. Mrs. Madeline Andrzejkowicz, one of our artistic
celebrities, has endeavored to supply this want by establishing recently at Warsaw a school of painting for
women.

I shall next touch upon the industrial professions, where
great progress has been made since 1870 in the interest of
both sexes. Industrial or professional schools have been
founded with the best results. The first was established
at Warsaw in 1874, and up to 1880 it had been attended

---

* Mrs. Oresko is herself the best example of what is said in the text.—T. S.

by seven hundred and forty-three pupils, of whom three hundred and sixty-five were from the capital, and three hundred and seventy-eight from the provinces. Ten of the graduates have opened similar, though more modest, schools, while seventy-six have created shops owned and directed by themselves. Thus, from one single industrial school have sprung in six years ten schools and seventy-six shops, not to speak of the graduates which it has sent forth, who earn their livelihood by means of the trades learned in this institution. Women flock to these schools from the provinces, since, for political reasons, none exist outside of the Kingdom of Poland.

Many private individuals are interested in this industrial movement. Mrs. Marie Lubienska, for example, gives lessons in engraving and painting on glass to ten pupils at her own house in Warsaw, while Mrs. Gabriel, who spent a long time abroad studying lace-making, now offers in the same city free instruction in this beautiful art. A school of lace-making, recently opened at the capital, had ninety applicants for admission on the first day, which proves that our women are fully awake to the need of an industrial education.

Among manual occupations, sewing holds the same place as teaching among the intellectual pursuits,—that is to say, the supply is greater than the demand, and the pay is, therefore, very low. Needle-women of ordinary skill, for example, earn only about eight rubles a month on plain sewing. The female workers in artificial flowers, of whom there are some two thousand at Warsaw alone, are much better paid than needle-women. The publishing department of newspapers, book-binderies, photographic galleries, and other callings, employ women. They are frequently at the head of business houses, and often act as clerks and bookkeepers, while many circulating libraries, and several large and well-known book-shops at Warsaw are managed by them. Many Polish women are devoted to agriculture, and they have often gained prizes for fruits, vegetables, seeds, cattle, and silkworms at the Warsaw agricultural and industrial exhibitions. Women have also made a creditable appearance at these exhibitions in artificial flowers, gloves, book-binding, shoes, lace, embroidery on silk, painting on porcelain, etc.

The unfortunate condition of Poland as a nation renders the political emancipation of women impossible. Even the entrance of women into the government civil service is met by the great obstacle that three-fourths of the men are also shut out of the departments because of their nationality. Complete legislative impotence, excessively limited means of propagandism, lack of a broad system of popular education, the right to teach taken out of the hands of Poles,—such are a few of the causes why so little progress has been made in the woman question in Poland. But our liberals and advanced leaders of thought are exerting every effort to remove these impediments to national and individual development, and the future is full of hope for Polish womanhood.

CHAPTER XVI.

BOHEMIA.

BY ELISE KRÁSNOHORSKÁ.

[Miss Elise Pech, known in Bohemian literature by her pseudonym, Krásnohorská, was born at Prague in 1847. Her father was a varnisher and sign-
painter. She acquired the rudiments of an education in a private school, but
as there were then no institutions in Bohemia for the more advanced instruction of girls, she was forced to give up the cultivation of her mind for the training of her fingers; she began to learn needle-work. A friendship for the
celebrated novelist, Caroline Světlá, decided her career: the humble sew-
ing-girl became an author. Elise Krásnohorská has given to the world
the following original works: Three volumes of poems, a score of novels,
a dozen librettos and other dramatic writings, stories for children, biographies, literary criticisms, essays on different phases of the woman question, and treatises on music and pedagogics. Since 1875 she has been
the editor of the *Woman's Journal* (*Ženské Listy*), a monthly published at
Prague, and has just produced a complete metrical translation of the great
national poem of Poland, *Pan Tadeusz*, by Adam Mickiewicz. Miss
Krásnohorská is at present one of the collaborators of the grand illustrated work, "Bohemia" (*Čechy*), a topographical, historical, and pictorial
description of her native country.]

AFTER its terrible disasters, Bohemia, towards the end
of the eighteenth century, had already disappeared from
among existing nations. Joseph II., the most remarkable of the Austrian emperors, in assuming the crown of
Bohemia, in addition to his other royal diadems, little
dreamt of the future which awaited a people, on whose
tomb he thought to plant the torch of civilization and

reform through the medium of the German tongue and the German intellect. The rays of this funereal torch pierced to the heart of the nation, and the burning pain awakened it to a new life. And while it was believed that serfs, beggars, and vagabonds alone composed this people, Bohemia was seen to rise again in the person of her noblest sons—thinkers, poets, savants, champions and martyrs of patriotic enthusiasm.

At their side stood Bohemia's women, who performed their part in the regeneration of the humiliated race. How repulsive these noble efforts were to the prejudices of a denationalized society is painted by Caroline Světlá, the most celebrated of our writers, in a true and touching manner in her excellent novel, "The First Bohemian Woman" (*Prvni Céška*). Many educated women threw themselves into the combat for the restoration of the vernacular tongue to the family and society, and came generously to the aid of those patriots who, having sacrificed everything to the struggle for nationality, found themselves reduced to poverty or, after the unfortunate effort of 1848, condemned to imprisonment and exile. Dobromila Rettig, Bohuslava Rajská, the nun Maria Antoinette, Vlastimila Růžičková,—women of letters; Maria Cacká, the tender poetess of maternal love; but above all, two persons of remarkable intellect and the grandest merit— the noble Polish-Bohemian, Honorata z Wišniowskich Zapová, and Božena Němcová,—are a few names selected from a long list of women, who took an active part in the battle for the resuscitation of their native land.

At a meeting of Bohemian women, called together to ask for the pardon of the political prisoners of 1848, the high-minded Honorata, wife of the Bohemian writer, Charles Zap, carried away by enthusiasm, proposed the establishment of the Slavonic Women's Society, for the education of girls in the spirit of Bohemian patriotism. In 1855 she accomplished this object, but scarcely was the school, which had been the darling dream of her life, opened, when it had to be closed on account of the founder's broken health. This excellent woman died on January 4, 1856.

Her contemporary, Božena Němcová, who was born in 1820 and died in 1862, was a superior writer. Her literary career began by a collection of folk-lore composed in a most graceful style. She also produced a considerable number of exquisite short stories, and at a later period that fine novel, "The Grandmother" (*Babička*), which has been translated into Russian and French, and which depicts the ancient customs of Bohemian family life in such a charming manner, that this single work sufficed to give the author a prominent place in the literature of her country.

Němcová had not yet passed away when a genius, more brilliant and rarer than her self, blossomed forth in our midst. Caroline Světlá was born in 1830, and, since the beginning of her literary life in 1857, she has been the successful and adored guide of the intellectual movement in favor of Bohemian women. Her eloquent poetry, her moral courage and energetic activity in defending and propagating every noble and salutary idea, have brought about many useful reforms and popularized more than one sterling principle. In her novels, Světlá paints with the most delicate art the inward life and aspirations of the nation's heart, in contradistinction to Němcová, who dwells rather on external qualities. She prefers extraordinary and remarkable characters, the eminent personages of our history, to those general and com-

mon types so often described. She has a broad and
highly cultivated mind, a warm heart and a rich imagination. Truth, virtue, patriotism, an ideal future compensat-
ing all the wrongs humanity has suffered,—such is the
spirit which animates those beautiful, fascinating creations, full of life and strength, drawn by the powerful
pen of a woman who was as grand a poet as patriot and
novelist. She it was—and this is not the least of her
merits—who introduced the woman question into Bohemian literature.

Her sister, Sophia Podlipská, an author of distinguished
talents, who possesses less imagination and fire than
Světlá, and whose acute mind has a tendency towards
philosophical meditations, has produced stories, novels
and didactic works full of charm, soul and exquisite ideas.
Her writings, which enjoy the highest respect of everybody, have a special attraction for the young girl and the
mature woman, who love to reflect on her experiences.
Besides her novels, Podlipská has written many charming
children's stories and several treatises of great value on
pedagogics.

These two sisters are at the head of a large and able
group of literary women, such as Renata Tyrš, who has
written very learnedly on the fine arts ; Stránecká, whose
beautiful productions give promise that Moravia will find
in her its Němcová ; Bohumila Klimeš, who devotes herself to similar studies ; the poets Irma Geissl, Božena
Studnicka, Albina Mráček and Berta Mühlstein ; the
novelist Věnceslava Lužická, who, like Maria Riegr,
Anna Bayer, M.D., Julia Gintl and Clemence Hanuš, is,
at the same time, a writer on moral and educational subjects ; the sisters Dora and Milina Hanuš, Maria Čer-
vinka, and many others, who occupy themselves with

travels, biography, etc.; the sisters Augusta and Amelia Šlechta, who are known not only as authors but also as designers and wood engravers; and, among the large number of translators, Eliza Peška, the actress, who has translated and adapted an astounding quantity of dramas.

The Bohemian theatre owes much to women, who as playwrights and actresses hold a high rank. Odile Sklenář-Malá, a tragedian of magnificent talent, of elevated taste and an earnest and captivating enthusiasm, stands first among our singers and actresses. Girls who wish to prepare for the stage must pursue their studies in private, or in the Prague Conservatory of Music, where the singers for the opera are trained,—the only public institution of this kind in Bohemia.

The opportunities for women's education in Bohemia are most lamentable. The Prague Academy of Fine Arts does not admit women, though an intermediate school of design and painting, established at the capital by the government a few years ago, is open to them. The universities are closed to female students.* The same thing is true of all polytechnic, industrial, commercial, agricultural and mechanic art institutions, and of all intermediate schools. Their doors are firmly barred against girls. In a word, the State did nothing, until very recently, for the education of Bohemia's daughters after they left the primary schools. Almost everything

---

* Our laws not only refuse to give women a higher education, but they will not allow them to use the learning acquired in foreign universities. Julia Keck, M.D., and Anna Bayer, M.D., who were graduated in Switzerland, may not practice medicine in their own country. There is but one female dentist in Bohemia, Mrs. Simon, who has met with success at Prague.—E. K.

they learn beyond the a, b, c's is due to private enterprise.*

It was not until 1863, that the Prague municipal council
decided to open, at the expense of the city, a high school
for Bohemian girls. It is a beautiful building, and what
is more important, it is well endowed. This foundation
called for imitation, and most of the other cities of
Bohemia followed the good example set by the capital.
Then the general government began to show signs of
waking up to its duty, and in 1867, a normal school for
Bohemian girls was established at Prague, where only a
German one had been up to this time. To-day there are
three schools of this kind in Bohemia and Moravia.

Associations of women look after the other branches of
girls' education. The Society of St. Ludmila, for example, has attempted at Prague a school of porcelain painting. Caroline Světlá founded in the same city in 1871 a
society for the industrial and commercial education of
Bohemian girls, composed of two thousand women, whose
donations, augmented by municipal and governmental
subventions, support a school frequented by over five hundred pupils, the greater part of whom pay no tuition fee.
Those who are graduated with credit are found positions.
Encouraged by the generous aid of the Bohemian Medical Association, the society conducts a school for the
training of nurses, the first ever established in the empire. This organization, which has done so much to dis-
arm prejudice, has a monthly organ, the *Woman's Journal* (*Ženské Listy*), devoted to the women's movement,
and edited by Elise Krásnohorská.

---

* Among the great number of these private institutions for girls may be
mentioned those of Mrs. Amerling and Miss Peška, which are the best at
Prague for earnest and patriotic work.—E. K.

As teachers, women are employed only in the elementary schools, and receive the same pay as men.* They
also find occupation in the government postal and telegraphic service, but the field of women's work is excessively restricted in Bohemia.

Charity in a thousand forms is the object of most of
the other associations. Those composed entirely of
patriotic Bohemian women, are devoted mainly to supplying clothing, books, etc., to needy school children of
both sexes, to founding infant schools and *crèches*, to the
education of orphans, to the opening of soup-houses
where the hungry poor may live cheaply, to the shelter-
ing of the homeless, etc., etc. The Red Cross Society
has branches among our women, and reading-rooms,
lecture clubs and musical societies are common.

The moment it was seen that the spirit of Bohemian
nationality was invincible, the disdain of its enemies gave
place to intense hatred, and there began a bitter struggle
to snatch the education of the youth from the hands of
our race. But Bohemia's women came to the rescue of
our threatened language and patriotism, and these numerous societies have accomplished not only a grand
charitable and educational work, but they have been an
important agent in keeping alive the idea of our nationality.

Charity and instruction unite in the aims of the American Club of Bohemian women, founded at Prague by
Mr. Vojta Náprstek, a liberal-minded patriot, who, like

---

* When I asked Miss Krásnohorská if there was not some mistake here—if
it were really so that schoolmistresses were paid the same as school-masters,—
she replied with apparent surprise : "Of course, the same." In spite of our
famous common school system, we find Bohemia our superior in this particular. How long will it be in the United States before we may answer this
same question with Miss Krásnohorská's " of course?"—T. S.

his philanthropic mother, the late Mrs. Anna Náprstek, has devoted his fortune to the public good by enriching the industrial museum created by her, and by succoring the poor to whom she had been a generous benefactor. Mr. Náprstek had spent several years in the United States, where he had witnessed the remarkable progress of the women's movement, and, on returning to his native land, he wished to introduce among us the ideas he had so much admired on the other side of the Atlantic. Such was the origin of the American Club of Bohemian women. Every Sunday, instructive lectures are given in its rooms, and during the first years the subjects were principally drawn from the brilliant examples set by the United States in this question of women's emancipation. Under the auspices of this club, Mr. Náprstek organized, some twenty years ago, an exhibition of sewing machines, which were unknown at Prague until that time, and here were given the first lessons in their use. He has also opened to the members of the club his polyglot library, containing many literary treasures, and his beautiful collection of objects of art.* It will thus be seen that Mr. Náprstek has every reason to be proud of the nickname which has been given him of "the women's advocate."†

---

* Some idea may be obtained of the difficulties which progress encounters in Bohemia, when it is known that this admirable club is not allowed to enjoy all the rights of an association, but is forced by the government to endure the restrictions of a sort of private society.—E. K.

† A lady writing me from Prague says : " The Club has always been in a most flourishing condition although it has never had a constitution or by-laws to hold it together,—nothing but the one bond of philanthropy. At first it had not even a name. But outsiders began to call its members 'the Americans,' because they adopted American improvements in their homes. The appellation was accepted by the Club as an honorable title, and from that time it formally called itself the ' American Club.' "—T. S.

Indeed Bohemian women need an advocate. We have already perceived that they have many rights to conquer, but there are still others which have not yet been mentioned. The Austrian code, for example, is not free from contradictions in its treatment of our sex. Thus, while the testimony of a woman is considered valid in criminal cases of the gravest nature, she may not sign as witness the simplest civil document. Again, if she be a widow with children, she has authority over their tutor, with the title of maternal tutor, and yet she may not be the tutor herself. The ancient law of the kingdom of independent Bohemia, on the other hand, recognized women as tutors. But the Austrian code is just to us in all that regards the rights of possession, inheritance, etc., where we are placed on the same footing with men. Dissolution of marriage is permitted, but divorced persons may not remarry.

The electoral law of the empire—and what I say here holds good for the whole monarchy as well as for Bohemia—treats women more fairly than is the case in other European countries. They have a voice in the municipal, provincial and national elections, though a male citizen duly authorized by them casts their vote. With this single reserve—a very important one, it must be confessed—our women are politically the equal of men. At Prague, however, this is not the case. The Bohemian capital preserves an ancient privilege which is in contradiction to the Austrian electoral law, and which excludes us from the elective franchise.

Universal suffrage does not exist in Bohemia, nor for that matter in the empire, but the payment of a certain amount of.taxes confers the right to vote. I do not enter into the details of the electoral law, which is somewhat complicated, which has its exceptions and contradictions, and is in fact an apple of discord in Austria in more than one respect; but, speaking generally, it may be said that a woman who owns property, who is in business, or who pays taxes, may designate a citizen, possessing her confidence, to represent her at the polls. Our women are satisfied with this system, and prefer it to casting their ballots in person.

It may be said, also, that women are eligible to office, or at least that there is no law against their accepting it, while there are instances of their having done so. In southern Bohemia, a short time ago, a countess was chosen member of a provincial assembly (*okresní zastupitestvo*) with the approval of the body, on the condition that she should not participate personally in its deliberations, but should be represented by a man having full power to act for her.*

But I cannot close this short sketch without devoting at least a page to the German element in Bohemia. There exists at Prague a society of German women for the promotion of industrial and commercial instruction, a lyceum for German girls, a normal school for the preparation of German school-mistresses, and several private institutions for the education of girls. A women's industrial society, composed partly of Germans and partly of Bohemians, is also found at the capital, while the two races work side by side in several charitable societies, etc. Encouraged by the prosperity of the Bohemian training school for nurses, which has already been mentioned, the

---

* At Agram in Croatia (Austria) a woman was elected some time ago member of the municipal council, and no objection was made. Of course these cases are very rare, but they have their significance.—E. K.

German women founded a similar institution, which, however, has not been so successful, because those who consecrate themselves to the care of the sick come from the people, and cannot profit by instruction given in German.

German society at Prague is not composed of the various classes of the population, as is the case with Bohemian society, but it is chiefly made up of shop-keepers and merchants, the greater part of whom are Jews, whose influence is felt in all the German business life of Bohemia.

Public opinion is, in one particular at least, and for economic reasons, favorable to women's emancipation. The population of Bohemia contains two hundred thousand more females than males, and the efforts to render the former capable of self-support are naturally encouraged. But this fact does not check the presumptuous from declaring, in Bohemia, as elsewhere, that women have less ability than men, and that the work of the former is inferior to that of the latter. A still graver charge is that women are too accessible to illiberal and reactionary influences, and that therefore they should be refused admission into posts of importance. In order to prove for all time that these assertions are false, it should be the task of those of us whose minds are open to the light to elevate our sex to a true comprehension of progress, liberty and patriotism, so that the full powers and noble qualities of Bohemian women may be known of all men.

CHAPTER XVII.

THE ORIENT.

BY KALLIOPE A. KEHAYA.

[Miss Kalliope A. Kehaya was born at Broussa, a city of Bithynia, in Asia Minor, of a noble family, her grandfather being a very conspicuous citizen, whence the name *Kehaya* or *representative*. Her father followed a commercial career in this same city. Kalliope was educated in Athens at the establishment of the American Philhellenist, Mrs. Hill, between whom and herself sprang up a warm friendship which still continues, and she entered later the Arsakion, the National Seminary for women, where she took her diploma. Miss Kehaya spent two years in London, and on returning to Greece was placed at the head of Mrs. Hill's college. For three years she performed the duties of secretary to the board of managers of an industrial home for the poor, which she was instrumental in founding at Athens. In 1874 she visited France, and, on the invitation of the Greek ladies of Marseilles, lectured before five hundred persons in that city. She was invited to Constantinople this same year to take charge of a Greek seminary for women, and in 1875 became principal of the Żappion, a grand female college in this same city, which position she still holds. Since her connection with the Zappion, Miss Kehaya has done considerable literary work. At the end of each scholastic year, she delivers an oration, which is published annually under the title of "Educational Memoirs, Serving as a Vade Mecum to the Students of the Zappion." "A Refutation of Lefèvre's 'Philosophy of Socrates,'" and four lectures delivered in the hall of the Hellenic Syllogos of Constantinople belong to this period. Miss Kehaya is also the author of a work entitled the "Elevation of Female Character," a "Manual of Domestic Economy," and a course of lectures, the "Duty of Nurses," given under the auspices of the Greek Women's Association of Athens, of which she was the founder.]

As COMPACT, national unity is entirely wanting in the

Orient, I cannot write of the situation in this portion of Europe as has been done in the preceding sketches, where the social life of England, France, Germany, etc., has, in each instance, been treated as a united and homogeneous body. I am obliged to make a distinction between the women of independent Greece and the Christian Greek women still under a foreign yoke—although they are intimately linked by the same language and religion, the solid foundation of Greek nationality—and then to discriminate between these two classes and Oriental women in general, by which I understand the Ottomans, Armenians, Jews and Bulgarians. I shall say but little concerning these latter races, for their women are in a state of lamentable inactivity which offers almost nothing worthy of record.

"The Ottoman woman," writes a Greek who has studied Turkey very closely, "on account of the religion of the Koran and the life of the harem, cannot be looked upon as either a wife or a mother. It is true that she has some good qualities which might make her a worthy member of society; but her ignorance, her humiliating position, and her exclusive and sensual existence dwarf all development and destroy every hope of amelioration. These poor souls often possess a poetical mind, which is always of a lyrical cast, and they sing of love and its relations. The chief amusement of their days is the reading of Arabic fables which dwell on the harem and the various aspects of polygamy. They are so wrapped up in their religious beliefs that they forget their duties toward their fellow-beings, although many are distinguished for sentiments of philanthropy and hospitality. They generally love luxury and are delighted with precious stones and rich cashmeres. Their manner of dressing is unique. Its chief aim is to hide every part of the body, and especially the face. Some time ago great efforts were made to introduce European fashions into Turkey, but the innovation met with little favor, on the ground that they were wanting in taste and elegance. Many Ottoman women, especially among the rich families, are striving to completely reform the national dress and to have intercourse with the women of other religions. It is no uncommon thing to see these bold innovators taking a walk through the markets, the public gardens, in the streets of the Pera, or rowing on the Bosporus; but as many disturbances have resulted therefrom, the ecclesiastic and civil authorities have several times vigorously enforced the old customs. There are examples—unfortunately too rare—especially in the harems of certain distinguished pashas, where earnest attempts have been made to establish true family life, and where the children are brought up under the care and eye of their parents by European governesses, either French, English or German, from whom they learn not only European languages but European habits.

"Although the establishment of girls' schools among the Mussulmanic population has been tried, social prejudices and religious fanaticism have rendered the attempt abortive; so that Ottoman women, often remarkable for mental power, are debased intellectually as well as socially, and find in the material and common things of life their only occupation. For all these reasons, the moral situation of Turkish women is far from perfection, although there are many noble natures who long for progress and reform. But fanaticism condemns everything to mortal stagnation. It can be easily imagined, therefore, that their civil condition is lamentable and their political position utterly insignificant. In the country, however, where the Turks lead an agricultural life, the women work in the fields with the men, and are therefore better off than their sisters of the cities."

Armenian women are a curious compound of different elements of education. The national language, which until very recently had no literature of its own, is correctly spoken only by the learned few who study its perfectionment, while the Turco-Armenian tongue, the ordinary vehicle of speech, renders intellectual and moral instruction difficult and imperfect on account of its poverty. Domestic life presents numerous odd and strong contrasts. Many rich families of Constantinople have European governesses for their children and adopt European dress, but this change being not the slow and natural growth of years but sudden and forced, the real Armenian character shows itself in spite of western fashions and education. Thus there is often a striking difference between parents and children. Most fathers and mothers walk awkwardly with toes turned in—a deformity not noticed in their offspring—and the bodies of the former are heavy and stiff, while the latter, and especially the girls, are free from these defects. Although large, they have supple and agile limbs, move gracefully and generally possess an elegant form. So great is this dissimilarity between parents and children, that it is sometimes difficult to believe that they are of the same household. This new generation dresses tastefully, speaks Turkish with a grace that their vulgar vernacular would not admit, and conducts itself with propriety and tact in the various duties of society.

As regards their manner of life, Armenian women resemble their Ottoman sisters in many respects. They
lead a simple existence. Questions of social and public
importance but too rarely occupy their attention, so that
women's associations, clubs, societies, meetings, etc., are
entirely unknown. Their intellectual state is utterly lacking in the spiritual element. If we except some primary
schools under ecclesiastical control, nothing is done for
female education. They do not of course participate in
public life, for politics do not exist in Armenia, and
while, as Turkish subjects, they are governed by the Ottoman code, it is the Christian religion and ecclesiastical
law which regulate the family relations.

As Salonica and Constantinople are the two principal
cities of Turkey where Jews are found in great numbers,
it is easy to form a general idea of the Hebrew women of
the Orient by studying them in these two localities.

In these cities, the Jews occupy special quarters in-
habited only by their own race, and have little to do with
those outside of their own sect. Even business transactions with persons of another religion are very rare, and
are not so honestly conducted as when Jews alone are
the parties. They have colossal fortunes, which they
employ only to increase their riches; they are laborious
and great producers, and their moral, social, civil and intellectual condition is very peculiar and very imperfect.

At her twelfth or thirteenth year the Hebrew girl becomes a wife and a mother, so that—the vitality of the
nation sapped by early marriage—we generally find the
women small, poorly developed, awkward, feeble and
nervous. They are clever with the needle, although they
have no taste; and, while many imitate European fash-

ions, their dress is inelegant. They cover their heads with a cap of Egyptian origin which is not becoming, especially in the case of married women, whom custom requires to hide entirely their hair.

The moral and intellectual existence of the Hebrew woman is centred in her religion, in which she is a fanatic. The sentiment of humanity is limited to those of her faith, for the God of the Israelites belongs only to themselves. The wives of several well-known bankers have formed from time to time societies for the benefit of their sisters, whence have sprung primary and normal schools for the education of Hebrew girls. These intelligent women began by stepping outside of their isolation and making the acquaintance of Greek circles, which greatly contributed to the opening of their minds, and which has rendered some of them leading members of society.

The Bulgarian women of the country lead an agricultural and pastoral life, while those of the cities, having so recently renounced their nomad existence—for it is only since the treaty of San Stefano that Bulgaria has entered the circle of modern civilized States—are not yet fully prepared to assume the new duties of the new order of things. My remarks on this division of my subject shall, therefore, be brief.

Their habits are very primitive, and their dress, on account perhaps of the climate, is very simple and quite characteristic in its simplicity. The whole idea of elegance consists in the embroidery of the tunic, chemise and belt. Their common every-day wants, which are very limited in number, are easily expressed by their imperfect language, and, as nothing worthy the name of society exists, social duties and occupations are unknown.

The subject of female education is only beginning to occupy the attention of Bulgaria, so that there is but little progress to report under this head. In the large cities something has been done for girls' primary instruction, while many Bulgarian women, who have received a Greek education and who speak Greek fluently, exert a beneficial influence on society. There are some rare instances in the upper classes of women who have enjoyed a European education, and a movement is now under way to send girls to foreign schools with the object of elevating and organizing Bulgarian society.

The natural traits of the Greek woman prove that the race, notwithstanding its political vicissitudes, has everywhere preserved intact the true national character. Her activity, the vivacity of her eyes, the dignity of her bearing, her devotion, her courage, her suppleness, her presence of mind, render the Greek woman interesting, earnest, imposing. She is not so passionate and prone to romantic love as Europeans have represented. She cannot be made to serve as a heroine for the novels and dramas of to-day, but she might furnish the ancient tragic poets admirable models of sincerity, earnestness, piety and patriotism. If Alceste, Iphegenia, Antigone and other women were the chosen types of the old poets, the Greek women of the nineteenth century offer examples as lofty and dramatic as those of the past. The women of Missolonghi during the revolution, the heroines of Sulli and the island of Chios, as well as those of Psara, attest that in their veins runs the same blood as did of yore in the veins of the high-spirited women of Ionia and Doris. The school of Phidias might find to-day, especially in the mountains of Arcadia, living portraits of Diana, while Homer's faithful Penelope and chaste Nausicaa still exist in the persons of many contemporaries.

The Greek woman is religious, but her religion differs essentially from the theocracies of Asia and the fanaticism of other sects, so fatal to the welfare of our sex. It is her guide in the practical duties of life,—not a mere form, the result of theological study and dogmatic theories. She worships her family, leads an almost exclusively domestic life, and loves to boast of the neatness and decorum of her home.

The principal centres of Greek civilization in the Orient are Constantinople, Smyrna, Salonica, Seres, Adrianople, Philippopolis and Janina. It is in these cities that are found the best schools for both sexes, and the most important associations of men and women for educational and charitable purposes. The primary and intermediate instruction of girls is similar to that of independent Greece, where the female teachers have been educated and a good normal training offered them. It is due to the liberal, elevated spirit of this culture that Greek women, along with their domestic duties, cheerfully sacrifice certain days of the week to philanthropic work. Grouped in societies, they conduct girls' schools, hospitals, orphan asylums, poor-houses and insane asylums, contributing their best energies to the cause of suffering humanity. It was this same enthusiasm and devotion, to cite but one of many examples, which created a few years ago at Constantinople an establishment where poor, honest working-women might find a means of support, without being forced to have recourse to the humiliation of mendicity.

Female education is limited for the moment to primary

and intermediate instruction, as the present moral and social needs of the country demand nothing more. But since intercourse with Europe has become more general, and since the French language—the international tongue —has been made a compulsory study in the schools, the question of female education has entered a new phase. The French classics, novels and dramas, and the French and German governesses have awakened new ideas in the Orient concerning the sphere of women. It has therefore been found necessary of late to afford girls an opportunity to acquire a higher education, and normal schools for the training of female teachers according to the improved pedagogic methods have been established, the best being at Seres, Smyrna and Philippopolis. At Constantinople, where the Greek population is very large and where there are many rich and cultivated Greeks devoted to letters and the cause of education, it has been possible to create two excellent institutions for the higher education of women, the Zappion and the Pallas, in both of which the curriculum of studies resembles, in all essential particulars, those of similar schools in Europe. The graduates may therefore consider themselves the equals of the educated women of Occidental Europe, and, Greeks at heart, they feel themselves inseparably identified with Greek religion and Greek patriotism.

But to this brief account of the condition in Turkey of the Greek women in general, I must add a few words concerning a remarkable little group at Constantinople, an aristocratic *élite*, whose daughters are particularly distinguished for their refinement and education. The Phanariots,* who are represented by the Mouronzis,

---

* The name given to the old Greek families who retired to Constantinople and became a separate class from which were drawn the bankers, office-

Ypsilantis, Caratheodoris, Caradgas, Mavrocordatos, Mavrogenis and other great families, count among their most brilliant members many women noted for profound erudition and wide acquaintance with foreign tongues. Mrs. Dosios, for example, has translated into verse Byron's " Giaour," Mrs. Lucie Caratheodoris, who is one of several similarly gifted women, can interpret the language of Homer, Pindar and the tragic poets as if it were the vernacular, and still others are accomplished in the fine arts, in elocution and instrumental and vocal music. Their manners are very polished and have a slightly European flavor, while their homes, instead of displaying Asiatic luxury, are simple and tasteful.

The intellectual condition of Greek women in the Orient is generally not inferior to that of many parts of Europe, and, it may even be said, that, as regards the daughters of the poorer classes, it is much better than in several Latin countries. From a moral point of view the Greek women of the Orient are to be praised for their many social and religious virtues. They are hospitable, philanthropic and progressive ; they make excellent mothers, and are the real companions and social equals of their husbands. Although it is true that work is not always held in such honor by Oriental women as by those of the West, and the movement for the amelioration of the industrial condition of the sex consequently finds no echo here, nevertheless the Greek woman is very active and laborious in her own household.

She dresses elegantly, speaks eloquently and writes correctly the vernacular. She has an irresistible passion for foreign languages which renders her a little superficial,

holders, diplomates, and governors of provinces.   The name is derived from a quarter of Constantinople.—LITTRÉ.—T. S.

and, although often avoiding serious studies, she argues with vivacity, grace and ability. When a Greek woman devotes herself to a social, literary or philosophical subject, she is admired not only for the force and beauty of the conception, but also for the profoundness of the thought and the precision of expression. As regards her mode of life, it must be admitted that it is Oriental in many respects: luxury and change are its prominent features. Physical exercise is irregular, and, notwithstanding her intellectual activity, there is a proneness to indolence, attributable in part to the Ottoman atmosphere which all dwellers in the Orient are forced to breathe. Family ties are very strong, and the wife, especially if a mother, is regarded with a respect akin to worship.

The woman of Greece differs entirely from her Oriental sister. Greece, as soon as she had gained her independence, pushed the past behind her, and turned her eyes toward Occidental Europe, there to find models for the formation of a new and modern national life. This uprising of a liberated people was not without its effect on Greek womanhood. Our women showed that they had a character of their own, warm patriotism, a religious nature untainted by fanaticism, and a philanthropic and hospitable heart. These grand qualities they forthwith devoted without stint to the regeneration of the young land.

Scarcely fifty years ago Athens, dead and in ruins, became an object of deep interest not only to Greeks, but also to many big-hearted foreigners, whose sympathy had been chiefly awakened by that great and noble poet, Lord Byron. On account of its past history, Athens was fixed on for the capital of new Greece, and many rich patriotic Greeks soon settled there and began to busy themselves seriously with the organization of the country. Almost at the same time, in 1835, some American women, as philanthropic as they were learned, Mrs. Emma Willard, Mrs. Sigourney, and Mrs. Phelps, contributed toward the foundation in Athens of a college for the education of Greek girls.* Mrs. Hill, who had a broad liberal mind and a strong love for Greece, was put in charge of the new enterprise, and has built up an admirable institution which has sent forth a whole generation of women who have taken high rank in social and domestic life. Mrs. Hill's college was the first to awaken in Greek women a love for the study of the works of their ancestors, pervaded by such a lofty spirit of patriotism, and it was only proper and right, therefore, that the king, three or four years ago, should thank her publicly, in the name of the nation, for her fifty years of devotion to the cause of the education of Greek women.

But our own countrymen and government were not backward. Almost at the same time as the foundation of this American college, a Greek association established a girls' normal school, which is now known as the Arsakion, from the name of its benefactor, Mr. Arsakis. This superb institution has accomplished a grand work by training an admirable body of well educated teachers.

The Government next began to move. Teachers were in great demand, and normal schools were opened. The young women, sometimes but sixteen or seventeen years old, who graduated from these schools, were sent out

---

* Mrs. Willard visited Europe in 1830, and published on her return "Journal and Letters from France and Great Britain " (1833), devoting the profits (about $1,100) to this school at Athens.—Johnson's Cyclopædia.— T. S.

annually by the hundred to cities, towns and the smallest hamlets all over Greece, where they founded girls' schools. The difficulties of travel, the poor pay, their own inexperience and youth, did not daunt these brave, earnest, patriotic missionaries of the spelling-book. Greece, just freed from the yoke of despotism, was soon made a unit in language and religion by these schoolmistresses, who have been the most powerful civilizing influence in Greece at home and abroad. There is no question, therefore, that my country owes its rapid progress and Greek instruction to its women.

It is easy to understand, from what has just been said, that, while in other countries it has been found necessary to awaken women to a consciousness of their rights and duties, our women were fully alive to their interest and responsibilities at the first appearance of national life. The wife of a public man often represents her husband before his electors, and takes an active part both in directing and supporting his political views. It is no uncommon thing for a woman to go off into the provinces in order to solicit votes for her husband, and she often defends his course with considerable ability in the drawing-room. Indeed these facts would scarcely be believed by foreigners unless seen by one's own eyes.

As Greece has experienced the influence of modern civilization but a short time, and as patriarchal customs still exist, the moral condition of women is not contaminated by the evils which characterize old societies. The Greek woman still remains deeply religious, just as she was when the day of deliverance came, for she well knows that religion was the rampart of Greek nationality and the savior of the country. But her religious ideas, practical rather than theoretical, planted on the earth, not soaring in the heavens, taught her that there were duties which she owed humanity as well as God, and saved her from both priestly servitude and heresy.

The Greek family is a product of the days of foreign domination rather than a growth of the period of independence. The husband, who then lived as it were in the camp, exposed to dangers and terrors of various kinds, and removed from all public affairs, found at the family hearth the centre of all his thoughts and happiness. In this deplorable state, the wife was his only companion in sunshine and storm, who shared with him the longings and dreams of the future country. Deprived of all intellectual development and shut off from an active life, he was ever with his wife, who came to be not only the partner of his solitude, but began to be looked upon as his equal.

The Greek woman—if we except some anomalies which have appeared since the independence of the country—has, along with a profound religious conception of her duties, a sober mind and heart; sentimental love is foreign to her. Devoted to her family and home, she will often work from morning until night with her daughters in order to put the house to rights. Her dress has lost much of the individuality which distinguished it before the days of independence, and has now become quite European. On this matter of costume our women, however, are divided into two groups; some adopt all the European fashions, while others choose certain ones and preserve at the same time some of the features of the national dress. The former often become so Europeanized by their attire, habits and reading that the Greek character is entirely lost. This class is fortunately very small, and is found only at the capital; but as travelers get their impressions and ideas concerning the Greek family in the drawing-rooms of these exotics, they often return home with a very wrong conception of the real domestic life of the country.

The active part taken by Greek women in benevolent work has been very remarkable since 1850. During the past ten years, especially, numerous associations have been formed for various objects. Well-organized charitable societies, composed of prominent ladies of Athens and the other large cities, are conferring great blessings on the needy. The capital possesses two of these noble organizations. The first was founded about ten years ago by some of our most distinguished women, with the patronage of Queen Olga, and is admirably managed by a board of twelve women, who often receive suggestions and advice from the beloved queen herself. Her Majesty has greatly extended the usefulness of the society by recommending it in circular letters to all the Greek colonies, so that it has become a close bond of union between the Greek women of the colonies and the mother country. The society at first turned its attention to the poor women of the lower classes, and established an industrial home which has proved a grand success in every respect. The work turned out by this institution received medals and honorable mentions at the Vienna Exhibition. The hospital for the poor and the training-school for nurses connected with it, both of which are patronized by Queen Olga, are two other successful creations of this society. Through the generosity of its members and its many friends, the society has quite a large fund at its disposal; and when we remember by whom it was founded, and by whom it is conducted, we perceive the virtues and capabilities of Greek women.

The ideas of Occidental Europe concerning women have had considerable influence on the women of Greece. They find an echo in the heart of the better educated, and have prompted many of those efforts of which we are so proud. But, at the same time, the woman question has not assumed here the radical form which it has taken in England and America. Although a woman lecturing in public before an Athenian audience on literary subjects is not an unknown occurrence, still Greek women as a body are very conservative, and consider that their sphere does not lie outside of the family circle.

THE END.

INDEX.

A.

W.

Z.